SWIMMING POOLS

A GUIDE TO THEIR PLANNING, DESIGN, AND OPERATION

FOURTH EDITION

M. Alexander Gabrielsen, PhD, Editor

Published for
The Council for National Cooperation in Aquatics

Published by
Human Kinetics Publishers, Inc.
Champaign, Illinois

Developmental Editor: Sue Ingels Mauck
Copy Editors: Olga Murphy and Laura E. Larson
Production Director: Ernie Noa
Assistant Production Director: Lezli Harris
Typesetter: Yvonne Winsor
Text Design: Julie Szamocki
Text Layout: Denise Mueller, Lezli Harris, and
      Leah Freedman
Cover Design: Jack Davis
Cover Photo: Central Park Aquatic Center, Wood
      River, IL. Photo courtesy of Unteed
      Scaggs Nelson, Ltd, Champaign, IL,
      architects. Consulting engineers:
      Henneman, Raufeisen and Associates,
      Inc., Champaign, IL.
Printed By: Braun-Brumfield, Inc.

ISBN: 0-87322-075-7

Library of Congress Cataloging-in-Publication Data

Swimming pools, a guide to their planning, design,
  and operation.

  ''Published for The Council for National Coopera-
tion in Aquatics.''
  Bibliography: p.
  1. Swimming pools. I. Gabrielsen, M. Alexander.
II. Council for National Cooperation in Aquatics.
TH4763.S83 1987   690'.89   86-15255
ISBN 0-87322-075-7

Printed in the United States of America

10 9 8 7 6 5 4 3 2 1

Human Kinetics Publishers, Inc.
Box 5076, Champaign, IL 61820

Policy Statement Concerning Publications

  The Council for National Cooperation in Aquatics develops or releases various publications to serve the field
of aquatics and expand the knowledge base of aquatics
professionals. CNCA maintains an open forum, and the
reader should not assume that all of our member agencies agree with every word of any publication. Publication of this information is a professional contribution of
the Council, reflecting the opinions of authors. It should
not be considered to be endorsed by CNCA. The publication contents do not necessarily reflect the views of
each member agency. It is presented in the interest of
education in aquatics.

Council for National Cooperation in Aquatics
National Headquarters
901 W. New York St.
Indianapolis, IN 46223

Contents

Council for National Cooperation in Aquatics

The Council for National Cooperation in Aquatics (CNCA) is an umbrella organization for over thirty national agencies and organizations that have strong interest and involvement in aquatics. Since 1951, this Council of cooperating organizations has had as its goal to enhance the field of aquatics. One of our basic objectives is to bring together national agencies with a common interest in aquatic safety and education, for the betterment of all. These combined efforts have impacted aquatics to a great degree because they *were* combined efforts: national agencies and organizations working cooperatively for the enhancement of the aquatic world.

CNCA conferences provide opportunities for individuals at all levels of aquatic programs and organizations to meet and hear national leaders, to exchange ideas with others involved in similar activities, and to become informed on research and educational information critical to their professional development. CNCA conducts the ONLY national aquatic conferences sponsored by so broad a group. The opportunity for agency interaction at this level and to this degree is unique to CNCA.

National conferences offer sessions in the broad spectrum of aquatics, and speakers present current research and excellent information. Intensive workshops on a variety of aquatic subjects are conducted. The conferences are always a valuable professional development experience for participants. Through conferences and many publications, CNCA endeavors to meet information needs in aquatics.

National Organizations That Constitute CNCA

Amateur Athletic Union of the U.S.
American Academy of Pediatrics
American Alliance for Health, Physical
  Education, Recreation and Dance
American Camping Association
American Red Cross
American Public Health Association
American Swimming Coaches Association
Boys Clubs of America
Girl Scouts of the USA
International Academy of Aquatic Art
International Association of Dive Rescue
  Specialists
International Swimming Hall of Fame
Joseph P. Kennedy, Jr. Foundation
National Association of Intercollegiate Athletics
National Association of Underwater Instructors
National Board of the Young Women's
  Christian Association
National Collegiate Athletic Association
National Forum for Advancement of Aquatics

National Employee Services and Recreation
  Association
National Jewish Welfare Board
National Junior College Athletic Association
National Recreation and Park Association
National Safety Council
National Swim and Recreation Association
National Water Safety Congress
President's Council on Physical Fitness and
  Sports
Professional Association of Diving Instructors
Royal Life Saving Society Canada
The Athletic Institute
Underwater Society of America
United States Diving
United States Lifesaving Association
United States Professional Diving Coaches
  Association
United States Rowing Association
United States Synchronized Swimming

Editorial Committee

M. Alexander Gabrielsen, PhD
Nova University, Fort Lauderdale, FL
Senior Editor

Arthur H. Mittelstaedt, Jr., EdD
Long Island University, C.W. Post Campus,
Greenvale, NY
Consultant to Planning Associates, Ronkonkoma, NY
Associate Editor

Ralph L. Johnson
Associate Professor and Director of Aquatics
Indiana University of Pennsylvania, Indiana, PA
Associate Editor

Charles Batterman
Former Diving Coach
Massachusetts Institute of Technology
Cambridge, MA

Robert Bignold
Architect
ORB Associates
Renton, WA

Walter Bishop
Pool Consultant, Professional Engineer
New York, NY

Robert Clayton
Board Member
Council for National Cooperation in Aquatics
Fort Collins, CO

Francis Cosgrove
Deputy Commissioner
Recreation and Parks
County of Nassau
East Meadow, NY

Milton Costello
Consulting Engineer, Professional Engineer
Amityville, NY

Dr. Robert J. Cunitz
Human Factors Psychologist
Rockville, MD

Stan Diamond
Consultant
Urban-Suburban Recreation, Inc.
Amityville, NY

Herman Druckman
Regional Supervisor of Parks
Nassau County, NY

Peter Dunsay
Professional Engineer
Energy Savers
Hempstead, NY

Michael R. Frank
Landscape Architect
Principal, Planning Associates
Ronkonkoma, NY

Robert Gabrielsen
Aquatic Research Technician, Nova University
Fort Lauderdale, FL

Dr. Joseph Hunsaker
Executive Vice President
Counsilman/Hunsaker & Associates
St. Louis, MO

Dr. Jane Katz
Professor of Health and Physical Education
Bronx Community College, NYC

Dr. Leon Kazarin
Biomechanist
Bevercreek, OH

Adolph Kiefer
Aquatic Equipment
Northfield, IL

Richard Korman
Recreation Administrator
Ft. Lauderdale, FL

Dr. George Lawniczak
Aquatic Safety Consultant
Ft. Lauderdale, FL

Thomas Mohrman
Commissioner
Parks and Recreation
Town of N. Hempstead, Manhasset, NY

Dr. Eric Mood
School of Public Health
Yale University
New Haven, CT

Renn Olenn
Counselor at Law
Providence, RI

George Peters
Professional Engineer, Counselor at Law
Santa Monica, CA

Gaston Rafelli
Professional Engineer
Princeton, NJ

David H. Robertson
Aquatic Consultant
Orlando, FL

Dr. Anthony Sances, Jr.
Department of Neurosurgery
The Medical College of Wisconsin
Milwaukee, WI

Dr. Donald Sinn
Recreation and Park Planner
San Jose, CA

R. Jackson Smith
Architect
President, Designed Environments, Inc.
Stamford, CT

Phil Sperber
KDI Paragon
Pleasantville, NY

Mary Spivey
Editorial Assistant
Plantation, FL

Dr. Julian Stein
Professor of Physical Education
George Mason University
Fairfax, VA

Dan Tully
Architect
President, Tully Associates, Inc.
Melrose, MA

Richard G. Ward
Landscape Architect
Ward Associates, Pool Consultants
Ronkonkoma, NY

Foreword

The design and operation of swimming pools pose technical and educational concerns of considerable magnitude. There are basic questions that must be answered for all those who own or operate pools, whether they are homeowners, motel or hotel pool operators, school districts, municipalities, or park boards. The questions may relate to aesthetic design, reasonable cost, safe operation, maintenance and supervision, or many other considerations. In an effort to answer these questions, the book *Swimming Pools: A Guide to Their Planning, Design and Operation* was first written in 1969. In its first three editions it was extremely useful to aquatics professionals. This fourth edition should be even more valuable because it is the most comprehensive publication available on this subject. *Nine* new chapters contain valuable, current information. The chapters on energy management, on potential use of solar energy, and on modernization of existing pools will be of particular interest. These and the other six new chapters add great depth and dimension to an already fine book. In addition, existing chapters in the 1975 edition were carefully reviewed and updated by the editorial committee, headed by Dr. M. Alexander Gabrielsen.

The CNCA is indebted to the professionals who have given considerable amounts of their time in the preparation of this book. The book will be a valuable resource to all persons involved in the planning and operation of swimming pools.

Louise Priest
Executive Director
Council for National Cooperation in Aquatics

SWIMMING POOLS

A GUIDE TO THEIR PLANNING, DESIGN, AND OPERATION

Clinton C. Martin Park, North Hempstead, New York

Chapter 1

The Community Swimming Pool

The community swimming pool's primary function is to provide a variety of opportunities for swimming, diving, and related aquatic activities at a low cost. Public pools may be under any one of the following jurisdictions: a village, city, park district, school district, public-supported college or university, or county. The elements included in the planning, administration, and operation of these pools are discussed in this chapter. Those details concerning design, water chemistry, enclosures, equipment, and pool safety features will be covered in other chapters of this book.

Chapter 1 is divided into five major sections: "The Development of Community Pools," "Planning the Community Pool," "Pool Administration," "Programming the Pool," and "Staffing the Pool."

The Development of Community Pools

The first municipal pool, as community-owned pools were once called, is believed to have been built in Brookline, Massachusetts, in 1887. About the same time, Dr. Simon Baruch, father of Bernard Baruch, convinced New York City officials to build several public pools, primarily to provide bathing facilities for dwellers in the many New York City tenements. These pools, or "baths," contained showers and dressing rooms in addition to a pool.

The modern era of swimming pools began in the 1920s, and in that decade several thousand pools were built in the United States. About two thirds of them were operated by municipalities, Ys, and Boys Clubs; the rest were commercially operated. The number of residential pools also increased during the 1920s and were usually referred to as "estate pools" at that time.

Officers' Club Swimming Pool Complex. Bolling Air Force Base, Washington, DC

Residential pool construction rose sharply in the 1930s, slowed down only by World War II and the Korean War. After the Korean conflict, however, a veritable boom in residential pool construction began. Simultaneously, the tremendous surge in nonresidential pool construction that occurred, particularly at hotels and motels, was of such significance that swimming has become the most popular form of outdoor recreation in America today.

Predictions indicate that in the next two decades, residential and community-sponsored pool construction will continue at a rapid pace. This demand will partly be the result of the "energy crunch" and spiraling inflation, which is expected to curtail vacation travel by automobile to far-away ocean beaches and inland lakes. The community pool may well become the substitute for travel to distant recreation areas. This trend will demand that community pools provide a greater variety of recreational opportunities to its patrons. Such facilities as tennis, racquetball, handball, par three golf, children's play apparatus, and other additional recreational facilities will be incorporated into future community swimming pool complexes.

Today, swimming is the greatest leisure-time activity in the United States, and participation is expected to increase significantly over the next several years. A recent A.C. Nielson study indicated that 103,500,000 Americans swim at least once a year. Some experts believe that this figure is low, and that in all probability at least 60% of the population (about 130 million) swim at least once a year. The difference in these estimates probably stems from what actually constitutes swimming. With the increase in all forms of water-related activities (boating, canoeing, wind surfing, scuba diving, fishing, snowmobiling on lakes, and ice skating), the ability to swim becomes essential to individual safety and constitutes a prerequisite to participation in these activities.

About 50% of all swimming in the United States today is in swimming pools. Although the community pool has the highest participation rate, only 10% of the number of pools in this country are community pools. A significant fact revealed by the National Safety Council states that only 8 to 10% of the annual drownings in the United States occur in swimming pools. This suggests that pools are the safest place to swim. (Pool safety is discussed in chapter 8.)

The major attribute of the community pool is its ability to attract the whole family. The underlying concept of the community pool is to serve the widest range of people of all ages and abilities. To achieve this objective requires careful planning of the pool and its related facilities.

With the increasing demands on the tax dollar, some communities have had to place pools on a self-supporting basis to sustain all or some of the pool's operating cost. A few pools even produce extra revenue that is used to defray costs of developing or operating other recreation facilities in the community.

Planning the Community Pool

At the earliest stage of planning for a community pool, it is essential for the planning group to develop a concept or image of what the pool will look like and how it will operate. The following principles profile a typical community pool complex:

1. The pool should be a beautiful facility that will blend into the decor of the surrounding area. It should be a distinct asset to the community.
2. The pool should be a place where parents may bring their children with complete confidence that their children will be safe and adequately supervised.
3. The pool should be planned so that parents may watch the activities of their children without having to enter the pool deck area.
4. The pool should be a place where families may come, not just to swim, but to spend most of the day.
5. The pool should incorporate opportunities for activities other than swimming.
6. The pool should avoid becoming a noise nuisance to the surrounding neighborhood.
7. The pool should be a place where participants may improve their skills and knowledge in aquatics, enjoy the wholesome benefits of swimming, or just swim for fun.
8. The pool should be expertly designed and engineered with a body of water that is "purer than drinking water."
9. The traffic flow around the pool should be carefully planned to minimize congestion.
10. The pool should be designed to include all safety features and should be supervised with qualified personnel whenever it is open for use.
11. The location of the pool in any existing park or playground should not reduce the quantity of other recreation facilities without adequate provision for replacing those facilities in accessible areas.

Objectives

A community swimming pool should have stated objectives to guide its operation. These objectives are just as various as people's needs in different communities. As a guide to communities contemplating the construction of a pool, the Editorial Committee has established the following broad objectives that it considers necessary in any community pool.

1. The pool should be designed so that it meets as many of the aquatic needs of the community as possible.
2. The pool should serve all age groups and not just concentrate on the needs of youth.
3. Young children, disabled persons, and senior citizens should be included in the pool's program with necessary modifications made to pool design to accommodate these groups.
4. Instruction in all aspects of swimming, diving, lifesaving, and water safety should be a basic part of the program.
5. "Swimming for fun" should be the dominant philosophy governing the pool's operation.
6. The pool program should provide performance opportunities for skilled individuals through competition, demonstrations, and water shows.
7. The pool should provide a healthful and safe environment.

Planning Factors

The components, size, and design to be included in a pool complex should relate to the following factors:

1. The density and characteristics of the population to be served, including such elements as age, occupation, nationality, and income of people.
2. The physical characteristics of the site, its suitability, accessibility, drainage, vegetation, and topography.
3. The needs and interests of the people of the community in various types of aquatic activities.
4. The safety and security of the area. Too often pools are located on sites that require children to cross major arterial roads or highways to reach them.
5. The availability of utilities: power, water, sewage, and communication.
6. The legal codes, laws, and ordinances, particularly those of local and state Boards of Health that regulate public pool facilities.
7. The type and quantity of existing public and commercial recreational facilities in the area including other swimming pools.

8. The scope and nature of the program to be conducted in the pool and the requirements of the activities that need to be met by the pool.

9. Requirements for parking, emergency access to pool, and support facilities.

The planning factors should be considered with regard to both immediate and long-range needs. Once the components of the complex have been established, the overall size of the complex may be determined; it may range from 3 acres up to 12 or 15.

Financing Community Pools

Community pools have been financed in different ways in the past. Pools, or baths, during the depression years of the 1930s were entirely supported from tax funds, which in some instances were supplemented by federal funds (mostly through the Works Progress Administration). Since World War II, the methods used to finance public pools have varied, depending upon the philosophy of the governing body. Some pools, as in the case of New York City, were completely financed through the general municipal tax structure. This included the acquisition of property, construction of the pool facility, and the operation and maintenance of the pools. Other municipalities have underwritten the original cost of acquisition of land and construction of the pool and have required a user fee to operate and maintain the facilities, thus reducing the burden on taxpayers. Still other municipalities have refused to underwrite the cost of swimming pool facilities as a general municipal responsibility. Instead, they have encouraged interested citizens to approve the creation of a "special park and pool district" for the purpose of funding a swimming pool. The special district is given the authority to tax residents in the district. A summary of these methods of financing pools is contained in Table 1.1. In many situations, the cost of public pool construction has been obtained by selling bonds that are payable in 10 to 15 years for cost of site work, 30 to 40 years for building cost, and 20 to 30 years for the cost of the pool. This may vary from state to state, but the average bonding time for municipal pools is 20 years.

Because of the increased demand for the tax dollar from most municipal departments, the trend to membership-type pools has increased. The philosophy behind this trend is that those who use the pool the most should pay for its operation and bonded indebtedness—thus, the self-sustaining and self-liquidating pool project.

Once a pool is under construction, management officials cannot afford to let the project enthusiasm wane, especially if it is to be supported by membership fees. Membership is somewhat of a misnomer because it does not grant exclusive use of the pool to the members. It really constitutes an annual or seasonal fee permitting the individual or family unlimited use of the pool, whereas other users are admitted on a daily fee basis. It also provides the city with immediate operating funds. Promotion of the pool in local papers during the

Table 1.1 Methods of Financing Community Swimming Pools

General municipal tax (state, county, town, village)	Entire citizenry is taxed to provide pool facilities in the same manner as roads, sewers, and other municipal services and facilities.
Special district tax (park/pool district, school district)	Taxes are obtained from a special district or a portion of a municipality where the people desire a pool facility and are willing to pay for it on their own.
Grants from states or federal government	There are a number of federal and state programs that provide part of the cost of swimming pools.
Grants, endowments, donations	Pools have been given to municipalities, universities, colleges, schools, and semipublic agencies who have in turn opened the facility to the general public.
User fees (memberships, single admission)	The people who use the pool pay for both the construction and operating cost. Seasonal or yearly membership fees and daily admission charges are the methods employed.

construction period, advance membership sales, visits to the project by pool committee members, and the mailing of brochures to residents all help to promote interest in the pool.

The Pool Complex

The modern community swimming pool is no longer an isolated, independent, special facility serving only the swimming interests of the people of the community. When people go to a swimming pool today, they expect a variety of services and recreation opportunities. Thus, the concept of the "aquatic complex" came into being. Swimming remains the major attraction augmented by supporting services and facilities. The successful pool manager recognizes the value of these support activities.

Studies have shown that approximately 25% of the people attending an outdoor pool will be in the water at any given time. In comparison, the number of people actually in the water at ocean beaches may be as low as 3 to 5%. This is because most people go to the beach merely to sunbathe. What provisions need to be made for those who are not in the water? Pool planners and administrators have wrestled with this question for years.

A great deal of thought goes into the development of a matrix of facilities, to adequately serve the requirements of patrons. Through cooperation and coordination with program specialists and planning consultants, the administration can prevent crowding and other unsafe conditions. Lack of understanding of people's behavior patterns on hot, humid days, on cold, damp days, or during a sudden rain or windstorm may lead to undesirable and even unsafe situations. Supplemental facilities may provide shelter during storms and additional activities for pool users.

Components of the Aquatic Complex

The ideal aquatic complex is composed of a matrix of facilities providing a year-round recrea-

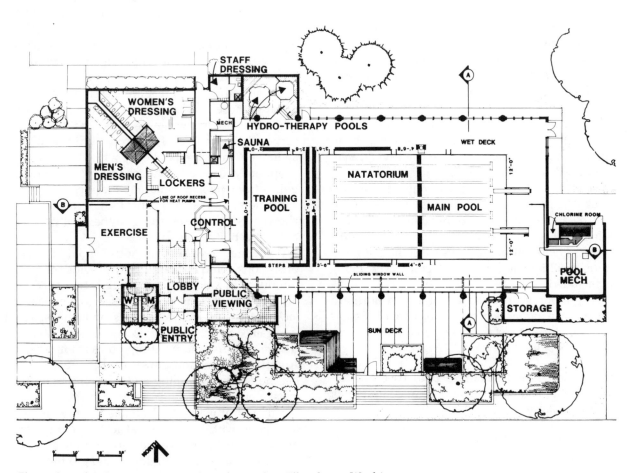

Floor plan of indoor natatorium, 3-pool complex, Ellensburg, Washington

tion area to serve fully the needs of the area. The aquatic complex contains facilities that are both recreational and operational in nature.

The pools. In a few instances only one pool is designed to serve all aquatic needs, but the current trend is to have separate pools, each serving a different function. The following are the components of an ideal outdoor pool complex:

The familiarization pool. Sometimes referred to as the "kiddy" or "wading pool," this pool is for youngsters ages 1 to 5 who do not know how to swim. Children play in the familiarization pool and get used to the water. The depth of water ranges from 6 inches to a maximum of 2 feet.

The training pool. Used primarily for teaching people to swim, this pool ranges in depth from 2 feet to 3-1/2 feet and varies in size according to the population.

The main pool. General recreation swimming, advanced swimming instruction, and competitive swimming meets take place in the main pool. The ideal size of a main pool is 50 meters long by 25 yards (or meters) wide, with depth ranging from 4 to 6 feet. (See chapter 14 on design characteristics for competitive swimming.)

The deep-water well, or diving tank. This pool is often referred to as the "diving pool." However, many other activities such as scuba diving, synchronized swimming, water safety instruction, lifesaving, and water polo are conducted in this pool. The pool size varies from the smallest of 30 feet by 40 feet to a full size of 60 feet by 45 feet, which will accommodate four springboards and a tower. The water depth stays constant at a minimum of 13 feet and up to 17 feet if tower diving is included.

To provide year-round swimming in northern climates, an indoor pool containing either a 25-yard or 25-meter course or a 50-meter long course should be added.

Recreational facilities in the pool area. The following list includes some important components of the pool area.

- Space for people to lounge in the shade
- Sunbathing area

- Eating area (concession)
- Dancing on a special terrace or portion of the pool deck
- Seating for spectators for shows and swim meets
- Portable stage for shows or concerts
- Children's play apparatus
- Shuffleboard courts
- Sitting area where table games may be played
- Walkways between facilities
- Public transportation area and drop-off point
- Changing areas
- Infant feeding area

Recreational facilities outside of the immediate pool area. A number of facilities might be located near the pool complex to serve directly or indirectly those who have come to use the pool. Typical types of facilities include basketball courts; baseball and softball diamonds; picnic areas; horseshoe courts; tennis, platform paddle tennis, handball, and racquetball courts; pitch-and-putt golf or a par three course; golf driving ranges; roller skating rinks; bicycle paths; children's playgrounds; and nature trails.

Usually, these facilities are classified into two groups: those that directly serve the swimmers while they are in swimming suits, and those that serve all the people of the community and the swimmers from the pool only when they are appropriately dressed. The control of swimmers going from pool to adjacent facilities is a consideration that planners must face. Availability of showers for those returning to the pool from an outside activity is essential.

Winterization of the bathhouse should be seriously considered because it may provide the community with valuable indoor recreation space at little cost. Judicious planning for conversion of locker-room areas, office facilities, and other spaces into game rooms, dancing, lounging areas, weight training rooms, and meeting rooms is important. Another combination, however, is the use of the bathhouse as a warming and changing room for ice skaters in the winter.

Although it is highly desirable to provide outdoor pools with supplemental activities, there are numerous problems related to design and engineering of the pools, building, and grounds that must be understood. Such questions as whether the participant should have direct access from the pool to the supplemental recreational facilities, and whether such supplemental facilities are open to nonaquatic participants, along with a host of other questions may only be answered after careful planning and programming of each particular activity and area. Other concerns related to supervision, safety security, and maintenance that affect the establishment of rules and regulations must be considered. Disadvantages and advantages must be weighed.

Operational facilities.   Operational facilities include such items as space for storing trash, benches, cleaning equipment, instructional equipment, the filter room, first-aid room, general office, manager's office, lifeguard dressing rooms, locker rooms, showers, toilets, and garage space. The deck area usually includes areas for lounging, shelter, and sitting, as well as control facilities for the pool.

Deck area.   The deck area immediately surrounding the pool should be constructed of impervious material, such as concrete, bluestone, quarry tile, or some other hard, nonslip surface material. One of the most common mistakes is to trowel or float a concrete surface smooth, which makes it very slippery and dangerous when wet. Painted pool decks can also create a slippery and dangerous surface.

The deck within 10 feet of the pool's edge is the wet area. It is the zone of activity for immediate circulation around and in and out of the pool. The deck is usually pitched away from the pool's edge so that the excess water is collected in drains located at least 5 feet from the pool's edge, 20 feet on centers. In the case of the deck-level pool design, however, the floor is pitched toward the edge of the trench cover, which is usually 24 inches wide and includes vertical drainage channels.

Behind this wet zone is the primary traffic, or circulation, area that extends around and through the pool complex and is usually designated as the walkway area. It should provide direct and safe pedestrian flow between areas of the pool complex without interference with the pool's wet zone or lounging areas. The lounge area is located on the outer periphery of the deck, situated either to take advantage of the sun or to escape from the sun under shelters.

The entire pool complex must be enclosed, preferably with a permanent 8-foot fence or wall. The fence, necessary for safety reasons, may also serve as a windbreak if it is made of solid wood, masonry, or wire fabric covered with canvas. A pool may actually become undesirable for lounging and swimming if noise, dust, or wind conditions are not controlled.

If grade changes are proposed between pool areas, traffic between elevations should be accommodated by construction of ramps. Steps are dangerous and will create difficulty for elderly, disabled, and young individuals in getting around the pool area.

For proper service of the pool, it is important that emergency vehicles and maintenance service trucks have some type of vehicle access. An area for off-street parking is also an essential consideration. The parking lot should be planned so that during the off-season it may be used for other recreation and community purposes (e.g., basketball).

The pool deck should have a low-intensity lighting system to provide security surveillance of the area at night when the pool is not open. Sufficient light must be provided to allow a security person to check the bathhouse, pool, and deck area periodically during the evening without being subjected to dark, hazardous conditions.

For nighttime swimming, the pools should have both underwater lights and area lighting that meet the requirements of the standards of the Illuminating Engineering Society (IES) and of state regulations. (See chapter 11 for details on lighting.)

Benches, lounge chairs, drinking fountains, tables and chairs, towel racks, and seat walls are all important equipment features within the pool area. The absence of these can detract from the convenience of the pool deck for lounging, viewing, eating, socializing, and resting.

Neighborhood Versus Community Pools

Whether a community should build one large pool or several smaller neighborhood pools has long been debated, especially in communities with a population of 50,000 or more. Although it is more costly to build several small pools than one large one, in most cases several neighborhood pools dispersed throughout the community will serve the needs of the population better than a single, large community pool.

Indoor pool of the town of North Hempstead, New York. Bulkhead moves up and down to provide separate areas; pool has variable bottom at one end.

Thus, it may be concluded that the best distribution of outdoor swimming pool facilities in a community is a series of satellite neighborhood pools strategically located among the heaviest concentration of people, a large community complex (one pool for each 100,000 to 150,000 people), and one indoor pool for every 50,000 people. The indoor pools may be located in schools or in such youth-oriented agencies as Boys Clubs, YMCAs, YWCAs, YMHAs, and community centers or as a part of the community pool complex.

Outdoor Versus Indoor Pools

At least 60% of a community's population will want to swim sometime during the summer months, 30% will swim at least once a week, and 15% will swim on a regular basis (4 to 7 days a week).

During the winter months, the interest in recreational swimming wanes. Not more than 10 to 20% of those who swim regularly in the summer will continue to do so in the winter, even when facilities are available. Thus, to be successful, community indoor pools should be coordinated with the physical education programs of the local schools. Supplementary activities such as birthday parties, scout merit badge programs, and other special events should also be planned. This will ensure regular use of the pool during the school day and yet make it available to the public after school, in the evenings, and on weekends.

Pool Administration

The successful pool is one that is properly administered. Good management involves many functions that require careful preparation and execution. The details of each function could not possibly be covered in this chapter because it would take a large manual to treat the many facets of pool administration adequately. However, this section will identify and describe each administrative function, and then offer authorities those suggestions necessary in pool planning and operation. Although major emphasis will be on the problems inherent in the summer-operated public pool, nearly all of the administrative functions discussed apply in some degree to year-round indoor or outdoor pools as well.

An essential principle in pool administration is that only one department should be responsible for the complete operation of the pool. In some communities the recreation department that operates the pool does not maintain it; rather it is maintained by another department of the municipality or school district. This arrangement may be unsatisfactory due to conflicts of interest, priorities, and interdependent responsibilities. If personnel are assigned to the pool from different departments, they should report to and be responsible only to the pool manager.

In most municipalities the personnel department is responsible for hiring personnel and establishing employment policies. Obviously, the policies established for all municipal employees will have a direct bearing on personnel employed for the pool whether they are classified as part-time, seasonal, or full-time.

Noteworthy is the trend to contract the pool's operation to outside firms specializing in pool management. Primarily directed toward private club, motel, and hotel pools, these firms usually furnish the pool manager, clerical staff, lifeguards, and maintenance personnel for an annual or seasonal fee.

The Operating Budget

Budgets for pool operation are influenced by the pool size, the type of program and services offered, the length of the season, and the pool's maintenance system. The budget for pools is often incorporated into larger recreation budgets as a separate line item. A tentative budget should be developed before fees are established, particularly in those cases where the fee is expected to pay for all or part of the operating cost.

Following is a sample pool budget. The specific amount needed under each item must be determined. It is important to realize that there are certain fixed costs that cannot be reduced regardless of the pressures to do so, such as the annual cost of amortizing the pool where bonds were floated to obtain the funds to build the pool.

1. Personnel
   - Professional: permanent, full-time, part-time
   - Nonprofessional: permanent, full-time, part-time
   - Fringe benefits: workmen's compensation, social security, group insurance, retirement, medical, dental, vacation, sick, personal days
2. Services
   - Printing, advertising, engineering, publications
3. Utilities
   - Electric, gas or oil, water, telephone
4. Instructional Supplies
   - Lifesaving, awards, kickboards, scuba, and other items
5. Maintenance Supplies and Equipment
   - Chemicals, vacuum cleaning, furniture, tools, uniforms, laundry
6. Safety and Emergency Equipment and Supplies
   - Life rings, shepherd crook, spine board, telephone, resuscitation equipment
7. Insurance
   - Liability, property, fidelity
8. Repairs
   - To building and equipment, replacement parts
9. Miscellaneous material
   - Pipes, paint
10. Indebtedness
    - Bonds, interest
11. Taxes
12. Contingency
    - Usually 5 to 10% is added to the total budget for emergencies or unforeseen costs. For example, additional lifeguards might be needed in order to extend the daily swimming period an hour or two on particularly hot days.

Insurance

All swimming pools and all personnel employed in the operation of the pool should be covered by insurance. It is inevitable that accidents will occur in and around the pool, with some resulting in legal action against the pool owner. The following types of coverage are available through various insurance companies or their brokers:

1. For Employees:
   - Workmen's compensation
   - Workmen's disability
   - Comprehensive general liability
   - Group accident, sickness, and life
   - Social security
   - Fidelity
2. For Structures and Equipment:
   - Comprehensive general liability (which contains a property damage floater or a basic form property damage endorsement).
3. For Members or Users of the Pool:
   - The managing authority must be protected against suits resulting from accidents. Such liability insurance can be included in a comprehensive policy or taken out as a separate policy.

It is possible to obtain other insurance such as protection against defective workmanship during the construction of the pool and protection against financial loss due to adverse weather. The latter type of insurance is usually employed only when a large spectator event is planned and where the anticipated revenue is essential to the operation of the pool.

C.T. Branin Natatorium, Canton, Ohio. Lawrence, Kydes, Goodenberger, and Bower, Architects. Photo by Balthazar.

Admission Systems

An important aspect of pool planning is determining what method or system of admission to the pool will be used. Pool admittance control is critical because it involves both handling money and identifying eligible patrons.

The following three basic admissions systems are used by pools throughout the country.

Attendant system.   This system employs one or more people (attendants) to collect daily fees and check membership cards of patrons. Identification is usually established by a card, badge, tag, or pin. A recurrent problem of this system is that these identification items are frequently lost.

If a pool is adjacent to a beach or other recreational facilities, it may be desirable to develop a system that permits pool users to leave the pool area and be readmitted. To date, the best system developed is by stamping the back of the hand. Then as the person returns to the pool, an ultraviolet light activates the image on the hand. This also requires an attendant.

Turnstile system. Turnstiles are becoming popular with pool operators. Turnstiles, however, are seldom used alone; an attendant must always be available to assist those who may have questions or who may have lost their identification. Turnstiles have become so sophisticated that they will take not only coins but cards, tokens, or specially prepared keys.

Open admission system.   This admission system is practical only in situations where control is not a factor or where control is exercised at an entrance of a larger facility that incorporates the pool as a part of a complex. Because this system permits anyone to use the pool when it is open, regardless of age or ability, it has some drawbacks.

Concessions

All community pools must resolve how the food and drink problem will be handled. Food is as much a part of the outdoor pool's environment as the picnic basket is to the beach. Food provisions must not be ignored; however, any dispensing or consumption of food must be kept separate from the pool itself. The serving and the vending machine systems are the two basic food and drink dispensing systems.

Serving system. A staff and facility are required to prepare and dispense food items. The service may be contracted with an outside firm or individual (a concession operation), or the stand may be operated by the pool management. Under no circumstances should bottles or glass containers of any type be used in serving food and drink to pool patrons.

Vending machine system. The vending machine is gaining popularity with pool operators. Vending machines are usually obtained on a contract with a company that services and stocks them. The pool realizes a percentage of the profits on the gross income from the machines. Contracts with vendors must include provisions for checking sales, accounting procedures, and maintenance service.

Emergency Procedures

Emergencies occur at almost every pool. Failure to act properly could result in unnecessary physical injury, as well as bad publicity and legal action against the pool. Detailed discussion of pool safety can be found in chapter 8, including a section on establishment of emergency procedures to follow if an accident occurs. Without question, the most important factor when confronted with an emergency is time, particularly when a drowning or near drowning occurs. The second most important factor is administering proper first-aid procedures.

Pool Safety Devices

Several recently developed devices are valuable supplemental aids in supervising a pool and guarding against possible accidents and unauthorized entrance to the pool.

Ground Fault Circuit Interrupter: Several companies are producing this extremely effective device that detects any electric leak around the pool and automatically and instantaneously cuts off the electric power.

Water Sensor: Reacting to the slightest disturbance of the water, this "night sentry" will sound an alarm. Anyone entering the pool activates the alarm, which may terminate at any point such as the local police station or recreational department night station.

Safe Light: A safe light is merely a night light that illuminates the pool area to discourage illegal entry and to provide security personnel with sufficient

visibility to supervise the pool during the night.

Other Safety Devices: Other safety devices have been developed for use when the pool is both open and closed. Some need to be tested further to determine their practicality. Examples of such safety devices are pool covers (plastic, mesh, or metal), fencing, closed circuit TV (for surveillance of remote areas of pool), electric mat (burglar alarm), electronic eye, and anti-intrusion devices (radar eye).

Daily Pool Maintenance

The pool manager should establish specific daily maintenance procedures. Effective maintenance is best accomplished by the proper delegation of various tasks to staff members. A daily maintenance routine is essential both to the efficiency of the pool and to the health and safety of patrons.

The following daily maintenance functions should be performed:

1. Taking water samples for chemical analysis (chlorine residual and pH, usually performed each day before opening and closing of pool, and at 9 a.m., 1 p.m., and 3 p.m.). See chapter 13 on water chemistry.
2. Taking water samples (for bacterial analysis)
3. Cleaning the bathhouse or locker room
4. Cleaning the pool's deck and surrounding area
5. Brushing the pool walls and vacuuming the bottom
6. Inspecting the pool's water, safety equipment, and other pool facilities such as the diving stands and boards
7. Checking the filtration system (backwash if pressure indicates need to)
8. Mowing any turf area, trimming shrubs, and picking up leaves
9. Recording water and air temperatures and weather conditions

Daily records should be kept of the pool's condition as revealed by the above maintenance procedures.

Public Relations

Once a pool has been opened for use, continuous publicity is essential if it is to meet its objectives. Every medium of communication—newspaper, radio, television, cablevision, pennysaver, brochures, mailing, and word of mouth—should be used.

An effective public relations program involves two aspects: The first involves releasing information to the public about the pool, its programs, the schedule, membership and daily fees, and any other pertinent information needed to inform people about the pool. The second aspect is concerned with reporting what is going on at the pool whether it be in the form of news stories about specific events, such as the results of a swimming meet, or in the form of feature stories that tell about someone or something going on in the pool.

A good public relations program is planned well in advance. Yearly plans are best with indications of what should be accomplished each month. Prepared press releases are usually the most effective and are preferred by newspapers. Photographs should also be available to newspapers.

An excellent public relations technique for membership-type pools is the weekly or monthly newsletter, which provides a means of stimulating and maintaining interest in the pool year-round.

Records and Reports

Keeping accurate records of pool operation is a problem that confronts every pool manager. The following list recommends necessary records and reports that should be kept:

- Daily attendance
- Daily receipts
- Membership list
- Sales from concessions or vending machines
- Personnel: payroll cards, duty log, certification or other qualifying evidence, and training and evaluation records
- Inventories: equipment, supplies, chemicals
- Daily maintenance: chlorine residual, pH, water temperature, air temperature, wind velocity, and weather conditions
- Program: record of daily events and special activities
- Accident reports
- Annual Report: prepared by the pool manager containing his or her recommendation for next year's improvements

The Operation Manual

An operation manual is a must for every pool. This document is prepared by the pool manager and should be approved by the appropriate managing authority. It contains all information about the pool's operation, provides detailed information, and outlines specific procedures for the items discussed in this chapter, including such duties and responsibility of lifeguards. Every year the manual should be reviewed and, if necessary, modified. Its value lies in standardizing the operation of the pool; then when a new manager is employed, a detailed guide is available. Certain sections of the manual may also be reprinted as a handbook for the pool's staff. Some people have developed specific instructions that define the function and establish goals and objectives for each position.

Pool Rules and Regulations

All pools should publish well-established rules and regulations that represent the policies and procedures under which the pool is to be operated. It is the pool manager's responsibility to prepare, promulgate, and revise the pool's rules and regulations. All rules and regulations pertaining to patrons must be placed on posters and displayed at strategic locations in the pool area and bathhouse.

Rules and regulations developed for both the operation of the pool and the use of the pool should be contained in the pool's operation manual. The following represent the usual subjects for which rules are written:

1. Staff Rules: Pertain to the conduct of staff in the performance of their jobs (e.g., lifeguards, attendants, engineer, and snack bar operator).
2. Patron Rules: Related to the manner and times patrons are to use the pool facilities.
3. Special Group Rules: Involve rules for special groups such as the swimming team, scuba diving group, and special interest groups.

Rules and regulations represent, in essence, legal statements. Many pools have been protected against liability suits by the fact that their rules and regulations, which were prominently displayed, explicitly prohibited the activity in which the person was participating when injured.

Municipal pool, Ellensburg, Washington. Photo by G. Karl Bischoff.

Recommendations for Pool Operators

Listed below are helpful recommendations for pool operators and managers.

1. The management of a swimming pool is a complex operation that may affect the health and lives of the patrons. The task must not be taken lightly. Remember that the safety of patrons cannot be delegated.

2. A resource library, which contains material on all aspects of the pool's operation from program to water chemistry, should be maintained. *Swimming Pool Weekly* and *Swimming Pool Data and Reference Annual* are excellent sources for current information on pools.

3. The success of any pool depends on the ability and performance of its staff. Time spent on supervision, counseling, and training of staff will yield rich rewards.

4. The higher the atmospheric temperature, the greater will be the pool's attendance.

5. People prefer warm water (80 to 86 °F) over cold water even for competitive swimming.

6. People will be less likely to go into the water if attractive supporting recreational and lounge facilities are available to them.

7. Although water slides are attractive to children, the dangers associated with their improper use make constant supervision necessary.

8. Membership pools have a higher daily attendance than the daily admission pool.

9. Children and youths will use a pool in far greater numbers than adults.

10. Diving is the most hazardous activity. The diving facilities must be supervised at all times and diving into shallow water (under 5 feet) should be discouraged. Other hazardous areas and activities are discussed in the pool safety chapter.

11. The manager should devise a general list of all possible programs that could be conducted at the pool to use as a reference. The list will serve as a guide to the development of a comprehensive program.

12. The pool manager should visit other pools to obtain information about successful programs.

13. Be sure that all groups and activities have equitable access to the pool.

14. Remember that a clean, well-maintained pool attracts customers.

Programming the Pool

Successful pools are those that have a comprehensive program of activities to satisfy the wide variety of interests of potential pool users. These varied activities must also be scheduled at times to accommodate the patron. The basic components of a good pool program are described below.

1. *Instruction:* A good pool program includes instruction at all levels of swimming ability, from beginner groups to the most advanced, from the youngest child to the senior citizen, as well

Lake Isle Country Club, town facility. Town of Eastchester, Westchester County, New York. Photo by John Scari.

as in special activities such as springboard diving, scuba, and skin diving.

2. *Recreation Swimming:* Often referred to as the "free swim period," this portion of the program should be scheduled at a time of day best suited for most people. During recreation swimming, people can participate in nonorganized aquatic activities of their own choice. All lifeguard stations should be manned during this period.

3. *Free Swims:* Free swim is designed to provide access to those who might not be able to afford the admission charge. Free swim is usually scheduled in the morning hours (8-10 a.m.) or during the noon hour and may involve both instruction and recreation swimming. A policy must be established and approved by the governing body before implementing free swims.

4. *Lifesaving and Water Safety Instruction:* This activity is usually conducted by scheduling groups who wish to acquire certification. It is possible to schedule such groups at the same time that other activities are being conducted such as diving instruction or a beginners class. This will depend on the design of the pool. Multiple pools lend themselves to this type of scheduling.

5. *Swimming Teams:* Both an age group swimming team and the so-called senior team

should be organized and scheduled for practice sometime each day. The two periods that these groups seem to prefer are in the early morning, 7-10 a.m., and in the evening, 5-6:30 p.m. Divers should be a part of the swimming group; however, it is sometimes necessary to schedule them at a different time if the diving well is located in the swimming course.

6. *Swimming for Disabled People:* Special sessions may be scheduled for individuals who are physically disabled. Once they have achieved a certain ability level, they should be encouraged to join the regular program.

7. *Synchronized Swimming Group:* This activity may be conducted on both a competitive and demonstration basis. The activity requires deep water; consequently, it must be scheduled so that it does not interfere with divers using springboards.

8. *Shows, Pageants, and Swimming Meets:* These activities are all special events to which the public is usually invited. Water shows and pageants bring together all the different aquatic activities, as well as special "show" events. These events give participants an opportunity to demonstrate the skills they have learned and often are used to help raise funds for the swim team or for other activities.

9. *Special Groups:* Some pools admit outside organized groups such as schools, Boy and Girl

Scouts, and day camps at designated times so that these groups might carry on their own special programs.

10. *Special Activities:* Special instruction in such related aquatic activities as canoeing, boating, bait and spin casting, fly casting, and model boat racing often has considerable appeal. These good off-season activities should be introduced only when they will not interfere with the regular program.

Guiding Principles in Program Planning

The following principles should be invaluable to pool program planners. Some principles will not apply to all pools because of their limited function.

1. Beginners classes should be scheduled at times when the pool conditions are the best. Too often they are conducted early in the morning when the air and water temperatures are least comfortable.

2. Beginners of comparable age should be grouped together. For example, 4-year-olds do not belong with 9-year-olds.

3. Pools should provide the best instruction possible for talented swimmers. Establish times when they might practice and schedule events where they may display their talents.

4. Special interest groups such as bait casting, scuba diving, and synchronized swimming generally are more successful when organized on a club basis with elected officers to direct and promote their activities. A member of the pool staff should act as advisor to the group if no outside qualified person is available.

5. The pool schedule should be flexible enough to permit immediate program adjustment if necessary. For example, if the swim team is scheduled to practice between 5 and 7 p.m. and the air temperature is 92 °F at 5 p.m., obviously many people other than the team members will want to swim to get relief from the heat. The swim team practice should be cancelled or rescheduled and the pool opened for recreation swimming.

6. Some children tend to overdo when not supervised. Lifeguards and other pool personnel should constantly watch for the youngster who looks chilled, has blue lips, or shows other signs of fatigue.

7. The most hazardous activities are diving from springboards and the sides of the pool into shallow water and scuba diving. Both should be carefully supervised, strict adherence to posted rules should be maintained, and only qualified certified leadership assigned.

8. A major function of the pool's staff should be to maintain a safe environment for public enjoyment in the pool. Lifeguards are on duty not only to rescue drowning victims but to prevent dangerous behavior that can lead to accidents. The pool staff should not be considered a baby-sitting service. Parents should be made aware of the real peril of water and should understand that they share the responsibility of watching their children.

Pre- and Postseason Programs

If the pool is operated on a seasonal basis (summer only), procedures for the opening and closing of the pool must be established. This involves developing a checklist of tasks to be done, including the time when each specific task is to be accomplished.

One of the most debatable questions of the seasonally operated pool is whether the water should be left in the pool. Leaving the water in the pool is preferable because it not only protects the plumbing system, but the weight of the water protects the pool against shifting, which is a result of the ground heaving by alternating freezing and thawing or by a variation of the underground water table. A shift in the water table or the expansion of surrounding frozen earth exerting extra inward pressure on the walls has caused many pools to crack. The engineer's or pool builder's advice should be followed.

It is important for management to realize that leaving the water in the pool during the off-season creates a potential danger. Undrained pools should be covered to protect youngsters from falling in or being pushed in. Fencing around a pool is not enough.

Preseason activity. The work to be accomplished before the pool can be opened may be divided into three time periods.

1. *Winter and early spring* is the time to buy equipment and supplies, repair deck furniture, start an interior painting program, and clean and

Plantation Park 50-meter pool, Plantation, Florida

repair bathhouse facilities and equipment including the refreshment stand.

2. *Late spring* (1 to 2 months prior to opening) is the time to paint the exterior of the buildings and the pool basin if necessary; inspect and repair all electrical fixtures and wiring; prepare grounds, especially flower beds and shrubs; drain and clean pool basin if painting is not necessary; and check filter plant and motors.

3. *Two weeks before pool's opening* is the time to fill the pool, start the circulating system, heat the water to the desired temperature, start the chlorinator, activate the filtration system through several backwash cycles, vacuum the pool, place all equipment in position, take daily water samples, and place the bathhouse in readiness for opening day and inspection for proper permit.

Off-season use of the pool. Can outdoor pools be used during the off-season? It is not only practical but desirable because it adds to the value of an expensive recreation facility ordinarily used for only 3 months of the year. Operators of both public and private pools should study the feasibility of converting some or all of their pools to year-round use. Some off-season uses of pools are as follows:

During periods when pool water is not frozen. This would be during the fall and spring in freezing zones and all year in southern areas where little if any ice forms on the water. Possible uses of pools under these conditions are as a fishing pond; for recreation and instructional boating and canoeing; for bait, spin, and fly casting instruction and competition; for model sail and/or motor boating; and for instruction and practice in use of wet suit scuba diving.

Situations where pools are drained in the off-season. Two possibilities exist for the off-season use of the pool in climate zones where temperatures are consistently below freezing. The first involves completely draining the pool to convert the bottom and deck areas into court games. Using plastic tapes as temporary lines, games such as volleyball, badminton, deck tennis, table tennis, paddle tennis, basketball, and shuffleboard can be laid out. The pool must be of the all-shallow-water type. A 50-meter pool that does not vary more than 12 to 18 inches from one end to the other is ideal.

Freezing the water in the pool for use as an ice rink is the second off-season pool activity. Water is usually lowered 30 to 36 inches below the deck or rimflow level.

An engineering firm in Toronto, Canada, has developed an interesting concept. The pool is converted to a skating rink by the placement of plastic pipes on the surface of the pool so that the refrigerant may be distributed by means of a portable refrigeration system.

Combination plan. In the combination plan, the pool is used for activities selected from both of the previous categories. For example, a program may be developed that calls for boating in the fall, court games in the winter, fishing and bait casting in the spring, and a full swimming program in the summer.

Use of bathhouse. Too many bathhouses only serve the patrons of the swimming pool in the summer months. With careful planning and at little extra cost the bathhouse can be converted in the off-season to a functional community center, or it may serve as the "warming room" and administrative offices for a skating rink located adjacent to the pool.

Staffing the Pool

Because a direct relationship exists between the success of a swimming pool and the quality and performance of its staff, the staffing of the pool becomes a critical function of administration.

Job Identification

The first step in staffing a new pool is to identify the jobs to be performed. Generally, the administrative functions fall into three categories: instruction and supervision (lifeguards), operation and maintenance, and food service. The number of people needed to operate a pool will depend upon the size, the capacity of the pool, its support facilities and bathhouse, the scope of the program, and the number of hours that the pool is to be open each day.

Instruction and supervision. This category includes the senior lifeguard (sometimes referred to as the supervisor or captain of the lifeguards or the head lifeguard), all lifeguards, coaches, instructors, and lifeguard aides.

The person who coaches the swim team is often a highly specialized individual. Although occasionally a volunteer will fill this position, in most situations, communities hire college or high school coaches to train their teams in the summer months. Obviously, the community's desires and ambitions regarding competitive swimming will determine the approach to take. A false assumption is that a "good" swim team can be developed by merely assigning one of the lifeguards to coach.

Operation and maintenance. The operation and maintenance staff includes the pool engineer (the person responsible for operating the pool's mechanical system and controlling the overall sanitary condition of the entire complex), locker-room attendants, custodians, groundskeepers, and other support personnel.

The food service program. A public pool or club pool usually has a snack bar that is operated during the hours the pool is open under the direction of a snack bar manager. This person will occasionally work behind the counter, but his or her primary function is to be responsible for ordering supplies, supervising the snack bar staff, scheduling work shifts, processing payroll time sheets, balancing end-of-day receipts, and overseeing the cleaning of all equipment in compliance with health department regulations and the manufacturer's recommended preventive maintenance procedures. Vending machines are an alternative to the snack bar.

Job Descriptions

After each job has been identified and analyzed, a concise description of the duties of the job should be prepared. The following examples provide models of job descriptions: one of a manager's position at a city-operated pool, and the other of the lifeguard's job in the same setting. These are only sample descriptions; every pool should develop its own to address its individual needs.

Duties of the pool manager. The pool manager is responsible for the complete operation and administration of the pool and will report to the administrative head of the recreation department or other supervisory agency. The pool manager's responsibilities may include but not be limited to the following:

1. Supervise the pool plant and all related facilities.

2. Assist in recruitment, selection, and assignment of all pool personnel.

3. Plan and organize a comprehensive program of activities for the pool and schedule the use of the pool.

4. Develop and conduct in-service training programs for the staff, including drills for handling emergencies.

5. Handle any grievances of staff members.

6. Evaluate performance of staff members and review this with respective employees regularly during the season.

7. Assist in the preparation, distribution, and enforcement of rules and regulations of the pool.

8. Handle all grievances and/or discipline cases involving patrons of the pool.

9. Keep records of attendance, maintenance, and other administrative matters as set forth by administrative authority.

10. Prepare an annual report of the pool's operation.

11. Supervise the collection and banking of all receipts taken in by the pool.

12. Keep an up-to-date inventory of all equipment and supplies.

13. Prepare requisitions for procurements of supplies and equipment for the pool.

14. Assist in the opening and closing of the pool.

15. Prepare public relations material for news stories, radio announcements, brochures, and other publicity items.

16. Assure the maximum safety of pool patrons.

17. Be prepared to assist the administrator of recreation in any phase of the pool's operation not outlined above that might be required.

18. Prepare reports on needed repairs for submission to proper authority.

19. Maintain and submit employee time sheets and payroll records.

20. Make regular inspections of the pool and its equipment to assure that their condition is safe and sanitary.

Duties of the lifeguard. Lifeguards perform the following duties under the direction and supervision of the head lifeguard or pool manager.

1. Prevent accidents through the enforcement of policies, rules, regulations, and ordinances governing the conduct of persons using the swimming pool.

2. When on duty, constantly be on the lookout for potential accidents occurring in the water.

3. Enter the water to rescue persons in trouble; resuscitate swimmers who need it; administer first aid to the injured; and make certain the emergency hospital is notified in case of any serious accident.

4. Maintain the swimming pool deck; keep gutters clean; assist in cleaning locker rooms when instructed; and make minor adjustments on filter and chemical system as requested by the pool manager or engineer.

5. Perform other duties such as being watchman or vacuuming the pool as may be requested by the pool manager or head lifeguard.

6. Maintain order in the pool and, as far as possible, anticipate trouble and take steps to prevent it.

7. Call head lifeguard or manager if assistance in maintaining discipline of swimmers is needed.

8. Be friendly, helpful, and cheerful to all pool patrons and fellow employees in the performance of duties.

9. Assist in the program of instruction or coach swim team when requested by the head lifeguard or manager.

10. Assist as needed in any area of the pool when requested by the head lifeguard or manager.

11. Report definite or potential physical hazards and unsafe pool or equipment conditions to head lifeguard.

12. Maintain an acceptable appearance of both uniform and personal hygiene at all times.

13. Be punctual when reporting for duty and appear in the prescribed uniform.

Wage Policy

Once all the jobs have been identified and described, they should be ranked by salary from the highest paying job to the lowest. Salary schedules should then be developed for each job level. Furthermore, within each job level a salary must be established with incremental steps to reflect years of experience, advanced education and training, and other pertinent factors. All employees, unless they are in a training status, must be paid at least at the rate of the existing minimum hourly wage established by state and federal laws. It is sometimes necessary to make a wage survey before fixing salary scales. This is done by phone calls or visits to other pools in the community or in adjacent communities to obtain their salary schedules and job descriptions (duties often vary even though the job titles are the same).

Other Personnel Policies

In addition to the wage policy, policies and definitions must be written for other personnel practices such as the work day, work week, vacation time, sick leave, holidays, disciplinary action, handling of grievances, separation notices, performance appraisal, severance benefits, death benefits, compensation, retirement plan, insurance, and completion bonus. All policies, procedures, and rules pertaining to personnel should appear in an employees handbook, which should be given to each person upon employment.

Recruiting Personnel

If qualified people are not hired, the consequence is a poorly managed pool that endangers the health and safety of patrons. Recruiting involves the search for the most qualified people. Recruitment should commence well in advance of the opening of the season. The manager or pool director is the first person who should be hired and then become involved in the recruiting process. Only qualified individuals should be hired.

Several steps are involved in recruiting:

1. Announcements of job openings. The announcements may appear in newspaper ads and may be forwarded to college placement offices and to such agencies as YMCAs, Boys Clubs, the local Red Cross chapter, and high schools. The announcement should include a listing of the openings available, the qualifications for each position, salary, and other pertinent job-related information.

2. Receipt of inquiries, filling out applications by prospective employees, and interviews. An application form needs to be prepared. When it is received, it should be acknowledged promptly and a date for an interview established assuming the applicant meets minimum criteria. After a candidate has been interviewed, a decision should be made as promptly as possible, so the applicant can be informed of the decision. An important step is to check the credentials (certificates) for validity.

3. Acceptance or rejection of applicant. As soon as the decision has been made, the applicant should be notified in writing. If an individual's application has been accepted, that person should receive all pertinent information regarding the conditions of his or her employment. This could be in the form of a letter of agreement or contract.

4. An optional step often used in large operations is some type of examination, written and/or practical.

Training Pool Personnel

It should never be assumed that people hired are completely qualified to step in and perform their job. Orientation to the job and regular drills practicing all phases of their work are necessary. For lifeguards this means all forms of rescue. The first step in the training process is to provide the employee with the description of the job for which the individual has been hired. The second step is issuing the employee the pool's operations manual, which the employee should study thoroughly.

The following steps should also be included in the training of pool personnel.

Attendance at lectures, courses, or clinics. These events are often offered by the local Red Cross chapter, colleges, or other agencies such as the YMCA. Usually, the tuition fees for these courses come out of the pool's budget. In some areas local or state health authorities offer courses in pool operation. Some state associations, for example, Texas Beach and Pool Association, offer short courses in various aspects of pool operation.

Preseason training. This involves 1 to 3 days of continuous schooling immediately before the opening of the pool. A curriculum or course outline should be developed, which should not include performing such duties as preparing the pool for its opening. Rather, the staff should be concerned with learning about the execution of the specific functions they are expected to perform during the season. During this training period, lifeguards should be tested on certain types of rescues. Each year lives have been lost because of the failure of a lifeguard to make a simple rescue. Fear and panic are often obstacles to a successful rescue, and training helps to overcome this fear.

In-service training. In-service training may be of several types. One type might be visits to other pools on days off to observe and discuss methods of operation with experienced aquatic personnel. Another type of in-service training might be staff meetings with the pool manager. A third type might consist of short courses conducted at the pool on such topics as first aid and CPR, which are offered to lifeguards during slack periods of the day. Daily workouts and drills should be a standard practice to assure that each lifeguard is in satisfactory physical condition. A swimming rescue is a strenuous experience and the proficiency of the lifeguard depends upon his or her skill and endurance in the water.

Personal consultations. These involve meetings between individual staff members and the pool manager or other supervisors to discuss problems related to the individual's work.

Using personnel from other city departments, such as the police, fire, and health instructors, should be considered because they are often experts in certain emergency and health procedures.

Staff Assignments

It is imperative that personnel be properly assigned by publishing and posting a pool schedule.

This schedule includes days off, the daily and weekly work program, and even the hourly assignments and/or events related to work schedules. The schedule should be posted in a conspicuous location so that all personnel know what is expected of them. Assignment of lifeguards is usually the responsibility of the head lifeguard. All schedules, however, should be approved by the pool manager.

An important point to remember is that lifeguards should never be expected to sit in a chair for longer than 1 hour at a time. Two practices that many lifeguards prefer are (a) a 15-minute relief period after 1 hour in the chair, and (b) a change to another type of activity such as instructing beginners or working in the office on a 1-hour cycle.

Such a rotation enables a guard to work effectively throughout the day.

Supervision and Evaluation of Staff

All employees should be constantly supervised. This is one of the major functions of the manager and the assistants such as the head lifeguard. Evaluation of staff performance is important and should be a continuous process. Supervisors should counsel staff members whenever there is a need to upgrade or improve their performance. A critical period is toward the end of the season when people tend to become lax in their work performance.

Indoor natatorium, YMCA, Darien, Connecticut

Chapter 2

Voluntary Agency and School Pools

The planning, design, and operation of community pools, most of which are tax supported, were discussed in chapter 1. This chapter focuses on the planning and operation of pools for schools and colleges (public and private) and pools for such voluntary agencies as Ys, Boys Clubs, and Jewish Community Centers. Some of the unique problems and features of agency and school pools will be presented. Elements common to all pools—water chemistry, design criteria, hydraulic systems, pool equipment, and safety features—are treated in detail in other chapters.

Agency Pools

Until the 1940s, if a person wanted to take a swim in an indoor pool in the United States, he or she usually had to go to a Y or some other voluntary agency that had a pool. Few schools and only a handful of cities had developed indoor pools. Even few hotels had pools. Today, practically every YMCA, YWCA, Boys Club, and Jewish Community Center being planned includes a swimming pool.

Pool Planning and Design

Before designing an aquatic facility, an agency should determine the need for an aquatic program, including the size and content. These predesign procedures are explained in chapter 11.

Experienced agency aquatic staff indicate the ideal aquatic facility for a comprehensive program would contain three separate pools: one for swimming and recreation; one deep pool for diving, lifesaving, and scuba; and a shallow pool for instruction. Few areas of the United States have a climate suitable for continuous year-round outdoor aquatic programs; therefore, indoor facilities are necessary for uninterrupted operation. Housing a three-pool complex indoors is expensive. Financial constraints usually limit agencies to one indoor pool in the majority of situations; consequently, most of the discussion applies to the single indoor pool facility.

Recent swimming pool surveys conducted by several agencies revealed that instruction and recreation programs account for perhaps two thirds of available pool time. Fitness programs, which in most situations involve lap swimming, are becoming an increasing user of pool time and are considered the third most popular activity. Exclusive use by swim teams still averages less than 10% of an agency's pool time. The surveys also revealed that a wide range of aquatic activities and variations exist in programs across the country and even between units in a single agency. Therefore, before accepting a swimming pool design, it is incumbent upon the agency to go through the predesign procedures to determine whether the facility will meet its program needs.

Pool Shape, Size, and Depth

Rectangular pool shapes are most common among agencies for indoor aquatic facilities because the pool is usually a part of a comprehensive facility that includes a gymnasium, game courts, meeting and game rooms, and support spaces. Pool size is determined by program needs and the number of people to be served. Most agencies desire to have competitive swimming in their aquatic program. Competitive swimming rules will, therefore, have an influence on the length and the width of the pool with four-, six-, or eight-lane pools being preferred. Many existing agency pools have 6-foot wide lanes, and some may have to continue to depart from current competitive rules that recommend seven 7-foot lanes.

Another departure often necessary from competitive rules is the depth of water at the shallow end of the pool. Many existing agency pools have only 3 feet of water at the shallow end, whereas the minimum requires a depth of 3-1/2 feet. Less shallow depths should only be permitted in special instructional pools or in divisible pools where shallow water is separated from the main swimming area by a bulkhead or lifeline. However, as much shallow water as possible under 5 feet in depth is desirable in all agency pools to accommodate the younger members.

An important decision for agencies regards the depth of water for diving. A program calling for training and events in competitive diving requires the pool be built to competitive standards. If diving is to be for recreational purposes only and springboards with lower performance than the usual aluminum boards are used, then the minimum depth may be reduced to 10 feet for a 1-meter high springboard provided the board is only 12 feet long. A sign should be posted reading—NO COMPETITIVE DIVING—on recreational pools. In Ohio this requirement is included in the regulations.

Competitive diving using high performance aluminum boards, if included in the aquatic program, should be limited to 1-meter springboards and should have a 12-foot water depth. Some pool operators have removed their 3-meter boards because of inadequate depth of water. A 3-meter springboard or diving tower requires extra supervision because it is more hazardous. Side clearance, distance between boards, and distance from board to ceiling are specified in the competitive swimming and diving rules discussed in chapter 14.

Pool Modifications for Diving

Pools that were built years ago with ''spoon-shaped bottoms'' in the diving area are now considered dangerous in light of the introduction of improved springboards, particularly the aluminum boards. A problem confronting agencies with such pools is whether diving should be permitted. There are a number of alternatives from which agencies may choose, including the following.

Remove the springboard. This is a drastic action which would eliminate one of the most popular aquatic activities.

Change the springboard. If the board is 14 feet or 16 feet long, change it to a shorter one, preferably constructed of wood with a fiberglass coating. Recommended length is 10 or 12 feet. The boards should not extend over the edge of the pool for more than 4 feet (3 feet is preferred) and should not be more than 20 inches (1/2 meter) above the water. The board should be placed on a stand with a fixed fulcrum, not the adjustable type.

Caution adults and adult-size teenagers against attempting to dive out too far. This may be accomplished by placing a warning sign on the wall near the board, calling attention to the danger of div-

Deerkill Day Camp, Suffern, New York. Note moveable bulkhead.

ing out too far. This action would also apply to the suggestion previously outlined if there is not sufficient depth forward of the board to permit unrestricted diving.

Change bottom profile of pool. This step would involve a substantial investment, which in the long run may be the best solution. It involves removal of the "hump" in the bottom. An architect or engineer will have to be engaged to draw plans for this alteration.

Lengthen the pool. If the pool is 60 feet long, for example, by lengthening it to 75 feet, the additional 15 feet of deep water will make the pool safe for diving. Similarly, if the pool is now 75 feet long, it can be lengthened to 82-1/2 feet (25 meters) thereby providing an additional 7-1/2 feet of deep water. Increasing the length of the pool usually involves extending the wall behind the board if there is sufficient deck space to permit this change. Again an architect will be required to draw plans for these changes in the pool enclosure. For outdoor pools the change can be made at less cost.

Perimeter Overflow System and Deck Design

The choice of design for the perimeter overflow system will be influenced by the agency program emphasis. The roll-out or rimflow design with a handgrip is preferred for instruction and recreation. In small agency pools, using skimmers can reduce costs. Piping from skimmers to the pool

filters, however, is usually buried under the pool decks and is inaccessible for maintenance, which increases cost if a break in the line occurs. With a roll-out rim, the water piping is preferably placed in a tunnel under the decks around the pool. In a deck-level pool (rimflow), which was first developed by the Boys Clubs, a trench in the deck is used and piping is placed in the trench and thus becomes accessible by removing the trench cover. A fuller description of overflow systems can be found in chapter 12.

Adequate deck space is essential. A wide deck about 10 feet minimum can be used for out-of-water instruction and with portable bleachers can provide spectator space for water shows and swimming meets. A wide deck on one side is recommended for pools up to 40 feet wide and wide decks on each side of the pool for pools that are over 40 feet wide. There should be public access to the wide deck space for spectator events. Permanent spectator seating is not common in agency facilities because of added cost. However, a viewing area for casual spectators is highly desirable.

Deck equipment should be as maintenance free as possible. The aluminum diving board placed on a stainless steel diving stand with an adjustable fulcrum is preferred. The rear fulcrum should be the hinge type to allow tilting the board up out of the way for competitive swimming. Grab rails at recessed ladders at each corner of the pool should be made of stainless steel and designed to prevent loosening of the anchorage. One or more lifeguard chairs are usually required by local health department codes. They must be placed so that lifeguards can achieve maximum visibility and can avoid looking into glare on the water surface. Removable starting blocks for competitive swimming should be placed at the deep end. Stainless steel or fiberglass blocks are best. All anchors for deck equipment should be bronze or stainless steel.

Another deck equipment item to consider is a system for getting handicapped persons into the swimming pool. A portable hydraulic hoist, a ramp, or wide steps are available alternatives and are described in detail in chapter 9. Access through the dressing rooms and showers to the pool deck should be barrier free, allowing wheelchair users to reach the pool.

Water slides and minitrampolines are not recommended because of the need for added supervision to ensure their safe use.

Other Design Considerations

Underwater lighting is desirable in the pool, particularly if water shows are to be programmed. The lights should not be located in end walls, but if included, they should be located between swimming lanes and have switches separate from other underwater lights. This lighting is necessary for safety when adequate overhead lighting is not provided. (See chapter 11 for more detail.)

A pool alarm system is a desirable safety feature that allows the lifeguard to call for help in an emergency. Pushing an alarm button in the pool area sounds an alarm at the attendant area where someone is always on duty and can call for help. The pool office or lifeguard station should be in full view of the pool and should have a telephone with emergency procedures posted over it. (Other pool safety features are described in chapter 8.)

In designing the enclosure for agency swimming pools, careful attention is needed to achieve good acoustics, absence of glare on the water, and conservation of energy. The heating and ventilating of the space is expensive. Heat recovery devices on air handling systems are effective in reducing operating costs. Solar heating can be used successfully for heating the pool water and water for the showers. (Refer to chapters 17 and 19 for more information on these subjects.)

When financing is available for more than the single 25-meter rectangular pool, the agency's program priorities can help determine whether or not to build a second or third pool. A 33-meter pool with a moveable bulkhead is one way to obtain separate pool areas that provide program flexibility. The enclosure for such a pool is more economical than for an L- or T-shaped pool.

Another way to have multiple pools is to enclose one pool and locate a second outdoors. This has been done in milder climates where the outdoor pool season can be stretched to 6 or 7 months.

There are situations where an agency is willing to omit programs requiring deep water. An all-shallow pool with depths from 3.5 to 5 or 6 feet can meet most program requirements. In such pools the ceiling can be lowered because diving is not included. The smaller volumes of water and interior space will substantially reduce the initial capital cost as well as the operating budget.

School and College Pools

Every child should have the opportunity sometime during the school years for instruction in the basic elements of swimming, diving, and water safety. In many instances this can only be achieved through a summer program because many schools still do not have indoor pools. Although it is both possible and desirable to teach children to swim during the preschool years, the ideal age to teach children seems to be between 6 and 8, or in the first and second grades.

At the college level, the objectives of the school's aquatic program should be the development and perfection of aquatic skills for recreation enjoyment both while the student is in college and later in life. An important objective in any instructional program in swimming must be the safe use of equipment, plus the safe conduct of the activity in various environments. It is not appropriate, for example, to teach people the technique of scuba diving without including every aspect of safety involved when the student dives in an ocean or lake environment.

Colleges and universities that have highly organized men's and women's swim teams often deny other students full use of their pool. The best solution appears to be the development of separate pools for student recreation use. Some colleges solve the conflict problem by constructing a large 50-meter pool: A portion of the pool is set aside for general student use while the swim team practices at the other end.

To assist school and college officials confronted with the task of deciding what kind and size pool they should build, the following guidelines are offered to planners.

Pools for Elementary Schools

The most important objective in any swimming program at the elementary school level is to enable every student to acquire a level of swimming proficiency and knowledge of lifesaving so that an individual will not only be safe in any water situation, but will be able to enjoy the values inherent in aquatic activities to the fullest extent.

The type of pool to be constructed at the elementary school level depends upon such factors as the

Training pool for preschoolers, University School at Nova University. Water depth ranges from 6 inches to 2 feet.

school's enrollment, the availability of other pools in the community, the amount of funds available, and the objectives of the program. Recent advances in pool technology have provided school officials with a wide choice in both design and cost. Pools for the elementary school may be classified as follows: training pools, comprehensive pools, and school-community pools.

The training pool. The training pool is designed for teaching youngsters to swim. These pools are small and usually contain shallow water throughout the pool, thus eliminating any springboard diving. Training pools may be portable, which means that the pool is placed on the ground, or they may be permanent, placed in-ground.

Portable pools (above-ground). The portable pool can be erected and taken down almost at will. Since its development in the United States after World War II, the popularity of the portable pool has spread throughout the world. The low cost of a portable pool has enabled many families to afford one.

Since its introduction in this country in the early 1950s, an estimated two million portable, or

"above-ground" or "on-ground," pools have been sold. Today's portable pools are larger, more attractive, more sophisticated in design, and possess greater structural reliability. They range in size from the small, circular 12-foot diameter pool to full-size 75-foot long pools but seldom are deeper than 4 feet. There is, however, a definite limitation to the type of activities that can be conducted in them. Because they have a maximum depth of 4 feet, diving into them is not safe; however, all the basic swimming strokes may be taught as well as fundamental lifesaving techniques.

In the summer of 1958, the Herrick School District of Long Island, New York, organized a program where over 500 elementary grade pupils were taught to swim in a 24-foot circular vinyl-lined above-ground pool. One of the advantages of above-ground pools is that they can be installed in one day. A suitable pool for use at an elementary school may be obtained for as little as $1,200. All above-ground pools, regardless of size and shape, have two things in common: They have some kind of prefabricated rigid wall structure (of wood, aluminum, steel, or fiberglass), and they have a vinyl or nylon liner inserted into the basin to contain the water.

In-ground pools. The second type of training pool suitable for elementary schools is the "in-ground" pool that is a permanent construction. The cost of in-ground pools varies widely. For example, a 20 feet by 40 feet in-ground shallow-water pool may range from $8,000 to $24,000. The less expensive pools use a vinyl liner rather than the conventional cement basin. The higher priced pools are constructed of concrete usually with a plaster finish. The typical sizes and dimensions of this type of pool are shown in Table 2.1.

Table 2.1 Typical Dimensions of an In-Ground Pool (in feet)

Minimum size	16 × 32
Desirable size	20 × 40
Minimum depth of water	2
Maximum depth of water	4.5
Minimum deck width	5
Minimum ceiling height	10
Desirable ceiling height	12 to 14

Today, many school systems find themselves with vacant classrooms because of declining enrollments. These vacant rooms can be converted to accommodate swimming pools if they are located on the ground floor. See page 29 for an illustrated explanation.

The comprehensive pool. The comprehensive elementary school pool is a facility in which most elements of an aquatic instructional program may be conducted; only springboard diving is omitted. The comprehensive pool is also suitable for recreational aquatics conducted for students and the community after school, on weekends, and during the summer months. Typical dimensions for such a pool are shown in Table 2.2.

Table 2.2 Typical Dimensions for a Comprehensive Pool (in feet)

Minimum size	20 × 60
Desirable size	30 × 60
Minimum depth	3
Maximum depth	4.5
Minimum ceiling height	10
Desirable ceiling height	14

School-community pool. This pool serves both the needs of the pupils and those of the adult population residing in the neighborhood. The dimensions listed in Table 2.3 are typical for this type of pool.

Table 2.3 Typical Dimensions of a School-Community Pool (in feet)

Minimum size	30 × 60
Desirable size	45 × 75
Minimum depth	3
Maximum depth	10
(for a 12-ft long diving board)	
Minimum ceiling height	15
Desirable ceiling height	18

The Junior High and Senior High School Pool

There is little difference between junior and senior high school pools. Both should be planned to permit a comprehensive aquatic program that includes public use of the pool. However, in some instances at the junior high school level it may not be possible to construct the size pool desired because of the cost. Obviously, even a small pool is better than no pool at all.

Table 2.4 Typical Dimensions of a Junior/Senior High Pool (in feet)

Minimum size	30 × 75
Desirable size	45 × 75
	or 82.08
Minimum water depth	3[1]
Desirable shallow depth	3.5
Minimum deep water	6[2]
Desirable deep water	12[3]
Minimum ceiling height	16
Desirable ceiling height	18

[1]Recommended only if pool is to be used extensively by elementary school children, otherwise 3.5 ft.

[2]Only if diving is not included in the program.

[3]See chapter 14 for appropriate water depth for diving.

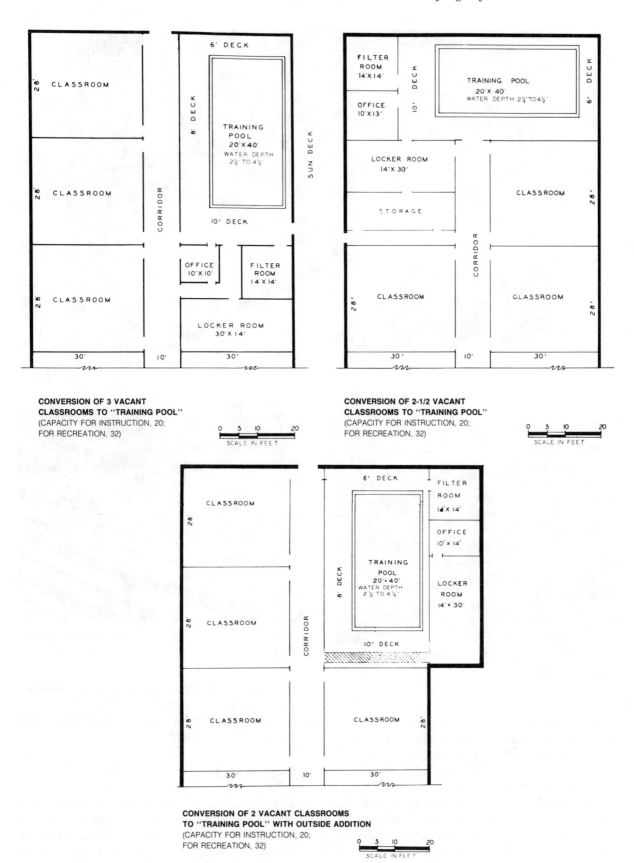

CONVERSION OF 3 VACANT
CLASSROOMS TO "TRAINING POOL"
(CAPACITY FOR INSTRUCTION, 20;
FOR RECREATION, 32)

CONVERSION OF 2-1/2 VACANT
CLASSROOMS TO "TRAINING POOL"
(CAPACITY FOR INSTRUCTION, 20;
FOR RECREATION, 32)

CONVERSION OF 2 VACANT CLASSROOMS
TO "TRAINING POOL" WITH OUTSIDE ADDITION
(CAPACITY FOR INSTRUCTION, 20;
FOR RECREATION, 32)

Sample classroom conversion plans

Two-pool complex, Downers Grove North High School, Illinois. Equipment by Kiefer.

Hughes Memorial High School, Washington, DC. Photo by Scurlock Studio.

Richwoods High School indoor natatorium, Peoria, Illinois

If possible, the high school pool that serves the aquatic needs of the community should contain a separate diving well to provide for all kinds of deep-water activities. This may also be accomplished by designing the pool in an L- or T-shape.

Some provision for spectators should be included either by construction of a balcony or through the use of roll-away bleachers placed at deck level or by the installation of permanent stands.

Detailed information regarding design features such as type of gutters, deck size, equipment, safety features, and filter systems will be found in other chapters in this book.

The College Pool

The swimming pool is emerging on many campuses as the focal point of the college's recreation program. A trend in recent years is the partial or complete financing of the pool through student fees.

Intramural-Physical Education indoor pool, University of Illinois at Urbana-Champaign. Architect: Holabird & Root. Consultant: Milton Costello. Photo by Chuck Mercer.

Probably the most important development in the design of college pools occurred during the 1970s and 1980s with the move toward 50-meter pools and, in some instances, multiple pools with separate facilities for diving and other deep-water activities. Colleges and universities have questioned whether it is more desirable to construct a single large, centrally located pool or several small pools strategically placed throughout the campus. The answer is increasingly in favor of the large complex. A good model is the pool at the University of Texas at Austin. Opened in 1977, it contains a 50 m by 25 yd, indoor eight-lane racing pool, capable of division into two or three separate training pools by the use of two moveable, floating bulkheads that are stored overhead in the roof plenum. This pool is 9 ft deep throughout and features an innovative underwater lighting system of continuous flourescent elements recessed in the pool walls 6 ft below the rim. A grid pattern of bottom inlets, coordinated with the tile racing lanes, is used to maximize water recirculation. A separate diving pool, 45 ft by 60 ft, center-staged and

theatrically elevated, features a white concrete diving tower, with 300 hp ''air cushion'' spargers. Both pools feature underwater observation windows, audio systems, ceramic tile finish, and precast rimflow stone overflows. Filtration is accomplished with a battery of regenerative-cycle D.E. filters controlled from an integrated control panel for total mechanical and also total chemical automation.

The University of Illinois at Urbana-Champaign, Indiana University-Purdue University at Indianapolis, New York University, University of Pittsburgh, University of Tennessee, Louisiana State University, and Cleveland State University are other schools with excellent aquatic complexes. All of these schools and others that either have or are in the process of constructing 50-meter pools, recognize the need for one or two additional small (25-yard) pools to serve the needs of professional physical education and aquatic instruction programs.

Factors that support the trend toward 50-meter pools may be summed up as follows:

1. Students seem to prefer being a part of a large group in a recreation setting that involves swimming. The large pool usually has a capacity from 500 to 1,000, depending upon the amount of deck space and water surface provided.

2. Pools that provide supplemental facilities such as lounge areas, sun decks, tables for eating or socializing, sauna baths, whirlpools, and other recreational facilities are the most successful in attracting students.

3. An important use of a university's outdoor pools is for summer school students and their families.

4. The faculty and their dependents find the aquatic center an enjoyable and attractive facility.

5. The large pool complex provides opportunities for holding major swimming championships, shows, demonstrations, and pageants.

6. The decks of the pool, if properly designed, may be used for dancing. The appropriate use of lighting (both underwater and overhead) enhances the beauty as well as the utility and safety of the pool.

7. The large pool permits the aquatic director to schedule several different activities or classes in the pool at the same time. At least three or four separate teaching or activity stations may easily be accommodated in a pool that is 50 meters long.

All indoor pools need to be properly heated, lighted, ventilated, and made acoustically comfortable if they are to be successful. Refer to chapter 11 for details on design of these and other important features. Where competition is to be held, every effort should be made to conform to the specifications contained in chapter 14.

Promoting a School Pool

When a community is contemplating the construction of a new school (high school, junior high, or elementary), it is time to consider the inclusion of a pool as part of the educational plant. Some hints to guide the physical education director and school officials in achieving the objective are given below.

Study the need for a pool. Accumulate supporting data on the number of pools available in the community, the range of swimming ability among students, the relationship of the pool to the schools, the physical education program, and the community's accessibility to natural bodies of water.

Make the pool a part of the total package. The pool should not be thought of as a separate entity to be voted upon as an optional facility but must be viewed as an integral part of the school's instructional facilities, not as a frill.

Be modest in your plans. Do not "shoot for the sky" in design. Propose a good functional pool but not an elaborate one unless the community wants such a pool and is willing to pay for it.

Involve the community in the planning. Use the "community pool" approach. In other words, design the pool to meet total community needs for aquatics rather than merely for instruction of schoolchildren.

Illustrate that the capital cost of the pool and its operation is low when calculated on the basis of its use. It usually is the most used facility in the school.

Set priorities. Be willing to reduce some of the areas of indoor physical education facilities in order to get the pool. The pool should be second in priority only after the gymnasium. It should have a higher priority than the wrestling room or separate gymnastic room when planning the physical education plant.

Provide leadership. One person must spearhead the drive for a pool. This must be a person who is respected in the community and is articulate and persuasive enough to be able to go before the civic groups and the public to sell the pool concept.

Nova University 3-pool complex, Fort Lauderdale, Florida.

The School's Aquatic Program

The following are three possible divisions of a school or college aquatic program:

- *The school day program.* Involves instruction for students as part of their curriculum.

- *After-school and vacation program.* This phase of the program is largely recreational; the swim team is one aspect. Many programs are combining the boys and girls swim teams so that they practice together. Every school and college with a pool should develop a program to teach preschool children.

- *Public program.* This may be both instructional and recreational and is directed toward all the people in the community. Evenings, Saturdays, and Sundays are the usual periods when this program is offered.

School and Community Cooperation. An excellent opportunity exists for cooperative effort between the school and the local city recreation departments, in using swimming pools during off-school hours. This type of cooperation may extend to the financing of the initial construction costs of the pool, which then becomes a joint operational venture. Here are some examples of cooperation between schools and municipalities.

1. A municipal outdoor summer-operated swimming pool is made available to the school for special instructional classes prior to the opening of the regular season. This may take place as much as 4 to 6 weeks in advance of the regular opening. Water temperature of 80 °F and air temperature of at least 65 °F are essential conditions.

2. A municipal indoor pool on a contract with a school district conducts a swimming instructional program for schoolchildren during school hours as a regular part of the school's physical education program, or the school's staff conducts the program. The school pays an annual fee for this service.

3. A school turns over the operation of its pools to the local recreation department during vacation periods, particularly during the summer months.

4. The city recreation department conducts special programs on Saturday and Sunday in a school pool. These programs, intended to reach the adult population, often include special instruction for police and firemen in such activities as the use of scuba equipment in rescue work.

5. Schools make arrangements with local motels or hotels to use their pools in the morning hours when guests seldom use the pool.

Indoor and Outdoor Pools. The indoor-outdoor pool concept works by opening large doors or by sliding the whole pool enclosure or roof away on a track, or by a removable "pillow roof" as in Mamaranack, New York. These types of indoor-outdoor pools have provided us with data on cost-effectiveness and maximum use. Some conclude that pool use has been increased, whereas others say its cost and problems have overshadowed any benefits. It is wise to compare the cost of constructing the structures to convert the pool to the cost of adding an outdoor pool.

The move to the metric system. The question of whether to build the new indoor high school or college pool at metric length (25 meters instead of the current official 25 yards) in anticipation that a change in the rules will occur sometime in the future is difficult. The best solution is to go with 25 meters and moveable bulkhead, which will shorten the course to 25 yards if necessary. Competition may be conducted in either one; however, when a school is bidding for a regional or national championship meet, the selection committee may restrict its choice to 25-meter pools.

Programming considerations. Scheduling various units of instruction in a block of classes (e.g., daily for several weeks instead of once per week) is best. It has been demonstrated that students learn most quickly when instruction is concentrated over a week or two.

The most important objective is to teach every student to swim as well as to teach basic lifesaving and aquatic safety. Classes should be split into levels of ability, such as beginner, intermediate, and swimmer. Ability levels also permit better utilization of the pool facility. Where possible, student leaders should be trained to assist the regular class instructor. The ideal ratio of beginners to instructor is one leader for each student. This pairing arrangement provides valuable training to the student leaders and also gives the instructor the opportunity to work with larger groups where a one-to-one ratio is not needed. This way one teacher can handle 15 to 20 students.

The physical education instructor assigned to the swimming program should be an aquatic specialist. Only a trained and qualified person should be responsible for pool supervision, regarding health and safety as well as the entire year's programming. The specialist should have a Red Cross Water Safety Instructor's Certificate or its equivalent and first-aid and CPR certificates.

Some Suggestions on Administration and Programming of School Pools

1. All instruction should be under the supervision of only qualified people.

2. Safety aspects of any activity being taught should always be included. The consequences of doing something wrong should always be pointed out to students.

3. The risk inherent in any activity should be minimized as much as possible.

4. A plan to handle any emergency that might happen in or around the pool should be established (see chapter 8).

5. When a class or group is scheduled for instruction, someone should lifeguard because the teacher's attention is usually directed to the instruction of the class.

6. Nonswimmers should not be included in a class of swimmers. If such situations do occur, a person should be assigned to watch nonswimmers at all times.

7. Fifty to 70 people drown in college or school pools each year, which is a small percentage in relation to the millions who swim in these pools. It is significant that most drownings occurred when no lifeguard was on duty.

8. Every pool should have a direct outside telephone line for emergency use and a portable inhalator-resuscitator.

9. All students at every level of ability should be instructed in making simple rescues and administering artificial respiration, including CPR (cardiopulmonary resuscitation).

10. The subject of safety should be included in every swimming class.

Variable deck levels add interest to the pool setting. Photo from Gary Pools.

Chapter 3
Residential Pools

The post–World War II era was a unique time in the United States. America was ready to forget 5 years of commitment and sacrifice to an effort that had drained its every resource. The war provided the impetus that finally brought it out of a great financial depression. Almost overnight the economy recovered, initiating an affluence never experienced in the country's history. The 40-year period since the war has produced the most dramatic advances in technology the world has ever experienced. Television, computers, nuclear power, solar energy, jet engines, and a nationwide interstate highway system are just a few of the remarkable developments that took place during this period. The baby boom, emphasis on the family as a unit, and the deep desire to repress the horror of 5 years of global conflict left Americans with a desire to recreate. It was this desire, coupled with many technological breakthroughs, that spurred the development of the residential pool industry that in the viewpoint of many has yet to peak.

The growth of residential pools in the United States is related to individual health, family recreation, changing life-styles, and a resulting increase to the value of homes. Americans are caught up in a wave of personal fitness. For many families the backyard pool is fast becoming the focal point for family recreation. Because of increasing travel costs, the home pool is substituting for long vacations with cars and campers for many American families. Undoubtedly, the home pool has made a significant contribution to the great increase in the number of Americans who know how to swim, which is reflected in the decrease of drownings each year. Being able to swim opens the door to many other aquatic activities such as sailing, canoeing, water skiing, boating, scuba diving, surfing, and fishing.

This chapter serves as a guide for residential pool designers, builders, and homeowners who have pools or are contemplating acquiring one. Every home pool should be designed and operated as safely as possible so that the health and safety of users is assured. The steps outlined in this chapter are designed to provide that assurance.

Elements Involved in Pool Planning

Most residential pools have been planned for people by pool builders and by firms that manufacture "prefab" and "package pools." Each offers many models from which homeowners may choose. Homeowners must recognize that residential pools, because of their size and depth, require strict limitations to the kind of activities that can be safely conducted in them.

Types of Pools

The three basic types of residential pools are the on-ground, above-ground, and in-ground pools. The terms *on-ground* and *above-ground* are often confusing because the differences are quite minimal. Residential pools usually serve an individual family but no more than three living units. Residential pools whether above-ground, on-ground, or in-ground are subject to the same dangers; they all require safety rules, good principles of administration, lifesaving equipment, fencing, an emergency procedure, supervision, proper sanitation, insurance, and periodic maintenance and safety checks—the same requirements as public pools.

There are many small "splash-type" pools ranging in size from 4 to 10 feet in diameter with water depths anywhere from 4 to 18 inches. These splash pools are sold in toy, hardware, and department stores. Because they hold water, they represent a potential danger to unattended youngsters and they, too, must be supervised at all times that children are in or around them.

On-ground and above-ground pools. On-ground pools contain rigid wall panels that are attached to each other to produce a straight-sided rectangular or other geometric shape. Much more versatility in shape and size is possible with rigid wall design. Another distinction of this type of pool is the full decking around it. This feature lends itself more to on-ground pools than above-ground pools, becoming a part of the external bracing system that serves to hold the straight walls in a vertical position. On-ground pools can also be identified by rigid piping and fixed electrical con-

nections. These permanent features distinguish these pools from the above-ground pools. An on-ground pool is not portable or capable of being moved to another location.

Above-ground pools are constructed with a continuous flexible wall that lends itself to round or oval shapes, which provide uniform distribution of forces from the water within the pool. Both on- and above-ground pools are sold in kits with plywood, aluminum, fiberglass, or steel wall components and a vinyl liner that holds the water. Either type can be "hoppered" to provide more depth for other activities.

The popularity of above-ground and on-ground pools has far exceeded the expectations of their early developers. Today, more than 50% of the pools in this country rest on the surface of the ground rather than in the ground. The advantages and disadvantages of these pools are as follows:

Advantages

- Relatively low cost
- Ease and reduced time of installation
- Portability, permitting their removal at season's end
- Usually no increase in property tax
- Instant recreation for the family
- Low operating cost
- Ease of maintenance

Disadvantages

- Not a permanent addition to the home
- Often does not match house design

Lomart's Woodcrest rectangular above-ground pool

- Hard to supervise

- Limited life span (usually 5 to 10 years)

- Limits types of activities (e.g., no diving) because of size, shape, and depth of water

- Frequent need to patch vinyl liner

In-ground pools. In-ground pools are of two types. The conventional pool is more or less permanent and is usually constructed of concrete (called gunite), fiberglass, steel, aluminum, and, in rare cases, concrete block. By far the most common of these is the gunite pool. Since the 1970s, the prefabricated package pool has become popular because of its lower cost.

The permanent pool in most instances is constructed of gunite and, if properly constructed and cared for, may last 40 to 50 years or longer. This pool also contains permanent plumbing, electrical fixtures, pumps, and filters, and often includes such features as heaters, a solar heating system, water slides, diving boards, underwater lights, and pool covers. One of the strong features of the gunite process is its versatility of form in that the pool can be shaped in any manner desired, including the kidney, lazy L, pear, figure 8, oval, and the always popular rectangular. Low-cost enclosures, such as air-supported fabric and lightweight metal frames supporting acrylic or fabric material fitted with proper heating equipment, enable the pool to be used year-round.

In-ground pools have many advantages, especially their larger size. As a result, more aquatic activities can be conducted in them. In-ground pools increase property value significantly and when properly located and landscaped, enhance the appearance of the property. The deck space and lounging area are limited only by the lot size. Disadvantages are the initial cost of the pool, the need for more expensive fencing, increased insurance cost, possibility of more maintenance, more extensive repairs, and often an increase in property taxes.

The package, or prefabricated, pool has emerged as the most popular in-ground residential pool. Most of the suppliers of this type of pool do not manufacture *any* of the component parts. Instead they purchase the components from subcontractors, then assemble the pools and sell them to dealers and retailers throughout the country. The major feature of these pools is the vinyl liner that serves as the water container. This replaces the concrete basin, thereby reducing the cost of these pools to about one half of the conventional concrete pool. The life span of these pools is directly related to the care they receive and how carefully the subsurface is prepared.

The component parts of the package pool include

- the walls, usually made of rolled aluminum or steel;

- support members that hold the wall in place;

- the coping that locks the vinyl in place;

- ladders or steps;

- filter, pump, and piping;

- optional items such as diving boards, water slides, and covers.

A disadvantage of package pools is that the pool components come from various manufacturers rather than one source.

Prepurchase Planning

A reliable, experienced pool builder can save the homeowner much time because of his knowledge of local building codes and health department requirements. This does not always apply when purchasing an above-ground pool from a local store or distributor. The following items should be considered before signing a contract or purchasing a pool.

- Local building codes that apply to residential pools

- Health department rules and regulations applicable to residential pools

- Permits needed

- Any deed restrictions

- The presence of any easements

- The probable use of utilities (gas, electric, sewage)

- Type of soil or rock that may influence excavation

- Ability to get heavy equipment onto the property

- The construction contract, including warranty and guarantee

- Cost of pool and accessories

- Pool shapes

Above-ground pools are usually limited to circular and oval shapes. On the other hand, the shape of in-ground concrete pools utilizing the so-called gunite process is virtually unlimited. From a utility point of view, the rectangular pool is generally considered the best design. Free-formed pools, however, have a greater aesthetic quality, befitting the style and decor of the home.

Before a homeowner decides to contact a pool salesperson, it is prudent to do some preliminary planning. Checklist 1 offers pool-planning criteria that should be considered before contacting a pool builder. Some of the preliminary planning may have to be modified as a result of suggestions from the pool builder.

Checklist 2, which follows, contains a break-

Checklist 1 Residential Pool Planning Checklist

---

1. Purposes or uses of the pool: _____

2. Secured copies of necessary ordinances:

   _____ Health   _____ Zoning   _____ Building   _____ Sewage   _____ Other

3. Secured copy of property survey: _____

4. Available space: Length _____   Width _____   Total square feet _____

5. Site accessible from road: _____   for large equipment: _____

6. Best location on lot: _____

7. Desired location related to house: Close _____   Away _____

8. Pool orientation: North-South _____   East-West _____   Other _____

9. Surface drainage rating: _____   Type of soil: _____

10. Shape: _____   Size Pool: Length _____   Width _____

11. Depth of water: Shallow _____   Deep _____

12. Type of construction material: _____

13. Deck size: _____   material: _____

14. Lighting desired: Underwater _____   Area (night swimming) _____

15. Required safety accessories (not optional):

    Reaching pole _____   Ring buoy _____   Spineboard _____

    First-aid kit _____   Pool cane _____   Test kit _____

16. Pool and deck accessories:

    Ladders _____   Leaf skimmer _____   Patching kit _____

    Heaters _____   Lounge chairs _____   Diving board _____   (Size: _____)

17. Equipment storage: Needs to be built _____   Available _____

18. Names of potential pool builders:

    A. _____

    B. _____

---

down of the various cost items related to pool construction. The homeowner is advised to request an estimate for each item from the pool builder.

Water Depth

The depth of water required in any pool must be determined by the activities to be conducted. Of all the aquatic activities, springboard diving is the most demanding with respect to water depth. For minimum safe water depth, see chapter 8. The depth of water at the shallow end of the pool should not be less than 3 feet. Diving from the deck should never be permitted where the water is less than 5 feet deep. Currently, springboards have been eliminated from residential pools because of their potential danger. When springboards are not placed in pools, the depth of water should range from 3 to 6 feet. The 6-foot depth provides a safe depth for normal dives from the deck of the pool. Diving should be prohibited in all constant depth above-ground pools that have water depths of 4 feet or less.

These dimensions are considered minimums and are the product of extensive diving research con-

Indoor residential pool

Checklist 2 Breakdown of Cost Items for Residential Pool (To be supplied by potential builder)

Item	Estimated Cost
1. Excavation	
2. Construction	
3. Plumbing	
4. Electrical	
5. Landscaping	
6. Accessories (safety)	
7. Accessories (pool/deck)	
8. Fencing	
9. Pump, filter, and supplies	
Total Cost	
Amount of Money Available	
Amount to be Borrowed	

ducted at Nova University (Gabrielsen, 1984) that included leading water safety specialists, engineers, architects, diving coaches, physicians, and diving champions. Of special concern are the ''hopper-'' and ''spoon-'' shaped pool bottoms. Both designs are potentially dangerous for springboard diving as well as diving from the side. A pool designed to accommodate diving in the deep end should have a constant depth bottom throughout the entire diving area with only a gradual slope allowed for drainage purposes. Pools must not only be designed safely but must also be operated safely.

Construction Materials

All types of above-ground pools utilize essentially the same basic construction materials. Walls are rigid and free-standing and usually made of aluminum or galvanized steel coil or interlocking panels. A few designs are made of wood. The panels are fastened together with vertical aluminum or galvanized steel supports to secure them in place. A liner is placed inside the walls that then forms the vessel that holds the water. The liner is usually made of vinyl.

In-ground pools are more permanent and therefore require materials that will withstand the forces of soil, water, and weather. Five types of materials are utilized in construction of the basin of in-ground pools: metal, wood, fiberglass, concrete, and vinyl. Each has its advantages and disadvantages. Selection will depend on cost, material availability, and soil consideration.

Metal Pools

The obvious advantage of metal pools is their strength. These pools successfully withstand cracks from freezing and loose fill problems. Metal pools do not require assistance from the soil to hold water and therefore are adaptable to hillside installation. Panels are prefabricated steel or aluminum sections that are trucked to the site where they are bolted, welded, plumbed, and equipped with various accessories such as lights and steps. Steel panels may be finished with porcelain, galvanized, or baked enamel. Panel size and weight can be a problem as a large truck with a crane is necessary to handle them and must be able to get close to the pool location.

Wood Pools

Wood is a material used mostly with above-ground pools today because of its low cost, light weight, and easy installation. Panels are made of specially treated wood and lined with .020 or .030 gauge vinyl. It is important to note that wood should never be treated with creosote as this chemical will react with the plastic liner and destroy it. Some in-ground pools utilize wood panels for the walls and a vinyl interior basin.

Fiberglass Pools

The early use of fiberglass for constructing residential pools proved to be less than satisfactory as many installations suffered from buckling, leaking, and adverse reaction to soil chemicals. These problems have now been solved, providing the industry with a satisfactory means of construction that offers many unique advantages including the flexibility so important in areas with expansive soil and severe freezing conditions. Fiberglass requires no expansion joints, is colorfast, requires no other interior or exterior finish, is completely resistant to algae growth, and is virtually maintenance free.

Pools constructed of fiberglass are available in two types: one-piece shells and fiberglass-walled models that require a poured concrete floor. The one-piece shell is just now coming into widespread use as more manufacturing plants are developing around the country. One disadvantage of this type is size and shape. Only a few sizes and shapes are available because each size requires a separate mold. Fiberglass-walled pools have become more popular because of flexibility. The panels are multilaminated with steel rib reinforcement and are used to build any size pool as the walls are embedded in a poured concrete footer.

Concrete Pools

Concrete is the most widely preferred construction material because of its strength, durability, and potential for free-form shaping. Three types of concrete construction are employed in today's residential pools, offering the purchaser a variety of advantages.

Poured concrete.   Poured concrete construction is the most expensive because of the labor costs involved in placing and removing forms. The use of forms results in some limitations as to the size and shape of the pool. Poured concrete pools do not lend themselves to the "do-it-yourselfer." Interlocking masonry blocks are used, which present some obstacles to free-form design. The blocks are layered on a footer and reinforced with steel rods. Then the walls are grouted, and a bond beam of poured concrete is poured around the top to form the coping.

Hand-packed concrete. The process of hand-packed concrete construction requires the skill of a professional mason and is not recommended for the home handyman. Once the pool site has been excavated, the concrete is applied to the hole without forms conforming to the shape of the excavation. The finished product will only be as good as the cement layer. After the concrete is hand packed, a layer of gunite is applied to the concrete to provide the finished surface.

Pneumatic concrete or gunite. Pneumatic applied concrete, or gunite construction, is the most popular concrete system in use today, requiring a professional with the proper equipment. The pool site must be accessible from a road to allow the vehicles with the application equipment close to the site. Gunite pools can be made in any shape.

After the hole is excavated, a steel mesh coupled with interlaced steel rods is added and the gunite (hydrated or very dry cement and sand) is blown into the hole utilizing a compressor, cement mixer, hose, and mixing nozzle. Once the gunite is "shot" into place, the construction crew begins to work the gunite, smoothing it out and making sure no pipes or drains are plugged.

Vinyl Pools

More pools use vinyl as the material to hold water than any other product because it is less costly and is easily installed. All above-ground pools utilize a vinyl membrane as their basin. Although well-installed and maintained vinyl will last at least 10 years, it is not permanent and will eventually need to be replaced.

Interior Basin Finish Surfaces

Regardless of the construction material used, the finished surface of the pool basin should be white, whether it has been plastered or painted. The most common finish used in concrete pools is plaster, which consists of white cement with a marbledust ingredient. Popular trade names are "Marcite" and "Marblelite." The white surface provides

Wood deck on two sides of pool. Photo courtesy of Weather King.

maximum visibility. Dark colors should never be used. Water imparts or reflects blue light and a white bottom will provide the maximum in safety and aesthetic value. Before filling the pool, lines should be painted at various locations as follows:

- A 2-inch black edge on any steps leading into the pool; all safety ledges (if used); and in-water seats

- A 4-inch wide line down the middle of the pool; at the breakpoint between shallow/deep areas of the pool; on all seams of hopper-bottom type pools; and at all points of slope change

This safety factor will increase visual acuity and the depth perception of swimmers and divers. Paint utilized as a final surface should be epoxy or a chlorinated-rubber base paint for longer wear as it is more resistant to the strong acids and bases inherent in community water systems and the pool chemicals used for disinfection purposes and water conditioning.

Decks and Deck Surfaces

Regardless of the type of material used, a deck has two functions: as a safe walkway and as a lounging area. It also forms an aesthetic transition between the pool and its surrounding areas. The area around a pool can be finished in many unique ways—some expensively and others inexpensively. The following materials are available for deck finishes and the lounge area:

Pool by Paddock of California. Photo by Julius Shulman.

- Patio stone
- Wood (tends to splinter after a few years)
- Flagstone
- Indoor-outdoor carpeting (usually placed over concrete)
- Turf
- Pavement block
- Brick or quarry tile
- Concrete, either brushed or keystone finish

A great deal of thought should be given to the desired effect, safety, and cost of the materials used. The least expensive is natural grass; however, the clippings, insects, and dirt that accompany grass and the fact that chlorinated water tends to kill grass often rules out its use. The lounge area should be large enough for the family and guests and should provide for drainage of rainwater away from the pool. All walkways should be constructed of nonslip, easy-to-clean materials. An area of concrete or patio stone has proven to be the best material to use adjacent to the pool. Recently introduced concrete stain has provided pleasing color to the otherwise drab concrete.

Pool Equipment and Accessories

The homeowner will need to consider many pool accessories and pieces of equipment. These additions are based on available funds, pool size and depth, and the functions the pool is to serve. Although some may be added later, there are several that must be considered essential to the safe operation of the pool.

Ladders, Handrails, and Steps

Children and adults must have an easy entrance and exit from the pool. Ladders are most commonly used for this purpose and are usually made of chrome-plated brass or stainless steel. Concrete pools lend themselves well to a safer design, utilizing steps that are recessed into the pool wall with a grab rail mounted in the deck. The stephole should be 5 inches deep and sloped slightly toward the pool. The handrail and recessed steps are preferred because they incorporate a basic pool design rule of keeping objects from protruding into the pool. Regardless of the type chosen, all ladders must be rigidly installed, corrosion resistant, and nonslip and should provide a good handhold for swimmers. Any pool 30 feet wide or more should have ladders on both sides—one at the deep end, the other at the shallow end.

Skimmer

Skimmer is the name given to the orifice through which the pool's surface water is circulated. The return of water to the pool is usually through side wall inlets or a bottom inlet. Skimmers have largely replaced the conventional perimeter overflow trough, or "scum gutter" as it is frequently called, particularly in home pools because of lower cost.

Underwater Lights

Two types are presently used, wet niche and dry niche. Wet niche are preferred for residential pools as they may be relamped from in the water. Dry niche lights are lamped through the deck or from behind the pool wall and present the possibility of considerable water loss should the lens be broken. Underwater lights are a safety feature because they help illuminate the bottom of the pool, which is essential in night swimming and diving. They also provide an attractive appearance at night.

Niches should be constructed at least 18 inches below the normal water line to prevent lens breakage in cold weather. Recently, pool ladders have come equipped with lights, including low-voltage models. A detailed description of pool lighting is provided in chapter 11; however, pool owners should consult local building and electrical codes before construction begins to avoid possible violations for improper installation of lights.

Overhead or Area Lighting

If the pool is to be used for night swimming, overhead lighting is strongly recommended to provide safe illumination of the deck, surrounding areas, and pool bottom. Mercury and sodium vapor or quartz iodide lights will provide maximum light at the least cost and are not as apt to attract insects as incandescent lighting. (See chapter 11 for type of light and required intensity.) No improperly lighted pool should be used at night.

Ground Fault Circuit Interrupter

All electrical lines, outlets, and equipment should be protected with some type of ground fault interrupter. These devices sense any electrical leak and trip the circuit breaker to prevent electrical shock to any pool user.

Heaters

By adding a heater, pool use may be greatly increased, starting earlier in the spring and extending later into the fall in northern climates. The cost of pool heaters, however, may add considerably to the total price of the pool. Because of the added cost, the owner may want to operate one season without the heater before making a decision to install one. The following basic forms of energy are presently used for pool heaters.

Gas: Either propane or natural gas is used. Gas is less expensive than fuel oil or solar units to install and less costly than electric to operate. At the present time the availability and supply of gas is a problem in some areas of the United States, and its use has been banned in some locales.

Oil: Next to solar heating, oil is the least expensive to operate, but initial installation costs are more than gas. Fuel oil heaters also can be noisy and give off an objectionable odor while in use.

Electric: Electric is probably the least practical of all pool heating methods. Installation costs are similar to fuel oil, but operating costs are high in most areas of the country. Some owners may be forced to install electric heat where there is a moratorium on natural gas. The owner is advised to make sure that his or her home is capable of handling the additional electrical load before installation.

Solar energy: For most regions in the United States, solar energy is the best source of thermal energy for the future. Although a variety of solar heaters are available, some problems still exist. The industry and solar energy's subsequent applications are still in their youth; therefore, some equipment and dealers are undependable, and cost of installation is still high. Reading chapter 17 is advised for more detailed information on solar heating.

Solar blankets: The term *solar blanket* is a misnomer, although there have been experiments using a so-called blanket to trap the thermal energy from the sun. Most solar blankets are intended to keep the heat in the water when the pool is not in use. They have proven to be effective in certain areas and are expected to find greater use as the cost of pool heaters and energy continues to rise.

Diving Equipment

Springboards and jumpboards can add a great deal of fun to the residential pool, provided the pool is constructed according to the dimensions recommended in chapter 8. Diving boards are made of laminated wood coated with fiberglass or plastic, rigid wood stringers coated with laminated fiberglass cloth, or aluminum. Boards are fixed on stainless steel mounts with adjustable or permanent fulcrums. The height achieved in a dive is determined by the diver's weight, the length and flexibility of the board, and the position of the fulcrum. Following are guidelines for the installation of diving boards:

- Do not purchase an aluminum board for a residential pool because of its high-performance characteristics.
- Use only stands with fixed fulcrums.
- Do not install diving boards over 12 feet in length unless your pool is 12 feet deep.
- No residential diving board should be placed higher than 20 inches above the water.

A jumpboard is a possible consideration where space does not allow for the inclusion of a full diving board. Jumpboards are constructed of the same materials as diving boards and range in length from 4 to 8 feet. They are usually mounted on a heavy-duty steel spring. The preceding recommendations for the design of the diving board are also recommended for jumpboards to ensure safe diving for adults.

Water Slides

With the possible exception of a diving board, a water slide will probably provide more fun for children than any other piece of pool equipment. Most slides are made from fiberglass and usually are mounted on an aluminum frame; they come in a variety of sizes ranging from 4 to 12 feet in height. Some models have a curve in the slide bed. All slides are lubricated; consequently, the slider experiences no friction. Slide use should be restricted only to children and only in a sitting position, unless the slide is located at the deep end of the pool (minimum of 8 feet). The U.S Consumer Product Safety Commission published a federal standard for slide installation in 1976. Water slide use should be carefully supervised under any circumstances because children are prone to go down in ways that are potentially dangerous. Some individuals will actually attempt to dive headfirst into shallow water from the top of the slide.

Hose Bibb

Hose bibbs are necessary for filling the pool and cleaning the deck area around it. Several bibbs should be included in the plan to allow all areas around the pool to be easily reached by one 75-foot section of hose.

Vacuum Sweeper

Every pool needs a vacuum sweeper to remove the leaves, dust balls, and other debris that accumulate in the pool. Several types of sweepers are available. One type attaches to a suction fitting built into the pool wall and works off the filter system. A clean filter is necessary for maximum suction; vacuuming with this type may require a filter cleaning when the job is complete. Portable, electric vacuum pumps are now available, but they present additional problems because water must be discharged to waste somewhere; this lowers the pool level and necessitates replacement of the lost water. Automatic vacuum sweepers, which alleviate the problems of the first two types are commercially available. They are self-operating devices, requiring no attendance by anyone.

Safety Equipment and Features

Several equipment and accessory items should be classified as safety equipment and at least one item, the safety ledge, should not be included in a pool design.

Safety ledge.   A safety ledge is a protrusion from the deep end walls, approximately 6 inches wide and located 4 feet below the water surface. Its original intent was to provide a place for people to rest while holding onto the pool's coping at the deep end. Realistically, a safety ledge presents a hazard to divers diving from the side and also attracts young children for play. Nonswimmers can slide off the ledge down the wall into deep water and, if not rescued immediately, could drown. Because several drownings and numerous near drownings have occurred as a result of these "safety ledges," these ledges are not recommended for any pool—residential or commercial.

Fence.   All residential pools should be fenced in some manner. Either the total property, or the area immediately around the pool, or the pool itself should be fenced. Innumerable possibilities exist in regard to size, shape, material, color, and price. Because the purpose of a fence is for protection of young children, a safe fence should provide for the following:

- No external handholds or footholds (vertical slats are best)
- Impenetrable by toddlers through or under it
- At least 6 feet in height
- A self-closing gate with a self-activated, positive-latching closure mechanism above the reach of a toddler (4 to 5 feet recommended)
- The capability of being locked with a padlock, or preferably with a combination lock, to prevent an older child from finding a key to open a keyed lock
- The maximum opening under any portion of the fence should not exceed 4 inches
- Where the home serves as part of the fence, the lock on doors from the house to the pool must be raised up to prevent children in the house from having access to the pool

The homeowner should check local, city, or county pool-building and zoning ordinances for any regulation pertaining to fencing requirements.

Pool covers.   No residential pool is complete without a cover. A cover provides the best security possible if properly placed. The pool cover will prevent leaves and dirt from entering the water, help keep heat in the pool at night, and provide an excellent safety device to prevent young children from falling in the pool. For the best results, a fitted vinyl or nylon cover should be selected that can be held down with deck anchor plates or tied to anchors in the soil. Whatever material is used, it must be resistant to weather and pool chemicals and should be equipped with grommet drains to avoid buildup of stagnant water. Accumulated water on the top of the cover is potentially dangerous to children, so steps should be taken to drain water off the cover.

Depth markings.   Depth markings, intended to communicate essential information to swimmers and divers, must be placed both on the deck, near the pool's edge, and on the interior wall. Location and marking should coincide with the breakpoint and every 1-foot increment in depth around the pool. All letters and numerals should be painted in a color contrasting with the coping (black, dark blue, or red) at least 4 inches high and 3/4 inch wide, with 6-inch high figures preferred.

Warning signs.   Signs listing the rules for swimming, diving, and water slides should be posted in appropriate and conspicuous places in the pool area. Rules for swimming should forbid running, pushing, ducking, horseplay, children swimming without adult supervision, swimming alone, swimming at night without lights, as well as any other "house rules" regarding open sores, toys, and so forth. Rules governing springboard diving should forbid double bouncing, diving without

Grecian pool with gazebo, Hollywood, California

checking to see if the area in front of the board is clear, prohibiting more than one person on the board at a time, and attempting dives beyond one's skill level.

Warning signs should reflect the seriousness of the consequences of ignoring the signs. For example, in areas where diving from the side or end is not permitted, an appropriate sign would be as follows:

DANGER—SHALLOW WATER—DO NOT DIVE

Lifeline. A nylon or polypropylene rope with floats placed on it every 2 feet is essential to identify the breakpoint between shallow and deep water. The line should be securely attached to the sides of the pool and located preferably 2 feet behind the breakpoint toward the shallow end. It should also be taut enough to support a young child with his or her head above water if the child should take hold of the rope.

First-aid kit. Every pool should have a first-aid kit. Many good commercially prepared kits are available today, or one may be developed using an inexpensive fishing tackle box. Advice from the local American Red Cross office or an emergency medical technician (EMT) should be sought. No kit is complete without an American Red Cross standard first-aid book or its equivalent, and all adults and children over 13 years old are urged to take a first-aid course. The local Red Cross office will provide information on the next available course. Every pool should have available a life ring, throwing lines, and a shepherd's crook.

Water test kit. Every pool needs a test kit to determine the levels and types of chlorine, pH, and total alkalinity. If cyanuric acid or any of the chlorinated isocyanurates are used in the treatment of water, a test kit that measures cyanuric acid is needed also. Kits are available in a variety of prices and need not be expensive. Remember to replace all chemicals every year because most have a shelf life of 12 months, except phenol red (testing for pH), which usually lasts only 6 months. For more information on water chemistry, see chapter 13.

Electronic warning devices. Warning devices, which set off an alarm or turn on a night light if someone disturbs the water or bumps the fence, are available. Contact any pool supplier for more information.

Telephone. A telephone should be available within a very short distance of the pool. A list of numbers including the police, fire department, and ambulance service should be posted near the phone and kept up-to-date.

Pool Activities

A properly planned, designed, and constructed residential pool provides a multiplicity of valuable family-oriented activities. The pool serves as a focal point of family recreation, aquatic learning, parties, and neighborhood entertainment. Some typical pool activities follow.

Teaching Nonswimmers

No other pool activity is more valuable than teaching children or adults how to swim. Swimming is a skill that every child should learn, and the potential of the residential pool as an instrument in this process has been untapped. Contact should be made with the local American Red Cross chapter or YMCA for assistance in developing a "backyard learn-to-swim program." Both of these agencies have already initiated such local programs, and other agencies are in the process of developing them. If no such formal program is available, seek out a properly trained and certified swimming instructor to conduct classes. A good source is the local college where a member of the swimming team or a physical education student qualified as a swimming instructor may be found. These qualified persons can be hired to teach children of the nonswimming family. By inviting some of the neighbors' children to participate, the cost can be shared between families. Once the children have learned the beginning skills, the more advanced level courses can be offered in swimming, water safety, lifesaving, and diving provided, of course, the pool is adequate in size and depth to accommodate these activities.

Family Recreation

The major use of a residential pool is family recreation. This may involve a variety of activities ranging from just taking a dip to cool off to enjoying structured activities involving games such as water basketball or volleyball.

Pool features Jacuzzi and inset seat

Pool Parties

Pool parties are rapidly becoming an American institution. However, the homeowner takes on added responsibility at these parties. Any pool party involving 20 or more people should have a paid or volunteer lifeguard on duty. Again, this may be accomplished by employing a college student qualified in lifesaving. If alcoholic beverages are provided along with swimming, unusual behavior is apt to occur. The lifeguard's duty is to prevent accidents from happening. Undoubtedly, parties are an important consideration in building the pool, but the owner must never forget the possible danger and must control behavior to provide the safest fun possible.

Swimming for Health

The home pool represents a great potential for improving the physical fitness of family members. Swimming laps three or four times a week for 20 minutes each time greatly improves a person's cardiovascular system. Kicking using a flutter board or any other device is an excellent exercise for strengthening the legs.

Accommodating Neighbors and Guests

As soon as the pool is filled, it becomes a neighborhood attraction. A safely designed and supervised pool may provide countless hours of wholesome entertainment for many of the neighbors' children, which in itself is a significant factor in building the pool. However, when the neighbors are invited to use the pool, the owner must either be prepared to supervise the pool or insist that adults come along to do so.

Supervision of the Pool

All homeowners with pools must recognize their responsibility not only to supervise the activities that go on in the pool but also to ensure the pool is maintained in a manner that assures the health and safety of users. The following are some reasonable guidelines for homeowners to follow:

1. Never leave children alone in the pool, even if they are good swimmers. Make sure some adult qualified in lifesaving (possibly a teenager, but preferably an adult) be present at all times that children are using the pool.

2. Post rules governing the use of the pool in a conspicuous location, and explain them to all children who may be unable to read.

3. Give neighbors and their children who use the pool an orientation to the proper use of the pool and help them become familiar with the pool rules.

4. Establish the hours when the neighbors may use the pool.

5. Neighbors and their children should obtain permission before using the pool.

6. Neighbors should never be allowed to use the pool when the homeowner is not present.

7. When hosting a large party, be sure to engage a qualified lifeguard to supervise the pool.

8. Pay particular attention to guests who swim after having consumed any form of alcohol. If they are drunk, do not permit them to use the pool.

9. Have lifesaving equipment readily available in proper locations around the pool.

10. If a pool is used at night, be sure to have adequate lighting in and around the pool.

11. When the family leaves the house unattended, as may happen when they go away for the weekend, cover the pool to prevent its use by neighbors.

Pool Maintenance and Operation

A swimming pool represents a sizeable investment and requires regular maintenance. Good maintenance begins with following the recommendations of the pool builder and equipment manufacturer because they are most familiar with the pool and its products. Following these instructions will ensure repair or replacement of damaged items under terms of the warranty.

Local and state ordinances must also be checked to become aware of health and safety requirements. Many communities and a few states are enacting such laws, and it is the homeowner's duty to be aware of and follow them.

With proper maintenance and repair, an above-ground pool should last 10 years, an in-ground pool 30 to 40 years. Proper maintenance, including adherence to the basic principles of pool chemistry along with daily and off-season care, will provide maximum pool life. The following routine and long-term maintenance are essential:

Daily
- Clean skimmers and decks.
- Inspect equipment: ladders, diving board, filter, chlorinator.

- Test pool water for chlorine and pH (three times a day).
- Skim leaves and floating debris.

Regularly
- Backwash filter (when needed).
- Test pool water for total alkalinity and cyanuric acid, if applicable (once a week).
- Vacuum pool bottom (when needed).

Off-Season Care: Above-Ground Pools
- Drain the pool.
- Drain all water lines.
- Disconnect and store the filter, motor, and chlorinator inside the home or garage.
- Remove and store the ladder.
- Place the cover on the pool and secure it.
- Lock the gate.

Pool Service Companies

In many communities pool service companies will maintain the pool for homeowners for a monthly fee. They clean and vacuum the pool, make chemical tests of the water, backwash filters, and usually clean the decks when needed. By employing a reliable company, the homeowner may be assured that the pool will always be clean and sanitary.

The preceding information represents only a small amount of pool maintenance information. (For more details read chapter 12 on the pool's hydraulic system and chapter 13 on pool chemistry.)

Guidelines to Effective Pool Operation

Maximum efficiency and comfort are traits desirable in all consumer products, swimming pools included. Comfort refers primarily to the temperature of pool water and the air around the pool, as a warmer environment will increase utilization time both daily and seasonally.

Ambient air temperature. The addition of a windscreen will eliminate or reduce the windchill factor on windy days. A natural windbreak of vegetation is popular with many owners, whereas others prefer wood-framed glass, wood baffle screens, or metal fencing with a nylon overlay. A windscreen may mean an air temperature difference of 10 °F and also prevents blowing debris from entering the pool.

Water temperature.   Control of water temperature for most pools means the addition of a pool heater. The heaters available today are reliable, efficient, economical, and highly desirable. However, a different problem exists in many southern states where pool water becomes uncomfortable during summer months due to high temperatures. Where water temperatures climb over 82 °F, a means of cooling should be considered. This includes some forethought during planning. Cooling may be accomplished through aeration with the addition of a spray or fountain in the pool or by burying some additional pipe underground, increasing the return time of water coming from the filter to the pool inlets. Some heat will be lost by convection to the ground, which tends to be a constant 55 °F.

Energy saving.   With increasing energy costs and decreasing energy supplies, the residential pool owner is obliged to be concerned about energy management. Included here are some measures that will keep the use of energy to a minimum and maintain the lowest possible cost to the owner. (For additional information refer to chapter 19 on energy management.)

- Purchase a good pool cover; this can reduce heat loss by 50%.
- Insulate concrete in pool walls to reduce heat loss to the ground.
- Add a windscreen.
- Use a mercury vapor or halogen light above the pool.
- Turn the heater down 10 °F when the pool is used only on weekends.
- Turn the heater off if the pool will not be used for a week or longer.

Pool shape follows contour of landscaping

- Add a time clock that turns the heater on or off during selected hours.
- Keep the filters clean.
- Turn the filter off for short periods of time during nonpeak hours.

Hints to Potential Home Pool Buyers

1. Where do you find out who builds residential pools? The most readily available source is the yellow pages under the heading "Swimming Pool Contractors (or Builders)." Some contractors take out ads in newspapers.

2. There are two distinct types of home pool builders. The first, the "local contractor," only builds pools (mostly in-ground concrete basin pools) in the immediate area. The second type is the distributors of "package pools" that are mostly vinyl liner pools, both the above-ground and in-ground variety. The latter pools are fabricated by firms dealing on a national basis.

3. It is advisable to have a qualified "installer" assemble the "package pool" unless the homeowner has some construction experience.

4. The homeowner should make certain to receive and read all the instructions for the operation of the pool from the "builder" or "distributor" at the completion of the job.

5. Regardless of what the builder or distributor may tell you about local ordinances and health regulations, check them out yourself to make certain you are in compliance.

6. Be sure to insist that the builder place depth markers in the pool's coping as previously indicated; or in the case of above-ground pools, all decals should be placed on the pool by the installer if they have not already been applied by the manufacturer.

7. The sanitation of the pool is the sole responsibility of the homeowner. Unlike public pools, the home pool is rarely inspected by the health department; therefore, it is incumbent upon the homeowner to set up a program of systematic testing and sanitation of the water as well as regular cleaning of the pool's basin and surrounding area.

8. A swimming pool should be covered under the homeowner's comprehensive insurance policy. It is essential that the homeowner notify the insurance company when a pool is installed because additional coverage may be necessary. A swimming pool can be a liability, and adequate protection is a part of the responsibility associated with owning a residential pool.

Safe Management of Home Pools

By 1990 it is estimated that 85% of all pools will be residential, numbering approximately 4.5 million units. These pools have significantly contributed to the number of swimmers in this country. It is a well-established fact that pools are the safest bodies of water in which to swim, as less than 10% of the annual drownings are attributed to pools. It is significant, however, that over 50% of these drownings occur in residential pools, and of this number, half are children under 6 years of age. Studies have revealed that almost all of them were nonswimmers. Many drownings of children in residential pools are preventable. Residential pools provide us with the largest number of improperly supervised aquatic facilities in the United States.

In order to help ensure that your pool is not included in the next set of accident statistics, a residential pool safety checklist follows. If the answer to each of the following questions is in the affirmative, a great step will have been taken to reduce the danger of drowning and serious injuries.

Safety Checklist

All homeowners should use the following checklist at regular intervals to determine whether they are adhering to recognized safety and health practices:

1. Have all members of the family learned to swim?

2. Is the pool properly fenced and does the fence have a self-locking mechanism?

3. If the pool is not fenced, is your property fenced to prevent intruders from wandering in?

4. Is someone in the family qualified in lifesaving, CPR, and first aid?

5. Is there an established emergency procedure?

6. Is there a telephone near the pool?

7. Are important emergency telephone numbers posted in plain sight near the telephone?

8. Are there posted pool rules for swimming, diving, sliding, and playing?

9. Do the pool rules cover the use of floats, toys, and scuba equipment?

10. Are the rules reviewed with and understood by each guest the first time he or she uses the pool?

11. Have depth markers been placed around the pool?

12. Have neighbors and other friends as well as their children been told when the pool is not to be used?

13. Is the water clear enough to see a dark object 6 inches in diameter, at the deepest point in the pool?

14. Are the chemical levels checked three times a day or more?

15. Have all state and local laws pertaining specifically to residential pools been reviewed?

16. Is there a cover for the pool, and is it placed on the pool when the family is away?

17. Relative to above-ground pools, are objects kept away from the pool walls that might be used as a ladder by a small child to gain access to the pool (filter, motor, pump, furniture, trash cans, cement blocks, wood or metal boxes, pool accessories)?

18. Does the homeowner's insurance policy cover the pool?

19. Is an adult present at all times to supervise children?

References

Gabrielsen, M.A. (1984). *Diving injuries: A critical insight and recommendations*. Indianapolis, IN: Council for National Cooperation in Aquatics.

Pool features a Jacuzzi and wood deck. Photo courtesy of Gary Pools.

Chapter 4

Pools for Motels, Hotels, and Apartment/Condominium Complexes

Today most motels have swimming pools, particularly those located in vacation areas and on major highways in the United States. Several major motel chains actually require their franchises to include swimming pools. Vacationing families usually inquire about pool availability before stopping at a motel. This trend extends to most major modern hotels throughout the world. At vacation centers, motels, and hotels, swimming pools with their accompanying support facilities such as saunas, bars, spas, restaurants, and lounge areas represent major amenities for attracting guests. A few of the more exclusive motels now provide "spas" in each room and are advertised as motel-spas.

With the tremendous interest in physical fitness, more and more hotels and motels are including fitness or health facilities with their pools. Complete sport centers are also emerging at some motels and include facilities for activities such as tennis, racquetball, and jogging.

Pools at apartment buildings and condominiums include many of the same features contained in motel and hotel pools. They differ significantly, however, in their mode of operation because, unlike motel and hotel guests, most of their users are permanent residents. There is even a difference in the way pools in rental apartments and condominiums are managed. In most instances, apartment buildings have single owners who may have an operating agent who establishes rules and regulations, whereas in a condo a group of resident owners makes up a board or committee that issues pool rules.

Directed toward architects and planners of motel/hotel and apartment pools, as well as owners and managers of these facilities, this chapter presents guidelines for the planning, design, operation, and maintenance of pools, specifically intended to serve the needs of owners, tenants, guests, and other users of these facilities.

For those details related to planning pools such as pool construction, type of equipment, water treatment, safety, and operation, refer to the chapters in this book dealing specifically with those subjects.

In most states, motel/hotel and apartment/condominium pools are classified as "public pools" or as "semi-public pools" and consequently are governed by the rules and regulations for public pools usually promulgated by state health agencies. Some counties and large cities have their own regulations and ordinances governing such pools, often exceeding the state requirements.

A review of state laws and regulations revealed that some states tend to modify regulations to accommodate small motels and to permit some pools to operate without lifeguards. The practice of not using lifeguards where there is no clear view of the pool or spa by other supervisory personnel of the motel is an invitation for accidents. This applies despite warning signs advising that there is "No Lifeguard on Duty" and exhortations to exercise special care in the absence of lifeguards. Similarly, apartment/condominium pools should be supervised by a fully qualified lifeguard at all times that the pool is open.

Motel and Hotel Pools

A common fault of many motel/hotel pools is that they attempt to provide everything normally contained in major pool complexes in a scaled-down model, which invariably leads to problems. Many motel/hotel pools, because of their small size, have distinct limitations concerning the type of aquatic activities that can safely be conducted in them. The most serious violation involves inappropriate diving equipment. For example, few motel/hotel pools can safely accommodate 3-meter springboard diving, but some try to do so, and too often with insufficient water depth for safe diving.

Schools, colleges, Ys, and other agencies that operate pools control their pool use. Students, for example, are assigned to a class with a qualified teacher for instruction, or they may belong to a swim team or use the pool just for fun during a recreational swimming period where lifeguards are usually present. In contrast, the clientele served by motel/hotel swimming pools is quite different: They are transients; they may range in age from a few months old to their 80s; some will not know how to swim and others will be expert swimmers. Some come as families on vacation; some as an individual on a business trip; some as members of a tour group, convention, or a special function such as a wedding or dinner party. The most eager to enter the pool are always the children of a family that has been on the road all day and often reach the pool before their parents have finished unpacking.

Most motels and hotels serve liquor, and some even have cocktail bars in the pool area. Thus, it is foreseeable that some of the guests may go swimming after consuming alcohol.

Of particular significance to motel/hotel operators is the fact that most of their guests have probably never swum in pools identical in size, configuration, and depth expectancies. They have had different swimming experiences in pools of varied geometric dimensions. Because of this variation in the background of guests, the job of the planner and designer of the motel/hotel pool is a difficult, important task and places great responsibility on the manager of the facility.

Apartment and Condominium Pools

Apartment/condominium pools have a much more stable clientele than do motel/hotel pools. Apartment tenants and condo owners may bring guests to the pool if only on a limited basis.

Apartment and condominium pool administration varies from the time the pool is constructed until it reaches the point of final ownership, and the following are some of the steps in the process:

1. The owner plans the pool, usually with the help of an architect, and hires a pool builder to construct it. For the first year or two the owner operates the pool by employing people to run it. He may even hire a lifeguard during this phase. Often, the pool is a part of a recreational complex that includes a clubhouse, tennis courts, and a children's play area. Far too often the owner fails to seek the advice of a pool consultant concerning design, operation, and safety aspects of the pool.

Multiple pools provide separation of activities. Pool by Gary Pools.

2. In the second phase the owner may turn the operation of the pool over to the tenants or condo owners but retains ownership of the pool and property.

3. The third step usually occurs when the owner turns the deed of the property and facilities, including the pool, over to the condo owners who then assume the full responsibility of all aspects of the pool's operation. When this occurs, the tenants' organization that takes over ownership should have a qualified pool consultant or engineer survey the pool immediately to determine if any conditions exist that the owner should correct before final agreement is reached.

4. In some situations the owner contracts with a management firm to run the whole apartment complex, including the pool.

The degree of supervision and control of the swimming pool should be consistent with the anticipated problems associated with the character and size of the apartment or condo, that is, turnover rate, age, and life-style of tenants, and variability in behavior patterns.

As contrasted with motel/hotel pools, many apartment/condo pools conduct regular programs for their clientele, such as "learn-to-swim" sessions, instruction in lifesaving and advanced swimming, a swim team, water exercise programs, splash parties, and water shows. And where children are included, special program needs arise and require attention.

Determining Size and Shape of Motel/Hotel Pools

The principle that "form follows function" certainly applies to the motel/hotel pool. Competitive swimming meets will not likely be held in many of these pools, although certainly it is possible. The old St. George Hotel in Brooklyn, the London Terrace Apartment Pool in New York, and the Ambassador Hotel in Washington, DC, are notable exceptions where many important swimming meets were once held. Pools in some apartment complexes may even have United States Swimming (USS) "age group" swimming competition. Modern construction techniques have opened up a wide range of pool shapes. However, planners must observe certain precautions. Refer to Appendix A, which includes a worksheet used in determining a pool's design.

The most important criterion in establishing the pool's dimensions is the pool's function. This involves a careful identification of the activities that will be conducted and, more importantly, permitted in the pool. Once the pool's purpose and use have been determined, planning can proceed;

the specifications governing the conduct of activities will mandate the pool's dimensions, including safe water depth. The following list includes the most typical swimming and diving activities conducted in pools:

- Free, unorganized recreational swimming for all ages
- Competitive swimming
- Instruction for people with varying skills and ages
- Springboard diving
- Lifesaving instruction
- Synchronized swimming
- Scuba diving
- Swimming for disabled persons
- Activities such as wading, nonswimmers sitting in water, sunbathing, and water exercise

Few of the previous activities are conducted in any organized manner in most motel/hotel pools, but many are a part of apartment/condo pool programs, particularly those with qualified instructors or lifeguards.

The number of people to be served will influence the specific size and shape of the pool more than any other factor. The crucial figure to establish is the anticipated peak load the pool must serve. Too many motels provide only a "residential" size pool as small as 15 feet by 30 feet for their guests, which is inadequate for any motel. To accurately plan the peak load, the figure should include any anticipated increase in the number of units (rooms or apartments). Based on the assumption that the pool will be used primarily for recreational swimming, the pool sizes shown in Table 4.1 (identified in terms of water surface area) are recommended as the minimum for motel/hotel pools.

The figures in Table 4.1 are predicated on the following assumptions:

- 10% pool occupancy at a rate of 3 persons per unit
- A peak utilization factor of 25% of the registered guests at the pool with a maximum of 50% of that number actually in the water at any one time
- That children will always be among the guests
- That adequate lounging area will be provided around the pool to accommodate those not in the pool

- That no springboard diving facilities be allowed in pools with less than 1,250 square feet of water surface area
- That any water slide will be at the deep end where the water depth is at least 8 feet, unless constantly supervised

Table 4.1 Recommended Size for Motel and Hotel Pools

Number of Units	Water Area (square feet)	Pool Dimensions[1] (in feet)
Up to 24	648	18 × 36
25 to 60	800	20 × 40
61 to 100	1,250	25 × 50
101 to 150	1,800	30 × 60
151 to 200	2,625	35 × 75
Above 201[2]		

[1]The rectangular dimensions are only illustrative and are not intended to restrict variations in shape to rectangular pools only.
[2]Consideration should be given to a multiple complex of pools, particularly where more than 200 units exist. This, however, increases the problem of supervision.

Table 4.2 Recommended Pool Size for Apartments and Condominiums

Number of Units	Minimum Water Surface Area (square feet)	Typical Pool Dimensions[1] (in feet)
Up to 50	800	20 × 40
51 to 100	1,000	25 × 40
101 to 150	1,800	30 × 60
151 to 200	2,700	36 × 75
201 to 250	3,375	45 × 75
Above 250[2]		

[1]The rectangular dimensions are only illustrative and are not intended to restrict variations in shape to rectangular pools only.
[2]Consideration should be given to providing a second pool in another location or adding a separate diving pool and familiarization pool to plans of the first pool.

Size and Shape of Apartment and Condominium Pools

In Table 4.2 are recommendations for a minimum water surface area for apartment/condominium pools. The tenants and their guests are the users of these pools. More apartments than condominiums are restricted to older people without children, so the pool design might vary considerably to accommodate the older tenants. The type of pool, its size, and accompanying recreational facilities greatly influence pool use. Attractive, well-maintained and operated pools will be better utilized.

The minimum sizes suggested in Table 4.2 are only guidelines and planners should, whenever possible, exceed these minimums.

Familiarization Pools

To every apartment/condominium where children also reside, a familiarization pool is essential. It should have a minimum of 250 square feet of water surface (for apartment units up to 100) and 450 square feet of water surface area for apartments containing more than 100 units. Proper water depth in these pools is important, ranging from a minimum of 6 inches at one end of the pool (or at the perimeter in circular pools) to a maximum depth of 15 inches. This depth is recommended only when the instruction of young children is not anticipated. If the pool is intended for instruction, the maximum depth of water should be 24 inches. Such pools obviously require close supervision. Motel/hotel pools should include a children's pool, if possible, along the lines previously discussed.

The water in these familiarization pools must be circulated, filtered, and chemically treated the same as in larger pools. A fence is desirable for these pools to keep youngsters from entering other pools.

Neighborhood Pool Versus Community Pool

To serve the needs of the residents in a large development (1,000 or more units), are several small, neighborhood-style pools better than a single, large pool complex? Studies done favor the community pool for the following reasons:

- The large facility provides a pool complex that offers many activities that the small neighborhood pool cannot.

- Maintenance costs are less.

- Because lifeguards must be employed, the supervision requirements provide for a safer environment.

- The large clubhouse often included offers many social activities that are not possible in smaller facilities.

However, the determining factor is the makeup of the condo or apartment residents. For example, if the complex is a large adult-oriented development, excluding children, and basically a retirement setting, the best plan includes several smaller pools, each with their own small clubhouse, such as Leisureville, in Boynton Beach, Florida.

Indoor or Outdoor Pool

Pool utilization studies have revealed that most people who swim in the summer seldom seek an indoor pool during the winter months. However, the motivation is significantly different when a family is on a winter vacation. The availability of an indoor swimming pool at a motel/hotel is attractive to many people.

Economics and location determine whether a motel/hotel should have an indoor or outdoor pool or a combination indoor-outdoor pool. Indoor pools require considerable space, and the cost of constructing an adequate structure to house the pool may be expensive. For that reason, some motel/hotels are incorporating within the pool area other facilities such as dining and cocktail lounges, game areas, and often space for lounging. The pool, however, is the focal point. Special lunches and dinners utilizing the pool deck area often necessitate closing the pool to swimmers. This multiuse concept of space has created supervision problems, which will be discussed later in this chapter.

The other planning factors are the geographic location of the motel/hotel and the climate. The further north, the greater the consideration of an indoor pool. Few motel/hotels having less than 200 units have indoor pools; however, many with outdoor pools are now considering adding indoor pools, especially at motel/hotels with high occupancy rates. This trend toward indoor pools is also being seen in large apartment and condominium complexes.

A recent trend is the construction of a connected indoor and outdoor complex, making it possible to swim from the indoor to the outdoor pool through a chute or tunnel. This scheme presents a problem of both supervision and maintenance of proper water temperature in the outdoor pool.

Diving Equipment

If springboard diving is to be included in the motel/hotel or apartment pool, the specifications for safe diving areas as established in chapter 8 should be strictly followed. Few, if any, motel/hotel pools should consider having 3-meter springboards unless they are prepared to add qualified staff to supervise this activity. Pools with less than 1,250 square feet of water surface area should not include springboard (or jumpboard) diving because too much water area is required, and this is detrimental to young children who need more shallow water. Those motels and hotels that placed springboards in pools that could not safely accommodate springboard diving subsequently needed to remove them.

Construction Material

For complete discussion of materials used in the construction of the pool basin, decks, and equipment, refer to chapter 11. A variety of options are available to the designer, ranging from poured concrete basins to pneumatic-placed concrete shells (gunite) and vinyl liners. Decks are mostly finished in some type of concrete. Tiles of various types are used on indoor pool decks but seldom, however, for outdoor pools. The most common basin finish is some form of plaster with a marbledust aggregate added to white cement. The painting of the pool's interior basin is not recommended—at least not at the initial stage. When painting becomes necessary, an epoxy paint provides the best and most lasting finish. The only disadvantage is that it is slippery. Pool basins should *always* be finished in white; dark colors should never be used.

Perimeter overflow gutters of the recessed type or one of the rimflow systems are more efficient and sanitary than skimmer types for circulating the pool's water.

Water Circulation and Treatment

For a detailed treatment of this subject, refer to chapters 12 and 13 for information on the various filter systems and methods of chemically treating pool water.

Heating Pool Water

To achieve maximum utilization, all pools should have a system for heating the water, unless they are located in the tropics. With the increasing energy costs confronting the country, planners of motel/hotel and apartment pools must carefully study alternate methods to heat the pool's water. The savings realized warrants careful consideration of solar energy. Chapters 17 and 19 describe the various solar systems on the market today and methods of energy management.

Pool Equipment

Certain types of equipment and accessories are essential to the safe and successful operation of motel/hotel and apartment pools; others fall into the "optional" category but may be desirable.

Hotel pools without fencing or other means of enclosing the pool are potentially dangerous. Photo by Manley.

Essential Equipment

Underwater lights. If pools will be used at night, underwater lights are essential. They not only are a safety measure but also add significantly to the general aesthetics of the pool. (See the section on underwater lights in chapters 8 and 11 for a full discussion.)

Lifesaving, first-aid, and safety equipment. The following lifesaving and first-aid equipment must be available at every motel/hotel and apartment/condominium pool:

- Ring buoys with line (number determined by pool size)
- Shepherd's crook
- First-aid kit and stretcher
- Blankets
- Spine board
- Lifeguard stand
- Telephone and/or alarm system
- Resuscitation equipment
- Lifeline
- Safety light
- Pool cover for safety purposes to prevent entrance when pool is closed
- Fence around pool to prevent unauthorized entrance

Gates should have self-closing, positive-locking devices to prevent children from entering the pool and locking devices to prevent unauthorized entry by adults. Most serious accidents happen when people use the pool when it is supposed to be closed.

Area lighting. Two distinct areas around the pool require adequate lighting if night swimming is intended. First is the pool itself, which should have a minimum of 30 footcandles of illumination at the pool's edge if the pool has underwater lights, and 50 footcandles of illumination if there are no underwater lights. The second area is the deck and lounge area, which should have a minimum of 20 footcandles when the pool is in use. During the evening hours when the pool is not open for swimming, a low intensity light that provides at least 2 footcandles of illumination is desirable as a safety measure. Higher levels are recommended when elderly residents or guests are present. (Refer to chapter 8 for further information on lighting.)

Maintenance equipment. For the proper maintenance of the pool, the following equipment is essential:

- Test kit for measuring chlorine and pH
- Vacuum cleaner (either automatic sweeper or conventional built-in type)
- Brush with long pole
- Leaf skimmer
- Hot water hose

Optional Equipment

Diving and sliding equipment. The installation of diving equipment such as springboards, jumpboards, platforms, and water slides is discussed in chapter 8. Those recommendations should be followed because these are facilities where serious accidents may occur.

Deck furniture. Pool patrons need a place to sit or lie down around the pool, which is best accomplished by lounges and chairs set back from the pool's edge by at least 10 feet (preferably 20 feet).

Water recreation equipment. Motels and hotels usually supply very little water recreation equipment. On the other hand, apartment/condo pools or the tenants themselves typically supply this kind of equipment, including the following items:

- Surfboards
- Kickboards
- Water balls
- Water basketball goals

Instructional equipment. This type of equipment is strictly for pools where organized instruction is a part of the pool's program. It includes kickboards and certain types of flotation devices used in the instruction of nonswimmers and for competitive swimmers.

Competitive swimming equipment. If competitive swimming meets will be conducted in the pool (most likely at apartment/condo pools), certain additional features and equipment must be added to the pool. The following type of equipment and pool features are needed for competitive swimming:

- The length and width of the pool must conform to USS and/or NCAA rules. The acceptable lengths are 60 feet, 25 yards, 25 meters, or 50 meters. The pool's width is determined by the required number of lanes. Although competition may be conducted in lanes 6 feet wide, 7- or 8-foot-wide lanes are recommended. Six or eight lanes are recommended, even though four lanes are the required minimum. (See chapter 14 for details.)

Other requirements include the following:

- Racing lines placed on the bottom of the pool
- Surface racing lines defining the swimmer's lane
- Starting blocks installed at the deep end of the pool
- Official diving stands and springboards (1-meter and/or 3-meter)
- Backstroke-turning pennants
- Recall line (for false starts)
- Pacing clock

Swimming competition may actually be held in any size pool, but for "official" meets, pools must conform to the specifications set forth by the rules and regulations of governing bodies.

Recreational and Support Facilities

An increasing number of motel/hotels as well as large apartment/condo complexes are adding various types of supplemental recreational and support facilities to their pools. The discussion of the specific design criteria and relative merits of each of these facilities is not possible here. Planners are advised to visit established motel/hotel and apartment/condo complexes to determine which of the facilities identified in the list below are most appropriate to their needs and settings.

First, the necessary support type of facilities include the following:

- Filter room
- Cleaning equipment storage room
- Lifeguard's and attendant's office
- Toilets
- Space for storing instructional equipment
- Locker rooms
- First-aid station

Some typical types of supplemental recreational facilities to include within or close to the pool are as follows:

- Spas or hot tubs (also called whirlpools)
- Sauna and/or steam room
- Snack bar and/or vending machines
- Video games
- Lounging area
- Table tennis
- Shuffleboard
- Music
- Children's apparatus area
- Spectator viewing platform
- Dance area
- Cocktail bar

Larger motel/hotels offer guests some recreational facilities not immediately adjacent to the swimming pool. The availability of space, the number of guest rooms, and the location are the principal criteria for determining which of the facilities listed below may add to the attractiveness of the motel/hotel or apartment/condo and provide service to the guests. The following are typical of such facilities:

- Tennis courts
- Indoor or outdoor racquetball courts
- Handball courts (could use the racquetball courts)
- Squash courts
- Basketball court
- Health club
- Jogging course
- Miniature golf
- Par three golf
- Putting green
- Roller-skating rink
- Playing fields
- Lake front with boating, paddle boats, and fishing

Attractive landscaping around pool. Photo courtesy of Gary Pools.

- Water flume (or slide)
- Game room
- Movie theater

Extending the Pool's Operation

Several of the major motel/hotels have initiated programs that extend their facilities to the local community, to both increase income and also render a service to the community. The major motivation is to achieve greater utilization of their facilities, particularly at certain times of the day. The two most popular types of supplemental activities are the health club and the swim club.

The Health Club

Various membership fees cover individuals, couples, and families. A successful health club should have at least a sauna, whirlpool, massage, showers, dressing room, and lounge area. The members have access to the available facilities such as the pool, racquetball and tennis courts, and other sports. Some motel/hotels even have a jogging course laid out within the property. Shown below is a typical announcement of a health club program by a motel located in a major city area:

Health Club Membership Includes: Sunroom, exercise room, year-round indoor-outdoor pool, summer outdoor pool, saunas, whirlpools, tennis courts, ice rink, game room, complimentary continental breakfast for ''early birds,'' towels, lockers, and discount rates on available rooms. Plenty of free parking, too. You'll enjoy all the personal attention you'll receive. Fees are as follows:

$325—Individual

$600—Couple

$700—Family

The Swim Club

This club is similar to the health club, but guests are restricted to the use of the pool and the facilities immediately within the area. Both family and individual memberships are usually available, and

Pool designed to fit into landscaping. Photo courtesy of United Pools.

the fee is less than the more comprehensive health club. The following is a sample membership announcement for a swim club operated by a motel:

Swim Club Membership Includes: Indoor-outdoor pool, locker room, showers, outdoor pool, sundeck, familiarization pools, towels, lounge chairs, swim club lockers, tennis courts (incoming charge), whirlpool, snack bar privileges, and free parking. Membership period runs from May 20 through September 4. Typical membership fees are as follows:

$175—Individual

$275—Couple

$300—Family

Leasing Facilities

A few motel/hotels, particularly those with indoor pools, lease their pools to schools for basic student swimming instruction. The pool is usually used in the morning when it is not used much by motel guests. The leasing requirements are that the lessee assumes all responsibility for students' safety, and that the lessee shows evidence of adequate insurance. Provision of some type of dressing room is essential.

Operating Guidelines

Too many motel/hotel and apartment/condo owners falsely believe that all they must provide their guests is a swimming pool and an established procedure for maintaining it in accordance with local and state health department regulations; the

rest is up to their guests. A number of court decisions have been made against many owners following a drowning or serious injury to a guest in their pool.

The swimming pool has proven to be the most hazardous facility within any motel/hotel or apartment/condominium complex. Each year approximately 160 people drown in these pools, and most drownings could have been prevented. The guidelines listed will help owners establish and operate a safe and sanitary pool environment. These guidelines apply to both motel/hotel and apartment/condominium pools; however, certain pool operations are significantly different and will be discussed separately.

General Pool Operational Procedures and Suggested Policies

1. The pool must be properly maintained to assure the safety and health of users. This implies the need for a trained qualified pool operator whose responsibility encompasses the following (starred items should be performed daily):

   • Testing water for chlorine and pH*

   • Taking water sample for bacterial analysis

   • Inspecting pool's water clarity and for presence of algae*

   • Cleaning deck (usually hosing down with hot water and looking particularly for spilled oil)*

- Inspecting all pool equipment (diving boards, lifeguard stands, lifesaving equipment, and emergency equipment)*
- Checking pressure gauges on filters*
- Checking lint strainer*
- Backwashing filters when needed
- Recording required data in log*
- Checking water level for need to make up*
- Seeing that lifeline is in place*
- Cleaning filter room

Note: If there is a bathhouse, locker room, sauna, whirlpool, and showers and toilets, the operator's job usually covers their maintenance as well.

2. Because children do unexpected things, they need to be watched constantly. Management must not assume that all parents are qualified to supervise their children's water activities, therefore lifeguards should be on duty. However, management should require parents to accompany and supervise their children.

3. A method for closing the pool when it is not open for use is essential. Covers and fences are most frequently used.

4. People may want to swim after consuming some form of alcoholic beverage. This dictates the need for careful surveillance of the pool (even when it is not in use), which may be accomplished with electronic devices.

5. When night swimming is scheduled, adequate light must illuminate both the pool basin and the surrounding deck area.

6. When the pool is secured for the night, a "safe light," giving sufficient illumination, must be on so that every area of the pool is visible, including warning signs and rules.

7. An emergency alarm system should be installed to alert proper authorities of an emergency in the pool. This may involve an alarm system, a telephone, or other types of electronic devices.

8. A daily record should be kept of pool attendance, names of personnel on duty, incidents that occurred in the pool requiring attention, and water condition.

9. Guests and tenants should be fully apprised of the rules governing pool use. Signs posted in and around the pool (particularly at the entrances to the pool) and written instructions posted in rooms or apartments best accomplish this.

10. Eating and swimming go together. Hence, provisions for dispensing food (vending machines or snack bars) and for disposing garbage must be made. It is best to isolate the eating area from the pool and deck area. Glass cups or bottles should never be permitted in any area around the pool.

11. Someone on the premises *must* be qualified to administer cardiopulmonary resuscitation (CPR) and other artificial resuscitation procedures. Where no lifeguard is employed, management should make certain that someone on the staff has been trained in CPR and other emergency first-aid procedures. This may be a clerk, a maintenance person, a bartender, or an assistant manager.

12. Spas, hot tubs, and children's pools should be separated from the main pool by fencing or some other appropriate type of barrier to prevent anyone from running from these facilities toward the big pool to dive in.

13. Daily inspection of pools and of the surrounding deck area is essential. Inspection should include checking all equipment and furniture for defects or breaks; the clarity of water; cracking and settling of concrete decks and patio blocks, which often occurs following winter freezing or heavy rains; broken glass and other debris on the deck including suntan oil; and properly positioned safety lines and signs.

14. To assure the safety of motel/hotel guests and tenants of apartments/condominiums, a qualified lifeguard should be present whenever the pool is open.

15. Because many motel/hotel and apartment/condo pools were constructed 10 or more years ago, they may contain unsafe and undesirable features. It is strongly recommended that a pool safety consultant, who may or may not be an engineer, be engaged to survey the pool to determine if any defects or conditions exist that may affect the health and safety of users. Laws, rules, regulations, and the state of the art are constantly changing. A pool that met all regulations 20 years ago may in fact today be a hazard.

16. The increasing number of foreign tourists visiting the United States and other countries has created communication problems for those hotels and motels that accommodate these

guests. Because their language skills are limited, they may find the pool rules, instructions, warnings, and pool markings ineffective. Special attention must be given to more universal, nonlanguage (pictorial) instructions and warnings. Pool rules can be printed in various languages on cards and given to guests upon room registration. Multilingual lifeguards are helpful in some situations as well. Pool depths should be marked in meters as well as feet.

17. Whenever a pool is drained for needed repair, the proper measures must be taken to assure that guests do not dive or jump into an empty pool. Special lights may need to be erected and appropriate signs and instructions given to guests as they register.

Need for Lifeguards at Motel/Hotel Pools

The presence of a lifeguard is the surest way to prevent accidents, particularly drownings. The protection of life is certainly equal in importance to making beds or tending bar, and yet many motel/hotels with more than 200 units do not provide lifeguards. Because the local or state boards of health do not require it, the owners are not legally relieved of responsibility in the event of an accident. The transient nature of the clientele, coupled with the great diversity of age, size, ability, swimming experience, and physical condition of the guests points out the need for careful surveillance of the swimming pool at all times it is open for use.

Any motel/hotel or apartment/condominium complex operating a pool without a lifeguard present is placing itself in a vulnerable position in the event a drowning or serious injury to a guest occurs. The mere placing of a sign stating "Swim at Your Own Risk" does not in itself relieve owners of responsibility. When a facility such as a pool is made available to guests, management automatically assumes the responsibility of the supervision of the pool and of the guests who use it. The cost of providing a lifeguard is so minimal that no guest would question a 25¢ to 50¢ addition to the room charge.

The responsibility for general pool maintenance in small motel/hotels (under 100 units) may be included in the lifeguard's duties. However, the policy of never leaving the pool unsupervised dictates the need for the guard to arrive before the pool opens to perform the necessary maintenance functions.

Management of Apartment/Condominium Pools

The management of apartment or condominium swimming pools may be quite varied, depending upon the existence of recreation leases, maintenance fees, tenants' associations, management companies, and other established administrative structures. The apartment owner and the condominium developer must assume the responsibilities for the design of the pool and for its equipment; therefore, if a defective design is the cause of an accident, they will likely be held responsible even though they may have turned the pool over to tenants either by deed or for operating purposes. However, if the tenants agree to operate the pool, through their association, they are then responsible for the supervision and maintenance of the pool.

Chapter 5

Spas, Hot Tubs, Saunas, and Steam Rooms

The use of water for therapeutic purposes and relaxation dates back thousands of years and circles the globe. Today's health clubs with their whirlpools, saunas, and steam rooms are re-creations of ancient facilities found in Rome, Greece, Japan, Scandinavia, and India, as well as throughout the Moslem world and among many Indian tribes of North and South America. During the Middle Ages, public bathing fell into disfavor in the Western world, and it took the age of imperialism for the conquerors to bring the idea back to Europe from the East. The 15th through 19th centuries saw a growing recognition in Europe of the healing benefits of water. The major growth in hydrotherapy as a procedure in rehabilitation and the return to the purely social and recreational uses of water have been the major contribution of the 20th century.

Health fads of recent years, in fact, have helped the spa/hot tub industry boom. An estimated 54,000 spas and hot tubs were sold in 1977, according to the National Spa and Pool Institute. That figure jumped to 85,000 in 1978 and to 140,000 in 1979. Projections for 1986 call for sales to reach 200,000. Manufacturers estimate that about half the current spas and hot tubs purchased are for home use, and the other half are for commercial and public facilities.

Spas and hot tubs are appearing in an increasing number of American homes and apartments. Many families choose to install larger spas in the backyard or in a recreation area indoors. Although already included as part of the swimming pool and recreational amenities provided for their guests, some modern hotels are also including spas in suites. Saunas and steam rooms are also gaining popularity in more homes and hotels. Currently, heaters and generators make it possible to convert enclosures, ranging from a bathtub to a 2,000-cubic-foot room, into a steam bath or sauna. Spas, saunas, and steam rooms as well as other types of therapeutic or relaxation-oriented facilities have become standard equipment at health clubs, public and private swimming pools, and other athletic facilities all over the country.

The current enthusiasm for spas may be attributed to the use of warm water as a modality for treating a variety of disabling impairments and diseases. Franklin D. Roosevelt made Warm Springs a household word. Sister Kenny's innovative approach to treating polio victims, and the use of water to treat military casualties in the early part of the century were also important in stimulating the 20th century's interest in the therapeutic uses of warm water. Therapeutic tanks (whirlpools) have become standard equipment in training rooms of high school, college, and professional teams in almost every major sport—football, baseball, basketball, and hockey. Sports medicine specialists prescribe water therapy as treatment for a wide range of athletic injuries.

Whirlpools with water-activated jets are for the most part an American development, following military use by the French in World War I. Whirlpool baths began turning up in more and more Veterans Administration Hospitals and in many civilian hospitals with physical therapy departments.

C.P. Hubbard designed a keyhole-shaped tank in the 1920s made of stainless steel for full-body immersion in water of controlled temperatures; it became known as the Hubbard tank. Jet hoses were added for the hydromassage effect as the tanks came into wider use. By the end of World War II, Hubbard tanks and whirlpools were standard equipment in virtually all physical therapy facilities in the United States.

Most ancient facilities were located at natural sources of heated water and springs, which came to be known as spas, and many had cold water immersion baths as well. Strictly speaking, the word *spa* only applies to those natural springs, but today it is generally used as another word for whirlpool or *hot tub*. By whatever name they are called, there is little doubt as to their relaxing effect and tension-easing benefits. Evidence of their medical uses and benefits has also been steadily accumulating.

Health Benefits of Spas and Hot Tubs

The hot water in spas and hot tubs is a muscle relaxant and aids in overcoming stress. They are ideal for easing the aches and pains often accompanying too much exercise or after exercising out-of-condition muscles. Subacute muscle strains and sprains as well as torn ligaments and bruises are among the injuries that respond well to whirlpool and hot tub immersion. Because the heat and jet action of the whirlpool act to lessen muscle tone, people should exercise before, not after, entering a whirlpool or hot tub.

Hot water also provides relief and is used as therapy for people with such conditions as arthritis, bursitis, rheumatism, and lower back pain. These and other problems, however, often require a doctor's attention and advice. In many cases, these conditions may be treated by medically supervised hydrotherapy, but individuals suffering from them should be especially careful when using whirlpools and hot tubs on their own.

Even more precautions are advisable in the case of individuals with certain other medical conditions, including pronounced hypertension, arteriosclerosis, aneurisms, and several serious organic diseases. The aged, pregnant women, and people who are in generally frail health should also use hot tubs and whirlpools with care, consulting their physicians prior to use.

Water is a safe place to do a range of motion exercises and other exercise regimens aimed at increasing muscular and joint strength. The buoyancy of water as well as its antigravity and resistance effects virtually eliminate drag and stress on the joints, reducing the chances of injury, whereas movements made against the resistance offered by the water increase strength in the extremities. According to physical therapists, water therapy helps maintain and extend the range of joint motion, a point that can be useful to individuals in normal health as well as to those recovering from injuries or illnesses.

Other medical uses of spas include treatment of burns, scars, some nerve injuries, painful amputation stumps, tendon repairs, and fractures. Hubbard tanks are used largely for treating certain orthopedic problems, for relieving muscle cramping and spasms, for underwater exercising, and for relieving many of the conditions treated in whirlpool equipment.

Hot and cold water contrast baths are used medically today for arthritis, fractures, bruises, and other conditions. This practice, too, dates back to the ancient world, and many health club habitués today alternate between the hot whirlpool, sauna, or steam room and a dip in the cold swimming pool or special cold water immersion pool.

Hydrotherapy and the use of water for recreational and social purposes work because total or partial immersion has certain physiological effects. As the use of whirlpools, hot tubs, cold immersion baths, and other special purposes pools increases, it is important for pool and health club operators to have at least a basic knowledge of their effects.

Briefly, hot tubs (98 °F and up) increase peripheral circulation by dilating the peripheral blood vessels causing the heart to work harder. After an initial decrease, heart rate goes up. Blood pressure rises at first and then falls. Breathing becomes fast and respiration becomes shallow. As the sweat glands are stimulated, metabolism increases and so does perspiration. Systemic temperature rises. The hot bath acts as a muscle relaxant and eases fatigue, but long immersion and/or hot water may be enervating, and individuals may experience feelings of weakness after leaving the whirlpool or hot tub. Whirlpool jets tend to enhance the effect of the hot water.

In a cold bath (60 to about 89 °F) the heart rate slows after an initial rise, respiration slows and breathing deepens, and blood pressure goes up. Rather than being relaxed and decreased, muscle tone and the general energy level increase. Staying too long in a cold bath may lead to shivering, stiffness, and goose pimples. People with severe conditions such as high blood pressure, myocardial weakness, and arteriosclerosis should not use cold immersion baths or at least should use them carefully and only after consulting a doctor.

In addition to the hot water pools and cold water immersion pools (designed essentially for relaxation, promoting socialization, and therapy), pools and other facilities have been developed for the serious athlete who may want to use the deep tanks (hydrostatic weighing tanks) to test for the amount of fat in body composition. These measure approximately 5 feet in diameter, are about 4-1/2 feet deep, with 6 to 8 inches above the water level allowed for displacement. Some are slightly bigger and some slightly smaller. A chair or sling to lower the athlete into the pool and an autopsy scale complete the equipment. Many university fitness assessment programs and professional sports teams use these pools.

Guidelines for Safe Use of Spas

Recent research and epidemiological studies and reports indicate that safety measures for proper management of spas and hot tubs have been successfully developed. Many states have enacted regulations to ensure safe and healthful use of these facilities. The U.S. Department of Health and Human Services published its first health and safety guidelines in 1981, whereas minimum standards suggested by the spa industry were developed in 1978.

Spa Hazards

The main hazards of spa usage have been identified by the Consumer Product Safety Commission (NEISS—National Electronic Injury Surveillance System) to include drowning, falls, and electrocution. Since 1980 an average of over 1,000 accidents have been treated in hospital emergency rooms. Drownings are caused by alcohol and the body's reaction to hot water, by hair entanglement in bottom drains, and by falling into the spa unconscious after striking the head. Many falls are also alcohol related. Electrocution usually involves electrical appliances used near the spa such as radios, record players, and video recorders. Human factors analysis shows that victims' blood alcohol levels range from .09% to .42% and water temperatures often range from 106 to 114 °F. In addition, up to one third of the victims of a spa death are alone at the time of the accident.

It is potentially dangerous to mix alcohol, tranquilizers, and sedatives with the use of spas and hot tubs because they may increase the muscle relaxant effects and general sense of enervation and possible weakness that accompany their use.

Some people become drowsy enough to lose track of time and stay in too long. When consumed prior to or during hot water immersion, alcohol can lead to chemical imbalances, which ultimately promote sweating. Alcohol is a diuretic and can increase loss of trace minerals such as potassium, which regulate heart beat and other body functions. For the same reason, individuals using diuretics should also use spas with caution (Lesser, 1979).

Children under 5 years of age, the elderly, and those in poor health should also use spa equipment with caution. As suggested earlier, this is especially important for heart patients and people with high blood pressure and certain cardiovascular conditions.

Recommended times for length of stay in spas and hot tubs vary according to the temperature of the water. Generally, at 98 °F, no limit is necessary, leaving it up to individual discretion and tolerance. From 100 to 104 °F, most health and medical authorities recommend stays of 12 to 20 minutes at the most. At the higher water temperatures—104° and above—an element of danger exists proportional to water temperature and health condition. Reddening skin and/or dizziness at any temperature are definite signals that it is time to get out of the tub. Many doctors and therapists take the attitude that "when you've had enough, you'll know it's time to get out of the spa."

Until more information is available, it may be useful to post signs with suggested time limits or to make sure that attendants are aware of them. Time clocks and thermometers should be placed in easy view of all spa and hot tub users. An adjacent pool or shower for cooling off after spa or hot tub immersion is also recommended. Spa personnel should be qualified both in safe operation and in emergency procedures and currently certified in CPR and standard first aid.

It is recommended that a sign similar to the one below be placed next to the entrance to the spa area.

Caution

1. Soap shower before entering the spa.

2. Enter and exit the spa slowly and cautiously.

3. Elderly persons and those suffering from heart disease, diabetes, or high or low blood pressure should not enter the spa.

4. Pregnant women are not permitted to use the spa unless temperature is below 102 °F.

5. Unsupervised use by children is prohibited.

6. Children under 5 years old are not permitted to use the spa.

7. Do not use while under the influence of alcohol, anticoagulants, antihistamines, vasoconstrictors, vasodilators, stimulants, hypnotics, narcotics, or tranquilizers.

8. Never use alone.

9. No diving permitted.

10. Observe a reasonable time limit (10 minutes), then shower, cool down, and if you wish, return for another brief stay. Long exposures may result in nausea, dizziness, or fainting.

11. No body lotions or oils permitted.

12. Street shoes may not be worn in spa area.

13. No food or drink permitted.

14. Do not submerge to the bottom of the spa; hair may be caught in the drain.

15. Failure to follow these rules may result in serious injury or death.

The immediate area around the spa must be designed to guard against accidents and falls. Copings should have slip-resistant surfaces, preferably of a type imbedded into the tub surface. A slip-resistant surface should also be used on any steps into the spa. Some manufacturers also make the bottom of the pool slip-resistant. Marking the steps in a contrasting color from the tub provides an additional measure of safety.

NSPI standards (1980) require steps, ladders, or recessed treads where the spa is deeper than 24 inches. Each set of steps, if there is more than one, must have at least one handrail. Depth markings should be placed on or within 18 inches of spas and tubs; regardless of their size and shape, "No Diving" signs should be placed in several locations around the spa. If they are located outdoors, whirlpools should also be protected by some kind of enclosure that will keep young, unsupervised children from getting into them. The fence or barrier should be at least 4 feet high, with no external handholds or footholds.

Covers are available to serve both as protection against unauthorized use and against accidental falls and may also serve as thermal aids, keeping heat in the spa. Most manufacturers offer both thermal covers and safety covers as optional items. Some covers can serve both purposes. Safety covers are more important for spas located outdoors. This also applies to thermal covers because the indoor temperatures are likely to be high enough to hold heat loss down relative to potential losses in outside areas.

Bottom drains must be covered with protective grates or covers that cannot be removed without the use of tools and should be designed to prevent the entrapment of fingers and toes. If only one drain is utilized in the design, it must be an antivortex type and should not pose a tripping or stubbing hazard.

Finally, a sign should be located near a telephone in the spa vicinity with emergency phone numbers: rescue or ambulance unit, fire, doctor, and/or hospital.

Health Hazards

Although spas and hot tubs are useful for relaxation and stress reduction, they are a breeding ground for many harmful types of bacteria. Hot water, high-density usage, low disinfectant levels, and infrequent draining provide an excellent environment for harmful bacteria. User density in hot tubs can be compared with swimming pool use. Two persons in a 400-gallon capacity spa are equivalent to 1,050 persons immersed in a 75-foot by 45-foot swimming pool with a 210,000-gallon capacity. Inattention to disinfectant levels and infrequent draining and refilling are the primary reasons for the frequent outbreaks of spa-related diseases.

Health hazards for spa users are often related to prescription medicines. Patients who are using diuretics, anticoagulants, antihistimines, vasoconstrictors, vasodilators, and tranquilizers should use a spa only with a physician's advice. Persons using recreational drugs such as narcotics (stimulants or depressants) or hypnotics should not use spas or hot tubs while under the influence of drugs.

Hyperthermia is a serious problem, displaying symptoms such as headaches and dizziness. Some people like to exercise in hot water and should know that once their surrounding temperature increases to 85 to 90 °F, they are risking hyperthermia. When the body temperature increases to 110 °F from exercise or prolonged immersion (beyond

15 minutes), the metabolic rate increases, the brain becomes greatly depressed, sweating decreases, and heat stroke results.

Persons who have sustained any type of injury treated with ice such as sprains should avoid the spa. Hot water will increase swelling and delay recovery.

Another spa-related health problem is dermatosis. According to Rycroft (1983), about 5% of spa users will develop a skin rash from spas that utilize bromine sticks (hydantoin bromine) as a disinfectant. Although this condition is not believed to be serious, a physician should be consulted if a rash occurs.

Pregnant women should use spas carefully. Maximum use has been defined as 15 minutes at a temperature no higher than 102 °F. Lower temperatures are recommended. At temperatures above 102 °F damage may occur to the fetus. A similar problem exists with children under 5 years old as their thermoregulatory mechanism is not fully developed until age 5, so using spas at temperatures above 102 °F may result in possible brain damage.

Pool ventilation in the spa area may produce "coughing disease"—a nonbacterial problem that produces coughing spells while in the spa. The disinfectant and nitrogen-ammonia compounds vaporizing at the water's surface produce an irritating condition for the mucous membranes of the nose and throat, resulting in coughing until the person vacates the spa area.

Disease-Related Problems

Because hot water is conducive to bacteria growth, a wide variety of diseases may be contracted from improperly maintained spas and hot tubs. Common problems range from staph infections that cause boils to vaginitis and urinary tract infections. Other more serious diseases that occur with some frequency include Pontiac fever and hot tub folliculitus. At this time the medical profession does *not* believe that AIDS (Acquired Immune Deficiency Syndrome) is transmitted through spa or hot tub water, as the virus is extremely susceptible to chlorine and bromine disinfectants, even at very low levels. It is also believed that the virus cannot exist outside the human body.

Pontiac fever, first identified in Pontiac, Michigan, is a hot water disease with flu-like symptoms.

Nausea, dizziness, headache, vomiting, and fever are the prominent symptoms. The bacteria causing Pontiac fever (legionella pneumophilia) is the same virus that causes legionnaires disease, which is also thought to be able to be transmitted in spas and hot tubs.

Hot tub folliculitus (pseudomonas aeroginosa) is another common spa disease. The bacteria is carried on the skin and enters the water when people do not shower before using the spa. Heat dilates the pores and the inlet jets jackhammer the skin, forcing bacteria into the pores. Symptoms usually begin to occur within 24 hours and consist of fatigue, swollen lymph glands, redness, tenderness, swelling of the breasts (men and women), and open, pustile-type sores that ooze, itch, and then become painful. The disease may cause blood poisoning, urinary tract infections, and penumonia. Although it usually lasts only 7 days, it may linger for as long as 2 to 3 weeks.

Whirlpool Design and Planning

Aside from the pool shell, the spa or hot tub package includes a hydromassage (or hydrotherapy) pump, inlets (jets), a heater, a filter, motor, filter pump, valves, drain, weir or skimmer, piping, disinfection system, and wiring necessary to the system.

Many hospital, athletic, and swimming pool complexes use concrete pool shells built into the ground or floor of the facility with liners of fiberglass, tile, or plastic. Current economics as well as convenience have increased the use of fiberglass and acrylic. Most manufacturers supply preplumbed packages delivered to the facility ready for hookup.

The use of the premolded fiberglass and acrylic materials allows for a great variety of shapes, sizes, and seating designs. Spas today may be round, square, oval, octagonal, or free-form, with seats that range from simple benches and steps to lounge-type and bucket-style. For health clubs and other facilities concerned with style and appearance, spas come in a wide range of colors.

Both above-ground and in-ground (or sunken) installations call for firm placement of the spa on a bedding compound such as sand or on a reinforced concrete pad. In on-ground installations, this helps prevent flexing. Most manufacturers also recommend wood cross-bracing under stairs, seats, and outer coping, after which a skirt can be attached to the bracing. Decking is recommended in above-ground installations.

The size, as with swimming pools and other facilities, is determined by the space available and anticipated usage. Fiberglass and acrylic spas on the market today range from bathtub-size for individual home or hotel installation, up to oval models 10 feet long. Even in locations where 25 or more people use the spa in the space of an hour, there should be no problem finding a prefabricated shell. And depending on cost and other considerations, it is always possible to build a concrete shell spa. The most powerful therapy pumps available, however, are 2-1/2 or 3 horsepower and can be used for about 10 jets. Most manufacturers of prefabricated shells can provide custom models where it is desired. Most commercially available shells tend to have depths of up to 40 inches and areas of up to 60 or 70 square feet. Volume capacity ranges from about 350 to 500 gallons. When planning the dimensions of a whirlpool, it may be necessary to consult local or state codes for size and volume capacity limitations.

Aside from the overall size, the number of users accommodated by a particular spa will depend on the number of seats and the number of jets. Based on guidelines from manufacturers and distributors, some appropriate sizes and usages are suggested in Table 5.1. Depths of most commercial spa shells made of fiberglass or acrylic vary from 37 to 40 inches.

Table 5.1 Spa Specifications

Dimensions	Seats	Jets
5 ft × 5 ft square or round	4	3
6-1/2 ft × 6-1/2 ft square	5	6
7 ft round	5-7	5
7-1/2 ft × 7-1/2 ft pentagon	6-7	6
9-1/4 ft × 8 ft octagon with steps	7	8
10 ft × 6-1/3 ft rectangle	10	10

Spas are often located near the main swimming pool in pool complexes and health clubs, allowing bathers to enjoy a cold dip immediately after using the whirlpool, or alternatively, to relax after swimming or other hard exercise. However, it is important to recognize the tendency of people to run from the spa and jump or dive into the pool without taking time to look around. Hence, signs should be prominently placed indicating the water depth as well as cautioning against diving if the area of the pool nearest to the spa contains shallow water.

The New York City code requires that whirlpools have at least a 5-foot walkway around their perimeters ''to facilitate cleanliness and safety.''

Spa Circulation and Aeration Features

In commercial-size spas designed primarily for health club and large pool complex installations, the hydrotherapy pumps generally require 1-1/2 to 2-1/2 horsepower (hp), depending on the number of jets. Four or five jets require 1-1/2 hp, seven or eight jets need 2 hp, and 10 jets require 2-1/2 hp. Bathtub-size whirlpool installations, having from one to four jets, usually require 1/2 to 1 hp pumps.

Jet-head sizes are standard and are mostly made of high-performance plastic. Different designs are available with adjustable and nonadjustable inlet or jet systems. Both work in accord with the well-known ''Venturi principle'': Air drawn into the system is funneled to the inlet heads and mixed with water in a continuous, even action. The air-water mix then flows into the spa shell, creating the whirlpool action. Adjustable inlets allow control of the direction and velocity of the water coming through. Most jets allow for a choice of a minimal amount of air to an equal air/water mix.

The whirlpool pump and circulation system usually operate separately from the heater and filtration system. This allows hot soaking without the whirlpool action, if desired, and cuts down on energy use as well.

Spa Filtration

Filtration circulation pumps for whirlpool systems are usually 1/2 hp in size. Regenerative cycle diatomaceous earth provides the best quality water for the least amount of operational dollars spent. Cartridge filters provide excellent water quality but

are more expensive to operate. The least appropriate filtration application for hot water use is sand. Hot water, body oils, and high mineral levels can make a pottery-like (clay) material out of a sand filter, necessitating replacement. If sand filters are chosen, a high-flow model is the most appropriate because it provides longer operational life.

The New York code also requires that the recirculation equipment provide a complete turnover of the water capacity at least once every 30 hours. The equipment should also be designed to return the water to a turbidity of 0.50 Jackson Turbidity Units (JTUs) at least once during the 4 hours following peak use.

Spa heaters allow for a wide range of temperatures. Some manufacturers include a two-thermostat arrangement that permits a range of water temperature of 50 to 100 °F. A desirable safety feature necessary for each spa is a thermostat that automatically shuts down the heater when water temperatures reach 104 °F.

Once the spa has been brought up to the desired temperature, most heat loss is from the water's surface. Heater size, therefore, should be based on surface losses. For outdoor spas, the factors to be considered, once the desired temperature is determined, are average temperature of the coldest month in which the spa will be used, the surface area of the spa, and the average wind velocity. Table 5.2 indicates the heat loss from the surface for outdoor spas. The correct heater size requires a BTU output that must exceed the heat loss. Heater output is determined by dividing the output by the actual efficiency of the heater. For indoor spas, the air temperature is generally close to that of the spa's water. For indoor locations, assume a heat loss factor of 100 BTU/hour. Spa covers may actually reduce loss by as much as 50% or more.

Equipment areas for spas measure about 4 ft by 6 ft or 5 ft by 7 ft and should be located no more than 20 feet from the spa.

Spa and Hot Tub Water Chemistry

Water chemistry and disinfection are discussed in chapter 13; however, due to the increased temperatures in spa and hot tub water, chemistry and disinfection procedures are somewhat different. These changes must be noted and followed if minimum health standards are to be maintained. Standards recommended by the U.S. Department of

Table 5.2 Heat Loss From Spa and Hot Tub Surfaces in BTUs Per Hour

Spa Surface (square feet)	Differential Between Average Air Temperature and Desired Water Temperature (°F)					
	10°	20°	30°	40°	50°	60°
50	5,250	10,500	15,750	21,000	26,250	31,500
75	7,875	15,750	23,625	31,100	39,375	47,250
100	10,500	21,000	31,500	42,000	52,500	63,000
150	15,750	31,500	47,250	63,000	78,750	94,500
200	21,000	42,000	63,000	84,000	105,000	126,000
250	26,250	52,500	78,750	105,000	131,250	157,500
300	31,500	63,000	94,500	126,000	157,500	189,000
350	36,750	73,500	110,250	147,000	183,750	220,500
400	42,000	84,000	126,000	168,000	210,000	252,000
450	47,250	94,500	141,750	189,000	236,250	283,500
500	52,500	105,000	157,500	210,000	263,000	315,000

Table 5.3 Public Spa and Hot Tub Operational Parameters

Parameter	Minimum	Maximum
Disinfectant Levels		
Free chlorine	2.0 ppm	4.0 ppm
Bromine	2.0 ppm	4.0 ppm
Iodine	2.0 ppm	5.0 ppm
Chemical Values		
pH	7.2	7.8
Total alkalinity	60 ppm	200 ppm
Dissolved solids	300 ppm	1500 ppm
Calcium hardness	50 ppm	500 ppm
Heavy metals (copper, iron, manganese)	0	
Biological Values		
Algae	none	
Bacteria	none	
Temperature Values		
Temperature		104 °F (40 °C)
Water Clarity		
Jackson Turbidity Units	0	1.0

Note: From *Suggested health and safety guidelines for public spas and hot tubs* (pp 15-18), by U.S. Department of Health and Human Services, 1985, Atlanta, GA: Author.

Health and Human Services with some modifications by slightly increasing the recommended levels of halogen disinfectants are presented in Table 5.3. Additional procedures include shocking daily by raising halogen levels to 5.0 ppm and shocking weekly to levels of 10.0 ppm. Temperature should be checked 30 minutes before opening and hourly thereafter unless an automatic shut-off occurs when water temperature reaches 104 °F. Bacteriological tests must be conducted weekly with samples taken during a period of heavy use.

Tests for the presence of residual halogens should be taken hourly each day. Tests for other chemical levels and water clarity should be taken as often during the course of a day as is necessary to ensure that the water is balanced and clear. A Langelier Saturation Index should be calculated after each refilling, and then necessary corrective steps should be taken. Water level must be maintained at midskimmer level so that oils and floating matter are constantly removed 24 hours a day.

Water must be replaced and the spa cleaned once a month and more often in times of heavy use or when chemical treatment difficulties occur. Spa surfaces should then be cleaned with an inhibited muriatic acid. Vacuuming may be necessary in larger spas between weekly draining.

A portable whirlpool spa by Jacuzzi

Hot Tubs

Hot tubs, made mostly of redwood and occasionally from other woods, are relatively new to the spa scene. They are purchased more for private home use than for commercial establishments, but this trend seems to be changing. A New York-based firm, California Hottub, one of the first in the field, offers models that are 12 feet in diameter with a seating capacity of 22 people. Hot tubs may be used just to soak in hot water, but most include jets that provide a whirlpool system. Most manufacturers of whirlpool equipment sell the parts of the system separate from the shell.

The redwood tubs, like the more common fiberglass and acrylic models, can be installed indoors or outdoors, above-ground or in-ground. The equipment package is essentially the same as that contained in whirlpools and spas: a circulation pump, filter, automatic chlorinator, heater, whirlpool pump, and jets. Most local building and health codes do not deal with hot tubs, considering them more of a private home product.

The tubs are generally available in round or oval shapes. For example, one company offers a total of 13 sizes. All except a 4-foot diameter two-seater are available in heights of 3, 4, or 5 feet. Models are available in 5- through 12-foot sizes. A 7-foot diameter tub seats 10 to 12 people, a 9-footer—14 to 16, 10-footer—16 to 18, and on up to the 12-foot, 22-seat model. An oval shape measuring 6-1/2 feet by 9-1/2 feet seats 12 to 15 people.

Chlorination, maintenance, and general upkeep procedures of hot tubs as well as planning steps are similar to those for spas, allowing for some special details because of the wood. For example, the tub should never be left empty for more than 2 days, and there should always be 2 or 3 inches of water left in the bottom.

A free chlorine residual of 2.0 to 4.0 parts per million (ppm) must be maintained at all times. Periodic superchlorination may also be necessary to overcome chloramine formation resulting from such agents as suntan oil, perspiration, and cleaning compounds.

The best filter media for hot tub use includes diatomaceous earth and paper cartridges. The pH should be kept in the 7.4 to 7.6 range, and a Langelier Saturation Index should be calculated and necessary levels adjusted every 2 days and each time the tub is drained.

Saunas and Steam Rooms

Sauna and steam room installations consist of an enclosure and the heat- or steam-generating equipment. In most settings, they are located in a locker-room area and frequently are placed adjacent to each other.

Commercial-size steam rooms and saunas generally require 80 to 140 square feet in floor space. Sauna ceilings should not be higher than 7 feet for maximum operating efficiency. Steam room ceilings may be higher because the steam rises. Both types of enclosures may range up to 1,500 or 2,000 cubic feet using standard equipment that is readily available. Most manufacturers can provide custom equipment if larger installations are planned.

Steam rooms contain vapor, and the temperature in the room should never exceed 120 °F. On the other hand, saunas, which produce dry heat, may reach temperatures in the 175 to 194° range. The maximum temperature should not exceed 194 °F. These are the extreme limits recommended by most equipment manufacturers and health codes.

Size guidelines are based on expected usage and available space. At least 2 linear feet should be allowed for each user; however, many people prefer to lie down while in the sauna or steam room.

The basic sauna package consists of what amounts to an insulated box with benches, a heater, igneous rocks for convection of heat, a thermostat, and a thermometer. The sauna heater must be Underwriters Laboratory (UL)-approved or the equivalent. There must be a guardrail around it to help protect users from accidental contact with the hot stove box containing the rocks.

Redwood is the most common wood used in construction of saunas because it does not develop high surface temperatures when exposed to high heat, although hemlock, cedar, aspen, and pine may also be used. The floor of a commercial sauna should not be solid because it absorbs sweat and is hard to clean. A latticework wood platform, called a ductboard, is commonly used for flooring.

Users should sit or lie on towels to minimize sweat absorption as well as to be as comfortable as possible on the wooden benches. Benches

should be periodically sponged with a solution comprised of 1 cup of sodium hypochlorite and 2-1/2 gallons of water.

Correct heater size depends on the size of the sauna room. A fairly standard size commercial sauna installation measuring 840 cubic feet generally requires a 14,300-watt, 47,000-BTU heater. The heater should be placed as low as possible in the sauna itself.

As a rough guide to deciding on the size of the enclosure and generator, a 400-cubic-foot steam room accommodates about eight people; one with 740 cubic feet is reasonably comfortable for up to 18; and a 1,500-cubic-foot steam room has enough room to accommodate as many as 30 people.

Saunas, less costly than steam rooms, are essentially freestanding rooms that may be put up anywhere, and are generally supplied in a prefab form. In contrast, steam rooms have to be built in as part of the building. But each provides users with relaxation and heat therapy.

Health Benefits of Saunas and Steam Rooms

Despite the rapid growth in the use of saunas and steam rooms in homes, hotels, and health clubs, there are no hard figures on installations and still relatively little in the way of medical data and studies on their possible health benefits or the dangers in their misuse. Some factors are evident, which users must clearly understand to ensure that they receive the benefits and avoid the dangers.

There is little dispute over the relaxing effect of both the sauna and steam room. Beyond this, both promote sweating, possibly helping to deep-cleanse the skin. The loss of body fluid from perspiration may also produce weight loss, although documentation here is poor. The amount of weight loss appears to vary in individuals, ranging from 1 to 3 pounds, and this results from loss of body fluids rather than body fat.

Use of steam rooms and saunas causes body temperature and blood pressure to rise. Generally speaking, individuals with heart diseases and higher than normal blood pressure should either not use saunas and steam rooms at all or should do so only after medical consultation and under the supervision of a doctor. People with serious respiratory conditions should also use these facilities with care. Both the sauna and the steam room act as cardiovascular stimulants.

Spa in attractive setting. Design by Gavin Brown.

Sauna and Steam Room Safety

Because of the health and safety problems associated with dry and moist heat, those responsible for sauna and steam room operation and supervision must take a variety of safety precautions. Primary to a safe operation is a complete set of rules, printed on signs made of metal and posted prominently on both sides of the access door. Letters should be large enough to read without a patron having to use glasses and of a color contrasting with the sign material. Rules should state the recommended length of duration (30 minutes) and should warn of dangers to those who have heart and hypertension conditions. The rules should also advise against sleeping and exercising in the sauna or steam room environment.

An emergency alarm should be installed with activator switches inside and outside the room. These switches should continue to sound an alarm at various building locations until someone moves the switch to the off position. A window should be included in the door and in at least one other wall so that facility attendants can make routine checks from the outside. Employees with responsibilities for these operations should also be currently certified in CPR and standard first aid.

Both a clock and thermometer large enough to see clearly without assistance should be located in a conspicuous area readily visible from anywhere in the room. A preset thermostat should automatically shut off heat or steam when the optimum temperature is achieved. If surveillance of these rooms is limited, a timer should be included to cut off the heat at one-hour intervals, requiring an occupant to leave the room and turn the heat switch back on from outside. All other controls should be inaccessible to patrons.

Facility operators also must be prepared for the possibility of an emergency (power failure) or an accident (cardiac arrest). Written and rehearsed procedures must be established. Such procedures require an attendant certified in CPR and standard first aid, a telephone with a list of emergency numbers located nearby, and a first-aid kit filled and readily accessible.

References

Lesser, G. (1979, October 15). Spas are a doctor's prescription. *Pool and Spa News,* **18**(20), 40.

National Swimming Pool Institute. (1980, February). *Minimum standards for residential spas.* Alexandria, VA: Author.

Spa and Tub Association of the National Swimming Pool Institute. (1978). *Minimum standards for public spas* (p. 21). Alexandria, VA: Author.

Rycroft, R.J.G. (1983, August 13). *British Medical Journal,* 287.

U.S. Department of Health and Human Services, Public Health Service, Center for Disease Control. (1985, January). *Suggested health and safety guidelines for public spas and hot tubs, pub. #99-960* (pp. 15-18). Atlanta, GA: Author.

Chapter 6

Pools of the United States

Arizona State University Aquatic Complex, Tempe

Pool features:

50 m by 25 yd competition pool

- Constant 7-ft depth
- Moveable bulkhead
- Underwater observation area
- Recessed rimflow system

25 yd by 25 yd by 18-ft deep diving well

- Tower with platforms of 5, 7.5, and 10 m
- Flanked by 4 springboards (two 1-m and two 3-m)
- Additional boards (2 each—1-m and 3-m) placed opposite diving tower
- Equipped for underwater speaker system

25-yd, 8-lane warm-up and teaching pool

- 3-1/2 to 6 ft depth
- Includes wheelchair ramp
- Deck rimflow system

Stadium seating capacity: 2,000

Consultant: Ward O'Connell

Engineers and architects: Sverdrup & Parcel and Associates

Contractor: Chris G. Evans, Inc.

Harvard University Natatorium, Cambridge, Massachusetts

Pool features:
- Main pool, 50 m by 25 m, depth of water 7 ft throughout, main pool divides into two 25-m courses
- Diving pool offset from center of main pool
- Two 3-m and two 1-m springboards, 7-1/2-m tower
- Whitten Uniflow s.s. gutters with wave quell grill
- Two underwater windows 36 in. by 60 in. and 60 in. by 21 in.
- Ceramic tile finish on interior of pool
- Seating capacity: 1,500

Architects: Architects Collaborative, Cambridge, MA

Contractor: Turner Construction Co., Boston, MA

Equipment furnished by: Whitten Corp., Mendon, MA

Cost: $4.3 million

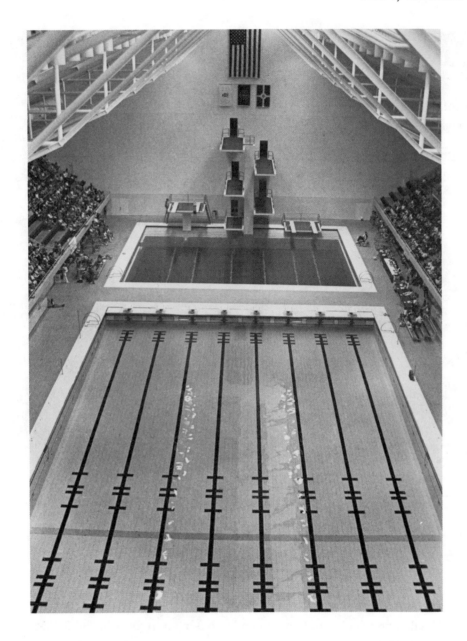

The IUPUI Pool, Indianapolis

The 1984 Olympic Trials for swimming and diving were held in this pool.

Pool features:

- The most unique feature is the dark blue bottom of the diving pool, which is 75 ft by 60 ft and 18 ft deep
- The pool is 174 ft long with two moveable bulkheads that permit pool to be converted to two 25-yd or 25-m courses or one 50-m course
- The diving pool contains two 3-m springboards, two 1-m springboards, a tower with platforms at 1, 3, 5, 7-1/2, and 10 m
- Seating capacity: 6,000

Consultant: Counsilman and Associates

Architect: Browning, Day, Mullins, Dierdorf, Inc.

Photo: Roy Hartill

Los Angeles 1984 Olympic Pool

The pool was financed by McDonald Food Chain and became a facility of the University of Southern California after the Olympic Games.

Pool features:

- One 50-m competitive swimming course with eight lanes
- One 25 yd by 25 yd diving pool with two 1-m and two 3-m springboards and 5-1/2-, 7-1/2-, and 10-m platforms and an elevator shaft
- Twenty-four underwater lights in 50-m pool
- Twelve underwater lights in diving pool
- Spectator seating capacity: 11,000
- Recessed overflow system

Consulting engineer: Dr. William Rowley

New York University Natatorium, New York City

Located in the Cole Sports and Recreation Center

Pool features:

- 25-m competitive swim course, 50 ft wide
- Separate diving well with two 1-m and one 3-m springboards
- Rimflow gutter system
- Water circulated through "tile tubes" that also form the bottom lines for competitive course
- Electrically operated lift for handicapped persons

Architect: Wank, Adams, Slavin, and Associates

Engineer: Walter Bishop, Long Island, NY

Consultant: Dr. M.A. Gabrielsen, Nova University, Ft. Lauderdale, FL

University of Texas Natatorium, Austin

Pool features:

- 50-m competitive swimming course, 25 yd wide, 9 ft deep
- Separate diving pool, 25 yd by 25 yd with 10-m tower, four 3-m springboards, three 1-m springboards, one on hydraulic for variable heights
- Rimflow gutter system
- Two bulkheads may be raised into ceiling by compressed air motors for 50-m course and may be lowered into pool to subdivide pool in 25-m or 25-yd swim courses or water polo
- Spectator seating capacity: 2,750
- Depth of water in diving well is 18 ft
- Diving pool is equipped with sparging system that creates a cushion of bubbles to soften a diver's entry into the water
- 880,000 gallons of water in the 50-m pool is kept at 79 °F; the temperature in 654,000-gal diving pool is kept at 82 °F
- Chemical balance of pool is controlled and monitored automatically
- Water is turned over every six hours and is filtered by diatomaceous earth media

Pool constructed by B.L. McGee Construction Co. of Austin, TX

Engineering Consultant: Milton Costello, P.E.

Architects: Fisher and Spillman, Dallas, TX

Photo: Frank Armstrong

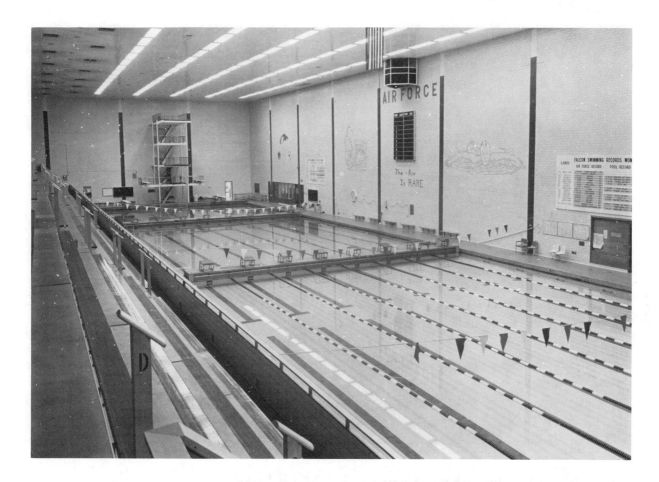

U.S. Air Force Academy, Colorado Springs, Colorado

Pool features:

- Moveable bulkheads permit pool to be converted to 50-m pool plus separate diving area or two 25-m or yd courses
- Diving equipment: Two 3-m or two 1-m springboards; 3-, 5-, 7-1/2- and 10-m diving platforms
- Recessed gutters
- Spectator seating capacity: 2,000

Architect: Skidmore, Owings, and Merrill

Photo: Stewarts Commercial Photographers

U.S. Naval Academy, Annapolis, Maryland

Pool features:

- Main competitive pool, 50 m by 25 m and constant depth of 8 ft; a moveable bulkhead permits team to train at any distance; bulkheads may be hoisted out of pool and stored in ceiling

- Separate diving pool measuring 60 ft by 52 ft with depths ranging from 14 to 17 ft; diving equipment: two 3-m and two 1-m springboards; a diving tower with 1-, 5-, 7-1/2-, and 10-m platforms

- Spectator seating capacity: 1,500

- Lighting is by overhead lights producing 100 footcandles of illumination on the deck

- The diving well has three underwater observation windows and underwater speakers

- Two skylights

Architect: The Eggers Group

Engineering consultant: Milton Costello, P.E.

U.S. Military Academy Natatorium at West Point

Pool features:

- 50-m course with submersible bulkhead for conversion to 25-m or 25-yd course
- Offset diving tower and 1- and 3-m springboards
- Underwater observation room

Walter Schroeder YMCA Natatorium, Milwaukee, Wisconsin

Pool features:

- 50-m pool with two moveable bulkheads
- Diving facilities: two 2-m and two 1-m springboards; tower with 3-, 5-, 7-1/2-, and 10-m platforms
- Variable bottom at one end of pool capable of reducing depth of water to 20 in.
- Separate training and therapeutic pools are part of the complex
- Hoist for use with disabled individuals

Mission Bay Aquatic Training Center, Boca Raton, Florida

Pool complex features:

50-m by 25-yd competition pool

- Eight 50-m lanes, 9 ft wide, 7 to 8 ft deep
- 8 starting blocks at each end
- Two 3-ft wide bulkheads providing flexibility of two 25-yd or two 25-m courses, or one 50-m course

50-m by 25-m warm-up pool

- 10 lanes, 4 to 5 ft deep
- 10 starting blocks at each end
- Eighteen 25-m lanes

25-yd by 65-ft age group training pool

- 8 lanes, 4 to 5 ft deep
- 8 starting blocks

25-yd by 25-m diving pool

- 9 lanes, 14 to 18 ft deep

- 9 starting blocks
- 1-, 3-, 5-, 7-1/2-, and 10-m platforms
- Four 3-m springboards on 2 concrete platforms and 2 durafirm platforms with 2 dura-maxi-flex springboards
- Two 1/2-m springboards
- Two 1-m springboards
- 2 trampolines, 2 dryland 1-m springboards
- Diving pool spa

Other features:

- Seating capacity: 4,500 permanent with 2,000 temporary
- 20 reverse cycle heat pump

Architect: Vander Ploeg and Associates

Sitework Contractor: Devcon of Florida

Engineer: Lawson Noble, Inc.

Consultants: Mark Schubert and Ron O'Brien

Chapter 7
Pools of the World

The Chandler Aquatic Center, Brisbane, Australia

Site of the 1982 Commonwealth Games

Pool features:

- Competitive pool: 50 m by 25 m, constant water depth of 2 m
- Pool basin: Finished with ceramic tile
- Diving pool: 27 m by 20 m with two 1-m and two 3-m springboards, plus tower with 5-, 7-, and 10-m platforms
- Spectator seating capacity: 5,000
- Lighting: LUX 1,800, suitable for TV transmission
- Electric timing by Omega

Architects: McDonald, Wagner, and Piddle, Brisbane

Photo: Bob Peisley

Crystal Palace Sports Centre, Swimming Pool Complex, London, England

Pool features:

- Racing pool: 50 m by 25 m by 6 ft 9 in. deep with electronic timing apparatus to .001 of a second
- Diving pool: 20.11 m by 15.84 m by 16 ft deep (5 m) maximum
- Learning pool: 18.28 m by 7.62 m by 2 ft 9 in. deep

Architects: Greater London Council Architects Department

Royal Commonwealth Pool, Edinburgh, Scotland

This magnificent pool was especially built for the swimming and diving events at the ninth British Commonwealth Games staged in Edinburgh, July, 1970.

The striking building houses a 50-meter competition pool with electronic timing and indicator equipment. A unique diving pit is built at an angle to the pool to allow most of the spectators to watch the divers in profile—the view taken by the judges.

Architects: Robert Matthew, Johnson Marshall, & Partners, Edinburgh, Scotland

Japan's "Super Swim" With Contractible Canopy

Pool features:

- Contractible canopy is manually operated
- Roof made of polycarbonate glass
- Tile used on pool basin
- Passive solar heat helps keep both water and room warm
- Glass panel designed to withstand winds of 139 mph and snow load of 39-1/2 in.

Architect: Nikko Corporation of America, Masami Kumode, President and Architect

Olympic Pools, 1960-1980

1960 Olympic Pool, Rome, Italy

1964 Olympic Pool, Tokyo, Japan

1968 Olympic Pool, Mexico City, Mexico

1972 Olympic Pool, Munich, West Germany

1976 Olympic Pool, Montreal, Canada

1980 Olympic Sport Center Pool, Moscow, USSR

Georgetown University Yates Field House, Washington, DC. Architect: Daniel F. Tully Associates. Photo by Edward Jacoby.

Chapter 8

Safety Guidelines for Pool Design and Operation

Factual safety information and guidelines for the pool industry are provided in this chapter. This includes pool planners and designers, pool operators and owners of both public and private pools, pool equipment manufacturers, and all pool supervisors in any capacity. Many pool accidents are the result of a lack of attention to known safety practices and standards. The purpose of these guidelines is to aid in reducing the number of pool injuries and also to strengthen existing pool standards and regulations.

The Incidence of Pool-Related Accidents

Swimming pools ranked number one in the development of recreation facilities in the post-World War II era. Now as many people swim in pools on any day in the summer as at beaches. Yet by its nature, swimming along with its related activities such as diving, snorkling, and scuba diving is a potentially hazardous sport because it involves a person's intrusion into an environment foreign to his or her usual habitat. Considering the number of people who use swimming pools and the number of times each person uses a pool during the course of a year, the pool accident rate is actually low. Pools are the safest place for people to swim; careful investigation of pool injuries and drownings has indicated that many could have been prevented.

It is estimated that as many as 50 million people swim in a pool somewhere in the United States on a hot summer day. The fact that the drowning rate has dropped from 10.2 per 100,000 to 3.4 per 100,000 in this country since 1900 is a tribute to those organizations and agencies that teach people to swim. Learning to swim and to effect simple water rescues combine as the single greatest prevention against drownings. And yet, drownings rank second to the automobile as the cause of accidental deaths for people up to the age of 45.

Significantly, of the estimated 7,000-8,000 annual drownings in the United States, only 10% (between 700 and 800) occur in swimming pools, and half of all pool drownings happen in home pools where supervision is often minimal or nonexistent. Approximately 50% of the home pool drownings are youngsters below the age of 5 who did not know how to swim. An estimated 30% of the pool drownings occur in pools operated by motels, hotels, and apartments. The remaining 20% occur in pools operated by cities, counties, voluntary organizations such as the Ys and Boys' Clubs, schools and colleges, country clubs, and commercially operated pools.

Several factors are usually involved in a drowning. The most frequent cause appears to be accidental falls into pools by children, accounting for nearly half of all drowning cases in residential pools. This accident frequently happens to youngsters below the age of 5, often because there was no fence or barrier around the pool to prevent the intrusion. Improper pool design, faulty equipment design, inadequate maintenance of the pool or equipment, lack of adequate supervision, and in some instances, the misconduct of swimmers themselves are other factors related to the proximate cause of drownings.

According to the National Safety Council, two thirds of the drownings in home pools involve members of the households. This fact indicates that fencing of pools or yards containing pools is effective in keeping out neighborhood children.

The creation of the United States Consumer Products Safety Commission (CPSC) by Congress in 1973 focused increased attention on pool-related accidents. Because many residential swimming pools were sold across the counter in department stores, discount outlets, hardware stores, and outlets specializing in pool sales, pools were labeled a product and hence came under the scrutiny of the commission. The commission held the term *swimming pool* to be the generic label for manufactured pool equipment and accessories such as diving boards, water slides, ladders, deck surface material, and instruction equipment. The National Electronic Injury Surveillance System (NEISS), administered by the Consumer Product Safety Commission (CPSC), provides data on the frequency and severity of injuries occurring in and around pools. An estimated 120,000 serious injuries are brought to a hospital emergency room each year. This number may seem small in relation to the number of people swimming in pools, yet the catastrophic nature of spinal cord injuries, often resulting in paraplegic or quadriplegic disablements, coupled with the astronomical cost of medical care, hospitalization, and attendant care, warrants the attention of all pool builders, owners, and operators.

Pool Accident Research

The first comprehensive in-depth study of the circumstances associated with swimming pool injuries, sponsored by the CPSC (1977a), was conducted by the Departments of Orthopedics and Rehabilitation and Neurological Surgery of the University of Miami Medical School and Nova University in 1976. Of the 72 case studies of serious pool injuries, 57 resulted in complete quadriplegia and 15 were injuries to the head and/or neck resulting in some neurological deficit.

Based on data gathered through the National Electronic Injury Surveillance System (NEISS), CPSC (1977b) estimated that between 8,000 and 9,000 serious diving-related injuries occur each year. The same source projects an annual rate of 1,800 water slide injuries. The number of people injured by diving from pool decks is not isolated in the statistical accounting, therefore, we infer their inclusion under the "other injuries" category.

The Consumer Products Safety Commission (1978), in discussing the swimming pool injury problem, stated that one of the "major accident patterns associated with swimming pools was striking the bottom or side of the pool because of insufficient depth for diving or sliding." The report further indicated that "in addition to striking the bottom of the pool, people are injured when they hit protruding waterpipes, ladders or other objects in the pool."

As the number of spinal cord injuries resulting from diving or sliding head first into pools and other water areas increased, several medical teams involved in treating these victims began to report their findings in the literature: that somewhere between 500 and 700 spinal cord diving injuries occurred each year, totally incapacitating the victims for life. The exact number of spinal cord injuries that occur in pools as contrasted with other water areas such as oceans, lakes, rivers, and quarries is not known; however, some authorities estimate that as many as 30 to 40% of the spinal cord injuries may be pool related.

Gabrielsen and others added to the data compiled in the original CPSC study. Of the total of 152 spinal cord injuries resulting from diving and sliding, 90% occurred in pools. A panel of authorities representing the fields of medicine, biomechanics, rehabilitation, and engineering, as well as coaches and teachers of swimming and diving, architects, and equipment manufacturers examined the data and subsequently prepared for publication a book entitled *Diving Injuries—A Critical Insight and Recommendations* (Gabrielsen, 1984). A summary of the findings of the study revealed the following:

- 88% of the victims were males.

- No victims were below the age of 12.

- 139 became quadriplegics.

- 35 injuries were the result of dives from springboards.

- 86 victims sustained their injuries by diving into the shallow portion of the pool, either from the deck or from a structure located adjacent to the pool such as a fence, shed, garage, porch, or water slide and platform.

- 66 occurred in pools with vinyl liner basins.

- In 118 cases there was no qualified person supervising the pool area.

- In 100 cases it was the victim's first time at the pool or facility.

- In 148 of the cases there was no warning sign calling attention to any potential danger.

- 79 of the accidents happened in home pools, 25 in motel and hotel pools, and 20 in apartment-owned pools.

From the previous data, a profile of the potential spinal cord victim emerges: usually a male, about 6 feet tall, over 175 pounds, and without formal diving training. It is his first visit to the pool, which is usually in one of the following facilities: home pool, motel/hotel pool, or a pool in an apartment complex. No lifeguard or any qualified adult is present to supervise his activity, and he dives or slides into shallow water. The panel's major conclusions are described as follows.

Springboard diving injuries. The following list summarizes the research findings related to springboard diving.

1. The recreational, or untrained diver, needs more, not less, landing area, and pool design must be able to safely accommodate a variety of water entries from left, right, and in front of the board.

2. The typical hotel, motel, or residential pool containing a springboard has either a "spoon" shape or "hopper"-type bottom, a bottom profile with truncated side and back walls. This design existed in every pool where springboard accidents occurred. The entry point of most springboard diving victims was from 12 to 15 feet from the end of the board. If a diver enters the water at this distance at an angle between 40 to 60° and maintains that angle, the in-water path will cause the diver to strike the upslope at nearly a perpendicular angle.

3. Insufficient water depth in the foreseeable landing area is the major cause of springboard diving injuries. Of the 36 springboard accidents, no victim struck bottom in the deepest part of the pool.

4. At all the motel and apartment pools where the diving accidents occurred, the maximum water depths ranged between 8 and 9 feet. In residential pools where the diving accidents happened, the maximum water depth ranged from 7-1/2 feet to 8-1/2 feet. None of the injured divers struck in the deepest part of the pool. None of the springboard diving victims were injured in pools that met the specifications for diving promulgated by the NCAA, USS, or FINA—the major governing bodies for competitive diving in the United States and throughout the world.

5. Some springboard diving victims claimed they had difficulty seeing the bottom of the pool as they executed their dives. This condition may have been a contributing factor.

6. If the diver makes contact with the bottom, the hands and arms are the diver's only protection in preventing the head from hitting the bottom of the pool. Several victims stated that their hands slipped as they struck the bottom, exposing their heads.

7. None of the residential pools in the study had depth markers to alert the diver to the water's depth at various locations.

Other diving. In 85 cases, injuries resulted from people diving into pools from locations other than from springboards or jumpboards. In every instance the victim struck the bottom where the water was less than 5 feet deep, and in most instances, 3-1/2 feet or less. Therefore, it was concluded that diving into the shallow portion of a pool is the major cause of serious neck injuries that occur in pools.

1. In areas where the depth of the water is under 5 feet, there is not enough water to safely accommodate a diver attempting anything but a shallow racing dive. Angle entries greater than 30°, coupled with a straight body alignment, will result in the diver interacting with the bottom of the pool at a potentially dangerous velocity.

2. The absence of depth markings (especially in residential pools) or any type of markings on the bottom (such as a black line or dots), which would have provided the diver with a better reference, appeared to be contributing factors in all but two of the cases. The presence of such markings may have overcome visibility problems.

3. Several victims claimed poor visibility of the pool's bottom because of inadequate lighting (either underwater or in the pool area) during night swimming.

4. The physical size of the diver is a definite factor in injuries resulting from diving into shallow water. The heavier the individual, the greater the loading on the spine if the head makes contact with the bottom.

5. The absence of adequate signs warning against the danger of diving into shallow water, particularly in the above-ground pools, is an apparent cause of many of the injuries to divers, for after the accident many of the victims stated, ''I didn't know,'' or ''Nobody told me not to dive.''

6. The slipperiness of the pool's bottom appears to have been a contributing factor in at least 16 cases where the victims specifically recalled that their hands slipped upon contact with the bottom.

Injuries resulting from sliding down water slides headfirst.   The 18 water slide injuries investigated included slides in pools and in other bodies of water such as lakes and ponds. These cases plus data from research involving water slides provide the basis for the following conclusions as to the causes of water slide accidents:

1. Body position of sliders. We believe that descending down water slides in a prone position (headfirst) into shallow water is potentially dangerous because it is difficult for adults to maintain the low angle of entry necessary to make a safe slide.

2. Location of slides. The factor that appeared to be the major contributor to injuries resulting from use of water slides was the shallow depth of the water below the end of the slide. All of the slide victims struck the bottom at a depth of 4 feet or less. No injuries were reported where the slide was located in water depths of 8 feet or more.

3. Size and age of individual. Adults and adult-sized teenagers are more prone to sustaining injuries than are children for the same reasons as previously stated in the springboard diving section.

4. Angle of entry. It was concluded that all the victims entered the water at an angle estimated to be in excess of 30° and probably for the most more than 45°, resulting in contact with the bottom at a dangerous speed and angle. A more desirable angle of exit from the slide is zero: that is, the slider is discharged from the slide horizontal to the water.

5. In-water velocities. Where headfirst water entry angles are in excess of 30°, the slider's head velocity continues to increase for the first several feet in the water. The height of the top of the slide above the water determines the entry and in-water speeds. It was concluded that the velocity a slider may achieve at a point 3 to 4 feet in the water is potentially dangerous.

6. Exit velocities of slider. It was concluded that all slides currently on the market are capable of producing an exit velocity sufficient to cause a serious neck injury if the slider's head comes in contact with the bottom. The slider's speed is mainly determined by the height of the slide, which according to the commercial/residential market ranges from 6 feet to 12 feet in height. Because all slides are water-lubricated, there is almost zero friction as the slider proceeds down the slide.

7. Height of slide exit lip above water. The higher the exit lip of the slide above the water, the more likely it is that the slider will alter his or her body angle at water entry. When the change in upper body alignment is downward, the slider will inevitably strike the bot-

tom if the depth is under 5 feet. The research has revealed that if the exit lip is at the surface of the water, the slider will not have time to change body alignment before entering the water and consequently will enter at a safer angle.

8. Warnings. The absence of appropriate warnings calling attention to the danger of proceeding down the slide in a headfirst position appeared to be a major contributing factor in most of the slide accidents.

Accident Prevention

The first step in preventing accidents in pools is to realize that swimming pools are inherently hazardous and using them involves a certain amount of risk. A *hazard* is defined as a condition that presents a potential for untoward injury or death. *Risk*, on the other hand, is interpreted as "simple probability of injury in percentages." For example, the risk is far greater for an individual diving from a platform 10 feet high into water 6 feet deep than it is diving into water 16 feet deep. Whenever a hazard exists, some risk of injury is present and that injury may occur at any time. *Danger* is the unreasonable or unacceptable combination of hazard and risk. Danger is usually unperceived or unrecognized by the swimmer. It is not foreseeable by the user but should be known and identified by those skilled in the field and/or responsible for facility management. Following "risk recognition" safety procedures requires elimination of either hazard or risk. When it is impossible to eliminate the risk or hazard, then it is incumbent on all persons involved to minimize the risk and take every precaution possible to guard against the hazard and to warn swimmers of the potential danger.

Responsibility for pool safety begins when the pool is actually in the conceptual stage; this involves the owner, the designer, the builders, the maintenance personnel, the manufacturers of pool equipment, the pool manager, and any others who play a role in this total design-construction-operation process. Each can be held accountable for the integration of safety principles and practices into a particular portion of the overall function of the pool. For the architect or designer, this accountability means adherence not only to all applicable safety and health codes and standards, but also to established safety practices; the builder and manufacturers of equipment must pay rigid attention to design and materials used; and the pool operator's responsibilities include the employment of the most professional and qualified personnel. Pool and equipment manufacturers have a responsibility to determine that their products are safely designed, that instructions for their installation and use are explicit, and that warnings of misuse are of the required intensity.

Within institutional facilities, accident-free operation is a management responsibility. Although certain authority and specific duties may be delegated to supervisors, lifeguards, instructors, and maintenance personnel, it is the pool manager or operating head who is ultimately held responsible for the safe operation of the swimming pool. The homeowner who has a pool assumes all the responsibility for the safe operation of the pool, which includes supervision of the activities of both family and guests.

Serious injury may happen to anyone at any time in a swimming pool, under almost any conditions. It is, however, a combination of the human factors with one or more of a variety of situations or conditions related to environmental factors, pool design, and operation that most often contribute to serious injury. The human factors may be physiological, psychological, or social. A person's physiological dysfunction is often a contributing factor. Such physical characteristics as visual acuity, perception, skill, neuromuscular coordination, fatigue, sex, emotivity, attention, drugs, and change in health status may be, and often are, related to a swimming pool accident.

From the psychological aspect, the human response to sensory stimuli such as depth perception, spatial discrimination, response time, and kinesthetics may contribute to the injury-producing accident. Social influences include the desire to be with others and to gain approval and self-respect.

The environmental conditions that may induce or contribute to the occurrence of an accident in a swimming pool are the design and geometry of the pool, the level of illumination (natural or artificial), the design and placement of equipment, the material used in construction of the pool basin and decking, the equipment used in the pool, restrictive barriers, and warning systems associated with potential hazards.

Regulatory Laws, Codes, and Professional Standards

Only two states have regulations governing residential pools, even though the American Public

Health Association and the National Spa and Pool Institute have published suggested standards and ordinances. Most state swimming pool regulations and laws are concerned with sanitation and health standards in public pools; little attention is given to safety regulations, equipment, and the need for lifeguards.

Legal requirements governing the design, construction, and operation of public swimming pools vary among states and local jurisdictions. It is essential that any person or organization assuming responsibility for pool acquisition or management obtain copies of local state codes and any municipal ordinances that relate to the safety and health aspects of pools. The interpretation of such legislation and the implications of court decisions may well require the service of an attorney familiar with the specific demands and exemptions that can be expected in any locale. The time to initiate this legal consultation is during the early planning phases of pool development. Matters of zoning, accessibility, physical dimensions, and other code requirements can prove difficult, if not impossible, to alter if a completed pool is found to be in violation of applicable laws or regulations.

Standards

In addition to legal requirements, some institutions such as the armed forces and youth service organizations have developed guidelines or specifications for a "model pool" available from their national headquarters. Such references are usually only advisory but often contribute to standardization and may reduce the necessary research and planning effort otherwise required by sponsors of local swimming pools.

Recommended codes for public, semipublic, and residential pools may be obtained from the American Public Health Association and local and state health departments. The NSPI publishes suggested minimum standards for both residential and public pools. It should be realized that minimum standards are just that: They do not necessarily represent the most desirable or optimum practice. Furthermore, they often become obsolete, as Peters (1977) has indicated. The criteria used to establish a design standard often change, resulting in outdated standards. Thus, as the adequacy of standards are tested, new criteria must be developed to serve as the basis for upgrading standards.

Guidelines for Pool Design and Management

Most of the safety guidelines contained in this chapter have been derived from material appearing in other chapters of the book. Because of the increasing interest in and concern for safety, the Editorial Committee considered it desirable to assemble, in one chapter, the design and operational elements related to pool safety. Many of the guidelines are statements of fact predicated on years of experience and/or research. Others represent the best thinking of professional people in the field of aquatics as represented by the Editorial Committee. The Committee is aware that research is needed in some areas to establish complete validity of some of the suggested guidelines.

Although many of the guidelines apply only to public pools, a number of them do apply to small motel and residential pools. Recommendations applicable to public pools may need some modification to accommodate smaller, private pools, such as those found in small motel and apartment complexes and in home pools. State and regulatory agencies at all levels and the swimming pool industry should seriously consider including many of these guidelines in their swimming pool standards, codes, and regulations.

Size, Shape, and Location of Pools

1. The *size* of any pool must be predicated on the expected "peak" use of the pool. In pools with depths of 5 feet or less, 20 to 25 square feet per person should be used to establish the safe-use capacity of the pool. (See chapter 11 for more specific details on calculating pool capacity, including deck area or total enclosure limitations.)

2. The pool *shape* should be determined by its function and the type of activities to be conducted. Irregular or free-form pools must not produce areas where visibility is impaired or in any way reduce the effective circulation of water. Walls and bottoms of free-form pools must be carefully delineated, especially where wall/bottom intersections are curved (gunite pools).

3. *Multiple pools* (two or more within a complex) are better than a single pool from a program

scheduling point of view but require more lifeguards than a single pool.

4. The *larger* the pool, the more difficult is the job of supervising swimmers. Pools that have over 10,000 square feet of water surface area generally contain areas in the middle where the bottom is extremely difficult to see, making the supervision job more difficult.

5. The *location* of the pool must be such that no structure, such as a bathhouse, garage, house, or shed is within 15 feet of the edge of the pool. Anything closer constitutes an invitation to people to dive from it into the pool. This also applies to trees that have overhanging branches that come close to the pool. When slides are placed in pools, people must be warned against diving from the top of the slide, a practice that has resulted in spinal cord injuries.

Entrance to Pool

Every effort should be made to orient pools so that swimmers entering the pool area from the locker room or bathhouse do so at the shallow end of the pool. It is important to have depth markings and warning signs specifically at the point of entry so that swimmers are made immediately aware of the depth of the water and rules of the pool at their first contact point.

Water Depth

1. The deeper the water, the more critical is the need for supervision of users to prevent drownings. The shallower the water, the greater is the danger of diving injuries.

2. Public pools designed primarily for recreational use should have the major portion of the pool less than 5 feet deep.

3. The slope of the bottom in the shallow end of large pools (5 feet or less) should not exceed 1:12 feet. A maximum slope of 1:15 is preferable for safety. Extending the shallow portion of the pool to create a shallow plateau of constant depth is dangerous because it is a deviation from conventionally designed pools with a gradual slope. Because people may not be aware of this unusual condition, warnings must be placed at the edge of the pool in

that section stating "DANGER—SHALLOW WATER—NO DIVING." In the deep portion of the pool (over 5 feet), usually the diving area, the slope of the bottom from the deepest portion to the breakpoint must not exceed 1:2 feet; however, a slope of 1:3 feet is preferred. To safely accommodate springboard diving, it sometimes becomes necessary to increase the slope to 1:2 feet to provide sufficient deep water far enough forward from the end of the board. (For safe water depth for diving, refer to the section on Diving Board, Stand, Jumpboard, Starting Block Safety.)

4. To safely accommodate young children (up to the age of 4), a water depth from 6 inches to a maximum of 15 inches should be provided. This is best accomplished by constructing a separate pool rather than attempting to incorporate this depth of water within the area of a larger pool. Children's pools (often referred to as familiarization pools) should be placed a safe distance from any deep water pool (recommended minimum distance—25 feet); should be enclosed by a fence or other suitable barrier at least 3 feet (preferably 4 feet) high; and should be supervised by a lifeguard. Incorporating shallow water portions (2 feet or less) as a section or wing of a large pool is dangerous because adults may dive into it without realizing the depth.

5. For safe springboard diving, adequate depth of water is imperative. (See chapter 14 for design specifications for pools intended for competitive diving.) Any pool having a springboard that is either 14 or 16 feet long must conform to competitive diving standards because it has been repeatedly demonstrated that the inexperienced diver often deviates more from the normal dive pattern than the experienced competitive diver.

6. The competitive diving standards related to required water depth for a 1-meter springboard (which is the height of the front end of the board from the water), call for a depth of 12 feet at the plumb line (the point immediately below the front end of the board). The 12-foot depth must be carried forward from the end of the board for 20 feet and back under the board for at least 5 feet. The lateral distance that this depth must be carried from the center of the board is a minimum of 10 feet. These

measurements provide a diving area of constant depth of 20 feet by 20 feet (NCAA, 1985; USD, 1985).

With respect to the safe depth of water for non-competitive-type springboards (usually found in home pools and most motel and apartment pools), there is considerable disagreement among authorities. As a result of recent studies involving a determination of the performance quality of boards measuring 8, 10, and 12 feet in length placed 20 inches above the water, it was concluded that the minimum depth at the plummet should be 9 feet (preferably 10 feet) and that this depth should be carried forward for a distance of 16 feet with a differential of not more than 6 inches at the point where the upward slope commences. The 9-foot depth should extend laterally from the center of the board for at least 9 feet (preferably 10 feet). This provides a diving envelope of uniform depth 16

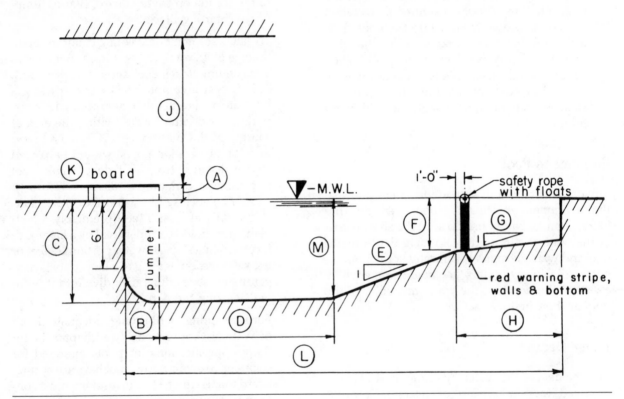

Dimension		Minimum	Preferred or Maximum
A	Height of board above water		20 in.
B	Board overhang	2 ft 6 in.	3 ft
C	Depth of water at plummet	9 ft	10 ft
D	Distance from plummet to start of upslope	16 ft	18 ft
E	Inclination of upslope of bottom		1:3
F	Depth of water at breakpoint	4 ft 6 in.	
G	Slope of bottom in shallow portion of pool	1:12	1:15
H	Length of shallow section of pool	8 ft	14 ft
J	Distance to any overhead structure	13 ft	15 ft
K	Board length		12 ft
L	Length of pool	40 ft	50 ft
M	Dimension not less than C minus	6 in.	

Figure 8.1 Minimum dimensions for pools with springboards or jumpboards other than competitive boards

feet by 18 feet (see Figure 8.1). It is further recommended that the maximum height of the board above the water be 20 inches.

Safety Markings

Safety markings represent one of the most important means of communication with the pool user. Safety markings are particularly important in situations where guests or other infrequent pool users are involved. Markings are used to communicate safety-critical information regarding the location of hazards such as breakpoints, shallow water, deep water, steps, and underwater ledges.

1. All *safety markings* in and around the perimeter of the pool should be installed during construction, not after the pool has been in operation for several weeks as is often the case.

2. Markings should be specified on the *pool's construction plans* and must meet local board of health regulations and recommended professional standards such as those promulgated by the NSPI and APHA. (*Note:* A recent court ruling in a Michigan motel drowning case established that posting of a required warning was no defense for inadequate supervision or full lifeguard services in "off" or low-use hours when the pool was made available to guests.)

3. *Depth markings* must be placed both on the deck near the pool's edge (or on the coping of the pool) and on the interior wall of the pool except in rimflow or deck-level pools where the wall is below the water level. Depth markings should be in a contrasting color (black or dark blue is preferred; red is acceptable) and should be at least 4 inches high, with 6 inches preferred (see Figure 8.2).

4. Depth markings indicating the point of *separation of the deep water* from shallow water (the breakpoint) must be located exactly at the breakpoint and must coincide with the exact depth of water at that point.

5. A *black line* (minimum of 2 inches in width, 4 inches is preferred) should be placed on the bottom of the pool 12 inches from the shallow side of the breakpoint (the bendline), which separates the deep end from the shallow end. A black line helps bathers and underwater swimmers see where the bottom begins to drop off. The bendline must always be a straight line across the pool and never include or allow any curvature of the bottom surface (see Figure 8.3).

Figure 8.2 Highly visible depth markings located on pool's coping. Clark High School, Hammond, Indiana. Photo courtesy of Filtrex, Inc.

Figure 8.3 Lifeline and line on pool bottom indicate the breakpoint separating the deep and shallow ends of pool. Photo by Lawyer's Photo Service.

Figure 8.4 Lines show pool's bottom contour

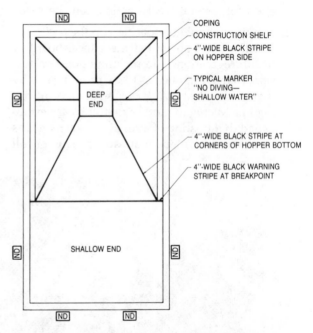

Figure 8.5 Markings on bottom of hopper type pool should be 3 to 4 inches wide

6. In pools that do not possess bottom racing lines for competitive swimming, it is desirable to place a *line along the bottom* of the pool, equidistant from the sides, in order to provide users with a visual image of the contour of the pool's bottom (see Figure 8.4). This line will help swimmers to determine the relative depth of the water at various points. For indoor pools, a practical depth indicator may be effected by painting in a 1-inch wide line on the wall parallel to the pool length. Such a line would indicate the pool depth profile in reverse or mirror-image. A bather may stand at any location along the wall and determine graphically whether or not the water is over his or her head before entering at that location. A concept recently advanced calls for finishing the bottom in contrasting colors, with the deep end one color and the shallow end another: for example, a white finish in the deep end to assure maximum visibility and a light blue color in the shallow end. The contrast should thus indicate to anyone approaching the pool that the water depth varies.

7. In *"hopper-bottom"* pools (pools where the side and end walls slope at an angle of approxi-

mately 45° to the bottom in the deep end), the bottom should be marked as shown in Figure 8.5. The sloping walls (some authorities identify this slope as part of the bottom) are such a marked deviation from conventional pool design that they may be dangerous to the unsuspecting swimmer. The bottom is not a true reflection of what the swimmer sees on the surface; consequently, as a person dives into pools of this configuration, the diver may strike the bottom before expected, or at an angle that could nullify the protection of the arms and hands.

8. The *top of the wall of the pool* at the water's edge (rimflow) should be finished in a contrasting color with background and/or adjacent surface. (Black or red is recommended.) In the recessed gutter system, this surface would be the overflow's edge. In skimmer-type pools, this surface is the tile band at the top of the pool wall. This effect maximizes the visibility of the overflow rim and top edge of the pool (see Figure 8.6).

9. The leading *edge of the steps* that are recessed into the deck or pool wall should have a black or red band 2 or 3 inches wide or black or red tiles to facilitate their identification for underwater swimmers and those descending into the pool. Steps protruding into the pool should have a leading edge or entire steps of contrasting color for maximum visual distinction. An alternate method is to finish the whole step in contrasting color.

10. All *underwater ledges,* even those 4 inches wide, should be either striped or finished in a contrasting color from the pool basin to make the

Figure 8.6 Markings highlight top edge of pool wall

Figure 8.7 Sample warning sign

ledges visible to divers and underwater swimmers.

11. To prevent underwater swimmers from striking the side wall, it has been suggested that *targets* in the form of a 6-inch black cross might be placed 6 feet apart all along the wall, about 3 feet below the water's surface.

12. Color-coding the pool's coping is one type of pool marking that would provide easy identification of depth for diving purposes. Areas where diving is prohibited (5 feet or less) are coded red; areas between 5 and 8 feet deep are coded yellow; and areas where diving from the deck is permitted are coded green. ''NO DIVING'' signs should be stenciled on the red coping with appropriate spacing; ''DIVE FROM HERE'' signs should be incorporated into the green coping; and ''DIVE WITH CAUTION'' signs should be designated in the yellow area.

Safety Lines

1. *Safety lines* separating deep water from shallow water are essential safety devices and must be included as a part of the pool's construction contract—never listed as an optional item.

2. Safety lines must be *kept in place* at all times, except when the pool is used for a special event such as lap swimming or a swimming meet.

3. Safety lines *separating the deep water* from the shallow water should be placed 1 foot toward the shallow end—away from the breakpoint (see Figure 8.3).

4. Safety *lines must be strung tightly* enough to permit a swimmer to hold onto the line for support without having it sink more than 6 inches below the water's surface. A taut, 3/4-inch diameter, 3-stranded, polyethylene, nylon, or an equivalent rope in contrasting strand colors with float markers at 1-foot intervals is recommended.

5. The *receptacle (eye cup)* to which the safety line is secured must be recessed in the wall to avoid creating an obstruction when the line is not in place.

Warning Signs

Signs located in and around pool areas are used to communicate important information to poten-

Figure 8.8   Markings highlight leading edge of pool steps

tial users regarding rules of the pool, the existence of hazards, and ways to avoid personal injury. Pools that are manufactured and sold to the public, such as above-ground pools that have definite activity limitations, should have appropriate warning signs placed on the pool by the manufacturer before sale to the customer. The communication of safety-critical information is a nondelegable responsibility of pool owners and operators and often can only be accomplished through the use of appropriately designed informational signs.

The purposes of warnings.   Signs accomplish the following three basic objectives:

1. To tell people about a threat to their well-being posed by dangerous conditions or products

2. As a safety measure to change people's behavior so that they act safely as opposed to acting unsafely

3. To remind people of (1) and (2)

If it is foreseeable that people will be injured when they act in a certain way and careful evaluation shows that when physical safety measures cannot be provided to ameliorate the consequences of their acts, then warnings to notify and remind those who are in danger are required. The existence of ''open and obvious'' hazards should not necessarily lead one to the conclusion that warnings are not needed because reminding people

about familiar hazards can prevent injuries. More likely, the danger of either risk or hazard is unsuspected and/or unobvious to the bather in the given circumstances. Warnings must be provided when known hazards remain as integral features of the swimming pool environment and human exposure to these hazards is possible despite design efforts aimed at identifying and removing the hazards or reducing or eliminating the exposure (see Figure 8.7).

Warnings in place of safety design modifications.   Warnings cannot be used to make up for inadequacies in design. Even the best of warnings will not consistently modify people's behavior at all times. Warnings are, in a sense, the last resort if danger still exists and has not otherwise been eliminated. A good warning causes people to not do something they otherwise (foreseeably) would do.

When to warn.   An inventory of hazards needs to be systematically compiled and revised as appropriate by either the pool designer, manufacturer, retailer, or the owner and maintainers of the swimming pool facility. One categorization of swimming pool hazards is as follows:

Physical Hazards

• Shallow water

• Internal stairs

- Springboards and diving towers
- Deep water
- Slippery surfaces
- Objects floating in pool

Chemical Hazards

- Chlorine gas
- Acid
- Liquid chlorine
- Chlorine-type granules
- Cleaning chemicals

Environmental Hazards

- Lighting in and around the pool
- Cloudy water
- Algae
- Glare on surface from either low sunbeams or artificial light

Behavioral Hazards

- Running
- Pushing people in water
- Throwing people in water
- Jumping on people
- Other forms of horseplay
- Unauthorized after-hours use of pools
- Diving or jumping in too shallow water

Every pool owner and operator must catalog and analyze the hazards that exist within the pool environment. It is recommended that a formal, written analysis be prepared with each hazard unique to the facility listed. Beside each entry, the person performing the warnings requirements analysis should identify possible methods for eliminating or reducing the injurious conditions of the hazard or for means of protecting the user. Those hazards that remain on the list and that cannot be eliminated or reduced are candidates for warnings. Each must be evaluated to determine whether a warning might work or if further effort can be made to eliminate, reduce, or guard the hazard.

Those hazards that survive this screening process must then be evaluated with respect to the intensity of the threat presented to the facility user. Warnings must be provided for all hidden hazards. The less obvious the hazard, the more compelling the need to warn. On the other hand, the so-called obvious hazards may not be obvious to everyone, and certainly those that present a serious possibility of harm should be considered for reminder warnings. In general, if it is possible to anticipate that a warning may prevent an injury, it is appropriate to provide that warning. Warnings are necessary for important hazards because society has come to depend upon the fact that hazards are always marked and that if no markings exist, the situation is safe.

Effective warnings. Warnings that successfully communicate a message and warnings that cause people to act safely have the following important characteristics in common:

1. Warnings attract attention to themselves by standing out distinctively from other features of the environment. Distinctive colors and shapes, the use of familiar signal words such as *danger, warning,* and *caution*, the use of warning colors such as red, white, and blue or black and yellow all serve to focus the attention of the people to be warned by the warning message. That is, effective warnings are designed to be attention getting.

2. Effective warnings are physically located in proximity to the actual hazard. In general, it is important to provide timely notice and reminder to those who must be warned. The greater the separation in time and place between the warning and the desired "safe" response, the less likely that the response will be made.

3. Warnings provide motivation to act safely by explicitly stating the consequences of failure to act appropriately by the use of the signal words *danger, warning,* and *caution* to refer to the severity of the threat to the well-being of the person being warned. In this latter regard, the signal word *danger* is used to mark the possibility of serious, permanent injury or death; the signal word *warning* denotes the threat of serious recoverable injury; and the signal word *caution* is used to mark the possibility of moderate to minor injury.

4. Effective warnings clearly and concisely tell people how to avoid being hurt in a way that is readily understood and followed by those who are being warned. The consequences of *not obeying* the warning are unmistakably illustrated for the unsuspecting bather.

5. Warning signs must be durable, legible, illuminated, in large type, unambiguous, serious, and simply stated.

Standardization, pictorials, testing. Using standardized warning formats (i.e., those in common usage) increases the likelihood that the warning will be seen and promotes rapid recognition and more sure adherence. (Refer to the American National Standards Institute publication listed under Suggested Readings at the end of this chapter.) The signal words *danger, warning,* and *caution* have standardized and well-known meanings. These signal words and the dangers they categorize are associated with color schemes that are equally well known (e.g., red, white, and black for *danger*, orange and black for *warning*, and yellow and black for *caution*). Similarly, warning signs are typically arranged with the signal word at the top (often in a standardized format such as the oval shape used with *danger*) and with a statement of the hazards and directions for avoiding injury. Deviations from these standardized formats should be carefully considered and well justified before being employed.

Pictorials, often referred to as graphics, present an opportunity to rapidly communicate the presence of a hazard or a behaviorally appropriate action to the pool user without requiring written language familiarity. Simple, clear, clinically tested graphic warnings have a minimum use of any language; plus, universally understood symbols are most preferable.

New, never-tried warnings need to be tested carefully for meaning, recognition, and potentially dangerous misinterpretation. The use of focus group interviews conducted by experienced clinical psychologists or safety experts using relatively simple market-testing methods is appropriate for the evaluation of new warnings. At the very least, a new sign should be shown to a representative sample of unsophisticated swimmers (20 or more) for comment to ensure that the intended meaning is communicated and dangerous reversals of meaning do not occur. Clearly, if even one dangerous misinterpretation in a group of 20 is discovered, the warning design effort must be repeated.

Summary. Warnings are required when hidden hazards exist or continue to exist despite engineering and other efforts to either eliminate or reduce the injurious potential of the hazard or to guard people from coming into contact with the hazard. The hazards at a facility should be systematically evaluated to determine the likely candidates for warnings. Warnings should be developed in standardized formats to promote rapid recognition and to maximize adherence. Mechanically, warnings should be legible, understandable, serious in tone, and durable. Warnings should be tested. Well-designed, carefully thought-out warnings can add considerable safety as they will help control the critical behavioral element involved in every facility-related injury. Also, manufacturers of above-ground and prefabricated in-ground pools should place appropriate warnings directly on their pools at the assembly plant.

Other Safety Devices

1. *Ground fault circuit interrupters (GFCI)* must be included on all electrical equipment and wiring around a pool, including the filter room.

2. A *water (alarm) sensor* is a safety device that may be an effective night sentry. In situations that warrant crowd control, it should be installed with its alarm located where it will signal someone in authority or will turn on a set of floodlights.

3. A *safety light* permanently "on" in the pool area is essential for monitoring the pool at night (never to be used for night swimming).

4. A *pool cover* should be placed over all outdoor pools retaining water during the off-season.

5. Depending on the need for night pool surveillance, such devices as an *electronic eye, closed circuit TV, or an electronic mat* may prove to be effective sentries in the prevention of unauthorized entry to the pool.

6. Automatic *emergency lights*, capable of energization instantly on power failure of the main lighting system, should be installed during construction in all pools where night swimming will be permitted.

Electrical Fixtures

1. All *electrical fixtures* in and around the pool must meet the standards of the National Electric Code.

2. All *electric wiring* should be placed underground in conduits.

3. Hair dryers and other electric drying devices should be placed in a dry area of the locker room or bathhouse, isolated on separate ground-fault circuits.

4. All *electrical service receptacles* accessible from the pool deck should be key-operated and individually ground-fault protected.

Underwater Light Fixtures

1. All *underwater lights* must be installed in accordance with Article 680 of the National Electric Code; however, where the local governing authority has stricter requirements, the local requirements become applicable. (See chapter 11 for further information on underwater lighting.)

2. The use of *amber-colored lights* has proven to be effective in minimizing insects normally attracted by lights.

3. Underwater lights must *never be placed at the end of a pool* in the center of a racing lane because they interfere with the swimmer's view of the end of the pool. Lights should be placed between lanes, under the lane float lines.

4. High luminous contrast (glare) from underwater lights may *reduce* an underwater swimmer's *visibility*. Where underwater recessed built-in pool steps exist, a light should focus on the steps.

5. Only experienced, *qualified personnel* should service underwater lighting fixtures.

6. All underwater lights should be angled slightly (5°) toward the pool's bottom.

Illumination of Pool Area

1. All *electric wires* leading to light poles should be placed underground in conduits and must conform to local and national electric codes.

2. As a general rule, *windows* should not be placed on the side or end walls of a natatorium because the exterior light causes glare on the water; this makes seeing underwater difficult for lifeguards or instructors when they look in the direction of the light source. Skylights and clerestories providing indirect illuminence are more acceptable sources of outside lighting.

3. Although *lighting levels* in this country have doubled every decade for the last 30 years, recommendations greatly affecting the demanding visual tasks of swimming, particularly the competitive phase and safety, remain unregulated or at inadequate levels. The fol-

lowing design guide is offered as a minimum recommendation for safety of competitive pool facilities. It covers the major areas of concern: decks, water surface from overhead source, and underwater lighting.

a. *On decks:* Recommended illumination should be a minimum of 100 footcandles at deck level of pools used for competition. All light sources used for deck illumination should be directed and shielded to minimize or preferably eliminate water surface reflections. Windows should not be installed behind diving boards or platforms. Generally, windows on these walls should not be permitted unless they are tinted or polarized to reduce glare and reflection on the water surface.

b. *On water surface:* Recommended overhead illumination of pool surface should be a minimum of 50 footcandles when underwater lighting is also provided. Without underwater lighting, a minimum illumination of 100 footcandles on water surface should be obtained by indirect sources having no reflections on pool surface, if possible. At night, it is extremely dangerous to swim in a pool that is not properly illuminated. Poor lighting makes it almost impossible for a diver to see the bottom. Without a distinct visual reference (ability to see the bottom), the diver (whether diving from a springboard or from the deck) may easily misjudge the depth and be injured by hitting the bottom.

c. *Pool basin:* Underwater lighting should be provided for all pools in accordance with minimum recommendations of the Illuminating Engineering Society (IES) Handbook, or the following:

Location	Lamp Lumens per Sq Ft of Pool Surface
Outdoors	60
Indoors	100

Underwater fixtures should not be installed in end walls of the competitive course above a water depth of 3-1/2 feet. In pools with deep water (i.e., over 5 feet) lighting may be installed in competitive end walls beneath competitive bounded water volume (as defined in applicable rules books).

4. Most residential and motel pools are inadequately lighted for night swimming. Both underwater and area lighting are essential for safe diving at night. To make a safe dive, the diver must be able to see the bottom clearly. The following guidelines are suggested:

- No pool should be used at night unless adequate area and underwater lighting are provided.

- A minimum of 60 lumens per square foot of water surface area should be provided by underwater lights.

- A minimum of 20 footcandles of illumination should be provided on the deck of the pool.

Drains

1. *Bottom outlets* (sometimes referred to as main drains) should incorporate covers or grates with openings no smaller than 3/8 inch in diameter and no longer than 1 inch, to prevent fingers or hands from getting stuck in them. Main drains should never be located directly under diving boards in the vicinity of the plummet.

2. The best form of *drain cover* is rectangular, covering a trench in which the outlet pipe is located. This design reduces the suction force from the outlet pipe and avoids the possible entrapment of swimmers. The grate should have a net-free area of at least 6 times (preferably 10 times) the diameter of the suction pipe below. In large pools, two or more drains should be provided, spaced no greater than 40 feet on center.

3. *Main drain covers* or grates should be securely fastened to prevent the possibility of removal by swimmers.

4. Generally, it is undesirable to have more than 25% of the pool water recirculate through the *bottom drains*. (The main drain pipe should have capacity, however, for 120% flowrate to facilitate rapid emptying of the pool when needed.)

5. *Floor drain covers* on the pool deck should be securely fastened down and should preferably be stainless steel, although some types of less expensive plastic drains have proven successful. Grate openings should be smooth at the edges to prevent injury to the pool user's bare feet.

Overflow or Rimflow System

1. The *top rim of the wall* over which the water flows into a gutter or trench should be finished in a color contrasting with the background to provide swimmers with the best possible visibility of the top of the wall.

2. *Recessed overflows* should not be made so wide or deep that they present a hazard to young children who might be entrapped.

3. *High recessed overflows* often create difficulties for swimmers getting out of the pool; these overflows also have the disadvantage of placing a young child at a height above the water, dangerously increasing his or her entry velocity when diving or jumping into the pool.

4. Generally, the *roll-out and rimflow* (deck-level) systems of top wall construction provide the most effective method of water circulation and, at the same time, facilitate the swimmers' pool entrance and exit.

Ladders and Steps

1. *Ladders* that extend into the pool and attach to the wall may well be an obstruction to swimmers and consequently are not recommended. Swimmers may easily collide with such protruding ladders, particularly while swimming on their backs, doing the crawl stroke, or swimming underwater.

2. The most effective and *safest method of egress* from the pool is via steps recessed into the pool wall with an accompanying grab rail so that the swimmer may walk out of the pool. This type of egress is especially helpful to elderly, disabled, and young individuals.

3. The *edges of all steps* should have a dark (black, blue, or red) stripe (minimum of 2 inches wide) to ensure their visibility to underwater swimmers and to those descending into the pool (see Figure 8.8).

4. The *tread of a step* should be a minimum of 1 foot wide with the rise no more than 9 inches (preferably 7 inches). The tread should be finished in white with a nonslip material.

5. A *hand rail* should be placed in the middle of any steps 4 or more feet wide and at the side of steps less than 4 feet.

6. *Steps recessed into the wall* should not protrude into the pool areas where they may constitute

an obstruction to swimmers. The insert should contrast in color with the wall.

7. *Stepholes* located in the wall should have a minimum depth of tread of 5 inches, a width of at least 1 foot, and a rise of no more than 9 inches.

8. Ladders or steps should be *located* at both the deep and shallow ends of the pool. A pool that is 75 feet by 45 feet should have four sets of ladders or steps; a pool that is 50 meters long by 60 or 75 feet in width should have five sets. The size of the pool is the determining factor. Steps or ladders should never be placed at the ends of pools where they interfere with the racing course.

Lifeguard Stands

1. The *number of lifeguard stands* needed in any pool and their location depend upon the size of the pool, the location and amount of deep water (over 5 feet), and the number of diving facilities. The pool configurations shown in Figure 8.9 suggest the number of stands needed and the most desirable location for them in typical pool designs. No less than one stand should be provided for every 2,000 square feet of pool surface.

2. In outdoor pools, lifeguard stands should be *located* so that the sun is at the back of the lifeguard during most of the day; this minimizes the effect of sun glare and light reflected from the water's surface when the lifeguard needs to look in the direction of the sun. The best locations for stands therefore are on the west and south sides of the pool where guards face toward the east and north.

3. Lifeguard stands should be *elevated* from 4 to 6 feet above the deck and should be stable enough to permit the guard to dive or jump from it in case of an emergency.

4. In large pools (50 meters) and multiple-pool complexes, lifeguard stands should be *equipped* with intercoms to enable the pool manager or lifeguard supervisor to communicate with guards at all times and to control the pool area via public address loudspeakers.

5. A desirable addition to the lifeguard stand in large pools is an *alarm system* that can be activated when an emergency occurs. This will alert all supervisory personnel present of an emergency and to immediately move into ac-

tion in accordance with preset emergency procedures.

6. *Other desirable additions* to the lifeguard stands are an umbrella to shade the guard from the sun and a signal flag.

Pool Obstructions

1. *Ledges* located on the side walls of pools (originally introduced into this country from Europe as a safety or resting ledge) constitute a hazard to swimmers and divers and consequently should not be permitted unless they are completely recessed in the pool wall (see Figure 8.10). Existing ledges should be painted a contrasting color to the pool finish, making them more visible to swimmers and divers. Young children are often attracted to these ledges and holding onto the deck, walk along them into the deep end of the pool. There have been several reported drownings and near drownings where children have slipped from such ledges into deep water.

2. All inlets, underwater lights, and main drain covers should be *flush with the surface* of the pool's walls or floor.

3. *Water slides and diving boards* should be placed at a sufficient height, usually 18 to 20 inches, from the water to ensure that swimmers will not collide with them.

4. There should be *no protrusions* into the pool basin of any equipment or device that could obstruct the free movement of swimmers.

5. In-pool seats should always be recessed into the wall of the pool in an alcove. They should never be attached to the interior wall of the pool where they protrude into the pool and constitute a hazard to swimmers or divers.

Orientation of Pool to Sun and Wind

1. *Sunning areas* should be located where people may receive maximum sun throughout the day. It is important, however, to provide shaded areas for swimmers to move out of the sun.

2. When outdoor pools are used for competitive swimming, they should be planned so that the *prevailing winds* strike the pool at a right angle to the racing course. Sun orientation in such pools is of secondary importance; however, if wind is not a factor, pools should preferably

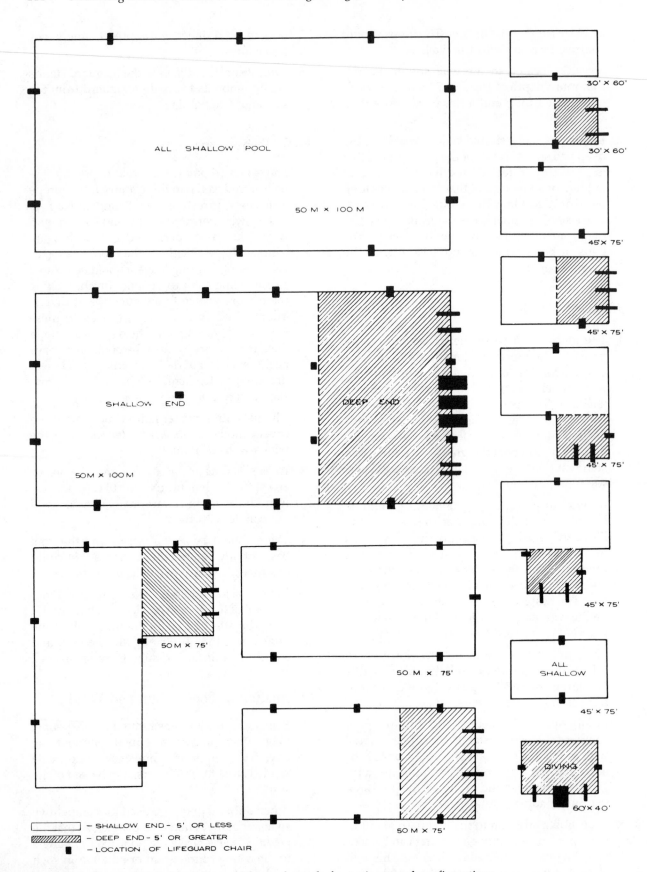

Figure 8.9 Recommended locations of lifeguard stands for various pool configurations

Figure 8.10 Recessed ledge where swimmers may rest.

be laid out so that the racing course lies in an east-west direction.

Water Clarity

1. The *clarity of water* is not always related to its sanitary condition; it is, however, a factor in providing a safe swimming environment. Highly turbid (cloudy) water prevents good visibility of the bottom. The larger the pool and the greater the depth of water, the more important the need for clear water will be.

2. A *standard* that is often used to determine water clarity is the visibility of a small disc (6 inches in diameter) of contrasting colors placed on the pool bottom. The disc should be clearly visible (both with natural and artificial light) from any area of the deck. A better measure is the JTU (Jackson Turbidity Unit) as measured on a nephelometric spectrophotometer. Investigators have established pool water clarity values: exceptional = 0.1 to 0.2 JTU; good = 0.2 to 0.3 JTU; acceptable = 0.3 to 0.5 JTU; poor = 0.6 JTU.

3. When water *lacks clarity*, it should be inspected for algae, fungi, or excessive amounts of iron or other chemicals. It is also important to check pumps and filter pressure to determine whether filters need to be backwashed.

Above-Ground Pools

1. Because most above-ground pools are shallow-water types (usually a maximum of 3-1/2 feet deep), *diving* of any kind as well as water slides should be strictly prohibited.

2. *Governmental regulations* for above-ground pools are practically nonexistent. Hence, homeowners who are the principal users and who are responsible to their guests must acquaint themselves with safe operating procedures for their pools.

3. *Manufacturers* of above-ground pools should supply adequate warning systems and instructional information pertaining to the safe use and operation of the pool as well as identify any unusual pool characteristics. Manufacturers of above-ground, portable pools should provide owners with operating procedures for the pool, and other materials to aid pool owners such as information from organizations like the American Red Cross, NSPI, YMCA, and CNCA.

4. *Signs* displaying rules for safe pool use, depth markings, and other safety considerations should be conspicuously posted. These signs should be placed on the pool by the pool manufacturer. Depth markings should be placed on both the exterior and interior walls of the pool.

5. *Steps* going up to a sunning platform or deck should be used in preference to vertical ladders terminating at the top edge of the pool. Ladders must be firmly secured to the pool structure and rigidly anchored to prevent motion due to wet, slippery soil foundation or to the weight of the user. Such ladders should be marked and designed so as to prevent diving or jumping. Ladders with platforms on the top are diving invitations; the platform on top should be eliminated (see Figure 8.11).

Figure 8.11 Internal ladders can be dangerous to underwater swimmers.

6. Portable and above-ground pools should be considered the same as in-ground pools concerning *fencing*. Every residential above-ground pool should have at least a 6-foot high, nonclimbable fence, wall, or other type of barrier around it to prevent intrusion (particularly by children) from the outside. If linked within the enclosure, the house or garage structure must meet the barrier criteria, and the locks on those doors leading into the pool area must be placed at least 4 feet (preferably 5 feet) above floor level to prevent children from going out into the yard.

7. If the pool is not contained within a fenced area, it should be *covered* when not in use, which may be accomplished by a portable cover.

8. The *location* of above-ground pools in the yard is important from a safety point of view. If located close to garages or houses, above-ground pools are an invitation for individuals to dive off the roof or porch. Similarly, a driveway adjacent to the pool invites youngsters to dive from the roof of a parked car. The pool should not be located any closer than 12 feet (preferably 15 feet) from any structure.

9. Certain *textures of vinyl* material used in above-ground pools (also in-ground pools) as a water container have proven to be extremely slippery when wet and may become even more slippery if fungus, algae, or silt is permitted to form on the bottom. A swimmer's hands must not slip when striking the bottom after a dive; otherwise, the head and neck could be exposed, resulting in serious injury.

Deck Finishes

1. Pool-related accidents frequently result from people *slipping* on the pool deck or coping. Three conditions contribute most to such accidents: (a) when the finish is too smooth (lacking tractive surface); (b) when oil, water, or some other foreign substance has been spilled on the deck; and (c) when surfaces around pools vary and are not the same material throughout.

2. Too often, concrete decks are brush-finished with too coarse a brush or with too much texturizing pressure. This technique creates a sandpaper-type finish that is *dangerously abrasive* in case of a fall.

3. The fully drainable *carpeted deck* is the safest of the available finishes; however, the cost of deck carpeting, its limited durability, its low resistance to algae, fungus, bacteria, and chemicals as well as the problems inherent in keeping it clean and sanitary are detrimental factors to be overcome. At present, few boards of health approve carpeting for public pools. Nevertheless, carpeting holds great promise for the future once the above criteria are met.

4. *Nonslip tiled decks* are probably the best safety surface for pools at present. However, the cost of the tile often prohibits its use in outdoor pools or large indoor pools. It is important that pool copings also be made of nonslip finish.

5. Recent *concrete stains* and *epoxy paints* containing an aggregate that provides a slip-resistant surface have been introduced and appear to provide not only a safe surface, but enhance the pool's appearance as well.

6. Until an absolutely safe deck or coping surface is discovered, a strict program to *educate users* against running, horseplay, and other risks of slipping must be maintained.

7. All *walk surfaces* within 10 feet of the pool, including horizontal sections of coping or overflows, should have a wet coefficient of friction greater than 0.70 with reference to bare feet, skin, and footwear.

Fences and Walls

1. All outdoor pools should be protected by a fence or some kind of *effective barrier* to prevent the intrusion of unwanted persons, particularly youngsters. Indoor pools must be locked when not in use. Where children (nonswimmers, below the age of 3) are members of a household with a pool, it may be desirable to use a "portable fence" around the pool to prevent them from gaining access to the pool when unattended.

2. Fences, walls, and other types of barriers placed around pools to keep intruders out should meet a *6-foot minimum height* (8 feet preferable for public pools).

3. *Spikes or barbed wire* should not be used on the top of fences because they constitute a dangerous hazard. Anyone, except the very young, who desires to enter a pool will not be kept out by a fence. Nevertheless, the fence

does explicitly indicate that intruders do not belong there.

4. Most residential pool drownings involve children below the age of 5 who just wandered into the pool from a neighbor's or their own house. Consequently, *gates to pools* and doors from homes must always be kept closed; they should contain self-closing and positive self-latching mechanisms at a height above a toddler's reach (4 to 6 feet high); and they must be provided with hardware to accommodate a permanent locking device.

5. Fences should be constructed of material that does not readily afford *handholds* or *footholds*. The "2 × 2" chain-link fence is far too easy to climb. Mesh size should not exceed 1 inch.

6. *Walls* used as barriers to keep intruders out of pools should be at least 6 feet high without handholds or footholds and without openings through which small children can squeeze.

7. *Exterior walls of bathhouses* or locker rooms that face the pool area should be constructed of smooth material (not stucco) to prevent possible injury to people falling against them as a result of slipping or being pushed.

8. The placement of *plantings* next to walls or fences helps create a barrier between the pool deck and the wall or fence.

Shrubbery and Trees

1. *Trees* within the pool area often are used to provide shade for swimmers. Trees that shed fruit or leaves, however, create maintenance problems. If debris is not immediately cleared away, it could interfere with the pool's circulation system.

2. *Flowering shrubbery*, which is likely to attract insects, should not be planted within a pool enclosure, particularly near sunning areas. This rule applies equally to flowers that attract dangerous insects.

3. Because some flowering shrubs and some flowers are *toxic*, pool planners and owners should check carefully with local health officials to determine which plants, trees, and shrubbery are poisonous and might have an adverse effect on humans. Obviously, these should not be placed within or in proximity to the pool environment.

Supporting Recreation Areas and Equipment

1. An increasing trend in pool planning is to provide *play areas* and supplemental facilities and equipment within pool complexes for children and adults. This practice dictates the need for the proper placement of these facilities. Children's play apparatus should be separated from the pool area with a fence to prevent anyone from running from the pool directly into the play apparatus area and to reduce risks of children running into swings and slides.

   Saunas and *whirlpools,* often referred to as spas or hot tubs, are becoming increasingly popular as supplements to public and semipublic pools. (See chapter 5 on spas and hot tubs for further information on location and operation.)

2. *Games* such as volleyball, badminton, tennis, handball, and shuffleboard should be separated completely from the pool area. Playing catch with a ball or any other device around the pool's deck should be prohibited. An excellent plan is to place these activities outside the pool complex, with direct access from the pool. Game participants should be required to shower upon returning to the pool.

Obstructions Around Pools

1. *Furniture* placed around the pool areas must be kept away from the swimmers' traffic lanes (area within 10 feet of the pool's edge).

2. For *separation of pool areas*, a fence, wall, or plantings hung 3 to 4 feet high may be used. Low-hanging chains or ropes suspended from stanchions or posts often cause falls because they cannot be readily seen.

3. *Equipment* should not be scattered about, particularly in traffic areas, because it may obstruct the free and safe movement of swimmers around the pool area.

Diving Board, Stand, Jumpboard, and Starting Block Safety

Diving facilities and equipment represent the most dangerous area in a swimming pool environment because of the nature of the activities involved. A high percentage of dives result in the diver entering the water in a headfirst position from activity-designated equipment such as springboards, fixed platforms, jumpboards, minitramps, and starting blocks. However, as indicated in the Nova University study of diving injuries (Gabrielsen, 1984), diving from the deck of the pool, from starting blocks, and from structures located adjacent to pools such as sheds, garages, houses, slides, cars, and trees into shallow water actually produces a greater number of injuries than dives from springboards and diving towers. If the guidelines cited in the following sections are followed, the number of injuries to swimmers and divers will be reduced.

Springboards

1. The *surface* of any springboard must be made of nonslip material and should be inspected daily and cleaned regularly. When the board's surface becomes worn (i.e., lost its nonslip characteristics), it should be refinished.

2. The *"take-off"* ends of diving boards, particularly metal ones, should be equipped with protective safety pads to prevent serious injury to divers who might strike the board (see Figure 8.12).

3. Adjustable *fulcrums* on diving boards should be used only by trained divers. The gear mechanism used should be covered so that fingers or toes cannot be caught in them. When not used by trained divers, the fulcrum should be locked in the maximum forward position to reduce the board's spring to prevent divers from "sailing" out too far.

4. Boards should be *checked regularly* to assure that cracks have not developed because both metal and wood fatigue after a period of use.

Figure 8.12 Diving board safety pad

5. Insufficient *water depth* in the area where divers may be expected to land constitutes the greatest potential hazard for divers. The most prevalent design defect is the failure to extend the maximum depth of water far enough forward from the end of the board. Where 14- to 16-foot long springboards are used, the pool's bottom profile and the depth of water should conform to the rules set forth by one or all of the following competitive diving groups: U.S. Diving, NCAA, National Federation of State High School Athletic Associations (NFSHSA), and FINA. (See chapter 14 for pool design specifications of these groups.) For all other springboards and jumpboards—ranging in length from 4 feet to 12 feet—it is recommended that the bottom profile of the pool conform to the specification set forth in Figure 8.1. Where existing pools do not conform to these specifications, it is strongly recommended that boards either be removed or restricted in their use to children.

6. The best *orientation for boards* at outdoor pools with respect to the sun is a direction that allows the diver to face north or east as he or she prepares to dive.

7. *Agitation of the surface* of the water by a bubbling or spraying device aids the diver in seeing the water's surface.

8. Boards should be installed *horizontal with the water*—not tilting upwards, as many do. When a board tilts up, the chance that the diver may come down on the board is increased. This condition is likely when divers perform reverse dives.

Diving Stands and Towers

1. All *stands* that accommodate springboards should provide a safety "bed" under the board to prevent a person who accidentally steps off the side of the board from falling onto the deck below.

2. *Handrails* should be placed on all diving stands that are above 1/2 meter in height. The safest design has the sides entirely closed. If the design does not include closed sides, intermediate rails should be provided so that no opening is more than 12 inches. Rails should be carried forward to a point at least 1 foot (preferably 2 feet) over the water toward the tip of the board (see Figure 8.13).

Figure 8.13 Guardrails extending over pool's edge

3. *Steps* leading up to diving boards are safer than vertical ladders. The angle of the steps should not be more than 50° from the horizontal, and the tread should be 6 inches deep and finished with a nonslip material. Handrails should be no more than 1.90 inches in outside diameter (1.5-inch standard pipe).

4. *Towers* ranging in height from 5 to 10 meters should be carefully supervised at all times. Multiple dives and jumps should never be permitted except as part of exhibitions by experienced divers.

Jumpboards

1. *Jumpboards* are a form of diving board and therefore should be treated the same as such. Insufficient experience and no published research are available at this time involving use of jumpboards to identify the potential hazards of this comparatively new equipment. The safety standards employed in the placement of jumpboards should be the same as those that apply to diving boards. Jumpboards with coil springs as the forward support and

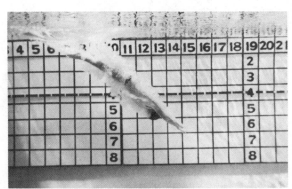

Figure 8.14(a) Underwater trajectory of swimmer making a racing dive

Figure 8.14(b) The angle of this dive will cause the diver to interact with pool bottom at a depth from 3 to 8 feet

fulcrum seem to provide greater spring than conventional boards and consequently possess the potential of projecting the diver further out, which may place the diver in too-shallow water, in the area of the upslope of the pool bottom.

2. The *jumpboard surfaces* must be slip-resistant and should be covered at the end with a safety pad.

3. *Instructions* on the safe use of jumpboards should be given before anyone is permitted to use them.

Minitrampolines

As with jumpboards, the *minitrampoline*, which is really a piece of gymnastic equipment adapted for pool use, has not been adequately studied to assess its potential catapulting hazard; therefore, minitrampolines should be treated as diving equipment to be carefully supervised. Only persons who have received proper training and instructions should be permitted the free use of pool minitrampolines.

Water Slide Safety

The origin of water slides dates back at least 60 years when they were first introduced in pools located in amusement parks and commercial swimming pools. Some amusement centers and commercial pools developed slides up to 30 feet above the water; some employed a toboggan-style sled on which people traveled down a chute. In the 1930s many major municipal pools introduced water slides without a device to sit on. The slide beds were made of galvanized steel with wood guardrails and were water lubricated. Most of the slides at that time were adapted from slides designed for playgrounds (see Figure 8.15). As injuries from slides began to occur in the 1930s, many public pools began to remove them so that by 1945 water slides were seldom found in public pools. In the late 1950s the water slide was reborn with introduction of fiberglass slides. Most of the slides at that time were sold to homeowners and motels. Few municipal or school pools installed water slides because of the supervision problem.

In 1976 the U.S. Consumer Products Safety Commission (CPSC) issued a swimming pool water slide standard. The guidelines set forth below differ in some ways from the CPSC standards, and are based on the study of a number of accidents resulting in quadriplegia. These recommendations do not apply to high "giant" commercial water slides (flumes) or to fully enclosed slides and chutes that are water lubricated.

Location

1. *Water slides* should be treated similar to diving equipment. They should be located in a minimum of 8 feet of water and be carefully supervised at all times.

Figure 8.15 Adaptation of playground slide to pool setting

2. If slides are placed in *shallow water* (5 feet or less), only feetfirst entries must be permitted, and the slide must be restricted to use by children.

3. There should be a clear *unobstructed area* for at least 16 feet in front of any slide and for 8 feet on either side of the center line extending forward from the end of the slide.

Proper Use

1. In many respects, going down a slide that is *water lubricated* is the same as diving. When a bather goes down a 10-foot high slide, the discharge speed is as if he or she dove off a platform 10 feet high. Accordingly, if a slide is to be completely safe for all types of entry, it should be placed in deep water, which means that all slide users must be good swimmers.

2. *Adults*, particularly, should not be permitted to use water slides unless the slide is located in deep water and unless they are experienced swimmers.

3. Wherever slides are installed, *careful instructions* should be given to all users by means of posted instructions placed on the side of the slide or on the ladder (or at both locations).

4. To prevent possible skin burns, *water should always run* or be sprayed on the slide to lubricate the bed.

5. Whenever any object such as a slide or lifeguard stand is placed adjacent to a pool or to any body of water, there will be those who are challenged to attempt to *jump or dive* from it. This has proven to be the cause of a number of serious injuries to teenagers. A warning sign calling attention to the danger and possible consequences of such action should be placed on any such equipment, particularly slides.

Giant Water Slides (Flumes)

An innovation of the 1970s has been the water slide "flume," or giant water slide. Most of these slides are operated as individual commercial enterprises or as part of water theme parks. Many of these giant slides contain a run of as much as 300 to 600 feet with multiple curves. They either contain a concrete bed with an epoxy finish or a fiberglass bed. These slides need to be carefully supervised. The most common accidents are the result of sliders striking other sliders or hitting the bottom of the landing pool. All water flumes must have a deceleration zone at the end of the slide where the slider's speed is reduced before being discharged into the splash pool. The deceleration zone helps prevent serious injuries resulting from striking the bottom at a high velocity or from people running into each other at the bottom of the slide.

The Communicable Disease Center of the U.S. Department of Health and Human Services published a booklet in 1981 entitled *Suggested Health and Safety Guidelines for Recreation Water Slide Flumes*. All giant chutes and water slides, whether located in pools or operated as a separate facility, should at all times be supervised by qualified personnel stationed at the top and bottom of the slide. The depth of water in the landing pool for a properly designed slide should not exceed 4 feet; otherwise, poor swimmers may need to be rescued. Only sliding in a feetfirst sitting position should be permitted, and appropriate warning signs should be provided. Sharp curves should not be included because they tend to throw the slider against the wall, which may result in injury to the head.

Filter Room Safety

1. The filter room should be *locked* at all times to prevent the entry of unauthorized persons. A sign to this effect should be posted on the door.

2. All *valves should be tagged* with numbers for easy identification. A chart identifying each tagged valve should be placed on the wall in a conspicuous location.

3. Filter room operators should *wear shoes* (preferably rubber-soled) when entering the filter room.

4. The filter room should be *ventilated* both mechanically by fans and naturally by windows.

5. A minimum of 75 to 100 footcandles of *illumination* should be provided in the filter room.

6. When *chlorine gas* is used, a room separate from the filter room must be provided. This room must be equipped with an electrically operated ventilator that is turned on (with the room light) when the door is opened. The room must be above existing grade level, or otherwise accessible via a single stairway and entrance platform only (i.e., no vertical access

ladder). The chlorine room door or entrance wall must have at least 2 square feet of wire glass for viewing all interior locations of the chlorine room. Discharge of the chlorine room ventilator must be to a remote, nontraffic location.

7. A *self-contained breathing apparatus* should be located immediately outside the chlorine room for use in the event that a leak in the chlorine gas line or tank is detected. It has been shown that gas masks offer only limited security in areas of high concentration of chlorine gas.

8. *Operating instructions* and valve schedule should be wall-mounted, preferably under glass. Any emergency procedures recommended should be included with the schedule.

9. *Ground-fault detectors* protect all motors on individual lines at no less than 20 milliamperes per 100 amperes of normal running current.

10. All valve handles used in main operation should be located so that they are accessible without reaching or bending and located within 2 feet to 7 feet above the floor level.

11. All *light fixtures* in the filter room should be shielded either with glass protectors or plastic louver wrap-arounds to protect them from direct spray of hose water or line bursts.

12. All *electrical outlets* in the filter room should be covered with U.L.-approved watertight snap-close covers.

13. Equipment *schematic drawing*, isometric drawing, or large-scale piping layout should be conspicuously posted for information of operators and identified in conjunction with operating instructions and valve schedule noted above.

14. Carborundum concrete floor or other *nonslip, integral safety finish* should be specified for filter room construction.

15. Standard *pipe marker flow arrows* should be posted on all main filter piping runs to facilitate operators' understanding of all operation and emergency procedures.

16. A *record-keeping book* with an informational form as may be prescribed by local or state health departments and with such other pertinent information essential to good record keeping of all operations should be provided. A strict routine of record keeping should be enforced by all facility operators.

17. If *suction intakes* or screens have to be serviced at locations remote from filter room water

pumps, outside disconnects must be provided at such service locations to prevent accidental flow connections and for emergency purposes.

Locker Room or Bathhouse Safety

1. The most hazardous area of any locker room or bathhouse is the *floor*. It must be made of slip-resistant material and kept as dry as possible.

2. Floors should have *drains* to facilitate cleaning.

3. *Carpets* or *rubber mats* should be easy to remove for cleaning.

4. *Electric hair dryers* should be located in a dry area of the room and should be individually ground-fault protected.

5. Floors in the *toilet and shower area* are the "wet areas" and should be finished in a nonslip ceramic tile.

6. The *water temperature* of showers should be controlled by a safety mixing valve from a central point away from the users to prevent scalding.

7. All *electric outlets and fixtures* should be waterproof, resistant to chlorine, and should be located where unauthorized persons do not have access to them. Otherwise, they should be key-operated.

First-Aid Room

1. The first-aid room should be *located* so that it is readily accessible to the street for easy transport of accident victims to an ambulance.

2. The room should be *furnished* with a cot, a lavatory, a toilet, and a shower room with hot water.

3. *Emergency equipment and supplies* should include an inhalator, resuscitator, and first-aid equipment of the type recommended by local health agencies or hospitals, including a spine board or other suitable device for removal of swimmers who sustain back or neck injuries.

4. There should be a direct (outside line) telephone available in the first-aid room or other location with clearly posted numbers to the hospital, police, fire department, and any doctor that may be on call. It is advisable to post

these numbers prominently on the wall adjacent to the phone. The telephone number of the immediate supervisor of the pool should also be listed.

5. In *small pool complexes* where it is necessary to economize on space, the pool manager's office may also serve as the first-aid room.

Safety Related to Pool Users

People who have any responsibility for the operation of swimming pools (homeowners, motel or hotel operators, apartment owners, pool managers, lifeguards, and administrative groups) must be familiar with the general characteristics of the people using their pools. This information helps in understanding the behavior of the pool users and helps to establish proper rules and regulations governing their conduct.

Infants

Children below the age of 2 are only safe in swimming pools if properly attended at all times by a responsible adult. The adult should hold a child just learning to walk. Some of the physical and psychological characteristics of children this age that relate to swimming and the pool environment are as follows:

- They do not generally follow verbal instructions.
- Their musculature is weak.
- They are not aware of the potential hazards of water.
- They tend to play, particularly with objects such as water toys and water balls if they are around the pool, and may fall into the pool reaching for them.
- When young children become familiar and comfortable with the water, they tend to become bold and must therefore be closely watched.

The following rules for supervision are suggested for infants:

- They should be held securely at all times in or near the water.
- Suntan lotion should not be applied to an infant prior to entering the water; the lotion makes the infant slippery and difficult to hold. If overexposure to the sun is a possible danger, the child should instead wear a clean, white shirt.
- Even if infants have had instruction in the water and feel comfortable in it, they must not be regarded as "swimmers." Watch them closely at all times while they are in and around the water.
- Infants must never be left unattended while floating in or on any type of flotation device.
- Leaving infants unwatched in a "baby pool" is unsafe, even if the depth of the pool is only a few inches. Children should always wear some type of safety jacket or belt until they learn to swim.
- The actions of infants around water are often unpredictable.

Nonswimmers

Nonswimmers are those who cannot swim a minimum distance of 50 feet. Here are some characteristics of this group:

- Nonswimmers may fear the water, some to a high degree.
- Some may have had a bad experience related to water or swimming.
- Most have come to the pool persuaded by someone else.
- Most respond best to group instruction because of the presence of peers.
- Nonswimmers exhibiting extreme fear are best taught separately from the group, with personalized instruction.
- Nonswimmers tend to imitate better swimmers.
- Nonswimmers often have difficulty with body balance in the water.
- "Breath control" is a nonswimmer's single greatest weakness.

Some suggestions for working with nonswimmers include the following:

- Nonswimmers should be restricted to the shallow portion of the pool where they can stand up.
- Nonswimmers should be watched constantly when they are not in an instructional group.
- There always should be a lifeline between the deep and shallow water to prevent nonswimmers from entering deep water.

- Nonswimmers must not rely completely on flotation devices such as rings, rafts, bubbles, and flutter boards; they should be watched when using such devices.
- Nonswimmers should never use face masks, snorkels, or fins except under the direct supervision of a qualified instructor.
- Nonswimmers should be given verbal instructions regarding what they can and cannot do.

Semiskilled Swimmers

Semiskilled persons are those who know how to swim but have not achieved a level of proficiency to be completely self-sufficient in the water. The following characteristics and guidelines pertain to semiskilled swimmers.

- Semiskilled swimmers may overestimate their ability and attempt a dive, distance swim, or an underwater swim too difficult for them.
- A sudden "dunking" may cause panic that often makes them temporarily forget their acquired skill.
- Semiskilled swimmers should be prevented from engaging in horseplay.
- They should generally be confined to shallow water.
- If they enter deep water areas or the diving area to dive, they must be watched closely.

Skilled Swimmers

Skilled swimmers are comfortable with the water. They have reached a skill level where they are able to perform all the swimming strokes and diving, as well as basic lifesaving skills. The following are characteristics of this group and guidelines for supervision:

- Skilled swimmers are bold and confident about their ability.
- Skilled swimmers need new challenges to keep them motivated.
- Skilled swimmers should be given responsibility in assisting others to learn to swim or dive.
- They should be warned of the hazards of hyperventilation and prolonged breath holding.
- They should be given activities such as competitive swimming, springboard diving, scuba

diving, lifesaving, fitness swimming, synchronized swimming, and water polo to keep them interested.

- They should be given advanced swimming and lifesaving instruction.
- They should be urged to stay within the bounds of their ability during recreational swimming and to seek professional instruction in advanced swimming techniques.
- They should be allowed to use such items as face masks, snorkels, or scuba gear only after receiving instruction in their proper use and in the presence of a qualified instructor.

Disabled Persons

Disabled persons may require one-to-one supervision while in the pool. Persons with certain disabilities may require a medical examination in order to establish swimming readiness. The supervisor and lifeguards should be made aware of any physical conditions requiring special attention or extra precautions. Pool operators should require organizations using the facility to make provisions for special or additional supervision where necessary. (See chapter 9 on facilities for disabled individuals for information on pool modification for swimmers with disabilities.)

Senior Citizens

Senior citizens often find swimming a healthful and relaxing activity.

- Many senior citizens do not know how to swim or lack advanced swimming skills. Special instructional classes should be set up to teach the nonswimmers.
- Senior citizens who know how to swim usually do not require special supervision or a special place to swim.
- A separate area of the pool or a special part of the day may be reserved for closer supervision and for a more relaxed atmosphere for senior citizens.

General Safety Rules

Every swimming pool should have posted rules of safety and proper conduct. They may not be exactly the same from pool to pool because facilities differ. Nevertheless, there are certain fundamental rules that apply to all swimming pools with some slight modifications. Listed below are rules that should be prominently displayed in conspicuous areas of the pool. Recommended letter size for rules is 1 inch; for warning signs 4 inches. (Facility operators should select those rules applicable to their situation.)

- Dive only where diving is permitted.
- When diving, keep arms stretched out in front to protect the head.
- Do not chew gum while swimming.
- Swimmers in the water have the right of way. Those entering the water from springboards, the deck, or from water slides must make certain that no one is in front of them.
- Obey lifeguards and other supervisory personnel.
- Do not run on the deck.
- Never push or throw anyone into the pool.
- Do not try to swim long distances underwater.
- Rest when tired.
- Be alert to help anyone in trouble. Go to their aid immediately, but also call for help. Do not remove injured people from the water who complain of back or neck pain.
- Take a shower before entering the pool.
- Do not talk with lifeguards who are on duty.
- Get out of the water before the approach of any electrical storm.
- Do not swim if you have an open sore.
- Never swim alone.
- Clear pool immediately when alarm is sounded. Follow instructions. Stay away from emergency locations.

Special rules may be needed to cover such items as food and beverages brought into pool areas, use of scuba diving equipment, flotation devices, water slides, and diving boards (particularly a 3-meter springboard or a tower for platform diving).

Management of Pool Users

Effective management of the people using swimming pools involves knowledge, leadership, tact, and, above all, constant alertness and attention to details. The various administrative aspects of public pools are discussed in chapter 1. The operation and management of home pools is covered in chapter 3, whereas the management of motel/hotel and apartment pools is discussed in chapter 4. This section focuses on the problems of supervision that relate specifically to safety. Some of the suggestions are not found in any published pool standards or in state or local swimming pool regulations. Nevertheless these suggestions represent the best professional judgment at this time of the Editorial Committee and are based on years of successful experience of many authorities in the pool management and operation field.

Lifeguards

No public or semipublic pool (e.g., motel, hotel, apartment) that caters to a transient clientele should ever be operated without qualified lifeguards. The number of guards needed and where they should be placed to be most effective are essential elements in providing a safe pool environment.

Numbers needed. Three factors must be considered in determining the number of lifeguards: the water area to be covered; the type of activities expected to be conducted in the pool; and the number of people in the pool and surrounding deck area. The following criteria should be used to establish the number of necessary guards:

- One lifeguard chair or station should be provided for approximately every 2,000 square feet of water surface area.
- The above formula may be modified upwards in terms of square footage where the pool consists of all shallow water (5 feet deep or less).
- One guard in a chair is usually sufficient in shallow pools up to 3,300 square feet of water area except during crowded periods. A pool of this size is considered crowded when there are 150 people in the water and surrounding deck area.
- In deep water pools (over 5 feet deep such as found in diving pools), more guards are needed, and the formula of one guard per 2,000 square feet of water area should be strictly followed.
- One guard should always be assigned exclusively to supervise diving activities and one or more, as needed, to watch the other activities and areas of the pool.

In large pools (e.g., a pool 50 meters by 25 yards), it is impractical to use the above formula because to do so would require five or six guards even if there were only six swimmers in the pool. The best policy in such situations is to restrict the small number of swimmers to a limited portion of the pool, which can be supervised by a single guard. When the number of swimmers reaches 50, a second guard should be added, and the pool area open to swimmers should be increased. For each additional 50 swimmers, another guard should be added until the number reaches 200. Then the whole pool area (12,374 square feet of water surface area) should be opened, and six guards should be assigned to the lifeguard stands.

The amount of deep water and the number of diving stations may necessitate altering the guard requirement upward. The center portion of a large pool (50 meters or more) is the most difficult area to supervise, particularly in outdoor pools where sunlight reflecting off the water's surface may make it difficult to see under the water's surface.

A sound practice is to assign one guard (the one who has the sun at his or her back) specifically to watch swimmers in the center of the pool. Guards should be rotated at regular intervals, at the least every hour, with every 30 minutes preferred.

Location of lifeguard chairs. Figure 8.9 indicates what is considered to be the best location of lifeguard chairs for pools of various sizes and configurations.

Responsibility of lifeguards. The major responsibility of the lifeguards is to prevent accidents from happening. (See chapter 1 for detailed discussion of a lifeguard's duties.) No person is in a better position to prevent accidents in a pool than the alert, prudent person sitting in the lifeguard chair. He or she is the ''radar,'' constantly scouting the assigned water area for any potential problems.

Where to Post Signs

Appropriate signs conveying instructions to pool users should be posted in the following areas:

1. *Entrance* to swimming pool from outside: to inform users regarding general rules as to eligible patrons, cost, identification needed, and other relevant requirements or regulations.

2. *Bathhouse or locker room*: to explain rules of conduct and procedures within the locker room.

3. *Entrance to pool area*: to acquaint patrons with the general rules for use of the pool.

4. *Others*: at any special facility or equipment such as diving boards, water slides, jumpboards, starting blocks, and wading pools to instruct and caution patrons as to their proper use.

Overexposure to the Sun

Sometimes children and even adults are unaware that they have had too much sun. Lifeguards should warn any person who appears to be approaching the point of severe sunburn to cover up or to get out of the sun.

Use of Flotation Devices

Flotation equipment brought to the pool by a swimmer should be inspected by a pool official or lifeguard to determine whether it should be permitted in the pool. Furthermore, it is good policy to instruct swimmers and parents about any limitations in the use of such equipment. It has been demonstrated that auto and tractor inner tubes are dangerous and hence should *not* be allowed in public pools. Certain flotation devices may be used if proper supervision is present.

Overexertion

Current lifeguarding courses taught by the American Red Cross and YMCA emphasize the need for guards to watch all swimmers for signs of overexertion and fatigue, and to provide immediate assistance to tired swimmers.

Contests among swimmers to see who can swim underwater for the greatest distance can be hazardous because swimmers may hyperventilate. Hyperventilation can cause shallow-water blackout, and has caused several drownings. Underwater swimming should be allowed only where it can be controlled and supervised.

Horseplay

Roughhousing or horseplay is common, but it has no place in a swimming pool. It must not be tolerated, and when it does occur, lifeguards should take immediate corrective action. The type of horseplay causing more injury than any other is pushing or throwing people into the pool. Although seemingly harmless, the danger lies in the possibility that the person may strike someone in the pool or dive incorrectly into shallow water where he or she may strike the bottom.

Running

Running around the pool deck is the most frequent abuse of the rules for safe pool conduct. The danger, of course, lies in the possibility of slipping on a wet portion of the deck or pool's coping. Lifeguards must be alert to prevent such accidents from happening.

Overcrowding and Congestion

All pools have a "rated capacity" that is usually established by the regulations of local health departments. These limitations must not be exceeded, both for reasons of pool sanitation and the possibility of accidents. Congestion may occur in one area of a pool when too many swimmers congregate in the area; guards should disperse such gatherings.

Supervising the Multiple-Pool Complex

The trend toward aquatic complexes involving as many as four or five pools is increasing. The proper supervision of multiple pools involves protection for each pool that is in operation. An effective supervision system involves a method of securing one or more pools or pool areas when attendance is low or special classes are being held. The use of aides who have been trained or who are in a lifeguard-training status (paid or volunteer) may be an effective method of improving the quality of supervision of large pool complexes, as long as they work under a qualified lifeguard.

Parental Supervision

No public or semipublic pool should ever place full responsibility for the supervision of children on parents. Many parents are not qualified to provide proper supervision of their children in all water situations. It is appropriate, however, to demand that parents who accompany their children to the pool see that their children remain in the area of the pool designated for them.

Principles of Safe Pool Management

1. Every person associated with the operation of a pool has responsibility for safety. In the final analysis, however, it is usually the city, school, motel, hotel, club, apartment, or homeowner that is charged with the responsibility when an accident occurs in their facility.

2. All equipment used in pools such as diving boards, platforms, water slides, ladders, starting blocks, and other pool accessories should be inspected every day. Equipment that is found defective should be secured until repaired.

3. Only personnel who are qualified through recognized certification or evidence of completion of a course of instruction in lifesaving, lifeguarding, CPR, and pool management should be employed as lifeguards, supervisors, or managers of swimming pools. Lifeguards under the age of 18 should be considered "aides" and in a training status. They should be assigned to older and more experienced lifeguards and never should be left completely alone in charge of a pool.

4. Emergency procedures for handling accidents should be posted in conspicuous locations and passed on by verbal and written instruction to the pool staff. There should be no uncertainty on the part of the staff regarding what to do in the case of an emergency. The procedure should be rehearsed frequently. Seconds may mean the difference between life and death, and the proper removal of a person with a spinal cord injury may make the difference between normalcy and quadriplegia.

5. Food and beverages go with swimming; consequently, they should not be eliminated but rather properly managed in order to prevent accidents or the creation of unsanitary conditions.

6. The chemistry of the water, that is, the condition of the water from a chemical point of view, is essential to a healthy and safe pool environment. The management of the pool's water should be in the hands of a qualified and conscientious individual. Automated recording equipment (Pool Chemistry Controllers or PCC) should be installed where possible during the initial construction period. Swimming should not be permitted if the cloudiness of

the water prevents the ability to see the bottom of the pool.

7. Spillage of oil on the deck from suntan lotions may cause accidents. Decks of pools should be constantly inspected for oil deposits. Even bodies covered with oil may deposit a sufficient quantity of oil while lying on the deck to cause a person to slip. People using suntan oil should be required to lie on towels.

8. Care must be taken to secure a pool properly during the off-season, especially when the water will be left in the pool basin.

9. Special attention is necessary when a pool is emptied for repairs during the swimming season to assure that people do not dive into an empty pool.

10. At least one telephone should be available in the pool area for emergency use. At every telephone located within a swimming pool complex (offices, lobby, locker rooms, and pool area), emergency numbers such as those of the police, hospital, fire department, and department heads should be posted in a conspicuous place.

11. First-aid equipment must be readily available and never locked up with a single key in possession of someone who may have left the premises. The type and quantity of first-aid equipment should, at a minimum, conform to the recommendations of local public health and/or safety officials and should include a spine board for the removal of any person sustaining a back or neck injury.

12. Good security of a pool comes only with careful planning. Doors and gates must always be secured. Proper illumination of the pool is necessary even when it is not in use. Where potential break-in is a problem, some kind of sensing device that signals the presence of intruders should be installed.

13. Accidents are bound to happen. Pool management must be prepared to handle any eventuality.

Handling Emergencies

This chapter has already alluded to many of the steps and procedures that must be taken when an accident occurs anywhere in the pool or pool area.

In this section the procedures to be followed whenever a pool is confronted with an emergency are summarized. This applies to all pools, but particular emphasis is placed on large pool complexes that employ lifeguards.

The most serious accident that may occur is a drowning or near drowning. In such an event, time is the most important factor. Getting the victim out of the pool and under proper resuscitation procedures, when indicated, must not be delayed for a single second. The lifeguard, pool attendant, or anyone else qualified to administer artificial respiration should do so immediately upon the removal of the victim from the pool, except if a cervical (neck) or back injury is suspected. In such cases, the injured bather should not be removed from the water until some type of rigid support such as a spine board is available, and artificial resuscitation should be started while the victim is still in the water.

Attempts to resuscitate the injured person should begin immediately. Do not wait for the ambulance or rescue squad to arrive; if the procedure is not started within 2 or 3 minutes from the time the victim has stopped breathing, the chances of reviving the victim are slight. It is strongly recommended that all personnel related to pool operation be qualified to administer cardiopulmonary resuscitation (CPR). (See the Suggested Readings at the end of this chapter for sources describing resuscitation techniques.) The following suggestions are offered as a guide in establishing emergency procedures:

1. A plan for handling emergencies should be established before pools are opened for operation. An emergency plan should contain what to do, how to do it, who to call, and where the first-aid and emergency equipment is located.

2. Every pool should have a direct outside telephone line, not one routed through a switchboard.

3. Every pool should have a portable inhalator-resuscitator. All lifeguards should be trained in equipment use.

4. All lifeguards must be certified in both first aid and CPR.

5. Visits by the pool manager to local police and fire departments are recommended in order to establish the role each will play in the event an accident occurs at the pool.

6. Every large pool complex should install an alarm system that lifeguards may activate by pushing a button located on or near their station. The alarm (gong or siren) alerts everyone to execute the emergency plan because an accident has occurred in the pool area. To reduce the time it takes for medical help to arrive at the pool, some pool complexes have a direct line from the pool office to local hospitals or rescue units that is used whenever a drowning or near drowning occurs.

7. Emergency drills should be conducted on a regular basis with all personnel employed by the pool as well as with the local police and fire departments participating in the drill. Everyone must be trained in what he or she is to do. Few, if any, commands are needed if everyone does his or her part. Success in handling emergencies depends on knowing what to do and on the proper rescue and emergency procedures so that they are accomplished effectively and expeditiously.

Some of the other types of accidents for which emergency procedures must be established include electric shock, cuts, abrasions, concussions, and fractures. Hitting the diving board has been the cause of a number of serious diving accidents. The use of a protective safety mat covering the end of the board may reduce the seriousness of these accidents appreciably. It is also recommended that emergency procedures be established to handle power failures, riots, and intoxication.

The Most Hazardous Pool Areas and Activities

It is inevitable that accidents will occur in and around swimming pools. A recognizable, inherent risk exists in the use of any swimming facility. Although pools are no doubt the safest of all swimming environments, it is a fact that some activities carried on in pools are more hazardous than others and should be so recognized. Similarly, certain areas of the pool and certain types of equipment are more dangerous than others.

Complete elimination of accidents is impossible; nevertheless, their number and seriousness can be reduced by the prudent attention to duty by lifeguards, by proper overall management of the pool, and by the alertness on the part of swimmers toward other swimmers who may be in trouble.

Listed below are the major hazardous areas and activities in the pool environment, along with some common sense practices and suggestions that, if followed, help to reduce accidents.

- Diving Equipment: All diving equipment, including jumpboards, should be supervised when they are in use. The chance of hitting the board is always a risk for the diver. Users of diving equipment who have not been given instruction should, if at all possible, receive some before being permitted to use the equipment. Divers should always be instructed regarding the proper exit from the diving area to avoid being hit by the next diver. Diving platforms up to 10 meters high are undoubtedly the most dangerous facility in any pool, and they must be carefully supervised because injury may occur from just hitting the water from this height in an improper posture. Multiple diving or jumping (2 or more people at a time) must never be permitted from the tower.

- Shallow Water: Diving into shallow water (anything under 5 feet) may be dangerous and should either be prohibited or carefully supervised. People who have been instructed in how to make a shallow dive seldom have any difficulty, but those who have not (and in addition are poor divers) may get into serious trouble. Diving of any kind should be prohibited in pools with constant depth—shallow water of 3-1/2 feet—such as is usually found in above-ground pools.

- Deep-Water Areas: This area is usually the diving pool or well. Inexperienced swimmers are at risk in deep water. Any deep-water areas should always have at least one lifeguard present. A lifeline should separate the deep from the shallow portion of the pool.

- Water Slides: Strict supervision of water slides is essential. Children or adults should never be permitted to go down slides in any position other than feetfirst, unless the slide is placed in deep water (8 feet or more).

- Decks and Copings: The pool decks and coping often become slippery when wet or if oil is spilled on them; consequently, running must be prohibited. Slip-resistant material should be used and kept clean and free of algae and fungus.

- Starting Platforms (or Blocks): The starting platforms used to start swimming races are usually

30 inches above the water and too often placed at the shallow end of a pool where the water is only 3-1/2 feet deep. Therefore, all swimmers other than swim team members should be prohibited from using starting platforms. Swimming team coaches should carefully instruct their swimmers of the dangers of an improper dive. The recently introduced start called "diving into the hole," or scoop dive, is dangerous for the inexperienced swimmer. Where possible, starting blocks should be placed at the deep end of the pool and should never be used in shallow ends where the water depth is 3-1/2 feet or less.

- Obstructions in Pool Area: Because furniture, tables, equipment, and rope barriers may obstruct the free movement of swimmers around the pool, they should be properly placed and stored when not in use.

- Underwater Swimming: Holding the breath too long or hyperventilating (often done in underwater swimming), may result in a person "blacking out." Long-distance underwater swimming should be prohibited unless carefully supervised.

- Scuba Diving and Equipment: No scuba equipment should be allowed in a pool except during an instructional class in scuba diving under the direction of a certified instructor.

- Underwater Obstructions: Ladders extending into the pool, steps going into the pool, eye bolts protruding from the wall, and underwater ledges or in-pool seats extending into the pool are all potentially dangerous to the underwater swimmer and diver.

- Other Conditions: Two other conditions may be extremely dangerous to swimmers and divers: insufficient lighting (both underwater and overhead) when the pool is used at night; and cloudy or turbid water. Visibility of the bottom is essential in order for a person to make a safe dive.

Need for Research

It is evident that more research is needed—not only in the area of injury causation, but in what constitutes a safe pool design. Pool design must be predicated on removing all potential hazards that can be realistically accomplished. The pool activities engaged in by children and adults must be studied in relation to their implications for design. An analysis of the variations in human performance based on age, sex, physical characteristics, and skill ability need to be conducted in order to provide a basis for understanding foreseeable action.

References

Communicable Disease Center, U.S. Department of Health and Human Services. (1981). *Suggested health and safety guidelines for recreation water slide flumes.* Atlanta, GA: Author.

Gabrielsen, M.A. (1984). *Diving injuries: A critical insight and recommendations.* Indianapolis, IN: Council for National Cooperation in Aquatics.

National Collegiate Athletic Association. (1985). *NCAA Swimming rule book.* (Available from NCAA, P.O. Box 1906, Mission, KS 66201.)

Peters, G. (1977, November). Only fools rely on standards. *Hazard Prevention.*

U.S. Consumer Products Safety Commission. (1977a). *Medical analysis of swimming pool injuries.* Washington, DC: Author.

U.S. Consumer Products Safety Commission. (1977b). *NEISS data highlights.* Washington, DC: Author.

U.S. Consumer Products Safety Commission Newsletter. (February, 1978). Washington, DC: Author.

United States Diving. (1985). *Diving rules.* (Available from USD, 901 W. New York St., Indianapolis, IN 46223.)

Suggested Readings

American National Standards Institute, Inc. (1972). *Specifications for accident prevention signs.* Publication no. ANSI-Z35.1. (Available from ANSI, 1430 Broadway, New York, NY 10018.)

American Red Cross. (1974). *Cardiopulmonary resuscitation.* Washington, DC: Author.

See also the Bibliography in Appendix D for other resources related to pool safety.

Chapter 9

Pool Facilities for Impaired and Disabled Persons

Today swimming programs and other aquatic activities for individuals with disabilities are conducted in both public and private pools of all shapes and sizes. Only a few programs, however, are conducted in facilities specifically designed and equipped to meet the special needs of individuals who are impaired or disabled. As aquatic activities for disabled swimmers have become more numerous, schools, colleges, universities, Ys, churches, community associations, country clubs, motels/hotels, and private homes are making their pools accessible.

Litigation, special education legislation, civil rights laws, and changing attitudes and philosophies recognizing the worth and dignity of every individual have resulted in new and expanded opportunities for disabled individuals regardless of the type or severity of their condition. This movement mandates that every individual have equal opportunities in programs and activities conducted in the least restrictive environment. The implications of these trends are especially pertinent to integrating mentally retarded and multiply disabled individuals with able-bodied persons in enriched early childhood experiences as well as in adult programs.

Explanation of Terms

For clarity, the distinctions among the terms *impaired*, *disabled*, and *handicapped* must be defined.

An *impairment* is an identifiable organic or functional condition. Some part of the body is actually missing or does not function adequately. The condition may be permanent as in amputations, congenital birth defects, cerebral palsy, and brain damage; or it may be temporary such as speech

Ramp built into adult pool. Town Park, Greenburgh, New York. Architect: Ward Associates.

defects, some learning disabilities, various emotional problems, certain social maladjustments, or specific movement deficiencies.

A *disability* is a consequence of impairment. The individual is limited or restricted in developing some physical skills, in doing specific jobs or tasks, or in performing certain activities. Individuals with impairments should not be automatically excluded from activities simply because the condition makes it appear that these individuals cannot participate safely, successfully, or with personal satisfaction. Many impaired persons attain high levels of excellence in activities in which they are not believed to be able to perform or participate: Congenital quadriamputees swim and dive; postpolio individuals participate in competitive swimming and scuba diving; paraplegic and cerebral palsied persons also swim and dive.

A *handicap* is a disadvantage that makes some physical tasks extraordinarily difficult. Every impairment does not necessarily become a handicap. The term *handicapped* is often used in a generic sense to also include the terms *impaired* and *disabled*; however, many impaired and disabled persons do not approve of such use. It is important to be aware of the needs and interests of every individual, regardless of the presence of any physical impairment.

Programs for Participants With Impairments or Disabilities

Regardless of the type, degree, or severity of conditions, three basic approaches may be applied to guiding, directing, or placing impaired or disabled individuals in swimming programs and other aquatic activities. The emphasis is upon functional abilities, not upon categorical generalizations that may or may not affect general swimming abilities or performances in specific aquatic activities. When an individual can take part safely, successfully, and with personal satisfaction in swimming or general aquatic activities—instructional, recreational, fitness, synchronized, or competitive swimming; diving; lifesaving; boating; fishing; scuba diving; and water skiing—it is impossible to justify or rationalize placement in special programs for those activities. In assessing each individual to determine activities and programs in which he or she can or cannot participate, three general groups become evident:

1. *General programs.* Individuals who can take part in regular activities safely, successfully, and with personal satisfaction should be guided and encouraged to participate in

school, community, and camp swimming programs and in aquatic activities where each participates with peers, classmates, friends, and families.

2. *Intermediate or "half-way house" programs.* Many individuals have the potential to participate in regular swimming/aquatic activities although they are now unable to do so. Something is lacking, whether it be confidence, experience, skills, physical strength, or conditioning. An intermediate care, or half-way house approach, serves to help each individual overcome such factors so that he or she may participate in regular swim programs and aquatic activities.

3. *Special programs.* Some individuals have physical conditions that require training and experience in special, separate programs. Individuals in this group should be reassigned to regular programs when they have mastered the necessary skills.

Placement decisions are made at the time each student is evaluated to determine specific needs in a particular area or for a given program or activity. Bases for placement decisions are individual interests, needs, and abilities, not categorical generalizations, labels, or impairments. Functional abilities in aquatic and swimming activities are key factors in determining placement of individuals in swimming programs and aquatic activities regardless of the presence of physical impairments.

Adapting Facilities

When existing facilities are used, instructional and recreational swimming programs and other aquatic activities for participants with impairments must be adapted at each facility. The following problems are often mentioned when existing aquatic facilities are used:

- Difficulties in adequately increasing water temperature
- Inability to use outdoor pools because of extremely cold water and air
- Difficulties in using pools at reasonable times on a continuous basis because of already crowded schedules
- Insufficient shallow areas for one-to-one and small-group instruction
- Difficulties in transferring individuals into and out of the water

- Architectural barriers that prevent use of locker, shower, and restrooms, or hamper entering and leaving the facility itself
- Lack of publicity about programs and availability of pools for these populations
- Difficulty in reaching the pools

Too often swimming pools and other aquatic facilities that are made available to individuals or groups of impaired or disabled persons go unused. So much emphasis has been placed on special needs, major facility and design differences, expensive extras, and extensive precautions that must be taken in sheltered environments and unique facilities that simple, commonsense ways to take full advantage of these opportunities are sometimes overlooked.

A major factor is transferring an individual into and out of the water. Because of preconceived ideas of what individuals can and cannot do, often unjustified limitations are imposed on persons with various conditions. To help an individual obtain access to a pool of any type, ask for his or her suggestions. When one has to deal constantly with barriers of all types, innovative, nontraditional, and unconventional approaches are learned and often become second nature. Consider the following examples:

- Bring an individual into the pool on a litter and let him or her float off to greater independence; only give the amount of assistance requested or required by each person.
- Use a wide board: An individual may slide or gradually progress down, forward, or backward into the pool.
- Take full advantage of wide steps; an individual may sit down on the top step and move down step by step into the pool.
- Take a wheelchair directly down a ramp or wide steps into the pool; the individual moves, or is helped, out of the chair and into the water.
- Carry a small child piggyback into the pool.
- Adopt various one-, two-, three-, and four-person first-aid carries so that an individual may be physically lifted and carried into and out of the pool.
- Let an individual roll from the top of the bulkhead ledge into the water; use as much control as dictated by functional abilities of the individual.

- Build a temporary or portable ramp appropriate to each individual's conditions.

- Build a platform near the side or wall of the pool so an individual may bring a wheelchair to it in a way that allows movement from chair to platform and then into the water.

- Use gym scooters or similar devices that help an individual move from the deck into the pool.

- Install a ramp in the ground or floor on one side of a pool; by going to the end of the ramp, the seat of a wheelchair is even with pool side, permitting easy transfer.

- Improvise sling seats with towels, canvas, and other materials as aids in moving an individual into and out of a pool.

- Install a commercial lift or hoist where need indicates and situations permit.

- Install a hydraulically controlled porch-type platform lift so that individuals in wheelchairs may independently enter and leave the pool by operating the lift themselves; when not in use, the platform sits securely on the bottom of the pool and does not interfere with routine pool uses.

- Build or purchase a platform that may be placed in sections of a pool so water depths are reduced and disabled individuals are better able to participate in programs with friends and families. By raising bottoms of pools many facilities become functional and usable by disabled individuals as well as by other groups including infants, toddlers, and some senior citizens.

In general, carrying and lifting individuals into or out of the water cannot be used to circumvent basic accessibility requirements. However, in some cases, carrying and lifting may be used depending upon severity of condition and whether an individual must be carried and/or lifted in other programs, activities, and situations. Direction should be to provide each individual with opportunities for maximum amounts of independence in all programs and activities, including swimming and aquatics.

Pools have been made more accessible and usable in the following ways:

- One individual, who can stand for only a few minutes, had his pool built 6 feet deep—2 feet above and 4 feet below ground level. The pool bottom slopes gradually up to 2 feet at the center so that when he wants to exit, he simply moves to the shallowest part and sits on the edge of the

Transfer tier for handicapped swimmers. Syracuse, New York. Design by Triad Technologies, East Syracuse, New York.

pool; someone turns his legs around and he transfers back to his wheelchair.

- A unique setup is used by the Veterans Administration Hospital in Miami, Florida. The 25 ft by 40 ft pool has a ramp 4 feet wide and 21 feet long sloping down at the shallow end. Handrails flank both sides of the ramp; a rope line mounted by pulley on a wall opposite the ramp can be hooked to a wheelchair, thus permitting another person to lower or pull out someone who is unable to walk.

- In Longview, Washington, the YMCA program makes use of a monorail system in conjunction with a truck hoist and special chair. This is used because pool decks are too narrow for wheelchairs to pass from the dressing rooms to desired points of entry into the water. A person is placed in the special chair at the dressing room door, is secured with a safety belt, is lifted approximately 2 inches above the floor by the hoist, and is pushed horizontally along the pool edge. At the desired point, an attendant in the pool manipulates ropes or chains on the hoist and lowers the person until the chair rests on the bottom of the pool. The safety belt is then unfastened and the occupant is assisted from the chair. When leaving the pool, the sequence of operations is reversed.

Some additional considerations for adapting and/or using existing swimming pools or aquatic facilities for disabled persons are as follows:

- Special chairs should be lightweight and corrosion-resistant. A chair with a rope or fabric back and seat is satisfactory, particularly a folding chair with tubular aluminum or magnesium tubing framework.

- Power associated with devices to aid entry into and exit from a pool should be mechanical or hydraulic rather than electrical to provide simplicity of operation and to avoid hazards associated with using electrical equipment in water or highly humid air.

- When a pool is used for programs involving both nondisabled and disabled persons, all aids to pool entry should be capable of being dismantled and stored when not in use.

- Exercise bars and extra handrails are simple but effective additions to a pool, adding to its accessibility and functional use by individuals having various ambulatory impairments.

Most existing facilities may be made usable and functional for participants with disabilities simply by adding or altering equipment and by reorienting pool operators to provide the best teaching and swimming environment for all individuals. When adapting existing swimming pools or aquatic facilities, avoid the trap of doing the obvious—installing some type of lift. Although this may be appropriate and necessary when the emphasis is on hydrotherapy and aquatic rehabilitation, lifts are not recommended when the focus is on instruction, recreation, and fitness programs. Lifts make individuals more dependent, call attention to and accentuate individuals' differences, and are not what most individuals themselves want and need. Providers of services must listen to those for whom programs and activities are designed.

Comfort and Safety Factors

Warm water and warm air are important to the health and safety of many disabled individuals and to the success of aquatic programs. The range of water temperature should be 80 to 90 °F, with air temperature up to 5° higher. Often when pools are used for therapeutic purposes or with individuals having multiple physical limitations or conditions, water temperature may be several degrees higher than this generally recommended range. Water must be clear, filtered, chlorinated, and must have a 4-hour turnover rate to accommodate any bather load.

Pools should have nonslip floors, decks, and access to both shallow and deep water by ladders or built-in steps; pool bottoms should have very gradual slopes. Recent developments show that ladders angled away from pool walls are more accessible for individuals with mobility problems than ladders that are perpendicular to or recessed in pool walls. Ramps of various kinds have been incorporated in different ways and for a variety of uses in many pools. Pool depths need to be clearly marked. Reaching poles, shepherd crooks, a buoy line separating shallow and deep water, and similar safety features should be installed and readily available. A large deck area or other dry space is desirable for drills and other selected teaching approaches.

Adequate shallow water area is important to the success of instructional swimming programs for participants who are disabled, especially the young and those with fear of water. Some instructors have advocated lowering water levels for some programs to facilitate beginning instruction. This can be both difficult and costly in most pools. Lowering the water level 1 foot in a large pool may require removing many thousands of gallons of water and usually requires a shutdown of several hours. Refilling usually takes longer and often the water must be heated, which is also costly. In addition, health authorities usually frown on lowering and raising water levels of pools or closing down the system. A wading pool or some device to raise the level of the bottom is a more satisfactory and effective practice for this purpose.

Portable ladder by Triad Technologies

Guidelines for Developing Facilities

Shower rooms, locker rooms, and toilet facilities should be accessible, functional, and usable by individuals with the variety of conditions being served. Guidelines and standards for these facilities within a comprehensive swimming pool or aquatic center are basically no different from those for other public buildings. Detailed information about such guidelines and standards may be obtained from the sources listed at the end of this chapter.

Specially Designed Pools

The Human Resources Center, Albertson, Long Island, New York, has an indoor swimming pool used by children at the school as well as by adults in workshop programs. The pool is 30 ft by 60 ft and has a depth ranging from 3 to 8 feet. This pool design has been incorporated in other facilities such as the Forrest Haven (Maryland) Center for the Mentally Retarded.

Although heating, filtering, and recirculating systems are standard, the pool includes a number of special features.

- Sides of the pool wall are 19 inches, the height of a standard wheelchair above floor level. Thus, a chair can be brought directly to the ledge so an individual may enter or may be easily transferred to the pool. Coping around the pool is made of natural finish marble with smooth, sanded edges. This ledge extends far enough over the outer edge of the pool so wheelchair pedals can fit comfortably underneath.

- Water in the pool is kept at a higher than usual level for easy movement into and out of the pool. Usual water level is about 12 inches below the top of the pool; at the center water level is only 6 inches below the edge. Water temperature is maintained at 80 to 82 °F because of children's impairments and their limited motions. Air temperature in the pool area is kept within 5° of water temperature for comfort and for preventing colds.

- Floor surface in the pool area consists of non-slip, heated tiles. Aisles around the pool are about 6 feet wide to allow two wheelchairs to pass at the same time. Benches and lounge chairs around the pool are wheelchair height.

- Access to water is provided in several different ways. There are five sets of parallel-assist bars set around the coping to aid individuals who can use their arms. The pool is equipped with two conventional ladders for ambulatory persons; nonskid pads are set in the coping between rails for safety. At the shallow end of the pool is a 19-foot ramp with a 15% grade. This ends in water 3-1/2 feet deep. Two 28-inch wide steps with a 6-inch rise lead up to the coping; six more steps descend into the pool for a distance of 8 feet and to a water depth of 3 feet. Double handrails along the steps continue into the water for a distance of 8 feet. This end of the pool also has 12-foot long parallel bars that are used for exercise and support. Portable water polo and basketball goals are also available.

- The pool is also equipped with a Hoyer (Ted Hoyer & Company) hoist that is easily controlled by an aide or lifeguard. A Hoyer hoist, consisting of a canvas stretcher suspended on a track, is used for quadriplegic individuals who may be transferred directly onto it from a litter or wheelchair and then lowered directly into the pool.

- The pool area contains an emergency button that rings an alarm in the medical department when assistance of a nurse or doctor is required.

Another outstanding swimming/aquatic facility is the CAR (Community Association for the Retarded) Swim Center in Palo Alto, California. This indoor H-shaped pool is 75 feet long, 45 feet wide at each end, and 20 feet in the center. Depth of the pool is 3 to 9 feet with a wide bank of shallow steps providing even greater variations of depth. A wheelchair ramp, a set of steps in the shallow end, and ladders in the deep end are provided. Water temperature is kept a constant 86 °F.

The Therapeutic Recreation Center in Washington, DC, also illustrates a facility with a functional pool for individuals with all types and levels of conditions. This pool accommodates instructional, recreational, fitness, competitive training, and therapeutic programs. The pool has dual, gradually sloping ramps so that wheelchairs may be taken directly into the water. Most of the rest of the pool has been designed for instructional purposes with water in which adults and children alike may feel safe and comfortable. An area blocked off from the main portion of the pool, yet still a part of the pool, provides water up to 8 feet deep for swimmers and advanced instruction. A small Jacuzzi is available in the pool area, which also has deck space for use in the variety of programs conducted in this facility.

Planning Criteria

Groups planning multipurpose community swimming pools or aquatic facilities should give considerable attention to pool design to ensure usable and functional facilities for all persons, including those who are impaired or disabled.

The following factors must be considered as part of comprehensive planning:

- Local need and demand
- General access and entrance into the building, including ramps
- Accessibility and accommodations for parking, first-aid rooms, entrance halls and corridors, rest rooms, offices, meeting rooms, telephones, drinking fountains, door widths, directional signs, and building furnishings
- General traffic movement and patterns into and within the building
- Pool construction including access, water temperature control, warmed rest benches, provisions for spectators, equipment, and aids in the pool area
- Changing, locker, and shower rooms including clothes storage and quick drying rooms
- Sauna and other special provisions

The pool should be easily accessible from parking areas. Walkways, approaches, and halls should be constructed of nonslip materials and ramped for changes in elevation. Doors and hallways should be wide enough to accommodate wheelchairs and passage of heavy equipment. Water fountains, telephones, lockers, and toilet facilities should be accessible from wheelchairs. Locker and shower rooms should be on the same level and immediately adjacent to the pool whenever possible; acoustical tile helps to control noise in indoor facilities. Adequate locker spaces at various levels are needed and consideration should be given to providing one or two horizontal locker spaces in addition to conventional vertical lockers. If possible, large padlocks with large keyholes and keys should be obtained for students having visual, neuromuscular, or similar impairments. Several shower heads and controls should be placed so they can be reached from a wheelchair. Handrails for support should be installed in shower and toilet

G.E.D. pool lift at Temple University pool

areas. Extension of toilet-flushing arms permits use by students with various physical conditions. Shockproof hair dryers and electrical fixtures are a necessity.

Many multipurpose pools have been designed to provide water areas of various depths so that instructional programs, physical fitness activities, recreational swimming, competitive activities, synchronized swimming, diving, and other special programs may be accommodated. There is great freedom in planning outdoor pool facilities. Oddly shaped, even free-form pools may be set apart in special areas. Indoor pools, however, do not have this degree of design flexibility. Rectangular swimming areas are most efficient for indoor pools if one must relate total available water space to structure span. Popular shapes providing multipurpose areas include L-, T-, H-, and Z-shaped pools. Multipurpose pools should be designed so certain areas may be roped off for special programs.

There should be adequate deck space all around the pool: Deck space should be related to programs and to those for whom the pool is designed and used. For example, pools used extensively by individuals in wheelchairs should have deck space at least the equivalent width of two and one-half wheelchairs. When types of programs and status of participants are likely to vary, a standard formula of deck/water ratio should be used to determine minimum deck space. One large deck area should be available, preferably near the shallow end.

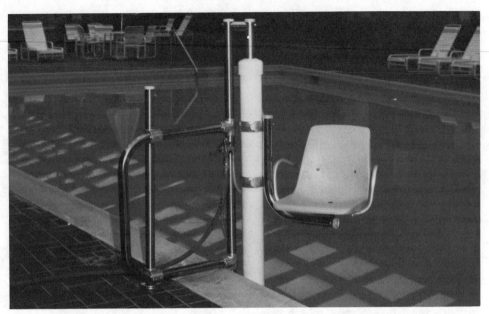

Nolan waterpowered chair lift for handicapped swimmers, Louisville, Kentucky

Areas to be used for these programs should have water depths ranging from 12 to 18 inches to 4 to 5 feet. Some pools provide shallow water areas by constructing 6 ft by 8 ft shelves or decks in 24 to 30 inches of water to provide the desired 12- to 18-inch depth. Several companies manufacture decks of this type. These portable decks take little storage space when not in use and can be assembled and disassembled in a matter of minutes by two or three individuals.

Various design treatments of deck level pools are available as well as innovations in recessed gutter-type pools. In both of these types, size, shape, and location of overflows are of great importance to efficient operation of the recirculating system. Architects designing these pools are urged to consult with competent hydraulic engineers or swimming pool consultants in the choice of a recirculating system. Other modifications that have been used for easy entry and exit are ramps going down into the water or underwater steps, with handrails for support also going into the water.

A pool should have a good filter and purification system as well as a heating system capable of raising water temperature quickly. In a multiuse pool, some method should be considered to raise pool temperatures in instructional or therapeutic areas to 80 or 90 °F. Ideally, air temperature and air flow should also be controlled to prevent evaporation that may chill a student when out of the water. Air-conditioning and heating specialists should be consulted because there is a 4 to 6° comfort zone between water and air temperatures, which also helps reduce condensation. Places for hanging towels and robes should be provided in pool areas so that students may dry and warm themselves when out of the water.

An emergency first-aid room with a telephone should open onto the pool deck. This room may be combined with one of the pool offices. A storage room opening on the pool deck should be provided as a place to store equipment and instructional materials. This leaves the pool area uncluttered and provides a better teaching environment, while ensuring that materials are readily available.

Other features found to be valuable include water inlets opening on the bottom to provide more uniform water flow and temperature throughout the pool; sleeves set in the bottom of the pool for removable rails or parallel bars to be used for support and handholds; a hydraulic or manually operated lift to help nonambulatory swimmers into and out of the pool; braille, color, and sound coding to indicate depths, exits, and other special features of the pool; music or sound system to provide soothing or stimulating music throughout the pool area; colored lines and shapes—circles, squares, triangles—of different sizes as part of the pool floor for introducing and/or reinforcing lateral and directional movements and patterns as well as spatial awareness.

The Learner Pool

A widespread misconception exists concerning water depth for impaired swimmers whose needs are supposedly met in learning pools where depths range from 2-1/2 to 3-1/2 feet. Without assistance of strong lower limbs, an impaired swimmer relies on the body's center of gravity being below pool water level to maintain buoyancy. To achieve this, an adult of average height requires a water depth of 3 to 3-1/2 feet. Usually only general pools meet these water depths. Certainly, a small impaired child and individuals who are especially timid or fearful of water may find satisfactory conditions in learning pools.

A good way to understand the role of the "learner pool" is to look at New Zealand schools where learning to swim has long been emphasized. In 1940 the first learner pool, a 40 ft by 15 ft concrete structure with a water depth of 30 inches to 3 feet, was built in an elementary school. This pool was built above ground so instructors did not have to bend over to speak to pupils and so that children would know their instructors were always close.

Since 1940, nearly 1,600 of these pools have been built in New Zealand elementary schools and have been used effectively. Shallow water encourages confidence: A handrail is never more than a few feet from a beginner, and water may be warmed quickly.

At first these pools were of the fill-and-draw type, emptied and refilled every week. Water was chlorinated and tested daily. Twenty years later filter plants suited to these small pools were developed. Today, most of them are filtered and have automatic chlorination systems. Standard pool size is now 45 ft by 18 ft, with water depths ranging from 2-1/2 to 3 feet.

Many times during the use of these pools, even 30 inches of water was found to be frightening to some children. In 1965 a learner pool was designed for a school for mentally retarded children near Auckland. This pool is similar to the usual shallow pool but has an addition, making it L-shaped. The L area is 15 feet long and slopes from 9 to 30 inches. This depth enables even the most timid child to lie down in the water, to kick, and to splash happily; thus, confidence is quickly established.

Children progress rapidly to hand support with body and legs floating. With faces in the water, they look at the bottom of the pool, pull along with hands on the bottom, and quickly move to the crawl stroke. Breathing practice is made easier by being able to move forward before actually being able to swim. Results have been so impressive in this pool that others of similar design have been built. A consideration is underway to adopt this design as the standard for New Zealand. For pro-grams for mentally retarded and elementary school-aged children, recommendations have been made for L-shaped pools 45 to 60 feet long by 18 feet wide with depths 27 inches to 4 feet for the main pool and an 18- to 20-foot L sloping from 9 to 27 inches in depth. This pool provides for children from kindergarten age up to 11 or 12 years of age and helps them rapidly develop the confidence so essential in learning to swim successfully.

Other successful approaches to learner pools that have implications for impaired or disabled persons include the following:

- A learner pool measuring 45 by 24 feet with shelving from 3 to 5 feet

- A private pool designed for physically impaired and disabled youth measuring 32 by 12 feet with shelving from 3 to 5 feet

- Portable above-ground pools of various types, sizes, and descriptions

- Special permanent and moveable learner pools providing a great deal of applicability and functional use in programs for these populations

Hydraulic controls make it possible to raise and lower pool bottoms and control water depths. Specially constructed sections come up and down out of the bottom and/or in and out from the walls to divide pools so they can be used for instructional, recreational, and/or competitive swimming at the same time.

In planning swimming pools, persons who are impaired or disabled should be consulted. Input and active involvement from consumers in every stage of the planning process, decision and policy making, implementation of the building program, and leadership evaluation are essential to the success of these efforts and programs.

Suggested Readings

American Alliance for Health, Physical Education, Recreation, and Dance. (1977). *Making physical education and recreation facilities accessible to all*. Reston, VA: Author.

American National Red Cross. (1977). *Adapted aquatics*. Washington, DC: Author.

American National Standards Institute. (1980). *American national standard specifications for making buildings and facilities accessible to and usable by physically handicapped people*. New York: Author.

Athletic Institute, & American Alliance for Health, Physical Education, Recreation, and Dance. (1985). *Planning facilities for athletics, physical education, and recreation.* Reston, VA: American Alliance for Health, Physical Education, Recreation, and Dance.

Council for Cultural Cooperation, Council of Europe. (1972). *Sport for all.* Strasbourg, France: Author.

Human Resources Center. (1976). *Modification of educational equipment and curriculum for maximum utilization by physically disabled persons.* (Studies 8-12). Albertson, NY: Author.

The Thistle Foundation. (1979). *Sports centres and swimming pools.* Edinburgh, Scotland: Author.

Organizations

American Society of Landscape Architects

Committee on Barrier-Free Design, President's Committee on Employment of the Handicapped

Council for National Cooperation in Aquatics

(Addresses for these organizations are listed in Appendix C.)

Chapter 10

Pool Equipment and Accessories

Every swimming pool, whether a small residential one or a highly elaborate and sophisticated public pool complex, requires a variety of equipment to assure safe and efficient operation. The terms *pool equipment* and *accessories* cover everything except the pool structure itself. The only equipment not discussed in this chapter is equipment that is associated with the mechanical aspects and with water treatment, which are covered in other chapters. Of concern here are those items that are built into the pool shell, mounted on the deck, or used in connection with the pool. Information concerning equipment installation during construction or by the pool management after construction is included.

Determining Equipment Needs

The necessary equipment items and accessories for a pool will depend upon the pool's size and shape, the type of activities to be conducted, the characteristics of the users, the requirements of competitive swimming and diving groups, and regulations of state and local boards of health. The major equipment items are usually illustrated in the pool design drawings and described in the written specifications. This pertains particularly to items built into the pool structure and to items mounted on the deck area. The equipment installation, the anchorage setting, and the assembly require a high degree of skill that only expert craftsmen can provide. The pool designer usually selects such equipment and incorporates it into the construction drawings and specifications. As part of the general contract, it becomes the responsibility of the contractor to furnish and install.

Additional items to be furnished are often added to the specifications. Safety equipment, maintenance equipment, or items required for competitive swimming and diving are typical additional

University of Alabama Pool

items. Because these items are not an integral part of the pool structure, they may be omitted from the construction contract and be furnished at a later date by the pool management. The general contract should include all equipment that requires anything beyond very simple installation procedures.

In addition to this book, several other standards or guides contain criteria that apply to the selection, location, and installation of pool equipment and accessories and are listed in Appendices C and D. The regulations and guidelines provide much useful information and constitute valuable reference material for anyone planning a pool.

Pool Deck Equipment

Deck equipment represents the most visible features of a pool other than the pool enclosure. The style and placement of deck equipment contribute much to the overall appearance of the pool. The equipment described in this chapter is usually part of the pool contract and is shown and detailed in the construction plans and specifications.

In most cases, deck equipment is installed by the pool contractor or manufacturer. Although budgetary limitations may restrict the installation of cer-

tain equipment such as starting blocks, anchors for such items should at least be included in the pool contract because installing the anchors at a later date may be difficult, costly, or even impossible. The equipment may be purchased and installed at a later date as funds become available.

Diving Stands and Boards

Springboard diving is the most exciting and the most hazardous of all pool activities. The selection of the proper equipment, including the type of springboard and stand, and the installation of this equipment is basic to safety. A function of supervision is the prevention of the improper use of diving equipment by providing adequate rules, warnings, and depth markers. Diving equipment may be used for recreation as well as competition. In an attempt to provide equipment adaptable to almost any size pool or pocketbook, a wide variety of stands and boards have been produced.

Short jumpboards, 2-1/2 feet to 6 feet long, may be set on a variety of stands, including coil springs, producing considerable variation in their flexibility. Conventional springboards with fixed or adjustable fulcrums range from 6 feet to 16 feet in length. Springboards for competitive diving under the NCAA and USD rules must be either 14 or 16 feet

Pedestal starting platform

long and 20 inches wide. Most are 16 feet long and made of aluminum. Shorter length boards of 6, 8, 10, and 12 feet are usually 2 inches narrower than competitive boards and are usually placed on "U"-shaped pipe frames or on pedestal stands.

Studies of diving accidents that occurred in public pools revealed that most springboard diving injuries were the result of hitting the bottom of the pool on the up-slope leading to the shallow portion of the pool. No accidents have been reported in pools that met the standards of the competitive diving groups. Studies have also revealed that the boards involved in accidents were those ranging from 6 feet to 12 feet in length. It is unfair to blame accidents on any particular design of a board if the pool water is not deep enough. On the other hand, improper installation, such as placing the board too high above the water, can be a contributing factor. (Refer to chapter 8 for detailed specifications for board and stand installation.)

Diving stands are available in heights of 3 meters, 1 meter, and 1/2 meter. If above 3 meters in height, springboard diving gives way to "platform diving." These platform towers are custom designed and built on the site. Competitive springboard diving is limited to 1-meter and 3-meter installations (see chapter 14).

A diving stand should be considered as a unit that includes the structure supporting the diving board, the anchors that bind the stand to the deck, the diving board, and the adjustable fulcrum. Competitive regulations define the diving height as the distance from the top surface of the board to the water surface. For a 3-meter installation, the requirement is 3 meters plus or minus 2%. For 1-meter diving, the diving height is 1 meter plus or minus 5%. The diving board must be 16 feet in length, 20 inches wide, and extend 6 feet out from

the edge of the pool. A fulcrum that is adjustable over 24 inches, designed to keep the diving board level, is required.

Because competitive regulations mandate a specific dimension from the top of the board to the water surface, the selection of proper anchorages or support foundation for the diving stand is essential. If the diving stand is being mounted on grade, a foundation pad of sufficient mass must be provided to ensure stability. If a diving stand is supported upon a framed beam or slab, the anchorage scheme must be compatible with the floor construction. In this situation, the board manufacturer is responsible for supplying information on the loading imposed upon the supporting structure, and it is the responsibility of the designer to design an adequate support.

The following checklist provides the planner with an insight to proper installation of boards and stands:

- The depth of water in the diving area must be sufficient to provide a safe landing area for divers, commensurate with the board's performance qualities. Many people have made mistakes in this area. To illustrate, a pool built in the 1930s or 1940s is unlikely to provide an adequate depth of water to accommodate today's high-performance model springboards. Installing these boards can create an unnecessary hazard, particularly for the recreational diver.

- All boards placed higher than 1/2 meter above the water should have guardrails that extend a minimum of 1 foot beyond the pool edge.

- All stands and boards should be selected on the basis that they will be used for recreational purposes by people of various skill levels and physical characteristics.

DuraFirm dive stand by Arcadia

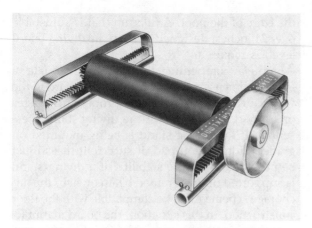

Adjustable fulcrum with rubber roller

- If springboards, 1 meter or more in height, are not placed on a concrete platform, provision should be made to close in the sides to prevent young children from falling through the opening of the guardrails.

- All ladders or steps leading up to the board level should have guardrails; the height of the steps should accommodate the youngest child who will be using the board.

- Board manufacturers should provide purchasers with instructions regarding any use limitations and installation of their equipment.

Lifeguard Chairs and Stands

Lifeguard chairs are usually required at all public swimming pools. Stands are available in a variety of styles and are either movable or permanently fixed. Most chairs incorporate a seat placed 6 feet above the deck. The chair is normally mounted upon a sturdy platform that permits the lifeguard to stand when necessary. The seat should be molded to conform to body contours and should swivel. Both features are desirable for safety and for minimizing lifeguard discomfort. The access ladder to the platform and seat is usually in the back. However, certain models incorporate ladders at the side. This feature is desirable for chairs located at the shallow end of the pool. At such locations diving from the chair is not possible, and the side ladders permit faster descent. (For information on recommended locations of lifeguard stands, see chapter 8.) Many states now require that a lifeguard chair meet Occupational Safety and Health Administraton (OSHA) regulations because the guard is an employee of the pool management.

Guardrails on such chairs are much higher and extend to the front edge of the platform. Umbrellas for shade on outdoor stands are desirable additions.

Moveable or portable chairs have become quite popular in recent years. Their advantage is that the chair can be moved directly to the most active part of the pool area or to an area with minimum sun glare. During the course of a day, the level of activity in different parts of a pool vary as activities and classes change. This is particularly true of pools containing one or more movable bulkheads.

Ladders and Steps

Providing an easy and safe means of exit from the pool is essential. Safe exit is best accomplished by ladders or steps recessed into the wall with grab rails. Ladders normally consist of two formed rails between which the steps are fastened. Ladders are anchored on the deck and project approximately 8 inches into the pool. Steps built into the pool wall require grab rails that are mounted on the deck. Because competitive swimming regulations require that the racing lanes be unobstructed, many designers choose the built-in steps and grab rails as the best means of egress from the pool. However, if a designer prefers ladders to grab rails, the

Lifeguard stand with ladders on sides

requisite for competitive swimming may be met by widening the outer lanes by a foot or two, by installing the ladders in a wall recess, or by using detachable ladders that may be removed for a meet. If the outer lanes have been widened to accommodate a ladder, it is desirable to stretch a racing lane marker along the outer edge of the outside lanes. In those pools with moveable bulkheads, the use of grab rails and steps is the necessary choice. However, the grab rails should either be readily removable or of a design and location that do not affect the movement of the bulkhead.

Maximum spacing between adjacent ladders and grab rails should be approximately 60 feet. A short course pool (25 meters long) usually has a ladder or grab rail near each corner. In 50-meter pools intermediate ladders or grab rails must be provided. Ladders or grab rails must never be located on the end walls of the racing course of a pool.

Starting Platforms

Starting platforms or blocks are required only for competitive swimming. The regulations require that the racers dive from a platform installed a maximum of 30 inches above the water. Because few pools have such a dimension from the top of the deck to the water level, "starting platforms" must be installed for competition. The top of the platform may be set either level or tilted a maximum of 10° toward the pool. Intermediate steps should be provided to make it easy to mount the platform, and the top surface should have a non-slip tread. For backstroke racing, a bar or hand-hold located flush with the pool edge approximately 18 inches above the water surface must be provided. One starting platform must be included in the center of each of the racing lanes.

In larger pools it is not uncommon to have two racing courses of different lengths. In such instances, starting block anchors should be provided for each lane of each course. However, only one set of starting platforms needs to be provided; these can be shifted to whatever course is being used. The platforms should be readily removable and easily stored because they are often erected only for competitive events and are dismounted after the meet. When the racing course runs the length of the pool, the anchors for starting platforms should be located at the deep end of the pool. Too many serious injuries have occurred as a result of swimmers diving off of starting blocks that were located at the shallow end where the water depth was only 3-1/2 feet.

Fixed lifeguard stand by American Sanitary

Stanchions

Stanchions, or upright bars or supports, are required at pools used for competitive swimming for the following purposes:

- To support backstroke pennant lines as markers at each end of the pool; a pennant line is required to warn backstrokers of the approaching wall

- To support a recall line for false starts

- To support a pennant line marking the finish of a course when metric distances are used in a 25-yard pool or if the course length is measured in yards in a pool built to a metric length

All stanchions should be removable and located on the deck whenever possible, measured laterally about 3 feet from the pool wall. However, when a pool has intersecting racing courses, it is sometimes necessary to locate a stanchion in the pool floor.

Water Polo Goals

Water polo has recently become a popular competitive sport. The special equipment required for this sport are goal cages at each end of the playing area. The regulations of both USS and NCAA stipulate the maximum and minimum lengths of a water polo course and the dimensions of the goal cages. Cages should be removed when not in use; therefore, they should be readily removable and storable. Competitive regulations for water polo require a specific location of the cross bar of the goal cage: In deep water the dimension is measured from the water surface; in shallow water it is measured from the pool floor. Goals are mostly mounted on the deck, and the distance from the deck to the water must be a certain height; consequently, the goal cages should be adjustable to provide regulation cross-bar height. Sockets set on the pool deck must be provided for installation of cages, and they should have caps to cover openings when the cage is removed.

Most of the items described in this section are items that may be included either as part of the pool contract or supplied by the pool management at a later date. However, in all pools that hold competitive meets, the anchors for the racing lanes and the stanchions supporting backstroke lines and recall lines should be part of the original pool contract. Although it is possible to add electronic touch pads to a completed pool, it is preferable to have this equipment incorporated in the original construction.

Slides

Slides are primarily for recreational use. They are usually available as complete units, including the bedway and the access ladder. The slides should be well anchored on the deck, and provision should be made for lubrication of the bedway with water. Standards governing the installation of water slides were established by the Consumer Products Safety Commission in 1976. They govern clearance between adjacent diving boards and between other slides and adjacent walls, as well as prescribe the minimum water depth. It is strongly recommended that the use of slides be restricted to children and that only feet-first entries be allowed unless the slide is placed at the deep end of the pool.

Safety Equipment

Safety equipment required at a pool is usually supplied by the pool management. Exceptions include lifeguard chairs and means for protecting the

Cover for safety and heat retention by Covermatic

pool against trespassers. Other safety devices needed are as follows:

Life rings: Every pool must be equipped with life rings. Each lifeguard chair should have at least one life ring; additional units should be around the pool on hangers. Each life ring should be equipped with a throw line of at least 50 feet.

Shepherd's crooks: Shepherd's crooks are long aluminum poles with a crook on the end. They should be hung on the wall or fence of the pool, enabling accessibility. The curve on the end has a wide enough opening so that it can be passed around a swimmer's waist. A shepherd's crook should always be attached to and hung with a pole at least 12 feet long for immediate use.

Lifelines: Lifelines, sometimes called safety lines, are used to delineate shallow water from deep water and to serve as a barrier to prevent a nonswimmer from wandering into deep water. Lifelines are usually made of heavy plastic ropes or cable with brightly colored floats. Proper location for a lifeline is at a point 1 to 2 feet on the shallow side of the breakpoint. The anchors for the lifelines must be recessed in the pool wall at each side. (Anchors should always be included as part of the original pool contract.) The lifelines should always remain in place except when swimming meets are being held or during team swimming practice.

Emergency and lifesaving equipment: First-aid kits should always be available somewhere near the pool area to take care of the minor cuts, nicks, and bruises of pool users. A resuscitator is also a necessary piece of safety equipment and should be kept in the pool area, ready for use. A spine board must be available for removing any person injuring his or her back or neck. A gas mask is a necessary safety equipment item, usually required by law, especially where gas chlorination is used. The gas mask must be hung just outside the room where the chlorination equipment is installed.

Protective pool barriers and devices: Some means of protecting the pool against unwanted intruders or trespassers when the pool is closed should be provided. This can be achieved in a number of ways. The method selected depends upon the type of pool, its usage, and the degree of necessary protection.

Fencing: Primarily used with outdoor pools, fencing is usually required by local ordinances and in some instances by state regulation. Such regulations usually stipulate the height of the fence and other requirements such as the need for self-closing and locking gates.

Pool covers: A pool cover is an effective barrier for smaller outdoor pools. Most covers are manually installed and removed, but many automated types are available. One type is a reinforced fabric cover, rolled over the pool electrically and wound up in a similar manner. Another type is a rigid decking system that is swung over the pool when it is to be closed. When the pool is to be used, the decking can be raised into an elevated position and can serve as a sun shade. A third type is a decking system on hydraulic lifts installed in the pool floor. This type of decking can be raised above the water level to serve as a pool cover and protector.

Night lighting: All public pools should have a security light on at night when the pool is closed. This light not only outlines the pool but identifies trespassers.

Closed circuit TV: Motels, hotels, condos, and apartments may monitor their pools by closed circuit television.

Electronic alarms: Several types of electronic alarm systems may be installed in the pool wall below water or can float on the water's surface. These alarms are sensitive to turbulence and pressure waves caused by a person entering or falling into the water, sending a signal to an appropriate place such as the inside of a home, a hotel, motel, or apartment manger's office, or a police station.

Equipment for Competitive Swimming

Pools to be used for competitive swimming and diving should meet equipment requirements man-

dated by the regulations of organizations such as USS and NCAA. Some of the equipment required for competition was discussed under the general heading of Deck Equipment and is covered in chapter 14. However, a few additional items require attention during the installation process.

Surface racing lane markers: Racing lane markers are required to separate the lanes provided for each swimmer. A marker consists of a set of continuous floats strung on a cord or cable, stretching the full length of the swimming course. Markers must, of course, be provided with hooks or snaps at each end so that they can be attached to anchors set in the pool walls or deck. Some means of tensioning is incorporated so that they can be stretched tightly to hold their position without lateral movement. Floats may be colored in a variety of ways. Most contain alternating colors; however, the last 15 feet of each line must be of a solid color to indicate to the swimmer the approach of the end wall.

In recent years, racing lane markers have evolved into devices to dampen the wave action of the pool and thus reduce turbulence. This type of antiturbulence float is approximately 4 inches in diameter and has a series of slots, grooves, or openings to absorb the kinetic energy of the waves. Racing lane markers of this type have achieved wide popularity and have contributed to the improved time-performance for most swimmers.

The anchors for the markers provided at each end of the swimming course should be substantial in order to absorb the tension. If the pool has moveable bulkheads, provision for anchoring of the racing lane markers must be incorporated into the bulkhead.

Backstroke indicator: Backstroke indicators are made of nylon lines containing a series of triangular pennants or flags strung over the pool at

Deck timer for swimmers

each end of the course. They are anchored to stanchions inserted into the deck near the edge of the pool. The horizontal location of the marker is 15 feet from the end of the pool in the short course (25 yards) and 5 meters from each end in the 50-meter course. The pennant line must be strung so that the distance from the water level to the bottom of the pennants is 7 feet above the water for the short course and 1.8 meters for the long course.

Recall line: A recall line is a rope hung at least 4 feet above the water, which is dropped in the event a false start occurs. The recall line is located 36 feet from the starting end in a short course and 15 meters from the starting end in a long course. The line is hand-held and dropped in the event of a false start to notify swimmers who may not have heard the sound of the gun or whistle.

Other Equipment

In addition to the items already described, such as diving stands, diving boards, and starting platforms, various other items are required for successful operation of swimming and diving meets. The quantity and type of these items must be determined by the coaches and administrators. The following equipment is needed to support swimming and diving meets:

- Diving judges' flash cards
- Stop watches
- Stands at finishing end for judges
- Scoreboard
- Electronic touch pads and accompanying recorder

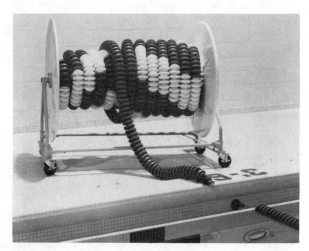

Reel for holding racing lane, by Kiefer

- Bleachers for accommodating spectators
- Splash curtains placed in front of bleachers to protect spectators
- Pace clocks
- Racks or storage bins for storing racing lines
- Spray device in the event no bubbler is provided to agitate the water's surface for divers

In some instances a number of items are necessary for successful operation of the pool while others are considered optional. Some need to be incorporated into the original plans of the pool because they are built-in equipment and include the following items:

- Underwater observation room
- Underwater speakers (for synchronized swimming)
- Underwater lights
- Special overhead lights for competitive swimming
- Color, spot, or flood lights for use in connection with water shows and synchronized swimming
- Portable ramps for accommodating disabled individuals
- Devices for lifting or assisting disabled individuals in and out of pool
- Benches for swim team members
- Electric outlets in pool area
- Bulletin boards

The details of design and construction of many of the previous items are included in other chapters of this book. Lighting levels and the most efficient types of underwater and above water, or area, lighting are important. New, more energy-efficient types of lights are now available. People planning pools need to carefully study all aspects of equipment availability and cost of operation before deciding on what is best for their pool. The subject of lighting is discussed in chapter 11.

Water Heaters

Swimming pool water heaters are becoming more popular each year. Heaters are included in most indoor pools because they are designed for year-round use and comfort. Pool heaters for outdoor pools have also proven to be a sound investment. In cooler climates, a marked increase in attendance has been shown after pool heating equipment has been installed in outdoor public pools. The additional revenue is usually sufficient to cover amortization of the cost of such equipment, plus the operating fuel costs. Currently, heating pool water may be accomplished with several different types of equipment, operating with a variety of fuel or energy sources. There are self-contained heaters that use natural gas, liquified petroleum (bottled gas), oil, and electricity. These units have their own burners or heating elements and heat exchangers within one compact unit. Self-contained heaters usually are equipped with controls to guarantee "fail-safe" operation. These devices will shut down the burners in the event of excessive temperature or low pressure caused by reduced flow in the recirculation system. Pool heating may also be achieved by means of separate heat exchangers working in conjunction with a centralized heating plant. With the tremendous rise in energy cost and the scarcity of some fuels, more people are depending upon solar energy as the solution to heating pool water. (See chapter 17 for a full discussion of the subject of solar energy.)

Outdoor pools are heated by self-contained units, which are quite compact and have relatively simple installation requirements. The choice of fuel or energy source is more often a matter of availability than of economics. Where available, natural gas seems to be the most advantageous. Units operating on bottled gas should be considered only for the smaller outdoor pool because operating costs with bottled gas are considerably higher than with other fuels. In addition, rather large, buried storage tanks are required as well as frequent gas deliveries. Oil is usually available as a fuel and affords operating economy; however, oil-fired units are generally more expensive in terms of initial cost. Because such a heater requires a fuel injector and a forced draft system, it is more expensive than a gas-fired unit. Heaters operated by electrical energy are available, but practical problems have precluded their use to any large extent. The power requirements necessitate a substantial service entrance and panelboard. As a result, the use of electrically operated pool heaters has been restricted to relatively small pools.

Self-contained heating units operating with gas or oil fuel are available in sizes up to 7,000,000 BTU per hour input. They are usually installed on the return line between the filter and the pool. The plumbing work consists of connections between

Pool water heater by Teledyne Laars

the return line and the inlet and outlet ports of the heater. A fuel line—for either gas or oil—must also be installed between the source and the heater. No outside electrical connections, except for oil-fired units, are required. They are usually shipped completely assembled with all controls and safety devices installed at the factory.

For indoor pools, the choice of heating units is somewhat wider. A central heating plant provides heat for the enclosing structure, permitting a choice between a self-contained heating unit and a heat exchanger. The heat exchanger is a unit in which one coil or circuit receives hot water or steam from the central heating plant while a second coil or circuit receives pool water from the recirculation system. A heat transfer takes place between the two, resulting in a rise of temperature of the pool water.

A heat exchanger is a simpler and more economical device than a self-contained heating unit. However, several factors must be considered in weighing the economics of one versus the other. The capacity of the central heating plant must be such that it can handle the requirements of both the pool enclosure and the pool water. Also, there is considerably more plumbing involved in the installation of a heat exchanger, particularly if the filter and the central heating plant are at a distance from each other.

The sizing of the heater for a particular pool is based upon several factors. The heat loss from a pool depends upon the surface area of the pool, the temperature differential between air and water, and the wind velocity. To maintain the pool water at a constant temperature, only the heat loss must be replaced. However, the heater must also be large enough to heat the pool water from its temperature at the time of filling to the desired temperature. The heater should be capable of bringing the fresh water up to the desired temperature within a 24-hour period. Most manufacturers of self-contained heating units have prepared charts that relate the unit to the desired temperature rise and the pool surface area in square feet. The desired temperature rise is defined as the difference between the average air temperature during the coldest month that the pool is operated and the desired temperature of the water. (Average mean air temperatures can be obtained from the local weather department.) In cooler climates, this figure is usually 15 to 25 °F; in southern climates, 10 to 15 °F. For indoor pools, where the air is heated, this difference is quite small, usually about 5 to 10°.

Another method of sizing heaters, which provides results fairly close to those of the first method, is on the basis of ability to heat the pool water at the rate of about 1 °F per hour. For indoor pools, where the heat losses are considerably smaller, the heater should be capable of heating the pool water at the rate of 1/2 °F per hour. (A BTU is defined as the amount of heat necessary to raise the temperature of 1 pound of water 1 °F.)

Pool heaters have proven to be reliable, efficient, economical, and highly desirable for swimmer comfort. They also have been advantageous in pools used for instruction of children. With the wide variety of models and sizes available, pool heaters have become an almost indispensable accessory for the well-designed and well-managed pool. Sufficient technical data are available from the manufacturers of such units to assure proper selection and satisfactory operation.

Maintenance Equipment

Maintenance equipment includes all the equipment and accessories used to clean the pool, not including the filtration equipment or chemical feeders. Maintenance equipment may be supplied by the pool management and need not be included as part of the pool contract.

Vacuum Cleaner

All pools accumulate dirt and debris on the bottom, brought into the pool by wind, rain, and bathers. The finer particles of dirt remain in suspension and eventually are removed by the filter; however, most of the dirt sinks to the floor of the pool, and normally is not dislodged by the recir-

Portable vacuum system by Kiefer

culating currents within the pool. This dirt must be removed by a vacuum cleaner or automatic pool cleaner by brushing or by skimming.

The vacuum cleaner consists of a vacuum head that rolls on the floor of the pool and that is operated by a long pole or by a tow rope. A length of floating suction hose is attached to the head. The other end of the suction hose can be attached to a vacuum fitting and piped to the recirculating pump or to a portable pump. The water enters the vacuum head, which is being moved over the pool floor with sufficient velocity to carry the dirt, silt, and sediment with it. If this water is fed into the filtration system of the pool, it is eventually returned to the pool. Pools of 50 or less feet in width can use a vacuum head operated by long poles. For larger pools, a tow-type vacuum cleaner or an automatic pool cleaner is necessary. The tow-type vacuum cleaners require two people for operation and must be worked blind over most of the floor surface, which is a distinct disadvantage.

Automatic Pool Cleaners

Several types of automatic pool cleaners are available. One type is an integral motor and pump unit that crawls over the bottom surface of the pool. This cleaner wanders in an erratic pattern over the floor of the pool and sucks up water and dirt. The built-in cartridge filter removes the sediment, and the water returns to the pool. This type of device is provided with a sensor that causes the cleaner to turn and start whenever it hits a pool wall. In the course of a night's operation, it covers the entire floor surface. (*Note:* Because this type of cleaner operates electrically, it should be used only at night when no one is in the pool.)

A second type of automatic pool cleaner, a floating cleaner, is powered by water pressure and moves about the surface of the pool. Long, flexible tubes are attached to the floating unit, and the ejection of water from nozzles at the top flail the tubes over the pool floor. The action of these tubes stirs up the dirt and debris, keeping them in suspension until they are removed by drains and skimmer, and so feed into the filter system. This type of cleaner needs an auxiliary pump to supply the pressure necessary for operation. Although swimmers may be in the pool while this cleaner is in use, it works best if the pool is empty during its operation.

Two types of automatic pool cleaners may be built into the pool shell. One consists of flexible tubes that whip about and move dirt and sediment

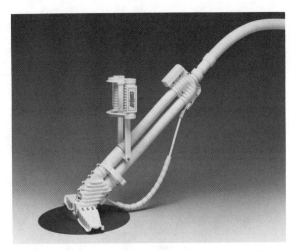

The Kreepy Krauly automatic vacuum cleaner. Photo by Jeff Smith.

toward the main outlet. The tubes retract completely into the walls when not in use. The other type uses inlet fittings of specified intervals around the lower pool walls and pool floor. Water pressure forces the sediment toward the main outlet.

Hand Skimmers

A hand skimmer, a frame with some type of netting plus a long pole, is used to remove larger debris such as leaves that float on the surface of the water or rest on the pool floor. Hand skimmers are essential for outdoor pool operations where debris is constantly being blown onto the water's surface.

Brushes

Brushes are available in various styles for cleaning floors and walls. Prior to vacuuming, walls should be brushed to remove dirt or algae. The floors may also be brushed to move the sediment toward the main drain where it is caught by the recirculating currents. However, brushing tends to raise large amounts of dirt, causing turbidity that may take considerable time to settle.

Test Kits

A test kit is essential for checking various chemical factors that control the chemical balance of the pool. Among these factors are residual chlorine, pH, and total alkalinity. There are also test kits for special chemical factors such as algicides in the

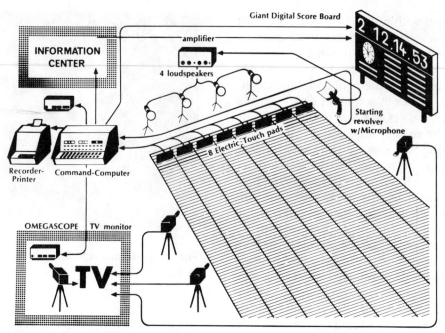

The Omega Swim-O-Matic Timing System, with an accuracy of .00001 second. Figure by Karl Heitz, Omega Electronics, New York City.

pool and cyanuric acid levels. All manufacturers offer combination test kits, which at least check the residual chlorine in the pool and the pH or alkalinity. Some also include a test for total alkalinity. The frequent use of a test kit indicates to the pool operator the need for adjusting chemical feed rates in order to maintain the chemical balance of the pool. (See chapter 13 on swimming pool chemistry for a fuller discussion of testing procedures.)

Instructional and Conditioning Equipment

Instructional equipment is usually purchased by the pool management as training aids for teaching swimming and for use by a swimming team during practice. Listed below are the items usually purchased by the pool administration on the recommendation of teachers and coaches.

The type of instructional equipment needed depends somewhat upon the method of instruction employed and the activities to be taught.

- Kickboards (flutter boards)
- Surfboards
- Swim goggles
- Hand paddles

- Nose clips
- Trainer tubes
- Swim fins
- Wet suits
- Scuba equipment (tanks, regulators, etc.)
- Special flotation devices
- Bulletin boards
- Whistles
- Megaphone (electronic)
- Turntable for playing records
- PA system
- Underwater speakers

Equipment for competition and physical conditioning include the following:

- Surface racing lines
- Recall line
- Backstroke turning indicator
- Stop watches
- Starting blocks
- Score board
- Timing devices
- Pace clock

Portable water polo goal by Kiefer

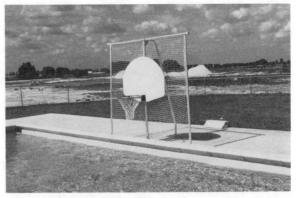

Water basketball backstop by Jayfro

- Racks for storing surface racing lines
- Wall pulleys
- Conditioning equipment (bar bells, universal gym, etc.)
- Video camera and monitor
- Score books for meets

Recreation Equipment

Most of the recreation equipment is supplied by pool management. The type of equipment purchased depends upon whether the pool is an indoor or outdoor one, the size of the pool, and the program to be conducted. An indication of some of the types of recreation equipment is listed as follows. Many of the instructional items may also be used in recreational swimming.

- Canoes
- Boats (dinghies, sailing prams, sailfish)
- Surfboards
- Basketball back stops
- Water volleyball
- Balls of different sizes
- Scuba equipment
- Snorkels
- Masks
- Swim fins
- Water polo goals

All equipment used in or around the pool should be inspected regularly, some even daily. Faulty or broken equipment may result in accidents; therefore, it is essential to take the time necessary to assure they are in proper working order.

Louisiana State University Natatorium, Baton Rouge

Chapter 11
Pool Design

The preceding chapters outline the steps involved in the overall planning of a swimming pool. During the schematic design and planning phase, or preliminaries, the professional designer in concert with the owner, prepares a design program. After approval by the owner's staff, this document provides guidance to the architect or engineer in preparing the contract documents, the plans, and the specifications. Specific dimensions and the actual shape of the pool are determined by the activities that will be conducted in the pool and by program activities that will take place on the surrounding deck area. (See Appendix A, Establishing a Pool Design Program.)

In the past pool designers were influenced by the rules and specifications for competitive swimming published by USS, USD, NCAA, NFSHSA, and FINA. (See Appendix C for addresses of these ruling bodies.) Meeting these standards for competitive swimming in conventional rectangular pools resulted in the compromising of other activity program needs. Where noncompetitive program needs were the dominant factor, the pool often ended up being "nonregulation" with respect to competitive swimming standards.

The problem of trying to meet all user and owner program needs continues to confront pool designers. Furthermore, it varies now between current competitive requirements promulgated by official organizations. When pool designers are also required to meet Olympic or international (FINA) competitive specifications, design accommodation can become extremely difficult. Basic design characteristics for swimming and diving competition that should be acceptable to all governing bodies have been described in chapter 14. Planners should follow these recommendations whenever possible.

The governing bodies for competitive swimming, however, are not the only groups that exert influence on pool designs. The major legal authority is the local or state board of health. These agencies publish various swimming pool codes to which the operation of all pools under their jurisdiction must conform. Local boards of health are guided by suggestions in the publications of the American Public Health Association (1985), whose Joint Committee prepared the booklet *Suggested Ordinances and Regulations Governing Public Swimming Pools*. The National Spa and Pool Institute (NSPI, 1985) has developed *Suggested Minimum Standards* for the design and construction of pools. The NSPI publishes suggested standards to guide its members and other pool builders, manufacturers, code authorities, and architects/engineers in the planning, design, and construction of swimming pools. There are separate, different standards for residential and nonresidential pools.

The trend today in community pool planning is to downplay or minimize the competitive swimming standards in favor of the need to provide recreational pools to better meet the needs of the general public—from the toddler to the senior citizen. Both needs, however, may be met by prudent planning. The rapid growth of the age group and Masters competitive swimming programs and the success of United States swimmers and divers in modern Olympics promote the need for better competitive pools and training facilities.

Another problem arises from the fact that architects too often design pools and natatoriums from a purely aesthetic point of view, ignoring the basic design principle that "form follows function." Sometimes planning goes to the other extreme. One such example is the International Swimming Hall of Fame pool in Fort Lauderdale, Florida. Faced with meeting the requirements for high-level competition (national and international), its two pools ended up with over 75% of their water area having a depth in excess of 5 feet, which reduced the potential value of the pool as a recreational facility.

The "multiple pool" concept appears to be the best solution to the problem of meeting all program needs. The Boys Clubs of America initiated this concept in the 1930s when they introduced the T-shaped or multiuse pool, which set off the diving area from the general swimming area. About the same time, New York City- and Chicago-area developments introduced a type of large, multiple-pool complex that provided a separate deep water tank for diving and other activities requiring water depths in excess of 5 feet, along with a separate wading pool and a large shallow water recreation pool.

The various factors that influence pool design will be discussed in this chapter. The discrepancies among various groups who "suggest" or "specify" certain standards will be identified, and certain logical compromises will be proposed.

Establishing Pool Size

The most important factor in determining the size of a swimming pool is the number of people to be served at the peak period of use (peak load). The maximum or peak demand is not always the best to use for planning purposes because it probably will occur only two or three times a summer. Even Long Island's famous Jones Beach, with a seemingly unlimited capacity, must close its gates on certain days—not because of shortage of beach area, but because of limited available parking spaces and servicing facilities. Jones Beach officials would rather have a capacity of 250,000 people, which meets the demand 98% of the time, than to overbuild and have acres of unused parking spaces most of the time. Few cities, particularly those with populations in excess of 100,000, have enough swimming facilities to meet the peak demand of the public.

A pool with a capacity of 1,000 (pool plus deck area) may serve between 4,000 and 6,000 people during the course of a day, particularly in hot weather. The question of how large to make a pool and still have a manageable facility has perplexed planners for years. When the capacity of a pool complex (pool and deck areas) exceeds 2,500, it creates a serious problem of management and supervision. At this point, it is better to begin to think in terms of a second facility in another location rather than exceed the 2,500 maximum.

Calculating Pool Capacity

In previous years a suggested standard for determining the capacity of a pool was 27 square feet of water surface area per person. A pool 75 feet by 45 feet would accommodate 135 people. However, this guideline fails to consider the type of activity conducted in the pool. To teach beginners requires more space than is required for ordinary swimmers, whereas divers require the greatest amount of water area. Each pool must be rated separately; relative proportions of shallow and deep water areas must be considered.

Table 11.1 provides a guide for determining the maximum safe capacity of any specific pool. However, communities must follow local health department regulations where these exist or obtain

Table 11.1 Maximum Safe Pool Capacity
(square feet per bather)

Activity	Indoor Pools	Outdoor Pools
Shallow water, under 5 ft		
Recreational swimming		
Beginning swimming instruction	40	45
Advanced swimming instruction	20	25
Deep water, over 5 ft		
Advanced recreational swimming	20	25
Diving, area within 30 ft of		
deep end diving wall	175	200

Note: From *Planning areas of facilities for health, physical education, and recreation* by Athletic Institute and the American Alliance for Health, Physical Education and Recreation, 1965. Reston, VA: AAHPER. Used with permission.

specific approval if they want to allow more people to use the pool than is prescribed in the health code.

Sample analysis of pool usage and capacity.
Capacity and usage for a pool in a community of about 17,500 people are analyzed here. Based on a subscribed membership of 1,260 families, the total number of potential users of the pool is 5,859 (4.65 users per family). It is interesting to note that the figure represents about 32% of the population. It is essential to plan facilities to meet the anticipated peak use of the pool; therefore, two questions regarding the capacity of the pool must be answered. The answers to the following questions should guide the administration and operation of the pool:

1. What is the safe, legal capacity of the swimming pools (actual bathers in the water)?

2. What is the recommended safe capacity of the total area of the pool complex?

Regulations Concerning the Safe, Legal Capacity of the Pools

The legal authority governing pool capacities in this example is the Sanitary Code of the State of New York. This code specifies the maximum pool capacity at any time to be one bather per 25 square

feet of water surface in the pool. In further interpretation of the previous regulations, Bulletin 27 on *The Operation of Swimming Pools and Beaches,* issued by the New York Superintendent of Health's Division of Environmental Health Services as far back as 1962 stated:

Experience has shown that many bathers actually are in the water for only a fraction of the time that they frequent a pool; consequently, the total number of bathers using all pool facilities may be considerably greater than the number actually bathing or swimming at one time.

This interpretation implies a judgment on the part of the designer regarding the safe capacity of the total area of the pool complex. It becomes obvious that certain basic assumptions as well as an estimation of usage must be made. In this example, the consulting engineer offered the following as a guide to the establishment of operating policies for the pool:

Underlying Assumptions Regarding Usage

1. Membership-type pools have greater use than daily admission pools.

2. The beauty of the facility's architectural statement and the availability of supporting facilities will affect the interest in and use of the pool.

3. The type of operating program offered by the pool may greatly affect the attendance.

4. In order to sustain interest in a pool over a 20-year period, a well-conceived and executed design program is essential.

5. The higher the atmospheric temperature, the greater is the use of the pool.

6. Children and youth are the greatest users of swimming facilities.

7. The more sophisticated and diversified the facilities, the longer people will stay in the pool.

8. Swimming after dusk is never as popular as daytime swimming.

9. People prefer to swim in warm water (82-85 °F) rather than cold water. However, the hotter the atmospheric temperature, the cooler the water may be. With an air temperature of 90 °F or above, the water in outdoor pools can be at least 10 °F cooler. (For indoor pools, an air temperature 5 °F warmer than the water is desirable.)

10. The success of any pool depends on the quality of the management running the pool.

11. Peak use of the pool can be expected to occur on weekends and holidays.

Anticipated Pool Attendance (Based on 5,860 potential users)

- Monday through Friday, 12 hours of operation. Average daily attendance (50% of 5,860)   2,930

- Peak daily attendance (60% of 2,930; 1,758 is about 30% of the 5,860 membership)   1,758

- Saturday and Sunday and extremely hot days, 12 hours of operation. Average daily attendance (75% of 5,860)   4,395

- Peak attendance (60% of 4,395; 45% membership)   2,637

- Estimated number expected to use the pool at one time (25% of 2,637; 11.2% membership)   660

Summary

The pool complex planned should be designed so that it will have a safe capacity of 660 people in the water. Deck space and supplemental facilities, including the bathhouse, must be able to accommodate an additional 1,977 people.

Legal Capacity of the Planned Pool Facilities

1. Main Pool:
   - Water surface area—12,375 sq ft
   - Capacity based on 25 sq ft per bather   495

2. Diving and deep water well:
   - Water surface area—60 ft by 45 ft = 2,700 sq ft
   - Capacity for diving (6 boards), 1 diver for each board plus 6 waiting to dive   42
   - Capacity when pool is used for general swimming with no diving permitted, based on 25 sq ft per swimmer   108

3. Training and orientation pools:
   - Orientation pool—800 sq ft; capacity based on 25 sq ft per swimmer   32
   - Training pool—1,000 sq ft; capacity based on 25 sq ft per swimmer   40

Total Legal Capacity
All Pools: 609-675 Bathers

Capacity of Balance of Area Within Pool Complex

The total estimated area within the pool complex is 4 acres. By deducting the area of the pools, the remaining area is 3.25 acres. The distribution of the 3.25 acres and the projected user capacity are as follows:

- 1 acre for picnic area; 43,000 sq ft at 100 sq ft per person   430

- 1 acre for lounging and sunning; 43,000 sq ft at 33 sq ft per person   1,303

- 1 acre for traffic areas around facilities; 43,000 sq ft at 200 sq ft per person   215

- .25 acre for children's play area; 11,000 sq ft at 100 sq ft per child   110

Total (not bathing)   2,058

Number in pools   675

Total capacity of complex   2,733

Conclusion

The pool complex as planned is capable of accommodating the peak load of swimmers expected from 1,260 family memberships. The number of people that may be accommodated within the bathhouse is not included in the above calculations. When the capacity of the bathhouse is included in calculating the ultimate safe capacity of the complex, an additional 50 families may be included.

The major responsibility of the pool manager is not to allow more than 675 people in the pool at one time.

Pool Design Factors

In addition to the steps involved in pool planning that determine aquatic program needs, some of the program elements must be translated into design characteristics. When establishing design criteria, three major aquatic use areas must be considered. These areas are for *competitive* swimming, *recreational* swimming, and *educational* swimming activities. Their ranking in order of importance should be established by the owner. Any major pool project will usually include design provisions for all three aquatic use interests.

Competitive Swimming Requirements

Design requirements for competitive swimming are covered in detail in chapter 14. Planners of new pools must decide for what level of competition the pool is to be designed and plan accordingly.

Recreational Swimming Requirements

When a pool must serve the total recreational needs of a community, its design is greatly affected. Preschool children cannot readily be accommodated in the same water depths that are required for competitive swimming. Some requirements pools must meet if they are to serve recreational swimming needs are as follows:

1. A greater proportion of shallow water for general swimming (up to 80% of the water area) should be less than 5 feet deep.

2. There should be large recessed (built-in) steps leading from the deck into the pool to accommodate the handicapped and elderly. A gradually inclined ramp with a handrail makes it possible for many people who cannot negotiate steps to use the pool.

3. The temperature of the water should be maintained at levels up to 86 °F, and deeper water should be provided in warm climates to keep the greater water mass cooler (i.e., shallow water masses warm up faster than deep water volumes).

4. Low diving boards (or deck-level boards 12 inches to 18 inches above water) and platforms should be provided for young children.

5. A deep water well should be provided for regular and scuba diving.

6. Special lift chairs may be needed to enable disabled children and adults to enter the pool.

7. The ratio of deck space to water area should preferably be no less than shown in Figure 11.1, based on pool size and type (i.e., indoor or outdoor).

Educational Swimming Requirements

1. Separate teaching stations should be arranged with float lines across the pool for classes of different ability levels.

2. A special warm pool section (86 to 92 °F) should be available for preschool children, senior citizens, and adapted aquatics programs.

3. Special underwater lighting and sound system capabilities should be installed for synchronized swimming.

4. Adequate deck space should be provided for class instruction and "dry-drill" exercises, including capacities for teaching aids, seating, lighting, and heating controls.

5. Storage areas should be available for large equipment (e.g., canoes, boats, kayaks, lane lines with floats).

Other Program Requirements

There probably will be a number of other design program requirements. Each should be checked to determine the design requirements that must be met. Some requirements are as follows:

1. *Instruction:* Shallow water (maximum of 5 feet) with a training pool for nonswimmers, ranging in depth from 2 to 4 feet. Variable depth bottom schemes allow multilevel pool activities in a common pool.

2. *Lifesaving and Water Safety Instruction:* No specific needs; however, it is desirable to have some deep water.

3. *Synchronized Swimming:* 2,000 to 3,000 square feet of water area over 6 feet in depth; underwater speakers and lights; overhead flood and spotlights.

4. *Water Shows:* Spotlights, floodlights, and underwater lights; area for permanent or portable stage.

5. *Water Polo:* Special deck and pool markings; minimum of 6-foot depth of water throughout playing area; receptacles (anchor sockets) to take goal nets.

6. *Safety Equipment:* Lifeguard chairs; racks for hanging ring buoys and reaching poles; spine

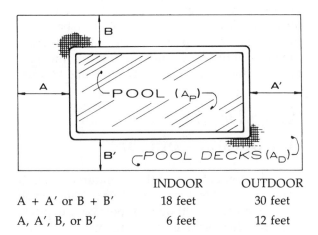

	INDOOR	OUTDOOR
A + A' or B + B'	18 feet	30 feet
A, A', B, or B'	6 feet	12 feet

Figure 11.1 Minimum pool deck dimensions

board; CPR equipment at pool manager's office; intercom/telephone in pool area and at each lifeguard chair.

Administrative and Supplemental Facilities

The requirements of any aquatic facility dictate the architectural arrangement of management elements and resources that are particular to local needs, available site restrictions, and budget. Prime factors should include the following:

1. Manager's office, locker area, toilet, and first aid

2. Control booth (cash booth where used)

3. Deck-accessible storage for large equipment (e.g., canoes, boats, racing line/float reels, game nets, and goals)

4. Remote storage for teaching aids, special program support equipment, regularly used equipment, additional deck seating, and lighting equipment

5. Steam and sauna rooms, suntan areas, spa or therapy whirlpool

6. Audio intercom system (local communication and control)

7. Lighting and special effects for games and shows

8. Direct emergency telephone

9. Trauma evacuation plan; emergency vehicle access

An optimum community pool complex must have at least two or more separate pools, or a combination with two or more separate pool areas for a full competitive swim program—one for swimming and one for diving and games. An optimum community recreational complex requires four pools: a main swimming pool (5 ft deep) for general swimming activities; a diving pool; a training pool for 3- to 5-year-olds; and an orientation (wading) pool for toddlers to 2-1/2-year-olds. If only a single pool is provided, a compromise in design program accommodations must be determined at the earliest planning stages.

Pool Shapes

Pool form must follow the functions outlined above to satisfy competitive, recreational, and educational requirements. For simplicity, this usually dictates rectangular form(s) or a combination for public pool designs because of the competitive requirement for parallel end walls (see Figure 11.2).

Many free-form shapes have been designed for residential, motel, and hotel pools. Hotel pools usually simplify to free-forms, "Ts" or "Ls." From these evolve the "lazy-L," "H," "fan," "boomerang," and "trapezoid"—a multiplicity of designs based on architectural choice and setting.

The trend since the 1950s has been the development of highly stylized (free-form) pools for private residences, motels, and hotels. Many of these are interesting and fit the surrounding decor, but few are functional athletic swimming facilities (although they will serve private recreational requirements well).

In the case of country clubs, apartment houses, and motels, uniquely shaped pools may provide diving, swimming, and wading areas requiring a minimum of supervision during periods of light bathing load and offer an economical approach to diverse swimming facilities for overall use. The municipal multiple-pool complex, however, is safer for heavy bather-load services.

On close examination, the more elaborate shapes are combined pool forms. The L-shaped pools are really two rectangular pools with a common wall omitted where they come in contact; Z-shaped pools are three rectangular pools with two common walls omitted; and so forth. In general, the large water surfaces created by these shapes introduce safety control problems that offset the apparent savings of the common wall omission. Pool programs are usually better served by separating the areas. Clear, paved deck space around such multiple pools is usually kept to a minimum for outdoor pools (see Figure 11.1). The result is an efficient and safe traffic pattern. For indoor pools the minimum clear walk space between pools should be 8 feet. Multiple pools can be better supervised and can better serve the differing aquatic ability levels and interests of the participants than can single, large, combined forms.

Water Depths and Bottom Contours

For the competitive pool, the minimum depth required is 3-1/2 feet and should be specified in all new construction, although 4-foot water depth is preferable for regional competition.

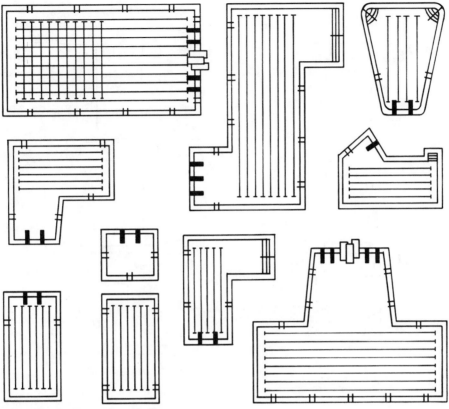

Figure 11.2 Typical pool shapes

For junior pools, serving the 6 and under age group, two types are favored. A familiarization pool serves the youngest bathers (toddlers to 3-year-olds) and should vary in depth from 6 inches to no more than 20 inches. The bottom slope of these pools should not be steeper than 1:15 for comfort and safety. It should be possible to enter the water readily from the deck, with the overflow or deck at pool level, but certainly no more than step-riser height of 6 inches above the water for convenient and safe access/egress to the pool by this age group.

For the preschool age group (4 to 6 years) an instructional or training pool with water depths from 2-1/2 feet to 4 feet best serves their aquatic program requirements. The bottom slope of this pool should not be steeper than 1:12, and preferably 1:15.

Depths for the main swimming pool are determined by the program requirements; for general swimming, water depth should range from approximately 3-1/2 feet or 4 feet to 5 feet or at most, 6 feet at the deepest part. The bottom should pitch uniformly and constantly at a sloped rate preferably 1:20 for maximum safety and comfort of the general bathing public, although steeper slopes as high as 1:15 may be allowed. For all pools, the bottom at all points must have some pitch, however slight, uniformly inclined to ensure complete drainage to the main drain location.

Perimeter Overflow Systems

Perimeter overflow designs have evolved through the years to meet design, hydraulic, and economic optimums. Hydraulic systems are reviewed in the next chapter, offering a complete review of pool surface water flow at the rim. Basic overflow techniques available to the designer include *fully recessed* overflows, *partially recessed, rollout, rimflow* construction, and *surface skimmers* (see Figure 11.3). On all pools, the overflow is used for skimming the water and removing the surface film. It is important that overflows be installed with the skimming rim dead level for maximum effectiveness (except on smaller pools where skimmers are allowed).

Perimeter overflow systems have developed greatly over the years from the *scum gutter*, which was merely a collection trough around the perimeter of the pool to collect dirty overflow water and promote gravity drainage of the skimmed pool

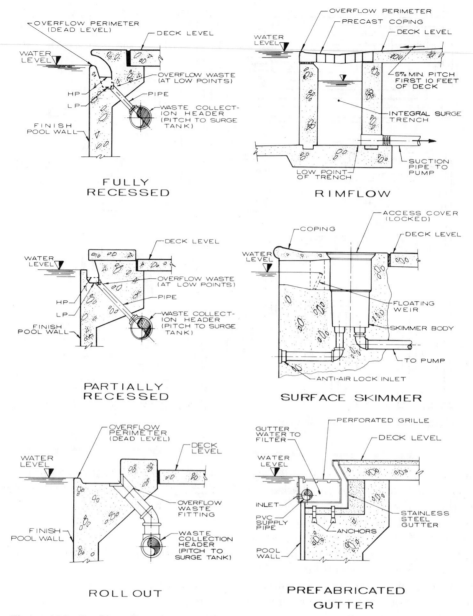

Figure 11.3 Pool overflow rim systems

surface water to the waste line. This meant that during use of the pool by bathers (BA or bathing period) and even with adverse winds, pool surface water flowed over the rim and was wasted. Unless the pool was kept continuously filled, the overflow system did not operate satisfactorily for continuous skimming of the pool and for removal of surface matter that interfered with the pool's hygienic condition.

During the late 1920s and early 1930s, attempts were made to recirculate gutter water by collect-ing it on the suction side of the pump, either through direct plumbing connection (poor hydraulic practice) or with a "balancing tank" that made little provision for adequately storing displacement water created by the bathers. Later developments provided for throttling the main drain water into a collection sump and allowing pool surface overflow water to cascade into the sump, thereby pumping the overflow water back to the pool through the recirculating system. Adequate surge water storage for bather displacement was again not provided, but the arrangement did allow the gutter system to operate with partial efficiency of pool return.

As the industry developed in the 1930s, the Boys Clubs developed a *deck-level* system using a collection trough, with cast stones installed around the perimeter of the pool, which was a slotted, stone-covered trench. Rim overflow water was conducted back to a detention tank, providing a fully recirculating overflow system together with throttling a portion of the main drain water so that a combination of both was available. This proved quite satisfactory, economical, and reliable. In 1984, a system at an outdoor pool constructed for a Connecticut Boys Club 30 years earlier was still in working order. Because the walkways around the pool drained into this collection trough, it was necessary to make sure the decks were washed down with proper disinfectants and nonfoaming detergents.

In the late 1950s surface skimmers were developed for residential swimming pools. These contained individual floating weirs 8 to 12 inches long and were placed around the perimeter of the pool to provide a unit for each 500 to 800 square feet of surface area. Skimmer units included collection baskets permitting removal of larger surface debris floating in the pool without overloading the strainer basket at the suction of the pump, eliminating the need to shut down the recirculating equipment for cleaning. Floating weirs also allow bather displacement water to be stored in the pool so that they operate both during periods of use and nonuse. There was and still remains, however, considerable resistance on the part of various state health departments to accept surface skimmers for public pools in lieu of the continuous (traditional) perimeter overflow system. For public swimming pools, skimmers are usually limited to pool sizes not exceeding 1,200 square feet (Iowa) to 2,000 square feet (New York). For larger pools their efficacy is questionable.

In the early 1970s the National Swimming Pool Institute (NSPI), in collaboration with the National Sanitation Foundation (NSF) in Ann Arbor, Michigan, formed a joint Swimming Pool Equipment Committee to develop standards for recirculation systems of swimming pools using surface skimmers. Their standards were given NSF approval for use in both public and residential swimming pools. Serious consideration was given to establishing a limit on the size of pools that could use

surface skimmers in lieu of perimeter overflow systems; however, no action was taken. The city of Los Angeles imposed a limitation of pool size not larger than 1,600 square feet as acceptable for the use of surface skimmers on public pools. The state of Florida does not accept surface skimmers for use in any public pools, regardless of size. There has been general acceptance of the use of surface skimmers for smaller public and semipublic pools and except in a few isolated cases, in residential pools as well. In the revision of the APHA (1985) Joint Committee Recommended Swimming Pool Ordinance and Code, the 1,600-square-foot limitation on the use of surface skimmers is endorsed.

In the mid-1960s and early 1970s, many developments led to greater utilization of the recirculating type perimeter overflow systems; and the use of built-in-place designs and prefabricated types was expanded. Because health authorities considered it advisable to have better documentation and test data regarding prefabricated units, a committee was formed in 1974 under the auspices of the NSF with the cooperation of the NSPI and with the participation of the various manufacturers of patented and prefabricated units. This committee reviewed performance of perimeter overflow systems through a subcommittee of public health officials and representatives of NSPI and the pool industry. Development of standards and test requirements for perimeter overflow systems, surface skimmers, and combinations of them provided a contribution to the state of the art. Much remains to be learned in the field of effective surface skimming and surface water flow dynamics. It is the designer's responsibility to consult with the local health authorities regarding existing regulations and to design a system that meets requirements for a satisfactory overflow system. This system must conform with local acceptable design practice and with those economical considerations necessary to optimize needs for surge volume accommodation in the recirculation hydraulics.

Recessed and Partially Recessed Overflows

Recessed and partially recessed overflows are the most difficult to install, especially as the deck height above the water is reduced to obtain more comfortable egress. Generally, the most expensive form to construct is the fully recessed gutter; the partially recessed gutter is slightly less expensive and easier to maintain. The fully recessed form is safer to use than the modified section, which has the potential for entrapment of limbs. Most coaches prefer an overflow with an elevated deck, but this tendency is diminished in view of the cost advantages of newer overflow methods.

Eliminating surface roughness is an important consideration in competitive pools; for this reason, it is necessary to use a full recess with a deep and extensive receiving trough to absorb waves and to quell the water surface when this overflow is used. The main pool at Indiana University-Purdue University at Indianapolis (IUPUI) is built this way. The 50-meter training pool, however, uses the deck-level (rimflow) method described next. If a large hydraulic receiving trough is not used with recessed overflow constructions, then it is necessary to pipe the gutter overflow to a separate surge tank of adequate size. The Chicago Circle Campus of the University of Illinois has pools exemplifying this construction technique.

Rimflow Construction

Rimflow construction is appropriate for recreational and educational pool use. This method was developed in 1968 for the Intramural-Physical Education (IMPE) sports complex containing two 50-meter pools at the University of Illinois, Champaign-Urbana campus. In 1977 the University of Texas at Austin chose this construction method for their 50-meter indoor swimming facility—an exclusive world-class natatorium—one of the few pool buildings in the world dedicated exclusively to international championship swimming.

Rimflow construction provides a deck-level pool, allowing the most comfortable pool use for recreational, educational, and competitive activities. The integral surge tank serves to eliminate surface roughness that develops with other forms of overflow construction due to wave rebound. Because of this wave-quelling feature, all four pools at the XX Olympiad in Munich, 1972, were designed for the first time in Olympic history as deck-level (rimflow) facilities. (For a discussion of rimflow control of natatorium psychrometrics, refer to chapter 15.)

Previously, older deck-level pool designs resulted in wet decks, involving the first 10 to 12 feet of deck space adjacent to the pool; this has been corrected by specifying a slope of 3-1/2 to 5%. This positive, one-directional slope makes it possible to eliminate expensive buried deck drainage piping

at the immediate pool deck area contiguous with the rimflow stones, with the elimination also of undesirable and dangerous "birdbaths" by using a single direction of deck slope for these critical, potentially dangerous decks. For competition it is necessary to define the turning edge of rimflow and all deck-level pools. This is done in several manners and works well in combination with the use of judging and timing touchpads and starting blocks that are required when regulation meets are held.

Surface Skimmers

Surface skimmers are self-contained units built into the pool wall structure at intervals around the pool. This overflow type eliminates expensive forming of the pool top wall. Cover plates set in the deck provide access to the skimmer body. There are several variations of this type, affording a freeboard of some 6 inches between the water level and the pool deck. Wave action is most severe with this overflow method, and their use is usually restricted in public pools to smaller construction as noted previously. Serious injuries to bathers have resulted when the top cover plates of skimmer units were not securely locked into their deck frames.

Automatic surface skimmers do not require separate surge considerations because the water level will rise and fall well within the limits of the skimmer opening (which is self-compensating). The skimmer weirs, however, may impose maintenance problems and require external anti-air lock protectors for the suction pump lines. Skimmer units are limited for public pools as previously noted in this chapter.

Prefabricated Gutter

Prefabricated gutter cross sections of different manufactured types are shown in Figures 11.4a and 11.4b to illustrate this top wall attachment method. These steel forms have the advantage of permitting independent leveling when installed on a concrete or metal pool, minimizing the extreme care normally necessary in setting formed-in-place gutters. These units are generally made of stainless steel or aluminum, but the designer must be aware that the collection troughs are generally of insufficient flow capacity to take the full quantity of recirculated water under gravity flow conditions of open channel flow. Collection troughs should be designed accordingly. On larger pools, in addition

Figure 11.4a Sylvan Pools' Speed-Flo gutter

to return water flow in the gutter, two or more large-diameter pipelines are required *external* to the gutter to handle the necessary pool water turnover. This results in higher construction costs, buried pipes, and potential piping problems that seriously negate the advantages of use claimed for the prefabricated gutters. In one system, a separate pump is also required to evacuate the flooded channel section: a questionable (long-term) use of energy for pumping water that bypasses the filters, the extra pump being required solely to correct the gutter flow deficiency. Prefabrication is always expensive—approximately twice (and even three times) the cost of other methods. Skilled labor trades are needed for field work or repairs.

It is also necessary with prefabricated gutters to install separate surge tanks for bather displacement in order to maintain continuous overflow of the sanitary skimming rim under all levels of bathing load. The serious pool designer is cautioned that so-called "in-pool" surge capacity is an impractical and unsatisfactory invention. There is no substitute for continuous, uniform skimming of the entire bounded water surface whether the pool is empty or is filled to capacity.

Roll-Out Gutter

The *roll-out gutter* is illustrated in Figure 11.3. This type has been used quite successfully and may be built-in-place or prefabricated. However, for competitive purposes platforms are necessary to define the pool limits at the competitive lanes. Care must be exercised to pitch the deck away from the pool to eliminate impounding of water when an elevated curb is required at the deck/gutter junction (as in the state of Florida). Surface texture of the horizontal, wet roll-out surface must be nonskid for safety since the bather usually steps

Figure 11.4b Whitten overflow and weir system

on the roll-out surface when entering or leaving the pool. This overflow system employs a separate surge tank in the traditional design method and works well for most pool designs.

Copings

The coping serves as a top or cap for the vertical wall, and generally forms part of the perimeter overflow system. However, coping is not used with attached metal gutters.

A well-designed coping must be of substantial, permanent material, have continuous surfaces without crevices or interior sharp corners, be *non-slip* when wet, be installed hydraulically true, provide a safety handhold from poolside, and be capable of being secured firmly to the pool shell. It should be frostproof when used on outdoor pools in freezing climates, must weather well, and last the lifetime of the pool.

Except for prefabricated metal overflow forms, almost all pools are finished with a tiled form for the coping, or cap, or a decorative precast shaped element. Precast stone construction offers a permanent, decorative, colorful finish. Cast stones are available for the many overflow forms, and when properly set, will last the lifetime of the pool. Cast stones are available in "high-tech" resin-concrete materials offering exceptional lifetime performance and a range of attractive colors. Chemical resistance of new products exceeds that of stainless steel. Structural strengths exceed the best concretes used in building construction by factors of 3 to 5, for long-term, maintenance-free ownership.

Precast concrete coping sections are available in sandcast forms, fiberglass, or metal molded finishes and can be found in a variety of colors, surface textures, aggregate detail, lengths, and widths. Lightweight resin-concrete products now allow use of some of these products at locations remote from the manufacturing plant, where higher shipping costs previously had been a drawback. New coping products have also been developed using lightweight shapes and materials, including aluminum, vinyl, and fiberglass and are available for residential and public pools.

When ceramic or quarry tile is used for public pool coping, standard tile shapes are available to the designer. These shapes are best installed in the "square edge" form to provide a smooth strike of the tile grouting, in order to obtain a uniformly smooth, sanitary surface. Tile is available in both unglazed and glazed finishes. In addition, small-percentage carborundum additives are available on specification for development of nonskid tiled surfaces. Tiled coping or deck installations require good craftsmanship and professional supervision to ensure a long-lasting finish.

Underwater Lights

Where underwater lighting is used fixtures and wiring must be installed in accordance with Article 680 of the National Electrical Code or to the stricter requirements that prevail in some localities. Consultation with the local inspection agency of the National Board of Fire Underwriters or other governing agencies should take place early during design planning to ensure operating approval.

The standard levels for general illumination have doubled every 10 years since 1920; however, no records are available on the trend in swimming pool lighting. It now appears that minimum energy values of 3.5 to 4.0 watts per square foot (using incandescent lamps) are required to provide the underwater lighting intensity needed for safe visibility requirements of a comprehensive aquatic program. Lower values of 0.75 to 1.50 watts per square foot, arbitrarily established by the pool industry, have been in common use for private (and semipublic pools) since 1970, but these values are much too low and dangerous for nighttime bathing, especially in residential pools.

The Illuminating Engineering Society (IES) recommendation has remained the same for the last quarter century and yields excellent and safe results. This recommendation is based more correctly on the lighting output (lumens) of the source rather than the energy input. This recommendation is related also to the surface area of the pool and requires 100 lumens per square foot for indoor

Figure 11.4c   Open gutter

Figure 11.4d Rimflow gutter system, University of Texas pool

pools and 60 lumens per square foot for outdoor pools. This is equivalent to a minimum reading on a light meter (photometer) of 100 and 60 foot-candles, respectively. (There are no underwater photometers.) By specifying luminous output rather than energy input, the pool designer can utilize more efficient lamps with higher output to advantage. For incandescent sources with an output of less than 20 lumens per watt, this indicates a design requirement, using incandescent lamp fixtures, of 3.5 to 5.0 watts per square foot. Obviously the development of underwater lighting fixtures using other lamp sources having higher lumen output would reduce the number of fixtures required for a given pool.

The IES recommendations seem to be most valid at this time, particularly in view of an increasing number of nighttime pool accidents. What appears to be needed by the designer is a volumetric method of calculation similar to "zonal cavity" computations now used in the lighting profession. Water volume, clarity, turbidity factors, and color have great influence on lighting levels throughout the pool shell, especially in the deep water and diving areas. More research is required as to how these factors affect design parameters. In the meantime, the underwater lighting designer should account for lumen reduction of the lamp considering the filament type, effectiveness of the fixture reflector, transmission illuminance loss due to uncleanliness of the glass and/or retaining

device, and other possible factors that reduce the maintained lumen output of underwater fixtures. Coefficients of Utilization (CU) in the range of 0.50 to 0.60 are recommended for designing safe pools when using the IES minimum published performance levels.

Placement of the lighting fixtures in the pool wall also has great influence on their effectiveness. Lighting fixtures should be at least 3 feet deep in the shallow areas and preferably 6 to 8 feet deep in the diving well, and they should be angled downward slightly. The use of a white interior finish optimizes light reflection and dispersion.

Colored underwater lighting should be avoided, although "white" lighting having a tinge of blue has been used successfully. Amber lighting, for outdoor pools that are lit for nighttime or architectural interest only, is effective in minimizing insect attraction. Other colors are less effective and therefore less safe.

Television interest in swimming pool events naturally requires higher overall swimming hall and underwater lighting levels. However, the use of high-wattage incandescent room fixtures has proven extremely distracting to the swimmers and can cause great visual discomfort because of brightness and high-luminous contrast. A more uniform use of closely spaced fixtures, strip lighting, or indirect illumination where possible should be considered above the pools, preferably directed and controlled to light the decks. Glare is reduced and underwater lighting enhanced by the use of parabolic wedge louvers with high-output flourescent sources in dry-niche strip windows. One of the finest underwater lighting systems in a world-class pool facility is at the University of Texas at Austin Olympic Swim Center Natatorium. Lighting design in excess of 150 lumens/square feet is achieved using VHO (80 lumens/watt), high power factor fluorescent lamps. These lamps are recessed in dry niches through the pool wall, 6 feet below the pool rim, in a continuous double-row, lighting strip on all four sides of both pools (see Figure 11.5). For additional information on underwater lighting and related area lighting levels, see chapter 14.

Construction Materials and Techniques

Basic materials and general construction techniques used for swimming pool construction should represent an optimum in foundation design. Every pool shell is a foundation structure with water on the inside and sometimes on the outside, too. Severe groundwater conditions that

exist or may develop must be investigated for their effect on structural design choices.

The designer usually has a limited choice of materials and construction methods, especially when there are budget constraints. For each possible site, the particular soil mechanics should be thoroughly investigated during preliminary studies by an experienced soils investigation service. Certified boring logs indicate changes of stratum, spoon and casing blows at 5-foot intervals, elevation of the water table, percentage rock core recovery, characteristics of all formations and rock, and any irregularities of the natural substrates. Sometimes a small plastic pipe test well may be left in place to further check diurnal changes in the water table. At least two borings are needed for a reasonable analysis of the support stratum. Digging an open pit is a quick, simple method for obtaining soil samples.

After boring logs are interpreted, a pool shell construction should be designed that best satisfies the natural parameters. For elevated pools or interior building constructions, the primary structural framing system is the optimum method of construction. For concrete buildings, pools using concrete support beams and a poured reinforced concrete system are usually most appropriate.

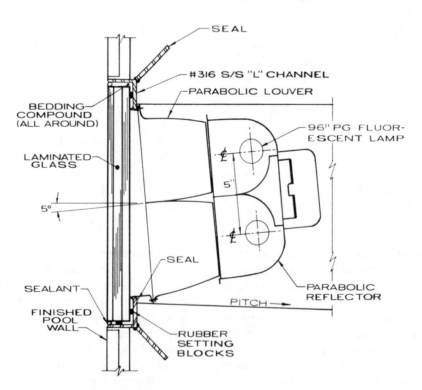

Figure 11.5 Underwater light fixture

With all-steel buildings, structural steel fabrication has many advantages. In-ground pools have been developed using many construction materials and techniques for the shell construction. Different pool construction and structural techniques are shown in Figure 11.6.

Poured reinforced *concrete pool shells* are durable and cost-effective. Pneumatically applied concrete (gunite) and other construction forms may prove to be more economical while providing the same substantial service characteristics under certain site conditions. Nonshrink concretes offer crack-free

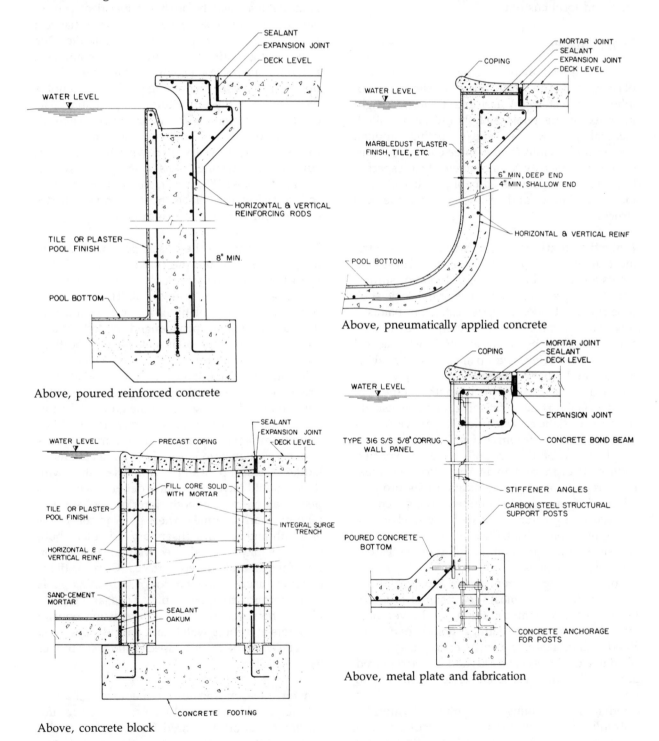

Above, poured reinforced concrete

Above, pneumatically applied concrete

Above, concrete block

Above, metal plate and fabrication

Figure 11.6 Pool wall construction methods

monolithic pours for 50-meter slabs, eliminating the installation of construction joints that require caulking and sealant, thus eliminating the servicing and leak potential. The decision regarding pool shell construction rests largely on site subsoil conditions and is influenced by the designer's preference and local custom.

Pool Finishes

Pool finishes may be classified as coatings, tile, plaster, or natural. Concrete pool shells are not inherently watertight and a test for watertight integrity of the pool shell should be specified. Generally, a two-part epoxy coating, applied greater than 10 mils (two to three coats), provides watertight integrity for a concrete shell, especially if the coating covers all pool-piercing fittings, niches, and pipes at their interface with the pool structure.

Protective coatings.　Protective *coatings* are the most diverse group of pool finishes. These materials are applied to the finished interior surface and fully reproduce the texture of the basic shell construction. Under the classification of ''paints,'' rubber-base applications are among the least costly and considered by many as the most practical short-term covering. Latex paints without noxious odors may be used effectively.

Care must be exercised in preparation of the pool interior shell surface for finishing. Concrete usually requires muriatic acid etch cleaning or even sandblasting. Coating systems having a minimum coating thickness of 15 to 50 mils have an expected service life of more than 5 years. However, inexpert preparation of the application may produce localized failures. Shell imperfections can be covered to a greater extent with the thicker system applications. Using silica quartz fines or other abrasives in the preparation will provide texture for nonslip finishes.

Coatings using neoprene rubber and hypalon are readily built up over most shell materials, regardless of surface or joint conditions, and cover most imperfections. (These coatings should not be confused with rubber-base paint.) Coatings may be applied in a thickness of 50 mils and can be replaced at the end of their expected service life of 5 to 10 years.

Other finish coatings use polyvinyl chloride, polysulphide, polyisoprene, polyurethane, and many new organic compounds to effect desir-able thick film qualities. Continued research and long-term field testing on all coating applications are required before comparative or optimum recommendations can be established. Many of the surface coatings have positive characteristics but require careful investigation with respect to substrate compatability before being specified. The advantage of these coatings is the lower initial cost when compared with permanent ceramic tile. One outstanding coating formulated from an aliphatic polyurethane polyester compound has been developed expressly for swimming pool use and holds promise as a tile substitute. Application costs (1986) of less than $1/sq ft are about one-fifth the price of tile. A 15-mil coating is expected to furnish 15 to 20 years of service life based on current field testing. This coating, known as ''Porcelaincote-S/P'' (manufactured by Fosroc Preco Industries), is available in white and six shades of blue and with nonslip additives.

Tile.　Tile remains the classic permanent swimming pool finish, but the cost of setting tile has restricted its use on many pools to a waterline band where service ability is essential. The long-term, service-free nature of tiling for indoor and outdoor pools remains unchallenged. Watertight and weatherproof (frostproof) installation specifications are available from the tile trade associations.

Square edge modules are recommended in preference to ''cushion-edge'' tiles to permit a smooth finishing strike of the tile grout. All floor-to-wall and also vertical inside corners should be at uniform radial curvature for sanitary purposes and ease of maintenance. Interior locations of ladder recesses, pool steps, and observation windows should have exact tiling details specified to permit an entirely smooth, interior pool surface, without sharp internal corners that can collect oils and filth and become unsanitary. Circular ''bubble'' tiles may be used effectively for installation on spherical and curved surfaces. Ceramic tile is generally used on the interior of swimming pools in preference to quarry tile. Tiles are usually glazed; however, tractive surfaces using nonslip elements at turning wall locations and steps must be detailed in the plans or specifications for proper use and safety.

Plaster.　Plaster finishes are medium-cost applications capable of 4 to 10 years of service life. Plaster mixes are prepared from hard, granular media; white cement; waterproofing; and plaster-hardening additives. Sometimes a light blue coloring is added. White silica sand may be used, although white "marbledust" or natural limestone fines may be employed with good effect. A brown sand truing coat of 1/4- to 3/4-inch thickness is usually applied first to the clean, rough shell surfaces, establishing a bond and truing the interior shell geometry. One or two hard, thin, white finish coats of the plaster are then placed as soon as possible. The plaster finish should be carefully cured under water for best results.

For long service it is best to avoid the use of strong acid solutions when cleaning plaster. Plaster finishes are indelibly stained by rusting hairpins and decaying organic matter such as leaves or windblown debris found in outdoor pools. Outdoor pools having plaster finishes must be covered during the off-season to protect the finish.

Other pool finishes. Natural or integral finishes are primary methods of ensuring low maintenance costs. Precast concrete sections having an integral mold-finished surface have been successfully used. Massive sections normally are shipped by truck to the job site, greatly reducing field work while providing a factory-finished pool face. After alignment and setting, the joints are caulked with one of many effective sealants now available for waterproof sealing.

Thin-set (approximately 1/4 inch) epoxy terrazzo and other topping finishes offer unusual permanence when applied to carbon steel or concrete pool shells. Several permanent epoxy matrix formulations in smooth or nonskid finishes can be used for trowel-on application. These products are available for use over concrete slabs for bathhouse and locker-room floors. These materials are useful for repair of deteriorated, existing construction.

Concrete pool bottoms poured with white sand, light-colored coarse aggregate, and white cement provide a pool finish with lifetime dependability. The white cement fines are carefully floated to the top by several passes of the steel trowel; then the required surface roughness is established for the bottom by brushing or float. Cleaning materials should be restricted to synthetic detergents; avoid acids. White toppings on an ordinary concrete base are also possible but require greater skill and labor, which may offset any material cost savings.

Thin-gauge construction featuring stainless steel or aluminum sidewalls and fittings offers permanently finished water surfaces for those pools where interior metal surfaces are not objectionable to the program requirements. Metal should be avoided in saltwater pools. All-metal pools are generally used for semipublic and smaller commercial installations.

Galvanic corrosion of aluminum pools in Michigan, Ohio, Alaska, and other locations in the country has raised concern about this type of pool. Cathodic protection using ribbons and bars of noble materials intended to protect the aluminum have not performed as specified; therefore, specific site conditions must be reviewed by experienced engineers familiar with local conditions before using this construction technique.

Pool finish color. Once the pool finish has been selected, color becomes an important consideration. For outdoor swimming pools, *white* is the only *color* that should be used. A light or medium blue (Munsell color No. 10B 7/8) may be used for pool walls, to enhance the water coloration. For junior pools only, a medium blue tile for walls and bottom is recommended and proves very effective. If a white coating or paint is used to finish an outdoor pool, it may tend to yellow after long exposure. A bluish white would be preferable for these applications. Avoid all other color applications of green, brown, or other dark colors.

For indoor pools, a dead-white color is best. Mosaic patterns or colors, other than light blue, should be avoided. Light blue ceilings for indoor pools with carefully controlled lighting sources can greatly improve the appearance of the filtered water.

It is important to note that properly filtered water is a monochromatic blue color: the deeper the water, the deeper the blue. The white finish, especially a reflective marbledust or coating, permits a greater degree of pool safety and maintenance of sanitary conditions than any other colored finish. A white finish also enhances natural light reflection, yielding the highly saturated blue chroma of excellent water.

Deck Area and Material Finishes

Outdoor pools require more space than indoor pools to accommodate their peak capacity, and decks should be sized no smaller than indicated in Figure 11.1. Deck-to-pool area ratios of 3:1 and 4:1 afford the most functional arrangements for handling peak summertime crowds. Decks are preferably located so that sunbathers are facing into the sun between noon and 4 p.m., while at the same time looking into the shallow pools and the main pool activities. This arrangement readily accommodates the diving section or a separate pool so that the high sun is oriented behind the diving boards (from the south). Generous deck widths are required behind diving stands. The recommended standards give the designer flexibility for arranging the decks so that outdoor walkways are never less than 12 feet wide. Large decks may be designed so as not to appear like overwhelming "seas of concrete" through the use of different textures and colors, arrangement of accessory planting, decorative walls, fountains, sunshades, and other vertical architectural elements.

Decks for outdoor pools require careful engineering and control during placement. Sufficient temperature reinforcements properly placed are a minimum requirement. Welded wire fabric road mesh (#44 × 44 WWF) or equivalent steel rods are appropriate for a typical 6-inch deck slab. Additional structural reinforcement of decks may also be required under specific construction conditions. Outdoor deck installations tend to settle into the area adjacent to the pool walls because of inadequate compaction practices. As previously discussed, a competent soil consultant can best advise on particular soil conditions, especially after review of the soil-boring data.

If at all possible, the construction schedule should allow for a maximum self-consolidation period after the pipe trenches are filled and before the decks nearest to the pool perimeter are to be poured. If the decks are to be supported on the pool wall, the design should not assume any subsoil support. The deck and pool wall should instead be made entirely independent and structurally secure. In certain soils, a 2-foot overburden placed for a short period prior to finishing the decks will develop the necessary soil density to prevent future settlement.

Impervious soils in freezing climates and expansive soils may cause serious problems for outdoor decks. The same is also true for decks on high capillarity soils. In either case, freezing water soon destroys the best designed decking. Engineering designs should provide a drainable base course for all decks. In addition, caulking of the deck joints, the use of water seals, and other measures to ensure run-off away from the deck, pool joints, and the base course should be employed.

Indoor pools, however, cannot be designed for generous deck areas. Walk areas, however, should at least meet the recommendations contained in

Figure 11.1. It is advantageous to the aquatic programs and for traffic control to maintain a minimum total width of 18 feet for indoor pool decks, the clear sum of any two dimensions in one direction about the pool.

Decks must be textured to prevent slipping when wet, and within a 10-foot perimeter area around the pool, all decks should be carefully pitched to provide positive drainage. A pitch of 1/4 inch per foot is a minimum nominal slope to guarantee the required drainage. Area drains when used in this manner should cover no more than 250 square feet and should be no more than 5 feet from the pool coping perimeter for most pool designs. The exception is the deck-level pool: The first 10 to 15 feet of deck adjacent to the pool is pitched in one direction toward the pool at slightly higher slopes of 3 to 5%. Deck drains are unnecessary in areas contiguous with the deck-level surge trench. Cricket lines, drainage flow direction, and exact finished elevations at the pool perimeter and adjacent deck areas must be carefully noted on construction plans to avoid "birdbaths" that result in health and safety problems during operation.

Although concrete is generally accepted as the finishing material for pool decks, textured and colored concrete, stone, tile, and brick pavings may also be used. These can be effectively utilized in conjunction with concrete flat work or by themselves. All decks must be self-draining, nonslip at wet traffic areas, and heat-reflective when used in warm climates outdoors. Deck materials must not retain puddles or moisture and must be capable of being washed with hypochlorite solutions routinely used for cleaning and sterilizing pool deck areas.

New materials such as polypropylene, vinyl, and rubber-based coatings are available as surface coverings and offer material and rug-like finishes, comfort, acoustic properties, and easy maintenance. Poured-in-place compositions and epoxy topping materials offer economical, permanent, and architecturally desirable methods for finishing pool deck surfaces and should be investigated as alternative methods within the guidelines noted previously.

Pool Markings

It is important that required markings on decks, walls, and pool bottoms be carefully specified on detailed plans and be included in construction specifications. Markings are required by local health department codes to indicate water depth, change of slope, and cautionary advice. Marks also are required for aquatic competition and for visual safety perception of the bottom. All markings must be installed with some degree of permanency and in a manner appropriate for the type of interior finish and form of overflow. See chapter 8 for further details.

For pools finished in tile, depth numbers, lines, and targets are set in contrasting color, usually black. For pools with coating finishes or those finished in the natural concrete, the line at the outside edge of all markings should be cut approximately 3/32 in. by 1/16 in. deep into the shell. These lines can be scored into the finish surface with a carborundum wheel, after which a contrasting color may be painted into the mark or target area. For plastered pools, lines are cut into the finish; then paint or a coating finish is applied within the mark. A preferable technique is to use ceramic tile strip inserts for lines and markers, placed on the shell prior to the plastering.

Marks for safety lines, step edges, recessed ladders, competition lanes, turnaround targets, diving references, water polo, swimming and underwater instruction, synchronized swimming, adapted aquatics, or other program requirements should be indicated in the original design and should be incorporated into the final pool plans.

Water depths should be indicated on the pool decks. The trend in the United States is to use both metric and English units. For public pools, it may also be necessary to indicate areas beyond which "street shoe" traffic is not permitted. Warning signs as described in chapter 8 are essential to safe pool management. Markings required for competitive swimming are discussed in chapter 14.

Diving Platforms, Stands, Springboards, and Other Diving Requirements

With careful placement and design, diving tower structures may be an eye-catching attraction. Many "package" forms are available to fit most budgets. Where more aesthetic expression is desired, unique stands and tower structures can be custom-designed and fabricated from structural steel, precast concrete, laminated wood, quarry tiles, and various combinations of these materials. In many situations, a single custom-engineered structure has replaced multiple "package" towers at lower cost. For natatoriums, diving facilities may be incorporated into overhead building structurals.

High-diving platforms (7.5 and 10 meters) are becoming increasingly popular for public installations. As a safety feature, all platforms of 3 meters and higher should be of an open grating construction to permit the highest divers to view the water area and platforms below. An elevator or man-lift access is desirable for 10-meter structures intended for an active diving program. Lift facilities should be designed to avoid distracting the back divers when they are in position on platforms or boards.

The design criteria for diving equipment is established by competitive regulations. In certain localities, the board of health or municipal building regulations also fix diving well requirements. These should be consulted in detail. It is essential that sufficient depth of water be provided under diving boards and in front of the plummet. Check standards of competitive groups, the local health department, and the American Public Health Association (APHA). Major hazards usually occur in lack of adequate depth forward from the end of the board (plummet). See chapter 8 and Appendices C and D for more information.

For indoor facilities, ceiling height above the highest springboard or platform should be verified for code compliance when construction plans are finalized. Ceiling marks above the divers' takeoff zone are employed increasingly as a safety measure, especially above highly competitive diving boards. The ceiling above the plummet location should be marked conspicuously at potential contact areas with a contrasting pattern to delineate the hazard (approximately 5 ft by 5 ft on board centerline, 3 feet forward of the diver).

Safety considerations dictate the inclusion of a protective handrail that extends fully over the deck-to-water surface, double railings, and "fall through" protection. Egress from the diving area must be such that divers will not pass in front of boards or towers.

Diving regulations require a method of agitating the water surface in the landing area below the board or platform to permit better visibility of the surface. Generally, this consists of a water spray located in the tower structure or overflow system. Jets should be designed to delineate the diving entry area. This will usually require an integral adjustment of the spray itself in addition to a readily accessible control for the water volume. Where a combined tower facility is planned, each entry area should be studied to determine the proper unit to provide agitation of the surface.

In recent years, air bubbles incorporated in the pool bottom have been used to serve the surface agitation function. These consist of a series of 1/4-inch underwater inlets located in the pool bottom, defining the entry area with a pattern of air bubbles. A series of 1-in. thick by 12-in. wide perforated plastic extrusions is available to provide air entrance patterns below the plummets of each platform and board. Because many pump rooms now use compressed air for operation of equipment, instrument indication, and automatic control of valves, the ''bubbled air'' may easily be supplied from the pump room compressor. If this method is used, it is important to provide volume control of the air that is conveniently located near the diving area, readily accessible, and preferably tamperproof.

Underwater Observation Windows and Classrooms

Underwater observation windows are becoming increasingly popular for their instructional value, in observing the competitive finish, swim turning areas, and the diving well. In addition, where underwater programs include scuba instruction, synchronized swimming, and research activities, underwater classroom instruction has been found to be valuable.

Window sizes vary from small ports to comfortable viewing galleries, from glass areas 2 ft by 3 ft to as large as 4 ft by 8 ft. Improved designs and construction techniques now permit these important fixtures to be economically installed. Laminated safety glass is the most acceptable type and may now be installed without the expensive heavy bolting, machine frames, and waterproof gasketing formerly associated with typical waterproof, submarine-type bulkhead design. A typical underwater window construction is detailed in Figure 11.7a-b.

In addition to the space, access, ventilation, lighting, and communication requirements associated with the observation window or classroom, remote television viewing should also be considered. Smaller port-type window installations may be used effectively to accommodate a remote television camera as illustrated in Figure 11.8. Space and access requirements may be limited to maintenance only. Underwater observations may be readily reproduced with closed circuit TV at the deck-side instruction or coaching location. This technique offers the promise of greater pool utilization along with valuable security provisions throughout the facility.

Pool Automation

Water filtration and chemical treatment are two areas where automatic controls are taking over. These equipment items are usually provided separately, but an increasing number feature a

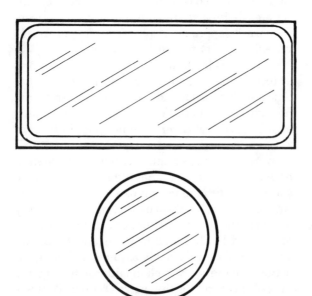

Figure 11.7a Underwater viewing windows

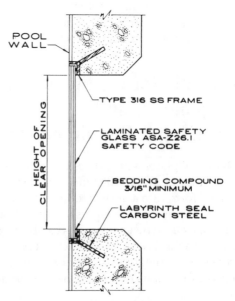

Figure 11.7b Underwater window, section view

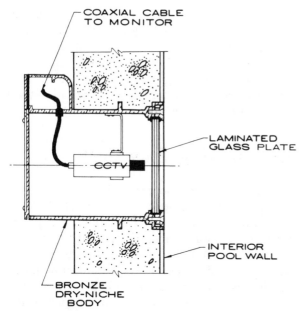

COAXIAL CABLE TO MONITOR

LAMINATED GLASS PLATE

CCTV

INTERIOR POOL WALL

BRONZE DRY-NICHE BODY

Figure 11.8 Remote television viewing port

single control panel employing both mechanical and chemical operation—the truly "automatic pool." Practical systems are available for reliable recording and controlling of free available chlorine (FAC) and pH levels in the water. Techniques for automating filtration plants are available at costs that pay for themselves in 3 to 5 years based on chemical, water, and labor savings. With material and labor operating costs steadily increasing, fully automated plants are increasing in prominence. At Ward Melville High School, Setauket, New York, a regenerative-cycle diatomaceous earth filter completed one year of fully automatic filtration before requiring backwash and recharge. The same system was used for 14 years before the automated filters were opened for inspection and servicing. After minor adjustments, it is believed the "like-new" stainless steel filter internals may be utilized for another 20 years before requiring service. Two slow-speed (1,200 rpm) recirculation pumps used for this pool installation had wearing rings replaced and new impellers installed at nominal cost. An epoxy coating applied to the outer perimeter of the impellers should allow the new impellers to perform for 20 years before replacement is required.

Construction Cost Factors

In considering construction costs, a planning committee is always concerned primarily with the initial construction sum. This total is affected by

general design factors basic to the site and by design elements of the construction that have been reviewed in this chapter. Although the general factors affecting the design are fixed for any location, the design elements have an important relationship not only to the initial cost, but also to the capitalized cost. Because of budget limitations, less expensive construction materials, methods, and equipment are often chosen that greatly affect operating costs over the life span of the facility. These operating costs, when reflected on a capitalized cost basis, show that good design decisions, although perhaps initially more costly, are overwhelmingly more economical in the long run. The following general design factors must be carefully considered with respect to the site and the need for optimizing capitalized cost versus the need for low initial cost.

The *water supply* for the pool is an important factor. The availability of a quality supply in sufficient volume is imperative and should be ascertained early in the design. A 3-inch fill line should be considered a minimum size for pools under 5,000 square feet; a 4-inch or larger fill line and supply is desirable for larger pools. The water should be of satisfactory quality and conform to prevailing health standards. An analysis of the water mineral content should be made, and consideration should be given to the natural pH, total alkalinity, total solids, and the presence of soluble iron or other elements that may be oxidized by chlorine with resultant treatment problems. Sometimes a deep well, even sea (salt) water or lake source of water, may be required. Here again, the cost of establishing a permanent, high-volume supply of a suitable quality is incumbent upon the designer. The cost of providing the water supply and also the necessity of special treatment must be considered in the initial job cost.

Sanitary waste and *water disposal* for the pool complex involves a large volume discharge of the pool contents. Various local regulations define the sewer type and/or water course to which the pool volume must be discharged and usually the rate or period of discharge and quality of effluent. In some cases, discharge to the sanitary sewage is mandatory, whereas in others it is strictly prohibited. Where pool volumes must be discharged to separate storm sewers the required connections must be included in the job costs. Discharge lines should be provided to accommodate pool water discharge in less than 8 hours, if possible. Where diatomaceous earth filters are used, many jurisdictions now require separate or preseparation equipment to remove spent powder from the effluent.

Also, the sanitary waste disposal of a pool complex may be a considerable expense; local law should therefore be reviewed in the early design stages. Early approval of tentative plans by local health and building departments may prevent extensive design revisions at a later time.

A reliable *power supply* is essential to any proposed construction. Three-phase electricity is necessary to run motors 5 horsepower and over. For large motors over 50 horsepower and/or a metallic-vapor lighting system at the pool area or parking facilities, a 480-volt source is preferable. A 208-volt supply may be used to advantage if a transformer is provided on the site near the distribution point, with a high-voltage primary brought to that point of transformation. Because of their influence on the system and engineering techniques, availability, local utility installation charges, and demand rate for heavy loads should be considered early in the design in order to minimize operating costs. For locations at a distance from transmission lines, 13 KV buried service will prove economical and practical.

The *fuel supply* varies from site to site and may be gas, oil, steam, or electricity, depending on the particular economics of supplying the energy at the pool complex and on the prevailing rates. It is important to consider the competitive merits of local fuels before finalizing the equipment design.

Energy conservation (see also chapters 17 and 19) and the use of solar collectors have greatly increased (15 to 30%) the initial cost of construction while lowering the capitalized long-term investment. It is this latter factor that is most important to the owner in the long term. The initial investment is usually in the form of increased thermal insulation and results in rapid pay-back. Solar collection takes several forms and may involve longer payback periods depending on the design idiom. For a simple system used directly (no intermediate exchange) to heat the pool water, the payback is immediate. For hot water heating, the annual load savings must be balanced against installation costs with consideration for annual insulation (sun exposure).

Passive energy collection systems relying on thermal glass walls, massive building elements (brickwork, concrete walls), or combinations (Trombe method) of building elements and using cleverly arranged gravitation circulation elements in the overall architecture will be one way of the future. The long-term operating costs must be considered when it is realized that a natatorium is a high energy-consuming building, requiring interior temperatures year-round greater than 83 to 86 °F.

Even hospitals and nursing homes do not approach this annual heating demand. When combined with the constant evaporative surface (cooling) and dehumidification needs, the potential for overwhelming operating costs due to inappropriate equipment and misunderstood economics is staggering.

Determining True Cost

True cost is much more than the initial construction price. All economic studies should be on a comparative basis of capitalized costs. Such costs reflect the amount of money required both to purchase (present) and to operate (future) a facility during a given life period under similar assumed conditions. Variables to be studied include amortization period, interest rate, maintenance and operating charges, energy charges, and other factors pertinent to an engineering cost analysis. For example, one type of filtration equipment may initially cost three times the price of a lower priced alternate. During the life of the pool, however, the less costly equipment may require service, operating, and replacement charges that far outweigh the initial cost consideration. Such a situation was discovered to be true for a large university installation (Costello, 1966). When the specific factors of initial costs, operating water charges, chemicals, yearly maintenance, replacement costs, value of space, and other pertinent variables were considered, the pressure D.E. system was found to be favored for this particular installation for economic performance reasons over the alternative granular media system. Interestingly, individual factors of the alleged "more expensive system," when considered singularly, may lead to the opposite conclusion. In the years since this installation decision, greatly increased interest rates and labor charges have overwhelmingly proven the correctness of the original comparative cost analysis.

Address

Fosroc Preco Industries, Ltd.
55 Skyline Drive
Plainview, NY 11803

References

American Association for Health, Physical Education and Recreation, & The Athletic Institute.

(1965). *Planning areas of facilities for health, physical education, and recreation.* Reston, VA: Author.

American Public Health Association. (1985). *Suggested ordinances and regulations governing public swimming pools.* Washington, DC: Author.

Costello, M. (1966). Sand and gravel vs. diatomaceous earth: A study in filtration engineering. *Swimming Pool Age, 40*(5).

National Spa and Pool Institute. (1985). *Suggested minimum standards.* Alexandria, VA: Author.

Filter room with small Perflex filter unit

Chapter 12

Water Circulation and Filtration

Before water circulation and filtration systems were required by health departments, the "fill and draw" method was used: Pools were filled with water and, when the water appeared to be too dirty, the pool was emptied and refilled. Today all public pools circulate the water so that it is turned over not less than every 6 to 8 hours, and wading pool water is turned over at least every hour. During this process the water is filtered, warmed, and chemically treated by the pool's hydraulic system. The mechanical equipment involved, such as pumps, filters, and chemical feeders, is usually located in a "filter room."

The principal function of the pool's hydraulic system is to cleanse and purify the water to assure that it is safe, healthy, and appealing to view and in which to swim. In order to achieve this, the system must efficiently flush the pool water from all locations where dirt and impurities tend to collect, skim the surface, filter it, sanitize it, chemically treat it, heat it, and finally recirculate it to the pool in the most efficient distribution manner possible. The components of the hydraulic system are the overflow (skimming) system, surge (displacement) storage, pumps, filters, chlorinators, chemical feeders, heaters, overflow, main drain, water fill system, and the inlet distribution network of piping through which the water flows. Supplementing the pool hydraulic system are the water supply, wastewater disposal system, and sanitary waste sewer.

Water Supply, Waste, and Sewer Connections

Whenever a public, potable water supply exists near a proposed pool, the health authorities prefer that it be used as the fill source. In remote areas, a problem of low volume may occur, necessitating careful consideration of the type of filtration equipment used (e.g., minimum backwash water) and careful planning for the fill periods and pool servicing times.

Well, lake, sea, or river water may be used only with specific permission of the health department. A well source must tap a dependable aquifer and be of the cased or rock-drilled type, with an approved sanitary seal at the well head. A potable well source may also vary considerably in mineral content. Following vigorous and sustained test pumping of any new water supply, a water analysis may be made for iron, manganese, high sulphur, and other elements harmful to bathing. Periodically, water quality should be verified during the first year of operation.

A large volume water supply under pressure or elevated storage is essential to any pumped water system. Well water usually may be discharged directly to the pool without treatment, although it may be extremely cold, and may require heavy chemical adjustment before chlorination.

Lake or river intakes are subject to variations in clarity and other variables. Pumping plants must be capable of taking suction under adverse conditions due to variations in temperature, hydraulic level, density, and pumping quality extremes. These water supplies may require filtration for removal of coloration and/or turbidity prior to discharge into the pool. Separate water-supply pumps are recommended.

Saltwater wells and screened intakes have been used successfully for coastal and island installations. The wells may be preferable because the water is of sanitary quality and constantly cooled in the hot summer months. Salt water is invigorating to swim in but may damage ordinary construction materials and equipment. Where a saltwater fill is used, the material specifications must provide serviceable items such as bronze or plastic pump casing, impellers, and internals; PVC, or other plastic pipe for pipe lines; porcelainized or rubber-lined interiors for strainers, tanks, and other normally ferrous items; type 316 stainless steel filters, internals, and deck equipment; cast stainless steel or plastic pool fittings and grates; all-plastic or rubber-lined valves; and cast bronze or Monel heat exchangers. In general, allow double the normal cost of piping and mechanical equipment for a saltwater system, unless PVC piping and a vacuum diatomaceous earth filter with concrete or plastic tank are used.

Where pool empty-water and filter wastes are discharged to a public water course, their correc-

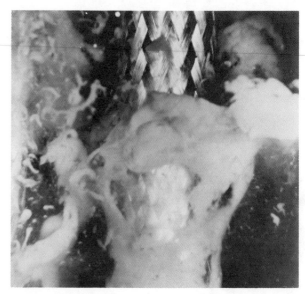

Figure 12.1   The bumping process of a regenerative filter system causes filter aid cake to be dislodged from tube

tive treatment is subject to ordinances of the local health, building, and environment control departments. Where possible, the pool wastewater is best discharged to the local storm sewer or designated water body. Chlorinated water, although safe, may be harmful to downstream fish and marine life. Discharge of any water into a tributary of a potable water supply normally is forbidden by law.

Diatomaceous earth wastes must not be permitted to accumulate and settle. Waste products may form a cementitious sludge if not kept moving and diluted. Some jurisdictions require separate settlement tanks and detention periods for D.E. effluent before allowing discharge to the public sewers. Leaching pools or tile fields become plugged and fail if used for this discharge without D.E. presettlement tanks.

Public sewer connections must be approved for all pool construction by the governing authorities (usually building and health departments). When pool wastes discharge to a sanitary sewer, an approved air break must be shown on the plans and installed to prevent any possible back siphonage and contamination. In many cases, filter rooms are lower than the local public waste line and must be drained by sump pumps. For these installations, only the immediate gravitational waste from the pump room sinks, hoses, and drip line should be handled, preferably by a duplex pumping unit. A ''direct empty'' drain line should be used to empty the pool through an air break into the waste line by means of the pool recirculating pump, which

Figure 12.2 Diatomaceous earth vacuum open type filter. Notice D.E. caked on sleeve.

discharges to an elevated sink connected for gravity flow to the waste system.

Pool Hydraulic System

Modern pools are designed with water recirculation and filtration systems that move pool water continuously through the filters. The rate of flow (gallons per minute, gpm) is determined by the total water volume in the pool basin (gallons) and the number of times a day it is necessary to move (turn over) this quantity of water through the filter. "Turnover" is specified by the health department and must be greater than three times a day, or once every 8 hours. A system to handle the water every 4 hours has a filter and pump rated at twice the capacity of that required to filter the same amount of water at a turnover of only 8 hours. Piping and accessory equipment capacity is increased when turnover time is decreased.

Larger capacity filtration plants may be installed initially if any doubt exists as to future requirements. It costs very little to oversize a filter when it is initially installed but much more to replace one that is inadequate for the job. Allowance for future addition of filter units—use of larger pipe sizes, larger pump casing, and provision of extra equipment space—is also often worth consideration in new construction with budget limitations. For this reason, the main recirculation pumps, for example, should not be installed with maximum size impellers.

In determining the required filter capacity and pump size, calculations for junior pools should be based on a turnover of less than 4 hours. Shallow wading pools are subject to severe load variations, especially if exposed to wind and sun, and should be designed for a 1-hour rate or less. Active, main swimming pools should be designed for a turnover of 6 hours or less; 5 hours is preferable. If possible, filtration piping should be sized large enough to allow a 4-hour rate. The best system is one using a dual pump arrangement, each unit capable of an 8-hour rate to provide high total filtration capacity (approximately 4 hours) when used together to meet peak conditions. The reliability of a dual system is worth the expense for swimming pools operated year-round.

The effectiveness of the hydraulic distribution inlet system depends on the technique used to introduce the filtered water uniformly to the pool basin. The treated water flow should traverse a maximum distance through the pool system, disperse uniformly, have no short-circuit paths, and be uniformly withdrawn at the farthest possible distance from the inlets. Each pool recirculation system must include a pump for moving the water, suction piping to take the water from the pool and pass it through the filter and treatment units, and return pressure piping back to the pool. Sterilizing and water-treatment additives are usually introduced into the pool return-water piping after filtration.

Pool filtration equipment falls into two general classes: vacuum or pressure method. Pool filter media may be granular (sand, gravel, anthracite, calcite, etc.); diatomaceous earth; or cartridge type. Granular media or cartridge filters are generally of the pressure system type, whereas the filtration method for diatomaceous earth units may be either pressure or vacuum system. Public pools may use any of these filter classifications; however, semi-public and residential pools normally employ granular media or diatomaceous earth in pressure systems.

Following are descriptions of the components of a pool's hydraulic system.

Surge Tanks

In designing the hydraulic system, it is most important to allow for water-volume displacement of the bathers, an operational consideration often neglected by health officials and pool designers. The average bather displaces 20 gallons of water. A typical pool of 10,000 square feet may serve a maximum 500 bathers in the water at one time depending on the occupancy allowed (see recommendations in chapter 11, Table 11.1). Thus a

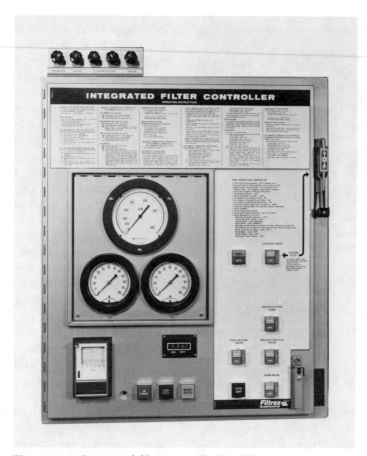

Figure 12.3   Integrated filter controller by Filtrex

surge displacement capacity of 10,000 gallons should be designed for this pool.

It is essential for safe, hygienic pool operation to maintain continuous skimming of the overflow perimeter edge. During active bathing periods if the surge volume is not readily absorbed by the system, flooding of the overflows occurs, negating the skimming action of the perimeter edge. Similarly, if many bathers leave the pool, they leave the pool deficient to the extent of their displacement, plus an additional amount of water equal to their body carry-off. The pool will then be below the overflow rim until the pool is refilled to an overflowing and skimming condition at the rim, a period called "recovery time."

At times of maximum bather surge, the overflows may be either flooded or the pool water level lowered more than 1-1/2 inches from the proper operating pool level. The retention capacity of bather surge volumes and the recirculation system's ability to absorb and replace surge water rapidly must be intrinsic to the design. A practical design formula is to provide 1 U.S. gallon of net surge storage capacity for each square foot of pool water surface. The recommended capacity, or Surge Volume (SV) in gallons, as a function of pool area (A) in square feet, is SV = A. Allow approximately 20% additional SV water capacity for controls and piping, drains, overflows, and freeboard, depending on the actual construction. This formula was recommended as a pool design parameter in the 1969 edition of this publication. It has since been adopted by many state health departments, public agencies, and design professions as the minimum standard for bather displacement surge capacity to be used in designing surge tanks and trenches on public swimming pools.

Surge tanks may be concrete, integral with the pool construction (trenches), or a separate chamber into which the perimeter overflow is piped. Many piping techniques are available to the designer for providing satisfactory flow and storage arrangements. Deck-level pools usually incorporate a surge trench in the pool construction below the pool coping.

Inlets

Filtered and treated water may be supplied at different locations throughout the pool shell. In large pools, it is advisable to supply water through bottom inlets to obtain uniform dispersion. The water surface below the 3-foot level may be viewed as a permeable interface with the active water volume above, having uniform injection points throughout the area. The flow of water upward from the bottom and outward over the pool rim is thereby preferable to any other inlet arrangement or proprietary alternates (see Figures 12.4 and 12.5).

Wall or floor inlets are commonly used. Wall inlets are essentially perforated spray heads, diffusing the water as it is injected into the pool volume. Eyeball inlets have a single large orifice that may be adjusted to direct the water stream in one direction. Floor inlets permit the water to be introduced at the interior pool bottom (the preferred location). Floor inlets project a shallow cone, 360° in extent, that sweeps the bottom. "Tile-tube," a plastic rectangular extrusion 1 in. thick by 12 in. wide, serves both as an inlet and as 12-in. wide racing lane lines, and is the most effective

inlet system currently available. (See Figures 12.6 and 12.7.) The black inlet tube has small perforations for uniformly admitting water at the pool bottom along the entire length of the lane marker. White inlet tubes are used at other locations, for introducing warmer pool water in special therapy sections, adapted swim programs, and so forth.

Main Drain

One or more main outlets or drains should be provided at the deepest location of the pool bottom. This is used for emptying the pool and for supplying a small percentage of the return water to the filters from the deep end, thus promoting uniform quality of the water mass.

A removable grate is set flush with the bottom and should have a net free area of at least 6, and preferably 10, times the area of the suction pipe to the pump or filters. At least two such drains are preferred, 8 to 12 feet apart, or 10 feet from each

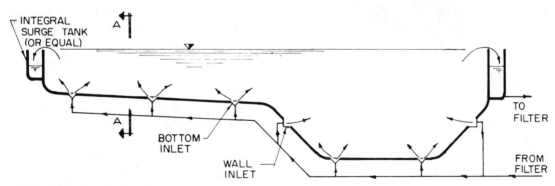

Figure 12.4 Waterflow hydraulics

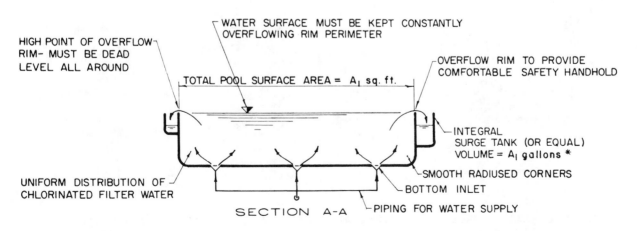

Figure 12.5 Water flow hydraulics, cross-section A-A

sidewall. The protective cover grate should be firmly secured in place or be heavy enough to prevent removal by swimmers. Openings should be no larger than 1/2 inch. It is also important to locate the main drain outside the diving trajectory area of the pool bottom to preclude any possibility of divers landing on the grate (with their hands or fingers) when they touch bottom. Precast concrete or reinforced fiberglass molded plastics are frequently used in preference to metallic grates to avoid the electrical bonding requirements for metal and the corrosion potential of metals in pool water.

When relative elevations of a given construction site allow, the main drain should be capable of an unrestricted gravity discharge (or pitched) to the storm or sewer wasteline. Bottom trenches similar to continuous main drains may also be used for the pool water inlet system, and styles to accommodate these systems are available.

Rim Overflows

As previously discussed, the primary purpose of overflows is to permit continuous skimming of the water surface. Typical overflow forms are illustrated in chapter 11, Figure 11.3.

It is essential that any overflow rim be installed dead level. For cast stones that cannot be field ground, this means care in workmanship and the setting installation. Equal care is required in placing prefabricated metal gutters, especially field-welded sections that must be joined to concrete walls. For cast-in-place concrete work, the overflow may be trued level prior to finishing with carborundum wheel attachments for industrial die-grinders. Tiled overflow rims use specially formed pieces that require expert installation.

The overflows and associated piping must be capable of accommodating the total water flow at the highest turnover rate. Overflows should lead directly to a surge tank (or trench) and have full flow capacity when flooded to quickly restore the original pool level in less than 20 minutes during the after bathing (AB) period. Generally this will mean frequent drainage fittings with protective

Figure 12.6 Tiletube serves both as an inlet and racing lane line. New York University Pool.

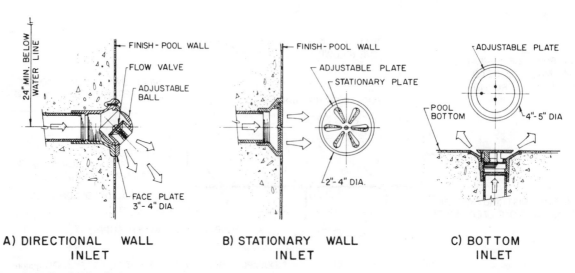

A) DIRECTIONAL WALL INLET

B) STATIONARY WALL INLET

C) BOTTOM INLET

Figure 12.7 Pool inlet fittings

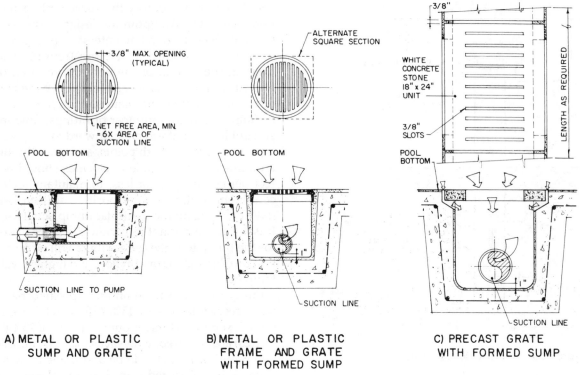

A) METAL OR PLASTIC SUMP AND GRATE

B) METAL OR PLASTIC FRAME AND GRATE WITH FORMED SUMP

C) PRECAST GRATE WITH FORMED SUMP

NOTE: METAL GRATE OR REINFORCEMENT MUST BE GROUNDED PER N.E.C. ARTICLE 680.

Figure 12.8 Main drain details

grates and large, unobstructed passageways. The overflow water collection header or open trough should be conservatively sized to permit maximum gravity flow needed to prevent flooding under extreme bather usage and wave action. Where deck-level copings incorporate an integral surge trench adjacent to the pool and below the coping, the elimination of overflow perimeter piping and fittings will effect a substantial saving in construction cost.

For smaller pools constructed with automatic surface skimmers, skimming occurs at 15- to 25-foot intervals in the pool walls, around the perimeter of the water surface. The automatically adjusting weir float compensates for an increased or decreased water surface level due to bather surge without impairing efficiency. It is important to maintain the mean water level of a skimmer pool at the approximate centerline of the skimmer opening to allow for level variations. Skimmer openings (approximately 6 in. high by 18 in. wide in the pool wall) must be at the same level. If the water drops below the level of the skimmer openings, the skimming action stops and the pump may become airlocked, unless an antiairlock feature is incorporated in the skimmer.

The overflows must be carefully designed and installed to preserve their primary sanitary function of skimming the pool surface at all times of pool operation.

Hydrostatic Relief Valves

Where a groundwater condition exists, this equipment is an important device for protection of the pool shell. Every pool, when empty, is essentially the same as a watertight boat hull. Water accumulation beneath the hull tends to cause the pool to float. Serious structural failures may occur when an empty pool is subjected to external hydrostatic pressures. Vertical poppet-type relief valves are used to admit water and to prevent a buildup of external shell pressures.

Relief valves should incorporate a quality well-screen placed in a suitable granular well-pack. Figure 12.9 illustrates a recommended design. Perforated pipes with a gravel pack, as commonly used, may be grossly inadequate in holding back a fine formation, which will enter the valve and cause the poppet to stick open or closed. A sieve analysis of the surrounding soil aids valve design. Valve design should employ a granular filter pack

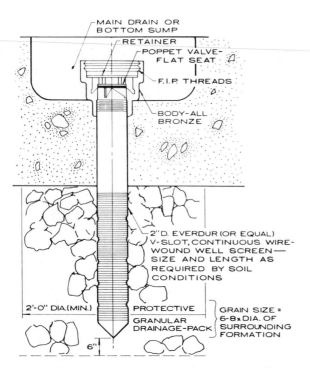

Figure 12.9   Hydrostatic relief valve

and well-screen opening sized to prevent migration of soil fines that would otherwise cause the poppet seat to malfunction.

Pumps

The main pool pump is the heart of the recirculation system. For swimming pool service, centrifugal pumps are used exclusively. These may be any of several types available, including end suction, double suction, split casing, close coupled, horizontal, vertical, turbine, and others. To minimize operating costs, it is important that pump performance satisfy peak operating conditions when the pump operating point is at maximum efficiency (or slightly to the left of maximum efficiency) on the standard pump performance curve. However, where flow rate is uncontrolled (no flow controller), the major part of the filter cycle is spent at some point less than the peak filter pressure. When a reduced (approximately 10%) flow condition is reached (maximum pressure before cleaning), the filter should be shut down and cleaned.

The pump should, whenever possible, be located at least 1 foot below the operating water level of the surge tank and as much lower as is reasonably possible for the particular design conditions. When this is not practical, self-priming pumps

should be used to empty the surge tank or main pool overflows. An optimum design exists when the pool main suction line enters the pump room on a level, or slightly lower, run from the main drain at the bottom of the pool. More often the recirculation pump is several feet above the main drain. In this case, the main suction line should contain a minimum number of fittings, flow in a straight line at uniform pitch upward to the pump, have no pockets or high points, and enter through an inline strainer. Suction velocities should be 5 feet per second (fps) or less, to maintain suction conditions within the net positive suction head (NPSH) rating for the particular pump being used. It is always important to review the NPSH curve for the pump to make certain there will be no suction problems at maximum flow and highest water temperature.

Pump motors with minimum specified nameplate service factors of 15% (SF = 1.15) are required; service factors for pump motors of 25% (SF = 1.25) are preferred, when available. The impeller and pump casings should be of durable materials such as porcelainized iron, bronze, plastic, and stainless steel. Monel and other high performance materials are available on special orders. Pumps should be installed with adequate service areas on each side and with provisions to permit electrical disconnection and motor removal without disassembling the piping.

Pipes

Piping for the recirculation system should be carefully selected because the materials are subject to many deteriorating actions, both inside and outside. Operating pressure is not a serious consider-

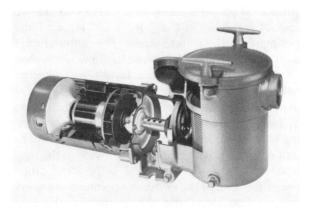

Figure 12.10   All-bronze pool pump by Sta-Rite

ation because most systems operate at 10 to 30 pounds per square inch (psi) or less. Pressure diatomaceous earth filters require the highest operating heads, usually in the range of 25 to 30 psi. Pumps for pool service usually have shutoff heads (maximum pressure) of less than 75 psi, thereby limiting the pressure in the recirculation system to lower values. Residential pool pumps normally have shutoff heads of less than 50 psi.

Recirculation piping should be hydrostatically tested in the range of 75 to 100 psi, depending upon the classification of the pool and the pressure limitation of components in the piping system (e.g., pump casing, filter tanks, etc.) Hydrostatic test pressure should be maintained for at least 2 hours without leakage. Extra care should be taken with the selection of pipe for the suction side of the pump so that it will not collapse under full vacuum.

It is possible to obtain a good piping system that meets these conditions, using iron, copper, cement-asbestos, aluminum, stainless steel, and plastic or plastic-lined pipes. Pipe size and corrosion are key variables in pipe selection. Pipe line size should be computed during the initial planning stage on a limited velocity basis of 5 fps for suction lines and 8 to 10 fps for the pressure lines. Economic considerations may dictate flows as high as 15 fps in the larger (over 6 in.) sizes. Corrosion and erosion influences at the higher flow rates should be investigated for the materials used. Certain materials cannot be used where they would be subject to the normal chemicals used in pool operation or deleterious conditions of the in situ soils when there is direct burial in the ground. Because brackish or acid soils are prevalent at many pool sites, the external soil chemistry should be carefully investigated before choosing pipe line materials that will be buried.

Subsoil support exerts a major influence on the choice of piping material. The piping must be designed to compensate for soil settlement, expansion and contraction under operating conditions, and hydraulic reactions (thrust) at changes of direction. Concrete support sleepers and thrust blocks must be provided at all changes of direction. Galvanic couples and stray electrolytic currents may be anticipated and corrected in the piping design by the use of isolating materials and/or cathodic protection.

Drainage and winter protection also are important design considerations in northern climates. Accessible cleanouts and servicing connections should be provided in the installation. The opportunity for gravity drainage for the main drain, surge tank, and large pipe lines is of great value.

The piping installation should incorporate specifications for neat and orderly placement, grouping and banking of lines, changes of direction at offset elevations, sufficient hangers and supports, and required air vents and drain plugs to facilitate the hydraulic service. Valves must be numbered and identified with permanent brass tags.

In the pump room, lines should be neatly marked with flow arrows and identifying legends. All pipes and mechanical equipment should be painted according to an identifying color code. Valve schedules and operating instructions are most valuable when wall-mounted under glass.

Recovery Time

Recovery time refers to the time interval during pool use, usually between intense activities, when the water level is below the overflow rim following active bather use. Water level may drop as much as 1-1/2 in. below the rim surface under extreme use conditions. Many older, heavily used pools require long time periods for the water level to return to normal after heavy use because of inadequate surge volume, flow capacity in overflow pipes or channels, inadequate pumping rate (turnover), inadequate fill water volume, or a combination of these design factors. Recovery time can be determined from the following expression:

$$\text{Recovery Time, RT (minutes)} = \frac{8 \, (\text{TO})}{D_{avg}}$$

where:

$$TO = \text{turnover time in hours}$$
$$D_{avg} = \text{average water depth of the pool in feet.}$$

For older pools built to a minimum standard of three turnovers per day, the time for one turnover is 8 hours. Therefore, such a pool with an average depth of 4 feet takes (8 × 8) ÷ 4, or 16 minutes, for maximum bather displacement to be recovered from the surge tank, holding tank, or surge trench. For the same pool with four turnovers per day (6 hours per turnover) the recovery time is only 12 minutes (8 × 6) ÷ 4. Recovery time is based on the full pump capacity (100% flow from surge tank) being used to withdraw water from surge storage when no displacement water is lost. Generally, recovery time is 25 to 40% longer when recirculation activity includes partial water flow drawn from the main drain line at the bottom of the pool.

The following factors help optimize recovery time:

- An external surge tank or trench capacity independent of the pool that contains a surge volume displacement from the bathers of 1 gallon per square foot of pool surface area

- Overflow pipes, channels, or trenches adequately sized for full gravity flow without flooding

- A pumping rate appropriate for the required turnover

An automatic fill system should be controlled to activate just above the lowest water level in the surge system, thereby providing continuous skimming action over the entire pool rim at all times of use.

Automatic Water Fill

In addition to the water displacement of bathers, which is temporarily removed from the pool during the BA (bathing) period, pool water is normally lost from the pool by evaporation and by carry-off of the wet bathers. This water must be replaced, usually during the AB period (after bathing) when undisturbed levels may be measured in the surge tank. Floatless, automatic level controls may be arranged to measure the water level and then pump up to a preset minimum water level in the surge tank. An automatic electric valve, one or two sizes smaller than the fill water line size, is installed in a bypass around the manual fill valve for the purpose of automatic control of pool water volume. This valve allows for continuous skimming operation with no interruption due to low water level occasioned by operating water losses.

Pool Shell Insulation

The least obvious thermal deficit of pool water occurs continuously, as heat is lost from the pool water mass to the surrounding soils. Ground temperature varies slightly but is generally assumed at 55 °F. In the middle United States, pools are generally maintained for comfortable aquatic programs at 83 to 86 °F. A practical design differential temperature (water to ground) is 30 °F (85 to 55 °F) for considering ground heat losses. This 30° differ-

ential is for the long-term equilibrium condition. A constant input of energy is required, therefore, to overcome heat losses to the ground that are a function of the area of the pool shell exposed to ground contact and the thermal resistance characteristics of the soils surrounding the pool shell. To overcome this constant thermal loss, the insulating characteristics of the shell may be improved by several techniques. Swimming pool walls may be constructed with rigid insulation on the outside, 2-inch Styrofoam sheets being a typical example. This material does not deteriorate, readily adheres to the outside pool wall, and sustains normal backfill (compaction) loading. Certain pool constructions have an inherent advantage over others in this regard. An integral surge trench (deck-level pool) has two walls of concrete with a large air space in between, which is a valuable insulator against thermal losses. (See chapter 15 for use of this construction idiom for psychrometric control of the natatorium.)

The underside of the bottom pool slab, however, cannot be treated with sheet insulation as recommended for the walls. The thermal resistance of the pool bottom may be increased by altering the base soils in contact with the underside of the bottom slab. Thermal conductivity of in situ soils has been determined by the U.S. Army Corp of Engineers. It is possible to examine soils at a given pool site and determine an adequate base course for the pool bottom in combination with the existing soils to obtain optimal thermal insulation for the bottom construction. This design approach minimizes heat loss through the entire pool bottom during the lifetime of the pool (having a constant differential temperature), resulting in a substantial savings in energy over the useful life of the facility. A professional engineer may provide additional information based on prevalent soil mechanics and construction practices. Typical values of thermal conductivity for 19 classes of identified soils are shown in Tables 12.1 through 12.3.

Types of Filters

Filter units for swimming pools are classified by pressure conditions and media. Pressure filters are those in which a closed tank contains the filtering elements or media. The influent water is forced through the filter under pressure. As the filter becomes progressively plugged, the pressure on the influent side increases with a corresponding decrease in the effluent pressure. Unless there is an automatic volume control (flow controller), the

Table 12.1 General Physical Properties of Soils[a]

| Soil No. | Soil Designation | Mechanical Analysis (percentage by weight) | | | | | | | Physical Constants | | | | | | |
		Gravel 6.68[b]	Coarse Sand 0.84 to 6.68	Medium Sand 0.177 to 0.84	Fine Sand 0.05 to 0.177	Silt 0.005 to 0.05	Clay <0.005	Silt and Clay <0.05	Liquid Limit	Plasticity Index[c]	Modified Optimum Moisture Content	Modified Maximum Density	Specific Gravity	Absorption (percent)	Textural Class[d]
P4601	Chena river gravel	56.0	26.0	14.0	3.4			0.6		N.P.			2.70	0.75	Gravel
P4703	Crushed quartz	0.0	44.5	37.3	12.7			5.5		N.P.			2.65	0.26	Coarse sand
P4704	Crushed trap rock	0.0	59.0	24.2	6.8			10.0		N.P.			2.97	0.20	Coarse sand
P4705	Crushed feldspar	0.0	51.8	34.2	9.8			4.2		N.P.			2.56	0.75	Coarse sand
P4706	Crushed granite	0.0	47.8	32.4	13.0			6.8		N.P.			2.67	0.56	Coarse sand
P4702	20-30 Ottawa sand	0.0	0.0	100.0	0.0	0.0	0.0			N.P.			2.65	0.17	Coarse sand
P4701	Graded Ottawa sand	0.0	0.0	98.3	1.6			0.1		N.P.			2.65	0.19	Medium sand
P4714	Fine crushed quartz	0.0	0.0	89.0	11.0	0.0	0.0			N.P.			2.72		Medium sand
P4709	Fairbanks sand	1.0	34.5	53.5	8.5			2.5		N.P.	12.0	122.5	2.67		Medium sand
P4604	Lowell sand	0.0	14.0	80.0	6.0	0.0	0.0			N.P.	12.2	119.0	2.74		Medium sand
P4503	Northway sand	1.6	5.4	86.0	7.0	0.0	0.0			N.P.	14.0	112.8	2.76		Medium sand
P4502	Northway fine sand	0.0	0.5	43.5	53.0	3.0	0.0			N.P.[d]	11.4	116.0	2.71		Fine sand
P4711	Dakota sandy loam	0.0	18.2	34.8	15.8	21.2	10.0		17.1	4.9	6.5	138.5	2.68		Sandy loam
P4713	Ramsey sandy loam	0.0	6.0	29.0	19.0	27.5	18.5		24.6	9.3	9.0	127.5	2.70		Sandy loam
P4505	Northway silt loam	0.0	1.0	2.0	19.0	64.4	13.6		27.3	N.P.	15.7	112.0	2.70		Silt loam
P4602	Fairbanks silt loam	0.0	0.1	0.5	7.0	80.9	11.5		34.0	N.P.	15.5	110.0	2.71		Silt loam
P4710	Fairbanks silty clay loam	0.0	0.0	1.0	8.2	63.8	27.0		39.2	12.4	18.0	102.0	2.59		Silty clay loam
P4708	Healy clay	0.0	0.0	0.7	0.9	20.1	78.0		39.4	15.0	17.0	108.0			Clay
P4707	Fairbanks peat									N.P.					Peat

[a] From *Soils* by M.S. Kersten, 1945, Minneapolis: University of Minnesota. Copyright 1945 by M.S. Kersten. Reprinted by permission.
[b] Size in millimeters.
[c] N.P. = non-plastic.
[d] U.S. Bureau of Chemistry and Soils.

Table 12.2   Tabulation of Thermal Conductivity (*k*) Values of Soils in Approximate Order of Decreasing Values[a]

Mean temperature—40 °F

Soil No.	Soil Designation	Moisture Content, %							Mod. Opt.[b]
		4	4	4	10	10	20	20	
		Density, lb per ft³							
		100	110	120	90	110	90	100	Maximum[b]
P4714	Fine crushed quartz	12.0	16.0						
P4703	Crushed Quartz	11.5	16.0	22.03					
P4701	Graded Ottawa sand	10.0	14.0						
P4709	Fairbanks sand	8.5±	10.5	13.5		15.0			19.0
P4604	Lowell sand	8.5	11.0			13.5			17.5
P4601	Chena river gravel		9.±	13.0					
P4705	Crushed feldspar	6.0	7.5	9.5					
P4706	Crushed granite	5.5	7.5	10.0					
P4711	Dakota sandy loam		6.5	9.5		13±			19.0
P4704	Crushed trap rock	5.0	6.0	7.0					
P4713	Ramsey sandy loam	4.5	6.5			10.0			16.5
P4502	Northway fine sand	4.5	5.5			8.5			9.5
P4503	Northway sand	4.5	6.0			7.5±			8.5
P4708	Healy clay	4±			5.5	9.0±	8.0	10.0	11.5
P4602	Fairbanks silt loam				5.0	9.0±	7.5	10.0	12.0
P4710	Fairbanks silty clay loam				5.0	9.0±	7.5	9.5	9.5
P4503	Northway silt loam				4.0±	7.0±	6.0±	7.0±	9.0

Note.   Soil P4702, 20-30 Ottawa sand is not included in the table since no tests were made at moisture contents of more than 2 percent.
[a]From *Soils* by M.S. Kersten, 1945, Minneapolis: University of Minnesota. Copyright 1945 by M.S. Kersten. Reprinted by permission.
[b]See Table 12.1 for values of modified optimum moisture content and maximum density for each soil.

water flow rate (turnover) is also reduced as plugging of the filter progresses.

Pressure filters normally use granular media, diatomaceous earth, or cartridge. The most commonly used granular media filters are rapid sand (sand and gravel); high rate sand (sand only); or anthrafilt (anthracite coal). Application rates on the rapid sand and anthracite filters are 2 to 3 gallons per minute per square foot of filter surface. Application rates for high rate sand filters are 15 to 25 gallons per minute per square foot of filter surface. Application rates for pressure diatomaceous earth filters are 2 to 2-1/2 gallons per minute per square foot of filter surface.

Cartridge filters may be either of the depth type or surface type. Depth type cartridge filters are designed for application rates of 3 to 8 gallons per minute per square foot of filtered area, whereas surface type cartridge filters are designed for .375 gallon to 1 gallon per minute per square foot of filter surface.

Vacuum type filters are limited almost exclusively to use with diatomaceous earth or filter-aid materials for swimming pool service. The influent is drawn through the diatomaceous earth septum, which is connected to the suction side of the pump. As plugging of the elements occurs, vacuum increases on the pump suction, throttling the

Table 12.3 Grouping of Soils on Basis of Mineral and Rock Composition (percentage by weight)[a]

Soil No.	Soil Designation	Quartz By Petrogr. Exam.	Quartz By X-Ray Analysis	Ortho-clase Feldspar	Felsite	Plagio-clase Feldspar	Pyroxene, Amphibole, and Olivine	Basic Igneous Rock	Kaolinite, Clay Minerals, and Clay Coated Minerals	Hematite and Magnetite	Mica and Coal	Others
P4702	20-30 Ottawa sand	99 plus[d]										
P4701	Graded Ottawa sand	99 plus[d]										
P4703	Crushed quartz	95 plus[b]										
P4714	Fine crushed quartz	95 plus[b]										
P4604	Lowell sand	72.2		20.5			3.0				1.3	3.0
P4709	Fairbanks sand	59.4		3.6	5.0	6.3	8.0			2.5	0.1	5.1
P4711	Dakota sandy loam	59.1		12.9		1.0	12.1	10.0	12.4			2.5
P4713	Ramsey sandy loam	51.3		11.8		5.6	12.6		15.9			2.8
P4601	Chena river gravel	43.1		11.6		12.9	27.0				2.1	3.3
4503	Northway sand	7.5			11.5	9.0	7.5	51.0				13.5
P4502	Northway fine sand	12.0			7.0	18.0	12.0	40.0				11.0
P4704	Crushed trap rock	3.0		10.0		50.0[c]	34.0			2.0		1.0
P4705	Crushed feldspar	15.0		55.0		30.0						
P4706	Crushed granite	20.0		30.0		40.0						10.0
P4708	Healy clay	22.5							55.0		22.0	0.5
P4710	Fairbanks silty clay loam	4.6	59.5				2.2		28.9	1.6	3.2	
P4602	Fairbanks silt loam	13.3	40.3						28.3		18.1	
P4505	Northway silt loam	1.5				31.5	19.5	4.5	17.5	10.0		5.5

[a]From *Soils* by M.S. Kersten, 1945, Minneapolis: University of Minnesota. Copyright 1945 by M.S. Kersten. Reprinted by permission.
[b]By visual inspection; impurities less than 5 percent.
[c]Andesine feldspar.
[d]By visual inspection; impurities less than 1 percent.

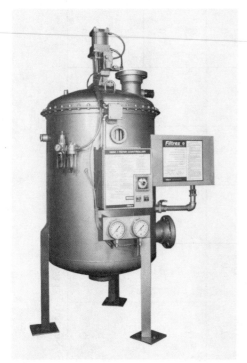

Figure 12.11a Regenerative D.E. filter by Filtrex

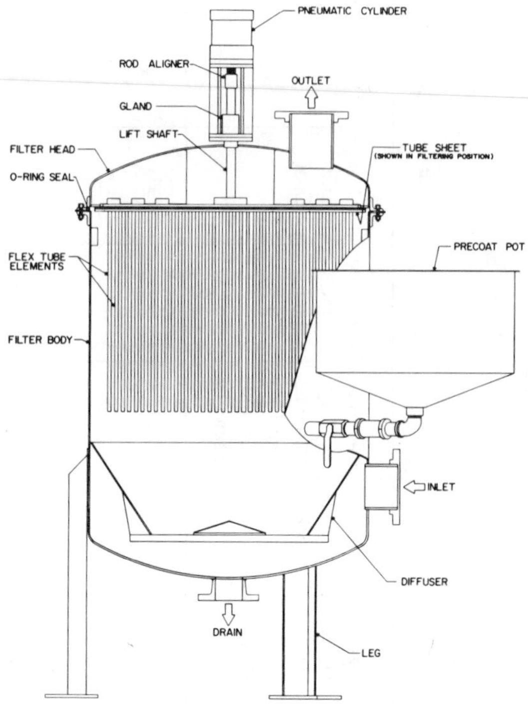

Figure 12.11b Schematic of Filtrex regenerative filter

flow as capacity of the pump is reduced. Cavitation and impeller damage may occur under high suction conditions, and vacuum applied should be limited for this reason. A vacuum switch is usually incorporated into such systems to give an alarm at a predetermined level and/or automatically shut the system down when the vacuum limit is exceeded. Vacuum diatomaceous earth filters are generally designed for application rates of 1.0 gallon to 1.8 gallons per minute per square foot of filter area.

Swimming pool pumps, filters, and multiport valves should be approved by the National Sanitary Foundation (NSF) and also conform to the requirements of the local board of health. Principal filter system arrangements are illustrated in Figures 12.12 and 12.13.

Filter Media

In granular media systems, water impurities are held on top of the media bed. The media itself is usually sand, sand and gravel, gravel, or anthrafilt. A coagulant in the form of a gelatinous floc is frequently used as a filter-aid to remove extremely small particle sizes. These systems are cleaned by reversing the flow through the filter tank at a high rate, thereby backwashing the bed of entrapped impurities.

When the filtering media is diatomaceous earth (D.E.) or filter-aid, the water impurities are removed as the flow passes through a thin layer of the material (precoat) covering the filter elements. When the filter elements become plugged with impurities and can no longer pass an adequate volume, the filter is cleaned by use of a backwash, by mechanically "bumping" flexible elements or by flushing fixed elements until they are clean. A fresh precoat of diatomaceous earth is placed on the element, and the filter is returned to service. During the filter cycle, the element coating may be kept porous and prevented from early plugging by the continuous addition of slight amounts of diatomaceous earth mixed with water, called slurry or body coat.

Diatomaceous earth systems have been developed using a "bumping" technique. These are known as "regenerative cycle" filters and feature a mechanical system in which the filter is periodically taken out of service and the flexible elements mechanically vibrated, or "bumped," to jar the caked impurities from the D.E. precoat. Backwashing and recoating are required every 1 to 6 months, depending on the pool situation.

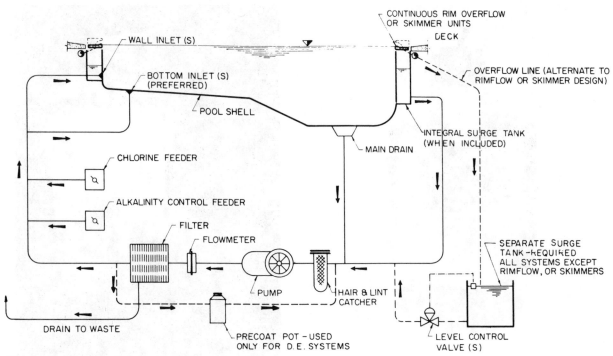

Figure 12.12 Granular media and pressure filters

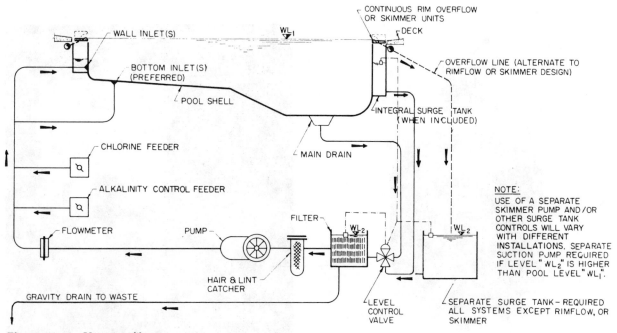

Figure 12.13 Vacuum filters

The most common cartridge filter uses plastic or impregnated paper that is pleated to give a large surface area. Water impurities are removed as the flow passes through the cartridge surface. Car-

tridge filters are not normally backwashed because of inherent structural weaknesses. They are removed for cleaning following which they can be reused several times until plugged.

Figure 12.14 Stainless steel high-rate sand filter

Figure 12.15 Lomart's sand filter with rotary 6-way valve

Figure 12.16 Fiberglass filter unit by Sta-Rite

Figure 12.17 Lomart's sand filter with push-pull valve

Typical cross sections of pressure D.E., granular media, and vacuum D.E. filters are shown in Figure 12.18.

Backwashing Filters

Commercial rapid sand filters are installed in multiple banks of three, four, or five tanks to facilitate the backwashing requirements of public pools. This is necessary because the water rate per square foot needed to loosen the filter bed and dislodge the filtrate particles is usually 3 to 5 times as great as the filter application rate. In some cases, an additional backwash pump is installed. It is usually more economical to install single or dual pumps with multiple filter tanks.

For rapid sand filters, the application rate is limited to 3 gpm/sf, when the recommended backwash rate is 15 to 20 gpm/sf. Although four or five separate tank compartments are preferable for backwash purposes, many installations use three or four tanks in conjunction with a pump capable of increased volumes at the reduced head of the backwash operation.

For anthrafilt (anthracite coal) filters, the media has a weight approximately one half that of a comparable volume of filter sand. The wash rate is correspondingly reduced to 9 to 12 gpm/sf. Effective

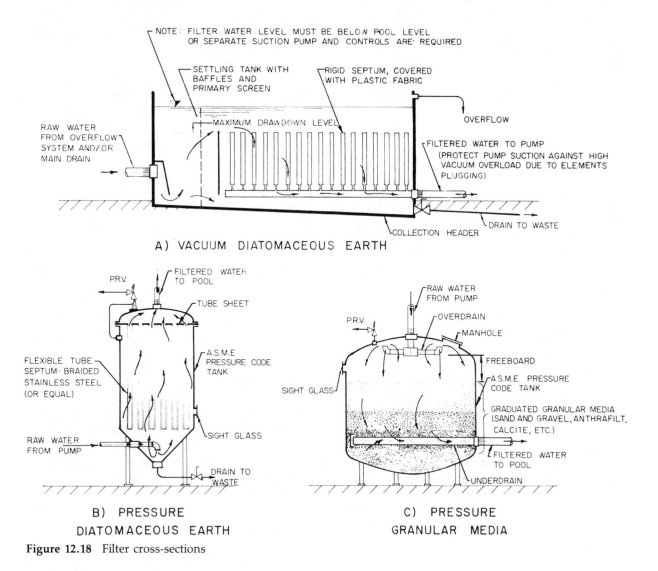

Figure 12.18 Filter cross-sections

installations featuring only two or three tank systems are in operation. Caution should be exercised in certain geographic locations where, due to the chemistry of the local water supply, anthrafilt may act as a solution indicator (titration analysis) producing a green color in the presence of residual chlorine.

It is necessary to backwash granular media systems at the indicated rates for at least 20 to 30 minutes per tank. The volume of water discharged may be considerable for large size pools. Because the pool water is used in the backwash operation, the expense of purchasing, filtering, treating, and heating the water must be considered when planning the installation. In certain areas of water shortage, the backwash requirement may be critical to continued pool operation, and alternate filters should be studied during design preliminaries. (For residential service, sand filter backwash is generally limited to 5 to 10 minutes per filter.)

With granular media systems, higher water discharge volumes must be accommodated by the waste system, and water and waste disposal costs must be reviewed at each locale.

Diatomaceous earth systems, both pressure and vacuum, have minimum backwash requirements. The vacuum D.E. systems are usually sluiced down after the open tanks are emptied. This involves at the most two or three tankfuls of water to clean the elements. External sluicing of the elements is not thought to be as effective as a true reverse or backflush, but there are many satisfactory installations of this type, particularly for seasonal operation.

Pressure diatomaceous earth filters may be sluiced, bumped, or reverse flushed, according to their design. For each of these methods, however, the quantity of water used is always less than several tankfuls unless a prolonged reverse flush is used. This can result in an average heating energy savings of 30,000 BTUH each time of backwash compared with sand systems, for the life of the facility.

With diatomaceous earth filters, however, settlement basins and high-volume sewer connections have to be considered, as discussed at the beginning of this chapter. Refer to the local health department or state environmental control agency for specific regulations.

Water Turnover Rate

The significance of turnover often is not properly understood. In order for pool water to maintain itself at necessary sanitary levels, free from harmful organisms and turbidity, it must be constantly recirculated. Continuous dilution of filtered and treated water must occur, based on well-defined mathematical relationships. Pumps must be run continuously every day. Too often filtration systems are shut down during "off-peak" hours, thus decreasing the system's effectiveness.

It is possible to improve recirculation turnover hydraulics by more effective use of the water flow principles illustrated in this chapter. These principles may be understood by examining Figure 12.19. After one turnover, 56% of the pollution in the swimming pool remains when the filters are operating effectively (100% removal of pollution passing through) and assuming all of the clean, filtered water is returned and uniformly mixed with the pool water. Some "clean" water and some of the remaining "polluted" water are continuously withdrawn from the pool—constantly mixed as a uniform solution by the pool inlets—and progressively filtered "clean" as pollution is reduced with each pool turnover. After two turnovers only 14% of the original pollution remains if no additions are made in the interim of the two turnovers. After three turnovers, less than 5% pollution exists in the pool. Following four full turnovers, the pool is virtually clear of pollution (< 1% remaining) and ready for the next day's bathers. This is especially true if water chemistry (discussed in chapter 13) and temperature have been adjusted to a desired level during the time of no pool use.

Turnover time to clean a pool to perfect water quality standards must occur in the time period when the pool is not being used (no pollution added). In many facilities, this may be as few as 6 to 8 hours. It is in this time that three or more turnovers must occur to prevent buildup of residual pollution levels in heavily programmed aquatic facilities.

If filtration equipment and pumping plants will not be increased unduly to accomplish four turnovers in the time interval allowed during the short AB period, an improvement in flow dynamics through the swimming pool is needed. Two criteria are apparent:

1. During the BA period, the inlet/overflow system should maximize mixing of the pool water during the bather's activities. In this manner, pollution introduced by the bathers is optimally dispersed through the pool water and removed by continuous skimming and uniformly mixed water withdrawal.

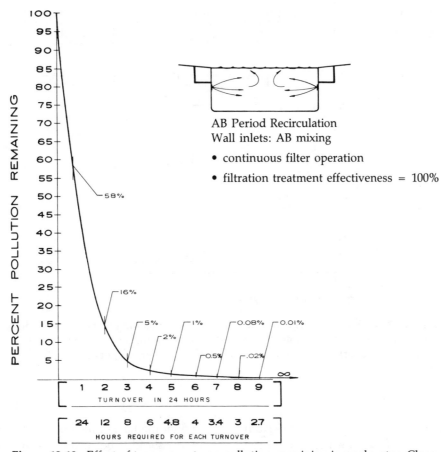

Figure 12.19 Effect of turnover rate on pollution remaining in pool water. Clear, clean, treated water is returned to pool. During AB period, filtered water entering pool completely mixes with polluted water before water is withdrawn for filtration and treatment.

2. During the AB period, mixing should be minimized with the cleaned, treated, pollution-free water returning from the filters. This treated, clean water should be "segregated" and used to "displace" polluted water remaining from the BA period.

Such a design may be effectively accomplished by refinements in water introduction to the pool via bottom inlet systems. A graphic description of the effectiveness of this system is shown in Figure 12.20. If the return filtered water is introduced through a bottom inlet method (several are commercially available), the water is diffusely and uniformly dispersed in the pool, flowing continuously and imperceptibly from the bottom upward and outward, to and over the overflow rim.

During the BA period the bathers promote mixing of the water by their activities, and pollutants that are introduced by them are effectively dispersed in the volume of clean pool water continually washing upward, especially in large pools where antiquated wall inlets are ineffective in reaching the most central areas. Filtration effectiveness is promoted during the BA period, especially when compared to pools with wall inlets and where those inlets are located at higher elevations on the pool wall, the worst position being just under the overflow.

By contrast, during the AB period, the hydraulic action (as shown in Figure 12.20) can be visualized by separating with an imaginary membrane the clean, filtered water permeating the pool volume upward from the bottom from the body of BA water. The water bottom inlet tubes are designed for minimum mixing of entering water during the AB period. At the start of the AB period, the invisible membrane is on the pool bottom separating the BA water from the entering clean, filtered water. After one fourth of the first turnover, the

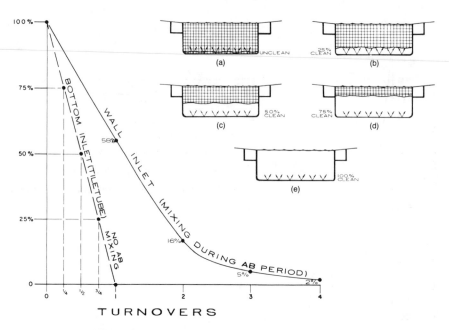

Figure 12.20   Effect of turnover rate on pollution remaining in pool water: no AB mixing, using bottom inlets. Inset: (a) pool at start of after-bathing period; (b) at 1/4 turnover; (c) at 1/2 turnover; (d) at 3/4 turnover; (e) pool after only one turnover.

membrane is up one fourth of the pool depth from the bottom and the polluted BA water is above the membrane, with 100% clean, filtered water below.

After one half of the first turnover, the membrane has moved up, separating the pool in half volumetrically, with only one half of the original polluted BA water remaining on top. After three quarters of the first turnover during the AB period, the membrane is three fourths of the wall distance above the pool bottom, and three fourths of the pool volume is now clean, filtered water under the invisible membrane. Finally, when one turnover has elapsed, the "membrane" is now at the pool surface; clean, filtered water fills the entire pool; and the design objective has been accomplished. The hydraulics of uniform, upward bottom water flow over a continuously skimming rim have promoted a clean pool in one fourth of the time required by less effective designs (i.e., wall inlets, internal pool skimming at lowered water level in the AB period, and other unsatisfactory devices available for public pool construction).

A very desirable and practical method at this time to implement the bottom inlet design is to have two pumps, both run at times of high demand and one pump used alternately for equal wear at times of low bather use.

After a period of use, water flow rates decrease as equipment wears, pipe lines corrode or clog,

and filter media become impacted. Flow-indication meters should be prominently installed and calibrated directly to read "gpm" and hours of turnover. Permanent lines should be marked on the meters indicating 5% and 10% decreases below minimum turnover rates, to signal servicing requirements. If difficulties are experienced in maintaining flow above the 10% reduction-in-rate line, the entire system should be checked, and necessary servicing should be effected. Enforcing authorities are encouraged to establish standards to accurately measure and maintain minimum design flow rates on this basis.

Operating Cost Factors

Better quality equipment, whether it be pumps, valves, filters, instruments, or pipes, usually returns the investment through reduced maintenance and annual operating charges. A comparison of system operating costs, for any quality of equipment, must be based strictly on local conditions. Factors affecting operating costs include chemical prices, water costs, electrical costs, sewage costs, heating costs, and labor services for repair or maintenance.

A system design that provides adequate capacity and quality equipment results in a minimum long-term cost. Specific installations must be examined in careful detail concerning annual operating cost factors. For an accurate comparison, the annualized operating costs may be determined as a present value in any time frame (usually 20 years) at the anticipated interest and inflation rates for the period. Alternative construction methods may then be compared on a basis of initial cost plus the value of projected operating costs for the given time period.

References

Kersten, M.S. (1945). *Soils* (pp. 391-409). Minneapolis, MN: University of Minnesota.

University of South Carolina Natatorium.   Consultants: Counsilman & Associates.

Chapter 13

Swimming Pool Chemistry

Few things in life provide such a beautiful and serene picture as a clear, sparkling swimming pool on a hot summer afternoon. Yet beneath the surface of that picture lies a seething cauldron of chemical, biological, and electrical activity. A swimming pool may be likened to a test tube utilized in an ongoing experiment: Many changes take place—some in seconds, others requiring hours or days.

Swimming pool water is an extremely unstable compound due to the many influences exerted upon it. Factors promoting the everchanging environment of a pool include disinfectants, buffers, alkalinity, pollen, dust, bacteria, minerals, plant life, gases, and electrical activity. In addition, pool water is responsive to changes in air temperature, water temperature, sunlight, humidity, air quality, people, addition of fresh water, and the effectiveness of filter media.

With all this potential activity, it is obvious that a pool requires almost constant attention, especially when environmental changes are sometimes rapid and continuous. The information contained in this chapter is designed to assist the home owner, aquatic facility director, lifeguard, or pool operator to manage his or her pool in a healthy, safe, and cost-effective manner. For planners of new pools, this chapter provides information on the different systems and chemicals used in the process of maintaining proper water conditions.

Health, Safety, and Cost-Effectiveness

Because a swimming pool is a public water supply, the health and safety of pool users is a primary concern. In most states the operator employed at the public water works must demonstrate his or her competency by successfully completing a water treatment plant operator's course before being hired. However, only a few states have such a standard for pool operators; as a result, an inexperienced person, recently certified in lifeguarding or water safety, may be hired to assume some of the same responsibilities for public safety and health as the operator of the local water treatment plant. It is a well-known fact that water is an excellent environment for the transmission and growth of bacteria, including those that produce typhoid and paratyphoid fever, amoebic and bacillary dysentery, hepatitis, pink eye, and impetigo. Bacteria prefer a warm, moist environment with an adequate food source—all of which may be found in a swimming pool. For these reasons, it is important that pool operators understand the fundamentals of water chemistry.

Clear, sparkling water is created only as a result of proper filtration, disinfection, and chemical balance. Improper management of any of these three factors may produce a degree of turbidity that may obscure vision of the pool bottom, even in shallow water. Many times each year accidental deaths by drowning occur as a direct result of cloudy water conditions. Turbidity stems from many causes, including environmental factors such as algae and dust, from the improper preparation and use of disinfection systems such as calcium and sodium hypochlorite, from poor filtration, and from precipitation of minerals in the water due to fluctuations in pH and alkalinity.

Two major problems that plague the aquatic profession today are energy costs and water treatment. In terms of energy, capital expenditure, and the cost of annual maintenance, an improperly operated swimming pool becomes an unnecessary "drain" of financial resources. Because commercial swimming pools are designed to have a lifespan of 40 to 50 years, pool managers and staff need to be educated and trained to obtain maximum life from the facility and to operate it on a cost-effective basis. Certification in pool operation and aquatic facilities management, implemented by agencies such as the Aquatic Council of the American Alliance for Health, Physical Education, Recreation, and Dance (AAHPERD), National Recreation and Parks Association, National Spa and Pool Institute (NSPI), and the YMCA of the USA, is essential for all pool managers.

The cost of maintenance and operation of some pools today is astronomical. Agencies, municipalities, and schools with pools are being forced to spend exorbitant amounts of money for new filters, plumbing, pumps, surface finishes, and heaters—after only 5 to 10 years of operation. Again, proper pool maintenance and operation, in most cases, greatly delays these expenses.

The Chemistry of Pool Water

The term pH is used extensively yet is hardly understood. Managers adjust it, lifeguards test it, and patrons talk about it. The symbol pH represents the *potential* of *Hydrogen* ions or the strength of the hydrogen ion concentration in a solution. Water (H_2O) is the solution with which pool operators and owners are concerned. In its natural state (rain), water is a neutral substance with a pH value of 7.0. Acidic properties of water are due to the presence of hydrogen ions or H^+. Basic properties of water are caused by hydroxide ions or OH^-. Water, or H_2O, may also be expressed H^+OH^- and is a substance that is constantly breaking up, or ionizing (disassociating), into an equal number of hydrogen and hydroxide ions. Because the number of each is equal, pure water is neutral.

All substances have a pH that can be established through any number of electrical and colorimetric tests. The pH test result of any substance (i.e., swimming pool water) is then compared with the standard pH table as summarized below.

pH Values

Acidic	Neutral	Basic
0.0-------6.9	7.0	7.1-------14.0

Because all values between 0.0 and 6.9 are acidic, any pH test result falling within that range indicates an acid water condition. Conversely, any result between 7.1 and 14.0 identifies the water as basic.

If a base substance such as soda ash is added to distilled (neutral) water, some of the hydrogen ions will be neutralized, showing an increase in hydroxide ions or a higher pH. If an acid is added to distilled water, the hydroxide ion concentration is reduced, showing a decrease in pH. Essentially, the same reaction occurs in swimming pool water.

A pH test, however, does not indicate by volume how acidic or basic a substance may be; it only indicates an acid or base condition. Of equal concern to a pool operator is the amount of alkalinity present in water, commonly referred to as total alkalinity, which is a measurable quantity expressed in parts per million (ppm).

pH Recommendations

All authorities agree that pool water must be maintained on the basic side of the pH scale. Most local and state health departments recommend that the pH be kept in a range between 7.2 to 8.2; the parts of the human body that have direct contact with water (i.e., eyes, skin, and mucous membranes) are compatible with a pH in the 7.2 to 8.2 range. If the pH is allowed to drop below 7.2, metal surfaces corrode (filter tank, pipes, heater coils, etc.). Skin irritations and excessive chlorine odors may also result.

High pH readings (above 7.6) should also be avoided. As readings approach 8.0, iron and calcium may form a precipitate causing turbidity (cloudiness). In addition, scale may form on the filters, pipes, and heater. High pH also has a negative effect on the formation of hypochlorous acid (bactericide formed from chlorine and water): At pH 7.2, 60% of the chlorine dissolved in water will convert to hypochlorous acid; at 8.5, the conversion is limited to 10%. Readings between 7.4 to 7.6 pH provide the most hypochlorous acid for the money spent on chlorine and still provide for maximum bather comfort. Higher pH levels result in chlorine converting to hypochlorite ion, essentially a useless by-product.

pH Control

It is recommended that a pH range of 7.4 to 7.6 should be maintained to provide pool managers and operators with the best results in bather comfort and balanced water. Many pools today utilize calcium or sodium hypochlorite, either of which usually increases the pH significantly. Pools equipped with gas chlorine have a problem with low pH, as it is a very powerful acid. A high pH may be lowered by adding an acid directly to the water when the facility is not in use or through a chemical feed pump. These acids include sodium bisulfate (powder) or muriatic acid (liquid). Sodium bisulfate is more expensive and less dangerous to use, whereas muriatic acid is less expensive but requires caution in handling and application.

Raising the pH involves the addition of soda ash (sodium carbonate), a fine white powder. It must be mixed with water and applied through a chemical feed pump. For pools with chlorine gas, the proper pH range may be maintained by using 1-1/2 pounds of soda ash for every pound of chlorine gas used.

The preferred method of increasing the total alkalinity is to add enough sodium bicarbonate (bicarbonate of soda) to the water to raise the level to a range of 100 to 120 ppm. A low alkalinity (50 ppm) may produce rapid changes or fluctuations in pH. An alkalinity level of 300 ppm or above makes pH extremely difficult to adjust. If the total alkalinity is less than 80 ppm, it may be raised approximately 10 ppm per 10,000 gallons of pool water by adding 1-1/2 pounds of sodium bicarbonate for each 10,000 gallons of water until the desired level is achieved.

Total Alkalinity

Total alkalinity is a measure of the extent to which a given amount of water is buffered or made to respond to pH adjustment. The pH value of water is an indication of the molar concentration of hydroxide ions. However, some alkalinity remains un-ionized and is not identifiable on a pH test.

Alkalinity in water represents the amount of bicarbonates, carbonates, hydroxide, and sometimes borates, silicates, and phosphates that are present. Total alkalinity is the sum of the concentrations of the first three in the proven absence of the latter three:

Total Alkalinity = OH^- + CO_3^{2-} + HCO_3^-

Bicarbonate: HCO_3^-

Carbonate: CO_3^{2-}

Hydroxide: OH^-

Water with only bicarbonates may have a pH value of 4.0 to 8.4 and cannot exceed the value of 8.4, even if the bicarbonate alkalinity reaches 20,000 ppm. Water containing bicarbonates and carbonates cannot exceed pH 12.0, regardless of amount. In water containing carbonates and hydroxide, the pH value may further increase with small amounts of alkalinity. Water containing only hydroxide alkalinity has a pH range of 9.6 to 14.0 and may be insufficient enough in alkalinity to prevent corrosion of plumbing or to maintain an alum floc on a sand filter. Therefore, it may be stated that pH has no significance unless the total alkalinity is known and that it is related to the number of hydrogen ions (H^+) in the water.

Bicarbonate alkalinity, in the amounts found in swimming pools, is not irritating to the body. At pH 8.3, some carbonate alkalinity may exist that is sometimes irritating to the eyes. If the pH rises above 9.4, hydroxide alkalinity may be present but cannot exist below this level. This type is extremely irritating but seldom occurs in swimming pools.

Generally, swimming pool water should contain between 100 and 120 ppm of total alkalinity. Numerically, this is the equivalent concentration of titrable alkali with an equal amount of standard acid (usually .6% sulfuric acid). The alkalinity of water is expressed in terms of milligrams of calcium carbonate per liter (ppm) determined by titration.

The addition of soda ash to pool water generally increases the total alkalinity: Soda ash combines with the carbon dioxide found in water to produce sodium bicarbonate. This is a desirable type of alkalinity because it provides a comfortable water condition for the bather and creates the least amount of corrosiveness. However, frequent testing for total alkalinity, adding bicarbonate of soda when necessary, is the best procedure for maintaining the proper alkalinity level.

Total Hardness

Hardness and alkalinity are closely related but are not identical. Hardness is a measure of the amount of calcium and magnesium ions found in water. Hardness can also be caused by metallic ions such as aluminum, iron, manganese, strontium, and zinc. Essentially, there are two types of hardness: carbonate and noncarbonate. Carbonate hardness (calcium) is usually equivalent to total alkalinity, therefore rendering the alkalinity measurement sufficient for water control. It is important that the pool operator understands some of the conditions produced by hardness.

Hardness can cause scaling and clogging of plumbing. Pools with heated water may experience trouble when calcium or magnesium precipitate forms a scale on heater coils or causes a scale to form on the plumbing. Such scale reduces heating capacity and can calcify and block sand filters.

Another consequence of hardness sometimes occurs with calcium and magnesium compounds that are in a soluble state in the form of bicarbonates. The addition of soda ash transfers these calcium and magnesium compounds into an insoluble state such as carbonates. Releasing these fine particles into suspension turns clear water cloudy. Calcium can also cause discoloration deposits on paint and tile. Although these deposits are unattractive, they cause no harm to those surfaces.

The amount of hardness in a pool is also affected by evaporation and the addition of make-up water. Disinfection systems such as calcium hypochlorite also increase water hardness. If the hardness level reaches 500 to 600 ppm, the pool should be drained and refilled with fresh water.

Soft water with no hardness is another undesirable condition because this type of water is corrosive. A minimum of 80 ppm is recommended. If the hardness level is too low, it may be increased by the addition of calcium chloride dihydrate (rock salt). A weak acid, this material should be predissolved in water before being added to the pool.

The Effect of Filtration on Water Chemistry

A granular filter medium such as sand removes most solid matter from the water, but in many cases clarity may be noticeably increased by the use of an alum compound. Among the most common alum compounds are aluminum sulfate, ammonium aluminum sulfate (ammonium alum), and potassium aluminum sulfate (potassium alum). Aluminum sulfate is the most commonly used coagulent for sand filters. Unless there is a specific reason for resorting to potassium alum, most filter authorities do not recommend it because it can cause chemical problems in some waters. Commercial coagulent mixtures are also available under various trade names. These mixtures have some advantages over alum compounds but are more costly.

How Does Alum Aid Filtration?

Aluminum sulfate dissolves in water, creating an acid solution. When this solution is allowed to mix with large quantities of pool water, the acid is neutralized and aluminum hydroxide is formed. The aluminum hydroxide then mixes with water; if the pH is in the proper range (7.2 to 7.6), it precipitates, similar to a white gelatinous snowflake. The precipitate then fills in the spaces between the sand grains and forms a gelatinous mat capturing solid particles from the water, which might otherwise pass through the filter.

Where, When, and How Much Alum?

The amount of alum to be added to the filter tank is usually 2 ounces for each square foot of filter surface area. In specific cases, this amount may be varied slightly.

After the alum is added to the circulation water, a brief interval of time is necessary for it to dissolve, for the acid to be neutralized, and for the aluminum hydroxide precipitate to form into a floc. For this reason, the alum must be introduced to the water at a point between the pool drain and the filters and preferably at a point that requires it to pass through the pump before entering the filters. This allows for additional mixing by the pump. If alum is added too quickly, too close to the filter, or in too great a quantity, it can pass through a sand filter, leaving alum in the pool, irritating the eyes, and causing the hair and skin to feel sticky.

Because pool water is only slightly basic, large quantities of water are required to neutralize the acid formed by the dissolving of the alum. The dissolved alum solution usually introduced to the line by a chemical feeder should be allowed to enter the circulation line slowly to ensure that sufficient pool water is mixed with it. The total feeding time should take approximately 4 hours.

The entire process of alum flocculation is sensitive to the acidity of pool water; if the pH is not maintained in the proper range (7.2 to 7.6), the flocculation process may not produce the desired results. Alum coagulents are used only with low-rate granular media filters having an application rate of 3 gallons per minute/square foot (gpm/sf) of filter surface area or less. Coagulents should not be used with "high-rate" filters unless specified by the manufacturer.

Effect of pH on Alum Floc

Alum is peculiar in that it flocs best in pool water at a pH of 7.2 to 7.6. If the pH moves out of this range, the alum floc begins to dissolve. Only experience and experimentation will determine the exact pH that is best for coagulation in a particular pool.

Consider a hypothetical situation in which the pH of the water is 7.4 and the optimum floc point is 7.2. Most of the alum has formed floc at 7.4, but some dissolved alum remains in the water, floccing out gradually as the addition of chlorine causes the pH to drop toward 7.2. Because the pool operator usually attempts to hold the pH above 7.2, soda ash is likely added at this point. If the pH is raised to 7.6, some of the alum floc holding the dirt in the filter dissolves, and the dirt is allowed to pass into the pool. The solution to this problem of maintaining proper pH in a sand-filtered pool is to add soda ash constantly in small amounts rather than occasionally in large amounts. If the pH drops below 7.2, backwash may be necessary before the gauge pressure differential is reached in order to adjust the pH without disturbing flocculation.

The addition of make-up water may also change the pH of the pool. If the make-up water has a pH higher or lower than the pool water, care must be taken not to disturb the floc when adding water to the pool. Alum produces an acid when it reacts with water and then lowers the pH. For this reason, the pH should be elevated slightly before adding alum.

Algicides

Warm water, high pH, and sunlight provide ideal conditions for red, green, brown, black, or blue-green algae to grow and to attach itself to the sides and bottom of a pool. Algae has been a problem for most pool operators, depleting chlorine, causing turbidity, producing slimy surfaces in and out of the pool, and sometimes causing a foul odor.

Preventive maintenance is the best solution to handling algae problems. This consists of maintaining a free chlorine residual above 1.0 ppm and a pH range of 7.4 to 7.6. However, some pool operators resort to commercially prepared algicides or to other chemicals known to be effective against algae. When used correctly, these algicides have a killing effect, but they also affect the chemistry of the pool water.

Quarternary ammonium compounds (QACs) are often used to control algae because they are considered much safer than the various mercury and copper compounds; however, ammonium ions may combine with chlorine, producing eye irritation through the development of chloramine compounds. Quarternary ammonium compounds (QACs) reduce chlorine effects, increase chlorine demand, collect on filters, and cause pool water to foam. Some types of algae have also developed a resistance to ammonium algicides.

For many years, pool operators have also used copper sulfate and phenylmercuric acetate, neither of which is recommended for use. Copper sulfate can cause discoloration of bathing suits, skin rash, green hair, a carbonate hardness precipitate, or an inky precipitate if sulfur (hydrogen sulfide) is present in the water. Mercury products are not recommended for use under any circumstances because mercury is known to be a cumulative poison.

Controlling Carbonate Stability and Corrosiveness of Pool Water

In addition to knowledge of disinfectants and pH, the pool operator must be aware of several factors at work in pool water. Of primary concern is a disinfection level (free chlorine) with a narrow range of pH and limited total alkalinity content. Additives required for control of each of these factors affect the other factors in some way. In addition, the changing bathing load constantly introduces organic and ammonia nitrogen along with microorganisms. If the pool is located outdoors, sunshine, wind, and windblown matter further affect chemical requirements.

All chemicals in the pool water affect the tendency of water to be either corrosive or to deposit carbonate scale. An optimum equilibrium is possible when factors affecting these properties of water are nearly balanced. In 1936, W.F. Langelier of the University of California developed a useful method for obtaining equilibrium. In a single formula, he expressed the relationship among pH, temperature, calcium hardness, total alkalinity, and dissolved solids. This method has been subjected to experimental study in the field, has been found to coincide with operating results in the treatment of municipal water supplies, and is recommended for use in swimming pools. A Saturation Index for a given temperature is used as a reference point for comparing values of pH against actual determined pH values of water. When these are in balance, the water is in equilibrium with solid $CaCO_3$ at that temperature. If the index is positive (+), the water is supersaturated with $CaCO_3$ and may deposit a protective coating or scale in the pipeline, particularly metal filters and valves, pumps, and such. When it is negative (−), water dissolves $CaCO_3$ and may be corrosive. In this case, the Saturation Index is negative; the quantity of soda ash required for corrective treatment may be determined, and

immediate steps may be taken to eliminate the corrosive condition of the water (i.e., metal attack).

For swimming pools a practical simplification of the Langelier Saturation Index accounts for five pool water variables:

1. pH
2. Temperature
3. Total hardness
4. Alkalinity
5. Calcium hardness

Each of these variable qualities of the water, except pH, must be converted to an appropriate factor for substitution in the formula:

$$S.I. = pH + \text{Temperature Factor (TF)} + \text{Calcium Factor (CF)} + \text{Alkalinity Factor (AF)} - 12.1$$

Sample Problem

Water analysis results reveal the following:
pH = 7.5
Water Temperature = 78 °F
Calcium Hardness = 140 ppm
Total Alkalinity = 20 ppm

Utilizing the Langelier Index Table (Table 13.1), analysis results are converted into the appropriate factors.

$$S.I. = (pH)\ 7.5 + (TF)\ .6 + (CF)\ 1.8 + (AF)\ 1.4 - 12.1$$
$$S.I. = -.8 \text{ (corrosive water)}$$

For swimming pools, a Saturation Index range of plus or minus ±0.5 is considered acceptable. Higher than +0.5 is scale forming; lower than −0.5 is corrosive. The recommended objective is to maintain a Saturation Index just slightly on the positive (+) side.

Because the Saturation Index in this example proves to be corrosive (−.8), the proper correction move is to increase total alkalinity by addition of sodium bicarbonate to increase the AF or alkalinity factor. Because the total alkalinity is less than 100 ppm, the minimum recommended value previously noted in this section, the addition of sodium bicarbonate will raise the alkalinity level to a desirable value and elevate it without increasing pH.

Increasing alkalinity of pool water in the above example from 20 to 150 ppm using sodium bicar-

Table 13.1 Langelier Saturation Index Table

Temp (in °F)	TF	Calcium Hardness	CF	Total Alkalinity	AF
32	0.0	5	0.3	5	0.7
37	0.1	25	1.0	25	1.4
46	0.2	50	1.3	50	1.7
53	0.3	75	1.5	75	1.9
60	0.4	100	1.6	100	2.0
66	0.5	150	1.8	150	2.2
76	0.6	200	1.9	200	2.3
84	0.7	300	2.1	300	2.5
94	0.8	400	2.2	400	2.6
105	0.9	800	2.5	800	2.9
128	1.0	1000	2.6	1000	3.0

bonate and rechecking produces the following Saturation Index:

$$S.I. = 7.5 + 0.6 + 1.8 + 2.2 - 12.1 = 0.0$$
(acceptable)

Disinfection Systems

Water has long been recognized as a transportation medium for disease. Centuries ago 1,300 miles of aqueducts were used to bring water to the city of Rome from the mountains. The Romans were aware of the value of the aqueducts that exposed the water to a form of aeration and to the ultraviolet rays of the sun, thus implementing a crude system of water disinfection.

Today the disinfection of swimming pool water is usually accomplished through the use of one of three of the four members of the halogen family of elements on the periodic table: florine, chlorine, bromine, and iodine. Florine is a very powerful acid and is not utilized for pool water disinfection.

Throughout the years many different methods of water purification have been attempted, including the following:

- Physical treatment—heat application
- Use of metallic ions—silver and copper salts
- Irradiation—ultraviolet light
- Alkalis and acids—sulfamic acid
- Surface chemicals—ammonium sulphate
- Oxidizers—halogens and ozone
- Electrical—chlorine generation from salt

Some of these methods have met with considerable success, a few have proved too expensive, and others have not provided quality results. Of the halogen disinfectants chlorine has proven to be the most widely used, with chlorine gas, calcium hypochlorite, and sodium hypochlorite being the most popular of the many types of chlorine. These three are discussed in order of their cost-effectiveness, beginning with the least expensive method presently known.

Gas Chlorine (Cl_2)

Gas chlorine is prepared commercially by the electrolysis of table salt. The gas is dried, cooled, and compressed into steel cylinders. In the pure form (99.9%) at room temperature, it exists as a green-yellow gas, 2-1/2 times heavier than air. When compressed into metal cylinders, it liquifies and exists as an amber-colored fluid, approximately 1-1/2 times heavier than water. The liquid returns to the gas form as it is emitted from the cylinder.

All chlorine containers must conform to prescribed guidelines established by the Chlorine In-

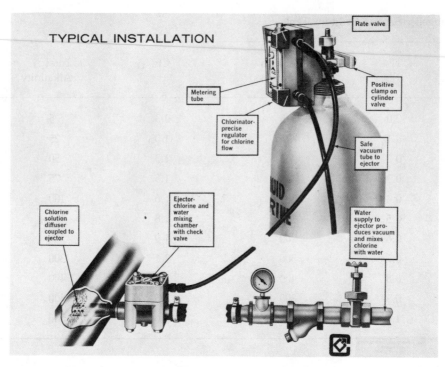

Chlorine gas vacuum system by Capital Controls Company

stitute, Inc. The valve is composed of a brass body with a Monel (nickel/stainless steel) stem. On the opposite side of the valve opening is a fusible plug designed to melt at 160 °F. The purpose of this plug is to prevent the container from exploding, which might result from high internal pressure caused by extremes of external temperature. The valve itself is protected with a cap that has nonstandard threads. Each valve is covered by a screw or cylinder "bonnet" attached to a collar on top of the cylinder.

In the gaseous form, chlorine is an excellent oxidizer and bactericide in concentrations of .4 ppm or more and is the most inexpensive form of chlorine. Expensive safety precautions are required because the system must be housed in a separate room ventilated to the outside, and at least one self-contained breathing unit is necessary for emergencies, repairs, and changing cylinders. Cannister masks are ineffective in high-chlorine density atmospheres and therefore are not recommended.

Because chlorine is an acid, attention must be given to the pH of the water. Continual addition of soda ash (sodium carbonate) is required, usually on a ratio of 1-1/2 pounds of soda ash for each pound of chlorine gas expended.

Advantages of gas chlorine

- Least expensive disinfection system
- No shelf life problems (heat, humidity, sunlight)
- Excellent oxidizer and bactericide
- pH easy to maintain with soda ash at ratio of 1-1/2 pounds of soda ash to each 1 pound of Cl_2 gas

Disadvantages of gas chlorine

- System installation is somewhat expensive due to safety requirements
- Training in use of self-contained breathing apparatus necessary for personnel who will work with the system
- Regular servicing of chlorinator necessary to maintain minimum safety (every 6 to 12 months)

Calcium Hypochlorite (CA[OCl]₂)

Commercial calcium hypochlorite is a dry and relatively stable mixture of chlorine (50%), calcium (28%), and oxygen (22%). It is a compound with an oxidation availability of 72% and is usually manufactured in granular and tablet form (about 100 tablets per pound). Because calcium hypochlorite is a strong oxidizer, care must be taken to keep it dry and away from fire and organic materials such as petroleum products, cleaning fluids, detergents, and paper products. If contaminated with any of these materials, a fire or explosion may occur.

Calcium hypochlorite, perhaps somewhat safer than gas, requires more time to prepare and demands more maintenance to the chlorinator than does gas. The granular type should be mixed with water in a plastic container and then permitted to sit while the calcium hydroxide and insoluble materials settle out. The green-colored liquid above the sediment should then be siphoned into another plastic container and fed through a hypochlorinator into the circulation line. Although most of the calcium hydroxide and insolubles are precipitated out before transfer to the second container, a small amount remains in suspension, and a gradual build-up of scale will take place in the hypochlorinator. Calcium hypochlorite may be applied directly to small pools but should not be applied directly to larger pools for any length of time, as a precipitate of calcium carbonate can occur, turning the water cloudy. Normal filtration removes most of the precipitate in time, but bathers will agitate this sediment during swimming hours, keeping the water turbid until cleaned by vacuuming.

Calcium hypochlorite is also an effective algicide. A few granules sprinkled on low spots in the cement, beneath diving boards, and on the other surfaces where algae may grow, eliminate slippery spots and odors stemming from algae. Caution must be exercised in using it on painted or plastic surfaces because bleaching may occur. This type of chlorine may be sprinkled into the pool over the algae growths on the bottom and is sometimes used on locker-room floors as a disinfectant.

A significant increase in pH normally occurs with calcium hypochlorite, thus requiring the use of muriatic acid or sodium bisulfate to reduce it to the 7.4 to 7.6 range. Compared with chlorine gas, it is more expensive because the dry compound has only 50% availability. No matter what type of chlorine is used, it is wise to keep 25 to 50 pounds of calcium hypochlorite on hand because of its multiplicity of uses. Shelf life of this product is approximately 1 year if stored at room temperature, in low humidity, and out of the presence of sunlight.

Advantages of calcium hypochlorite

- Less expensive than other systems except Cl_2 gas
- Keeps pH levels up
- Can be used for disinfecting decks and locker-room floors

Disadvantages of calcium hypochlorite

- Must be prepared ahead of time (mixing, settling, and siphoning required) if used properly
- Some types flammable and explosive
- Increases calcium hardness levels and scaling
- pH must be lowered with acid
- Shelf life of 12 months, if stored properly

Sodium Hypochlorite (NaOCl)

Sodium hypochlorite (household bleach) is used in much stronger concentrations for pool disinfection. Common bleach, available in most supermarkets, is a 5 to 5.25% strength solution. Stronger concentrations of 10 to 16% are required for swimming pool use. Sodium hypochlorite is produced by two methods: It is manufactured commercially by passing chlorine gas through a solution of sodium hydroxide (a strong base—pH 14.0); and can also be made on site by adding soda ash to a mixture of calcium hypochlorite and water, allowing the contents to settle and siphoning off the dark green liquid. This method is time-consuming and serves no useful financial purpose.

Liquid chlorine (12 to 16% NaOCl aqueous solution) is added to pool water through a hypochlorinator or can be applied directly to the pool. Direct application is not a recommended procedure because periodic fluctuation occurs in free residuals. Although it is virtually sediment-free, some precipitate may occur in the storage container if the supply is not fresh or immediately used.

Sodium hypochlorite is an unstable compound that cannot be manufactured stronger than 16% because sodium hydroxide becomes completely saturated at that point, and no more chlorine gas is accepted. It is extremely susceptible to deterioration, especially if stored in a warm, humid area or if exposed to sunlight. Although it is manufactured at 16% solution, it rarely reaches the pool operator above 15% and may be as weak as 10%. Rapid deterioration results in a shelf life ranging between 60 and 90 days.

One of the advantages of using the liquid form is that the sodium hydroxide elevates the pH, thus eliminating the need for soda ash. This is also somewhat of a disadvantage because the pH rises to a point where sodium bisulfate or muriatic acid must be used on a daily basis to maintain a range congruent with maximum chlorine efficiency (7.4 to 7.6).

When added to hard water, calcium hydroxide or calcium carbonate deposits may form at the point of injection in the water line. Dilution of sodium hypochlorite is sometimes necessary before application, and care should be exercised not to use hard water because a precipitate may result, clogging the chemical feeder. Frequent purging of the chemical feeder (once a month) with muriatic acid is desirable to remove sodium hydroxide deposits.

Advantages of sodium hypochlorite

- Ease of use, no mixing unless diluted
- Keeps pH levels up
- Little danger involved in storage and use
- Low cost, if used appropriately

Disadvantages of sodium hypochlorite

- More expensive than calcium hypochlorite and chlorine gas
- Increases sodium levels in pool water
- pH must be lowered with acid
- Short shelf life (60 to 90 days), even if stored under ideal conditions
- Causes scaling if pH not maintained between 7.4 to 7.6

Discussions of other types of less frequently used disinfection systems follow.

Lithium Hypochlorite (LiOCl)

Lithium hypochlorite is commercially processed and occasionally used as a disinfectant in swimming pools. It is a dry and fairly stable compound of chlorine and is closely related to calcium hypochlorite in its basic properties. Pure lithium hypochlorite contains approximately 61% available chlorine by weight; however, some lithium hydrates contain only 35% availability. If purchased at full strength,

lithium hypochlorite may be less expensive than calcium hypochlorite. If purchased in the hydrate form (35%), it proves more expensive than calcium hypochlorite (50% availability).

The shelf life of this product is about 1 year at temperatures below 80 °F. Above 80 °F it deteriorates at a much faster rate than the calcium type or the chlorinated cyanurates.

Lithium hypochlorite may gain more use in the future if a less expensive method of production is discovered.

Advantages of lithium hypochlorite

- Could be relatively inexpensive if 61% available chlorine compound is purchased

Disadvantages of lithium hypochlorite

- Shelf life stability is poor at temperatures above 80 °F.
- Hydrate forms (35% available Cl_2) are expensive to use

Dichloroisocyanurates ($C_3N_3Cl_2ONa$) Sodium Salt ($C_3N_3Cl_2OK$) Potassium Salt

The chlorinated cyanurates are one of the more recent additions to the group of pool disinfectant products; however, this method of disinfection is as controversial as it is recent. Chlorinated cyanurate is marketed in white tablet form and contains approximately 60% available chlorine by weight. The most frequently used types are the potassium and sodium salts because they are the most stable and soluble.

Potassium and sodium dichloroisocyanurates have many of the same properties as calcium hypochlorite: that is, appearance, feeding, and handling. Although its reaction with water is not completely understood, it is generally accepted that hydrolysis does take place, resulting in the formation of hypochlorous acid. The controversy stems from this point, however, over how much of the available chlorine exists in the free or combined state.

Prior to using this type of chlorine, pool water must be stabilized by conditioning it with 25 to 50 ppm of cyanuric acid. Conditioning helps to lock in the chlorine when it is added and slows down dissipation due to sunlight. The pool should then be superchlorinated with 1 gallon of sodium hypochlorite per 20,000 gallons of water. This completes the conditioning requirements; approximately 2 to 3 ounces of sodium or potassium dichloroisocyanurate per 10,000 gallons of water should be applied to the pool every other day. Weekly superchlorination is necessary with some other type of chlorine because chlorinated cyanurates are completely ineffective in retarding algae growth. The chlorinated cyanurates offer several advantages as well as several disadvantages.

Advantages of dichloroisocyanurate

- Safe handling
- Easy application (by hand or chlorinator)
- Residual stability
- No insoluble material to form precipitates or scale on plumbing or on the chlorinator
- Little or no fluctuation in pH

Disadvantages of dichloroisocyanurate

- Less free chlorine
- Slower bacteria kill (5 to 10 times slower than gas or hypochlorites)
- More expensive than other types of chlorine (because of conditioning of water and weekly super chlorination)
- Not an effective algicide
- Deterioration of chlorinated cyanurates produces ammonia (ammonia nitrogen or chloramines— an excellent nutriment for algae)
- Combustible (flammable and explosive)
- Levels of cyanuric acid above 100 ppm prohibited in most states by public health departments
- Cyanuric acid levels above 100 ppm linked to kidney and liver damage in humans

Organic Bromine ($C_4H_4O_2N_2BrCl$)

Bromine in the elemental form is not like chlorine (gas) in that it exists at room temperatures as a red or red-brown liquid 3 times heavier than water. It is extremely dangerous to handle, damaging almost any surface and severely burning skin; and fumes from an uncapped bottle will injure eyes and mucous membranes. For this reason, liquid bromine is always shipped in special, unbreakable glass bottles.

The obvious dangers of elemental bromine (Br_2) have led to the development of a safer type called hydantoin or stick bromine. Hydantoin bromine is comparable to the cyanurates and hypochlorites and has a total halogen availability of 62% (Br + Cl) by weight. It is manufactured in cylinder or stick form and is more expensive than elemental bromine. Application to pool water is accomplished by eroding the sticks with water in a brominator-dissolving tank and pumping the mixture into the recirculation line to the pool. Free residual levels fluctuate with bromine because erosion of the stick is not always constant.

Advantages of bromine

- Less eye irritation
- Effective oxidizer and disinfectant
- Effective algicide
- Adds no insolubles to the pool

Disadvantages of bromine

- Danger in handling elemental bromine
- Organic stick form combustible (flammable and explosive)
- Lowers pH slightly (requiring soda ash)
- Emits a strong odor around pool (due to excessive amounts)
- Causes water to turn dark green (safety hazard)
- Can stain pool walls brown (when used in excess)
- Using a dissolving tank prohibits a quick increase if the residual falls to an unsatisfactory level (stick form)

Iodine (KI)

Iodine (I_2) exists in the free state as a bluish-black solid and is the only member of the halogen family that occurs as a solid at room temperature. In the free state, iodine (I_2) has a very low solubility in water. Therefore, potassium iodide (KI), which is very soluble in water, is used instead. Potassium iodide has an iodine availability of 70% by weight and is approved by most public health agencies in concentrations of 1.0 ppm and higher.

Preparation of a potassium iodide solution requires dissolving 4 pounds of crystals in 40 gallons of water in a plastic container. This solution is pumped via a chemical feed pump into the water similar to liquid chlorine. An iodine system also requires a small amount of chlorine to be added almost continually. Chlorine is added to supply hypochlorite ion that can oxidize iodide ion to hypoiodite ion or hypoiodous acid (HOI). The use of liquid chlorine or calcium hypochlorite, therefore, requires a second chemical feeder.

Upon liberation, the free iodine combines with water to form hypoiodous acid (weak acid), a good disinfectant that has virtually no effect on pH. As long as make-up water has a minimum total alkalinity of 50 ppm, no soda ash should be required to maintain the ideal pH range (7.2 to 7.6).

Iodine is also very responsive to changes in pH, and a green-colored water, along with the characteristic iodine odor, occurs if water is not tested and pH frequently adjusted.

Advantages of iodine

- No eye irritation, bleaching of hair or bathing suits
- Safe and easy handling
- Effects on pH insignificant
- Effective as a bactericide
- Very stable, requires little iodine adjustment
- Converts back to iodine ion after being used as a disinfectant and may be reconverted as many as 10 to 13 times to free iodine by continuous addition of chlorine to pool water

Disadvantages of iodine

- Can promote skin rashes
- Produces an iodine odor (neglect of pH control)
- Requires two chemical feed pumps
- Completely ineffective against algae
- More expensive than chlorine (chlorine and related equipment necessary to use iodine)
- Necessary to burn out ammonia compounds by breakpoint chlorination or other chemical means
- Is unstable and tends to decompose within a few minutes to iodine and iodate ions
- Discolors jewelry not removed before swimming
- Requires a different test kit

Many improvements are necessary in methods and control of iodine if it is to be universally accepted.

Ozone

The use of ozone as a swimming pool disinfectant began as early as the 1940s in the United States and South America. However, these attempts were unsuccessful as some installations applied ozone directly to the pool and bubbles caused difficulties in visibility. The technology used to produce ozone also proved too expensive to be cost-effective at that time, resulting in this disinfection system's disappearance for 30 years. In the 1970s a company in the United States introduced a new innovation in ozone production that eliminated some of the earlier usage problems.

Ozone is a form of oxygen consisting of three atoms, whereas the oxygen contained in air consists of two atoms. Ozone is a powerful oxidizer and disinfectant—two widely recognized qualities. As an oxidizer, ozone can eliminate tastes, odors, and colors from pool water. Various studies have shown ozone to be extremely effective in destroying all types of bacteria and viruses.

The production of ozone is accomplished through an on-site system connected to the pool circulation line. This system consists of a chamber into which air is compressed over a short wavelength ultraviolet light. As air passes over the light, ozone is produced and then injected into the circulation line where it mixes with pool water.

Ozone offers the advantage of not having to order, handle, or store anything, along with reducing the staining and scaling properties of iron and other metals dissolved in pool water. Its major disadvantage lies in the installation expense: Ozone equipment may double the price of a pool disinfection system.

Some states require the removal of ozone from the water; for this purpose, a carbon absorption system may be included to remove the ozone from the water before persons enter the pool. All states require some sort of halogen residual, usually a minimum of .4 ppm of chlorine or its equivalent, to ensure that some residual bactericide remains in the water. This, of course, means two systems of disinfection or a double expenditure.

Chlorine Generation

One of the newest innovations in swimming pool disinfection systems was developed in Holland and the United States. This system involves the generation of a sodium hypochlorite solution in a pool's circulation by the electrolysis of salt dissolved in the water.

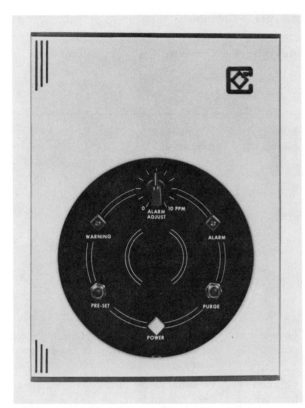

Chlorine gas leak detector by Capital Controls Company

The required salt content lies between .017 and .023 lb/gallon, which equals a salinity of 1,250 to 3,000 ppm or about 1/15 the concentration of sea water. A quantity of food-grade salt is added directly to the pool to bring the salinity up to the required level. From this point, only small additions are necessary after the initial application to make up losses from splash-out and backwashing.

Chlorine is generated from an electrolytic cell incorporated into the circulation line, operated by a transformer-rectifier and controlled by a hand-operated switch. The circulation pump forces water through the electrolytic cell, past anode and cathode plates. Chlorine evolves from the platinum anode plates, and hydrogen is formed at the cathode plates. A 220-volt electrical supply is utilized initially but is reduced in the transformer to 24 volts. Production of chlorine is controlled by varying the electric load on the cells, allowing free residuals of up to 20 ppm to be achieved with this system.

Of the several advantages built into the generation of sodium hypochlorite, regeneration is one of the most important. Active chlorine is converted back to chlorine during its disinfecting action; hence, there is no salt consumption. This system also eliminates ordering, transporting, mixing, and storing—common practices with other halogen disinfection systems.

As is the case with all disinfection systems, there are some disadvantages. Chlorine generation is contingent upon electricity, a form of energy that will continue to increase in cost significantly in the future. Some chlorine odor is discernible, and the pH increases slightly, requiring the use of small amounts of acid. The corrosiveness of salt water is also a factor to consider. Using PVC pipe, fiberglass, and stainless steel components in the circulation system and pool equipment that is in daily contact with salt water unquestionably lengthens the life of the pool and its associated equipment. Perhaps the most significant drawback is the cost of installation, which now ranges between $10,000 to $15,000 for a pool containing 150,000 to 300,000 gallons of water. However, with a lower daily cost of operation, the savings are much greater in the long run.

Water-Testing Procedures

Testing for the various residuals found in swimming pool water requires great care to ensure the quality and accuracy of the findings. Most testing procedures employing reagents are relatively simple; as a result, it is often tempting to delay routine water analysis. The following general water-testing procedures, if performed as recommended, enable the maintenance of a clean, safe pool.

1. Wash your hands with soap and rinse well with clean water prior to testing.

2. Use covers and tops provided in test kits when shaking the vial containing the water sample and reagent, or be sure to use different fingers. (False readings may occur otherwise.)

3. Keep all plastic and glass test kit components clean by washing with soap and rinsing with distilled or de-ionized water.

4. When collecting the sample, be careful to avoid the area in front of the water outlets.

5. Cover the vial with its provided top or with a finger, and take the sample by opening it at a depth of 8 to 12 inches below the surface.

6. Collect the correct amount of water.

7. Take two disinfectant tests: one in shallow water and one in the deep end. The shallow-water disinfectant level is always lower.

Table 13.2 Advantages and Disadvantages of the Common Types of Chlorine

Chlorine Source	Available Physical Forms	Other Chemicals Required in Conjunction With Its Use	% Available Chlorine	Advantages	Disadvantages	Comments
Gas	Gas	Soda ash (Na_2CO_3) to neutralize HCl formed	100%	Lowest cost/pound Cl_2	Potential safety hazards Equipment necessary for operation Operator training required for safe use Not stabilized against Cl_2 dissipation caused by u.v. rays of sunlight pH control continually necessary	
Ca(OCl)$_2$	Granular tablet		50%	Lowest cost/pound Cl_2 Can be fed by hand or with a chlorinator Can be used with a feeder to provide continuous chlorination	Causes precipitation (cloudiness) in hard water areas Potential safety problems caused by it being a strong oxidizing agent Not stabilized against Cl_2 dissipation caused by u.v. rays of sunlight	Hydrated form is fire-resistant
Chlorinated isocyanurate	Granular tablet	Pool must be stabilized initially with 25 to 50 ppm of cyanuric acid to stabilize u.v. caused dissipation of Cl_2	Usually 63%	Stable against Cl_2 dissipation caused by u.v. rays of sun Can be used in hard water areas Low cost/performance to use due to improved chlorine stability	Higher initial cost	Hydrated form of the sodium dichloroisocyanurate is fire-resistant
NaOCl	Liquid	Acid to neutralize high pH	Usually 90%	Low cost/pound solution	Requires acid to neutralize the high pH Not stabilized Container breakage High-cost performance to use	Potential safety problem

8. When utilizing a hand-held color meter, give preference to fluorescent light, indirect sunlight, or incandescent light (in that order) to provide the truest color for comparison.

9. Use only fresh reagents for testing. pH indicators have a shelf life of only 6 months, and DPD liquid and tablets kept under normal conditions (room temperature) must be changed every 12 months.

10. Use reagents for testing that are manufactured by the same company that manufactured the test kit. Variations occur among companies in strength of solutions as well as in chemical components.

11. Keep reagents away from extremes of heat and cold and out of direct sunlight.

12. Use caution in handling reagents because chemical burns and irritation to eyes and mucous membranes may occur.

Testing for the various residuals found in swimming pool water is usually accomplished through the use of some type of comparator slide, titration, or turbidity analysis. Other methods are also available.

Testing for Halogen Residuals

The most common method of testing for free chlorine directly is the Palin or DPD method. This method is based on the use of diethyl-p-phenylene diamine. It may also be used to measure the chloramines in the swimming pool water.

Another method for reading free chlorine (as well as pH) uses a simple test strip. In contact with the pool water, the test strip changes color, and the resulting color is compared with standards supplied by the manufacturer in the test kit. These test strips measure free chlorine only. Ortho tolidine, once the mainstay of pool test kits for identifying free chlorine levels, is no longer recommended. The opportunity for error is too great to warrant continued use; in addition, ortho tolidine has been identified as a carcinogen (cancer-producing substance).

Residual bromine may be tested very easily with the same DPD colorimeter test kit. If a chlorine test kit is used for testing bromine, however, the reading must be doubled. Thus, the 0.3 ppm chlorine sample becomes a 0.6 ppm standard for bromine unless the test kit manufacturer's instructions indicate otherwise.

Test kits for free chlorine determination and pH determination are essential items for pool operation whether the pool contains 3,000 or 300,000 gallons of water. Small, inexpensive test kits are also available for the home pool owner; however, a professional pool operator may desire a more comprehensive kit.

Similar test kits are available for cyanuric acid and iodine. Regardless of the type of test kit used or of the manufacturer, be sure to follow the directions provided with your test kit. As test kits are updated and accuracy increased, procedures sometimes change from year to year in test kits with the same model number and manufactured by the same company.

Testing for pH

Determining the pH of pool water is a relatively simple operation. There are certain chemical indicator solutions that are sensitive to acids and bases. The three most commonly used indicators are bromthymol blue (pH: 6.0 to 7.6), phenol red (pH: 6.8 to 8.4), and cresol red (pH: 7.2 to 8.8). Of the three, phenol red is the most often used. The test is conducted with the same type color comparator used for testing chlorine residual except that a separate set of color standards for pH and the proper indicator solution are used.

In water that has a high chlorine content (1.0 ppm or more), chlorine may bleach the pH indicator and give false pH readings. In this case, a drop of sodium thiosulfate (photographer's hypo) must be added to the vial before adding the indicator. The hypo reduces, or "neutralizes," the chlorine. Many indicator solutions already contain the neutralizer. Be sure to follow the manufacturer's directions for your kit.

Thoroughly clean vials are essential for accurate test results. If a vial is covered with a finger before inverting to mix the solution, a false reading may result unless the hand is clean.

Common Water Problems

The pool operator who has been exposed to basic water chemistry probably will not experience turbid, cloudy, or colored water. Conversely, the operator who is unfamiliar with these basic principles may easily experience these conditions along with eye, skin, and mucous membrane sensitivity and damage to plumbing, to the pool heater, and to other related equipment.

Solutions to common problems in water management are provided in the following sections. These solutions, however, serve only as guidelines and may not always solve problems to the pool operator's satisfaction. There may be other conditions present due to water supply, geographic area, and other regional differences that may have significance in each particular case.

Turbid Water

Turbidity implies the presence of dirt or impurities causing discoloration of water. This condition can be caused by a contaminated water supply, faulty filter operations, or improper chemical procedures. Exposure of water to air is another factor as pollen, dust, and automobile exhaust fumes can cause cloudiness. The easiest method of coping with turbidity is to prevent it and may be achieved as follows:

1. Maintain an adequate chlorine residual (.4 to 1.0).
2. Maintain the proper pH and alkalinity level (7.4 to 7.6 and 100 ppm) and a Langelier Saturation Index between −.5 and +.5.
3. Keep the water level up to the skimmers or to a point of overflow into the gutters.
4. Backwash when necessary; do not overextend filter runs, especially on hot or crowded days.
5. Keep decks and pool entrances clean.
6. For outdoor pools, keep the grass cut, discard the trimmings, and plant shrubs and trees around the area for protection from airborne contaminants.
7. Vacuum the pool every other day.
8. Drain the pool annually.

If a turbid condition exists, use these guidelines:

1. Check immediately for chlorine and pH levels.

- If the chlorine residual is very low (.1 to .2 ppm) or nonexistent, the pH is high (7.8+), and the water is green, suspect algae.
- If the chlorine is high, the pH is low (below 7.2), and the water colored (green, brown, black), suspect metals in solution or in suspension.
- If the water is cloudy or milky and the pool uses diatomaceous earth filtration, suspect a torn cover on a filter element that is leaking D.E. into the pool. In this event, the filter cover must be replaced.
- If the water looks dirty and the pool uses sand filters, recheck your backwash procedure to

determine if the valves were opened and closed at the proper time.

2. If the water is clear early in the day and cloudy late in the afternoon or evening, suspect overloaded filters or a torn D.E. filter cover. Overloaded filters need to be backwashed or cleaned on crowded days and may not be able to keep up with the load; therefore, increase the chlorine residual to help oxidize the organic material. If the cover on a D.E. filter is to blame, replace it.

Algae and Its Control

Algae is a single-celled green plant, which thrives in sunlight and water of high pH. Although about 46 species of algae grow well in pool water, three types are particularly bothersome to pool operators: planktonic algae (floating), bottom algae (creates sediment), and sessile algae (grows in cracks and cement pores).

Algae spores are introduced into pool water in raindrops or by wind-borne dust. Once in the pool, the spores grow rapidly and can take over a pool in as little as 24 to 48 hours. The spores are nourished by nitrates (ammonia compounds and dissolved carbon dioxide). Other conditions conducive to algae growth are low chlorine (below .2 ppm), warm water (over 80 °F), and mineral and chemical content.

Algae is not directly responsible for disease or infection, but should be eliminated because it decreases visibility, creates odors and slippery surfaces, and imparts objectionable tastes.

The best method for treating algae is to prevent it and may be done as follows:

1. Maintain a good chlorine residual (1.0 ppm).
2. Maintain a pH between 7.2 to 7.6; keep pH close to 7.4 during July and August; minimize CO_2 development.
3. Periodically (once a week) superchlorinate or use breakpoint chlorination to burn out ammonia compounds. Superchlorination should take place at night (no sunlight or bathers). Readjust chlorine and pH before permitting bathers to enter the pool the next day.
4. Maintain 24-hour filtration with maximum turnover.
5. Vacuum the pool every day if possible.
6. Paint the pool once a year (fill cracks and pores, maintaining a smooth surface).

7. Watch for unexplained, sudden rises in pH as this is usually a warning signal of algae growth before it can be seen.

Should algae gain a foothold in your pool, take the following steps:

1. Superchlorinate to 3.0 ppm overnight, killing the algae.

2. The next morning, brush the pool walls and bottom with a stiff-bristled brush to loosen the dead algae from pores and cracks.

3. Vacuum the bottom of the pool.

4. Adjust the chlorine residual by adding fresh water and keeping the chlorinator turned off until the desired level is reached.

5. If breakpoint chlorination is used, the chlorine level decreases automatically. Maintain careful checks throughout the breakpoint cycle.

6. If this procedure does not give satisfactory results, the pool must be drained, scrubbed with muriatic acid, rinsed, and refilled.

Hard Water (Chelating or Sequestering of Minerals)

Hard water is a common problem in the Southwest, Gulf States, and the North Central regions of the United States. Water becomes hard as it passes over or through calcium (limestone) deposits and magnesium. Hard water causes scale to form on plumbing and filters, clogging them. The formation of scale and/or cloudy water is affected by the amounts of dissolved solids in the water, temperature, amount of calcium hardness, total alkalinity, and pH. Of the five factors mentioned, only alkalinity and pH can be controlled significantly enough to reduce hardness, unless the water is softened before the pool is filled. If the pH is maintained between 7.2 and 7.6, scaling or cloudy conditions are unlikely.

Hard water problems can be reduced by following this procedure:

1. Add sodium hexametaphosphate to the pool at a rate of 1/2 pound per 10,000 gallons of water upon filling the pool at the beginning of the season.

2. *Do not chlorinate before softening.*

3. Add 1 ounce of sodium hexametaphosphate per 10,000 gallons of water every 2 weeks during the season. (This chemical is very inexpensive and available from almost all pool supply dealers.)

Colored Water

Colored water is caused by the presence of metallic ions in solution or fine metal particles held in suspension. These metals are either present in the water supply or may result from corrosion of plumbing due to low pH and alkalinity. Each metal imparts its own characteristic color. The most common dissolved metals and their resultant colors are as follows:

Copper: imparts a blue or blue-green color.

Iron: imparts a red or red-brown color. May also be green if the iron is dissolved and not oxidized and the pH has dropped close to 7.0 or below.

Manganese: imparts a brown or black color.

The following procedure should be initiated to alleviate this condition:

For pool with diatomaceous earth filters—

1. Adjust the pH to 7.2 to 7.6 range.

2. Superchlorinate to 4.0 ppm.

3. Scatter aluminum sulfate (alum) over the pool at a rate of 2 ounces per 1,000 gallons of water.

4. Flocculation similar to snowflakes forms and both alum and color compounds settle to the bottom. Allow 12 to 48 hours for settling.

5. Vacuum the pool bottom and maintain filtration at the maximum rate of turnover.

6. Adjust the pH range to 7.2 to 7.6.

7. Adjust the chlorine residual to .4 to 1.0 ppm before permitting bathers to enter the pool.

For pool with sand filters—

1. Adjust the pH to 7.2 to 7.6.

2. Superchlorinate to 4.0 ppm.

3. Add alum at the rate of 2 ounces per square foot of filter surface area *ahead of the filter*. This forms a gelatinous coating on the sand, trapping the color particles.

4. Maintain filter operation at the maximum rate of turnover. Allow 24 to 48 hours for filtration to clear up the water.

5. Backwash the filters to waste.

6. Check and adjust the pH to 7.2 to 7.6.

7. Adjust the chlorine to .4 to 1.0 ppm.

8. Vacuum the bottom of the pool.

With both filter types, it is important to check the pH before and after treatment because alum creates acid when added to water.

Breakpoint Chlorination

Frequent articles have appeared in swimming pool literature about the values of breakpoint chlorination. Operators of large pools that have a high organic content in the water would do well to investigate this method for controlling algae, eliminating chlorine odors and water tastes, and reducing irritation to the eyes. Breakpoint, or superchlorination, should be practiced whenever combined chlorine is detected in the pool water. There are test kits that detect combined chlorine levels at 0.3 ppm chlorine; therefore, when the difference between the total and free chlorine readings (combined chlorine) is greater than 0.3 ppm, one should superchlorinate the pool to breakpoint by adding an amount of chlorine equal to 10 times the amount of combined chlorine present. Consider the following example: A pool contains 2.1 ppm total chlorine and 1.5 ppm free chlorine. The combined chlorine is 2.1 minus 1.5 or 0.6 ppm. Hence this pool should be treated with 10 times 0.6 or 6 ppm of chlorine to remove ammonia and organic matter as discussed next.

Breakpoint chlorination is a process of chlorinating that is based on the following: First, chlorine added to a pool is immediately absorbed by two forms of nitrogen that develop in swimming pool water—ammonia nitrogen and organic nitrogen. Ammonia nitrogen responds rapidly to chlorine and is destroyed without much difficulty; however, organic nitrogen may be a problem. As various dosages of chlorine are added to water containing only ammonia nitrogen, monochloramine is formed, followed by the presence of dichloramine. A fall in the measured chlorine residual occurs as chlorine is continually added during formation of dichloramines.

In summary, breakpoint chlorination stresses (a) that most of the effective chlorine compound is free available chlorine—HOCl or hypochlorous acid; (b) that the proper concentration to be maintained in a pool is that in which the free chlorine is not less than 75% of the total chlorine residual (e.g., if a pool

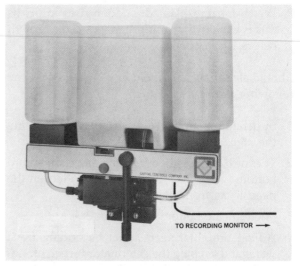

The Capital RR Chlorine Residual Analyzer and Monitor

has 1.3 ppm total chlorine, 1.0 ppm should be free chlorine and 0.3 ppm combined); (c) that differentiation between "free" and "combined" residual is the key to success of the free residual technique; and (d) that proper control of the free residual chlorine level greatly reduces eye irritation complaints, disagreeable odors, and black algae growths.

As noted above, because a great part of the so-called chlorine odors and taste is due to combined residuals, these odors and tastes also disappear after reaching breakpoint. As chlorine is added beyond the breakpoint, most of the chlorine in the water is in a free state, with combined chlorine remaining fairly constant.

Dosage Calculations for Other Disinfectants

Determine the percentage of available disinfectant in the compound used by reading the label. Change the percentage to a decimal by moving the decimal point two places to the left (85% to 0.85). Divide 1.3 by the decimal obtained to learn the number of ounces of compound per 10,000 gallons of water to produce 1 ppm disinfectant.

Example: Assume a compound has 63% available bromine. How much must be added to a pool containing 160,000 gallons to equal 1 ppm bromine?

63% = 0.63

1.3 ÷ .63 = 2.06 ounces per 10,000 gal.

2.06 × 16 = 32.96 ounces for pool.

Table 13.3 Operating Ranges for Pertinent Pool Characteristics to Avoid Green Water, High Chlorine Demand Water, Scaling, Corrosion and Stains, and Cloudy Water

Characteristic	Recommended Level	Means to Control	Means to Measure Level
*Free chlorine, ppm	1.0 to 1.5	Regulation of continuous feeding device.	Intermittent tests with suitable test kit.
*CYA, ppm	25 to 50[1]	Add acid if below 20.	Turbidometric melamine procedure.
**Alkalinity, ppm	50 to 150	Add $NaHCO_3$, if low; HCl if excessive	Suitable test kit (titration).
**Calcium hardness, ppm	50 to 150	Add $CaCl_2$ if low. Remove water or ion exchange; demineralize if high.	Suitable test kit (EDTA titration).
**Dissolved solids, ppm	<300[2]	No problem if low. Remove water on a regular schedule, ion exchange demineralizes if high or incoming water is high.	Weight of residue dried at 105 °C.
**pH	7.2 to 7.8	Adjust with acid or soda ash.	Suitable test kit (phenol red).
**Temperature, °F	82 ± 2	Adjust pool heater, use sprays to cool.	Thermometer.
NH_3, chloramines, or combined Cl_2	<0.2	Add >5 ppm Cl_2 if exceeds maximum. Remove water if persists over max.	Nessler method, DPD Palin test kit.
Added halogen	None	None recommended.	
Added algistat	None	None recommended.	
Bacteria count			
a. Total	<200 on 85% of samples	Regulate level of chlorine in range.	Standard 35° plate count.
b. Coliform	None	1.0 to 1.5.	
c. Other	To be determined		
Algae	None	Add >5 ppm chlorine if detected.	Visual inspection, water clarity.
Water clarity	Clean and clear	Proper operation of filter system, chlorine in proper range, removal of H_2O to control suspended "fines" buildup.	Visual inspection, black disc observation.

*Control of the variable indicated thus (*) required by most health departments.
**Values of these quantities can be used to measure the Langelier Saturation Index.
[1]May be limited to 100 ppm max. by local or state health department.
[2]May be operated at higher levels under certain conditions when hardness and alkalinity are reduced from values in this table.

General Guidelines

- When gas chlorine is used, approximately 1.25 to 1.5 pounds of soda ash must be added for each pound of chlorine to maintain the pH.

Exact amount depends upon other factors affecting pool water.

- Caustic soda is sometimes used in larger pools to obtain desired pH levels. Other pH control problems should be solved by trial addition of small amounts of sodium carbonate to raise pH or sodium bisulfate or acid to lower pH. Start with 1 pound of solid or 1 quart of acid and adjust as needed. Adjustment tables based on chemical readings are available from test kit manufacturers to guide pool operators with dosage calculations.

- For coagulation on granular media filters, use 2 ounces of aluminum sulfate for each square foot of filter surface area.

- For algicides, follow manufacturer's recommendations for dosage.

- For diatomaceous earth filter precoat, use about 5 ounces of diatomaceous earth for each square foot of filter area.

Pool operators find that optimum conditions of water clarity and chemical balances prevail when the following variables are scrupulously maintained at these levels:

pH	7.4 to 7.6
Free chlorine	1.0 to 2.0, but never lower than 75% of total residual chlorine
Calcium hardness	100 to 200 ppm
Total alkalinity	100 to 150 ppm
Temperature	78 to 82 °F
Langelier Saturation Index	(−) 0.5 to (+) 0.5

Chemical Calculation and Dosage

- 1 part per million equals 1 pound of chemical per 1 million pounds of water.

- 1 part per million equals 1 milligram per liter of water.

- 1 part per million equals about 8.3 pounds of chemical per million gallons of water or .13 ounces per thousand gallons of water.

Calculations for Chlorine Dosage

- When chlorine is added to water, it immediately begins acting on impurities. The amount of chlorine needed depends upon the amount of impurities present. For that reason, it is impossible to predict the amount of chlorine any given pool will use in a day. General guides may be used, however. Basing the calculations on absolutely pure water gives the minimum dosage

Weekly chlorine recorder by Capital Controls Company

necessary to maintain a desired residual in addition to that necessary for reaction with impurities.

- A chlorine dosage of 1 part per million means 1 ounce of chlorine for 1 million ounces of water; therefore, 1.3 ounces of pure gaseous chlorine per 10,000 gallons of water equals 1 ppm.

- About 2 ounces of granular or tablet calcium hypochlorite (70% available chlorine) per 10,000 gallons of water equals 1 ppm.

- About 1 cup of liquid sodium hypochlorite solution (15% available chlorine) per 10,000 gallons yields 1 ppm.

- About 1.5 ounces of trichloroisocyanurate (90% available chlorine) per 10,000 gallons yields 1 ppm.

- 1 pound of calcium hypochlorite (50% strength) equals 0.5 pounds of available chlorine.

- 1 gallon of sodium hypochlorite (15%) equals about 1.5 pounds of available chlorine.

- 1 pound of sodium dichloroisocyanurate (63% available chlorine) equals 0.63 pounds available chlorine. 1 pound of trichloroisocyanurate (90% strength) equals 0.9 pounds available chlorine.

- For scrubbing and sanitation of decks, use about 1 ounce granular product or 1/2 cup of liquid sodium hypochlorite in a gallon of water. A dramatic dip occurs when the level of chlorine to ammonia nitrogen reaches 10:1. This is the breakpoint beyond which continued addition of chlorine causes an increase in the free chlorine residual directly proportional to the dose added.

International Swimming Hall of Fame pool, Fort Lauderdale, Florida

Chapter 14

Pool Design Features for Competitive Swimming

Meeting the design specifications of the governing bodies for competitive swimming, diving, water polo, and synchronized swimming in the United States has long confronted architects, engineers, and others involved in planning swimming pools. The ruling bodies' requirements differ on a number of the pool's dimensions. Furthermore, the requirements of the other elements of an aquatic program such as springboard and tower diving, water polo, synchronized swimming, recreational swimming, instruction for nonswimmers and handicapped swimmers, and scuba diving frequently conflict with the requirements of competitive swimming. All these variations imply the need for compromise or the need to provide for meeting these program requirements in other ways, such as building separate facilities for diving or for teaching nonswimmers.

Of primary consideration to the planner is the pool owner. Whether the owner is a school, college, city, or private club is the major consideration in designing the pool because these owners represent different levels of swimming competition, each governed by their own ruling bodies. Fortunately, the basic requirements for the three major ruling bodies for competitive swimming in the United States are similar. Nevertheless, when a public pool owned by a city is used by high schools, colleges, and U.S. Swimming (USS) teams, each with their own level of competition, it becomes necessary for design compromises to be made in certain areas. When such a situation exists, the requirements of USS should be followed. However, it should be realized that when design compromises are made, it is desirable to provide a separate pool for instruction and for the recreation of nonswimmers and children. Because the rules of most competitive swimming bodies call for a minimum water depth of 4 feet or more, this level may be too deep to safely conduct instructional programs for children, 6 years old and under.

As of 1986, the six recognized ruling bodies in the United States and who they govern are as follows (see Appendix C for addresses):

The National Federation of State High School Associations (NFSHSA)
Rule books: *Swimming and Diving, Water Polo*
Jurisdiction: All high schools and prep schools; both men's and women's teams

The National Collegiate Athletic Association (NCAA)
Rule books: *NCAA Men's and Women's Swimming and Diving Rules, Water Polo Rules*
Jurisdiction: All colleges, universities, and YMCAs; both men's and women's teams in swimming and diving

United States Swimming, Inc. (USS)
Rule book: *U.S. Swimming Rules and Regulations*
Jurisdiction: All open amateur swimming in the United States, including masters programs

United States Diving, Inc. (USD)
Rule book: *Diving Rules*
Jurisdiction: All other diving in the United States

United States Water Polo
Rule book: *U.S. Water Polo Rules*
Jurisdiction: All other water polo in the United States

United States Synchronized Swimming (USSS)
Rule book: *Synchronized Swimming*
Jurisdiction: All synchronized swimming in the United States

Swimming meets may be conducted in any length pool with some modification as to swimming distances and lane width. Only when official meets under the sanction of one of the previously mentioned ruling bodies are conducted is adherence to specifications required. A pool not meeting the specifications of a ruling body will unlikely be approved for any conference, regional, or national championship meet. An unfortunate trend occurring among schools, clubs, and agencies is that springboard diving competition is being eliminated because of the pool's failure to meet

competitive diving standards. Installation of new, high-performance competitive springboards in older pools also has made competitive diving more dangerous than it used to be. Because these springboards are incompatible with water depth, hopper bottoms, and insufficient distance and depth in the entry area forward of the diving boards, they provide conditions that are dangerous to divers.

Other important considerations in the planning of new pools are local and state ordinances and regulations that must be met before plans are approved. These regulations do not address the many detailed specifications of competitive swimming; nevertheless, most do include details for the pool diving areas, including such specifications as the minimum depth of water, the height of the board above the water, and the spacing between boards and other related dimensions. Unfortunately, their recommendations often fall below the minimum dimensions contained in competitive diving rule books. For example, many state swimming pool regulations permit 1-meter springboards to be installed in pools with a water depth of only 9 feet, and 10 feet for 3-meter springboards, as compared to a minimum of 13 feet for 3-meter boards recommended by USD and NCAA competitive diving rules. Anyone planning a pool where competitive diving will be conducted must follow the rules of the governing body to ensure the safety of both the competitive and recreational diver.

Architects, engineers, and all others involved in the planning of a new swimming pool that will include competitive swimming and diving must first consult the applicable rule book as well as use the supplemental information contained in this and other chapters of this book.

Planners who design pools that may be used to conduct international swimming and diving competition are urged to conform as much as possible to the specifications set forth in the FINA rule book.

Federation Internationale de Natation Amateur (FINA)
Rule book: *Constitution and Rules Governing Swimming, Diving, Water Polo, and Synchronized Swimming*

Yards Versus Meters

For the past 20 years, pool designers and coaches have wrestled with the question of "yards versus meters'' in pool dimensions. At this time it appears that the United States government will continue with its present system of measurement; however, it is recommended that whenever possible, future pools should be constructed in accordance with the metric system. All national and international groups have recommended this change in swimming, diving, and water polo. Nevertheless, pools that now are measured in yards will always be eligible to hold competition. The metric system will probably be used only in championship meets when recommended by college conferences, USS, and NCAA.

To aid planners, the specific requirements and specifications of the three United States ruling bodies as contained in their 1986 rule books have been recorded in this chapter. Additionally, two sets of guidelines to assist planners and pool administrators in design and operation of the pool are presented.

Design Guidelines

These guidelines serve architects and all others involved in the planning process.

1. The architect should seek input from all those who are expected to use the swimming pool (i.e., instructors, coaches, and aquatic director) before developing preliminary plans.

2. A great deal of thought must be given to the level of competition to be conducted in the pool most frequently and to the possibility of any potential changes in program emphasis in the future before preliminary drawings are drafted.

3. All current rule books from the governing bodies establishing competitive standards must be read thoroughly, and correspondence must be made with the various competitive committees for anticipated, unpublished changes prior to drafting the preliminary drawings.

4. The safety of both competitors and other pool users must always be kept in mind throughout every aspect of the design. The following items must be considered:

   - *Depth markers* should be a minimum of 4 and preferably 6 inches in height, of contrasting color, with numerals and the appropriate measure (feet, FT, meter, etc.) to prevent patrons or foreign visitors from misinterpreting the depth. Both English

   and metric units should be used at each depth location (i.e., 13 FEET, 3.96 M).

   - *Starting blocks* should be located at the deep end of a single pool facility. Far too many spinal injuries occur each year from swimmers striking the pool bottom with their heads while diving off starting blocks located in the shallow end of the pools. It has been well documented that the ''scoop'' or ''pike'' racing dive if improperly executed in shallow water is the primary cause of most of these injuries. Roll-in or somersault recoveries of false starts are other areas of major concern with blocks located in shallow water. If races must be started at the shallow end of the pool where the water is only 3-1/2 feet deep, it is recommended that blocks not be used and that starts be made from the pool edge.

   - *Diving boards and stands:* Both 1- and 3-meter diving stands should be equipped with at least two and preferably three horizontal railings that extend at least 1 foot and preferably 2 feet over the edge of the pool. Springboards, particularly 3-meter boards, placed on a solid concrete or metal bed that extends a minimum of 12 inches laterally from each side of the board are most desirable. This will help prevent children from falling onto the deck. Another safety feature to prevent people from falling through guardrails is closing the sides with plexiglass or some other appropriate material. Remember that people of all ages and ability levels will be using these facilities and not just the trained diver.

5. A separate pool for diving is strongly recommended.

Shallow water warning sign placed between two starting blocks

6. Diving towers located outdoors should have a plexiglass windscreen 5-feet high around all sides except the take-off edge.

7. It is recommended that bottom targets be placed on the bottom of pools in the form of a 3 feet by 3 feet cross, consisting of lines 12 inches wide. The center of the target should be exactly 6 feet from the end of the board.

8. Proper orientation of the pool with respect to the sun and prevailing wind is essential in all outdoor pools (see chapter 8 for details).

9. In areas of high-prevailing winds, it may be desirable to construct some kind of a windscreen to block out these winds. This may be accomplished by locating maintenance buildings, trees, or spectator stands on the side from which the winds are most apt to come.

10. Regardless of whether or not electronic touch pads are installed at the time of construction, it is strongly recommended that the pool's length be increased to permit their installation at a later date. (Consult appropriate rule book for space required.)

Operational Guidelines

These operational guidelines are for pool administrators after the pool has been constructed.

1. Pools designed mainly for competitive swimming will also be used by other people for instruction, recreational swimming, adapted programs, and by young children at certain designated times.

2. When starting blocks are not being used by the swim team, they should be secured to prevent recreational swimmers from using them. Removing the blocks is recommended, but if blocks are permanently installed, warning

Diving well at Plantation Park pool, Plantation, Florida

signs and constant lifeguard and staff supervision must be employed.

3. Swim team members must be informed of the danger of making an improper dive from starting blocks located in shallow water. Swimmers must be told that during any false start, they must execute a regular racing dive and that under no circumstances should they somersault forward in a "roll" dive. Lead-up skills must be used for beginning competitive swimmers, starting with instruction from the coping in deep water, progressing to a wall in the shallow end, and culminating with practice on the blocks in the shallow area.

4. If it is anticipated that the pool will be used by non-English-speaking people, all warning signs and pool rules should incorporate the predominate language of visitors. The use of pictorial, graphic, or universal-designed signs is strongly recommended.

5. Both visitors and adults who bring children to the pool like to observe the swimmers and divers, so provision should be made for an appropriate observation area.

6. Pool managers and coaches who use the pool for practice and meets should stay up-to-date on swimming and diving rules by purchasing new rule books each year, by subscribing to competitive publications, and by attending clinics, workshops, and conferences.

7. When a meet or a special event such as a water show is to be held, food and beverages may be provided as well as adequate and comfortable facilities.

8. Providing areas for swimmers to rest and receive massages between races or heats is desirable.

9. Proper water temperature, water clarity, and correct chemical balance is essential for peak performance times for swimmers and divers.

10. Adequate lighting must be provided for night meets. Temporary flood lights may be necessary to raise the level of illumination at major meets. (See chapter 11 for recommended levels of lighting.)

11. Underwater lights should be beamed downward at an angle to strike the bottom midpoint between the pool's edge and the pool's bottom. In the deep portion of the pool or in separate diving pools, underwater lights should also be located at the midpoint between the water's surface and the bottom of the pool.

12. A person currently certified in lifeguard training, CPR—Basic Life Support, and standard first aid must be on duty during all competitive activities.

13. A first-aid kit, a backboard, a telephone, and written emergency and accident management procedures must also be provided.

Competitive Swimming Requirements

The requirements presented in the remainder of this chapter come from the following sources: NCAA (1986); USS (1986); NFSHSA (1986); USD (1985); U.S. Water Polo (1985); FINA (1985); and USSS (1985).[1]

Short Course Length

NCAA.[2]
Preferred: 75 ft 1 in. (22.89 m)

USS.[3]
25 yd or 25 m (82 ft and 1/4 in.)

NFSHSA.
75 ft (22.86 m) or
25 m (82.021 ft), measured from the inside walls or from tile and timing devices attached to the walls

Long Course Length

NCAA.
Preferred: 50.025 m (164 ft 1 in.)
Acceptable: 50.025 m (164 ft 1 in.)

USS.
50 m (164 ft and 1/2 in.)

NFSHSA.
None provided

Note: All pools must be constructed to permit the touchpads of an automatic timing system to be used without reducing the length of the pool below the minimum of 75 ft, 22.860 m, or 25 m.

Short Course Width

NCAA.
Preferred: 60 ft (18.29 m)
Acceptable: 45 ft (13.72 m)

USS.
22.86 m (25 yd)

NFSHSA.
Preferred: 60 ft (18.288 m)
Acceptable: 45 ft (13.716 m)

Long Course Width

NCAA.
Preferred: 75 ft 1 in. (22.89 m)
Acceptable: 60 ft (18.29 m)

USS.
Preferred: 22.89 m (75 ft 1 in.)

NFSHSA.
None provided

End Walls and Bulkheads

NCAA. For competitive course end walls, the finishing surfaces should be in parallel planes: vertical for a depth of no less than 3 ft 6 in. (1.07 m), measured below the plane of the perimeter rim overflow. Walls should be parallel and vertical within a tolerance of 1/4 inch (0.64 cm). There shall

---

[1]This material is used with the permission of the NCAA, USS, NFSHSA, USD, U.S. Water Polo, FINA, and USSS.

[2]These pool dimensions for swimming and diving are reprinted by permission of the National Collegiate Athletic Association and are subject to annual revision or change. These dimensions are only recommendations and as such, represent standards that the NCAA Men's and Women's Swimming Committees believe should be met for competition involving NCAA member institutions. These recommendations are not binding on member institutions or any other institutions or organizations.

[3]From *United States Swimming, Inc. Rules and Regulations, 1986*; used with permission. Local swimming committees may waive strict compliance with some of these requirements in sanctioning local competition, predicated on facility availability. Consult the most recent edition of *U.S.S. Rules and Regulations* for more detail. It is not the purpose of the *Rules and Regulations* of U.S. Swimming to set standards of care for the safety of the swimmer. Safety considerations are to be addressed by the swimmer, the officials, the swim coach, and the local public entity or pool owner where events are held. Recommended depth dimensions of competitive facilities, for example, are suggestions only for ideal competitive conditions.

be no protrusions, light fixtures, underwater windows, or inlets in the 3 ft 6 in. (1.07 m) finished planar surface described above. End walls should be finished with a nonslip surface. These specifications also shall apply to moveable bulkheads.

USS. Walls enclosing the racing course shall be parallel and vertical. The end walls shall be at a right angle to the water surface and shall be constructed of solid material with a non-slip surface that extends no less than 0.8 m (2 ft 7-1/2 in.) below the water surface. These specifications also apply to moveable bulkheads but with the additional provision that such bulkheads must be rigidly constructed to minimize distortion on impact and must be equipped to ensure locking at competitive distance settings.

NFSHSA. End walls and moveable bulkheads serving as end walls, shall be parallel and vertical for a distance of approximately 3 ft 6 in. below (1.0668 m) the overflow level of the water, with no protrusions or inlets below the surface. Touch pads for automatic timing may be used if they do not shorten the race course beyond minimum specifications. It is recommended end walls be finished with a nonslip surface.

Overflow System

NCAA. The overflow system is a method of conveying water beyond the perimeter overflow rim of the pool. The overflow system should guarantee the level of the water in the pool is not lower than the overflow rim of the pool at all times; maintain a smooth, quiet surface in the pool during competition; and prevent the accumulation or overflow of pool water onto the deck area where meet officials work. It shall effectively skim the water surface at all times.

USS. The overflow system is a method of conveying water beyond the perimeter overflow rim of the pool. It should guarantee the level of the water in the pool at all times; maintain a smooth, quiet surface in the pool during competition; prevent the accumulation or overflow of pool water onto the deck area where meet officials work; and effectively skim the water surface at all times. The pool circulation system shall be turned off during the swimming of any event if, in the opinion of the referee, the resultant water movement interferes with the conduct of the competition.

NFSHSA. The level of the water shall be at the overflow rim of the pool.

Water Depth

NCAA. Long and Short Course
Preferred: minimum of 4 ft (1.22 m)
Acceptable: minimum of 4 ft (1.22 m)

USS. Long and Short Course
National and International Competition:
2 m (6 ft 7 in.) deep throughout the course.
This requirement may be waived for National Championships.
Minimum: 4 ft (1.22 m). Predicated on facility availability, local swimming committees may waive strict compliance with these requirements in sanctioning local competition.

NFSHSA.
Minimum of 3 ft 6 in. (1.0668 m) in all pools

Racing Lane Size

NCAA. Long Course
Preferred: eight 9-ft (2.74 m) with additional width outside lanes one and eight
Acceptable: eight 7-ft (2.13 m) with additional width outside lanes one and eight

NCAA. Short Course
Preferred: eight 7-ft (2.13 m) with additional width outside lanes one and eight
Acceptable: six 7-ft (2.13 m) with additional width outside lanes one and six

USS.
National and International Competition:
eight 9-ft lanes (2.75 m) in width with approximately 0.43 m (1 ft 6 in.) of additional width outside lanes one and eight
Minimum: 7-ft wide lanes (2.13 m)

NFSHSA.
The width of lanes shall be a minimum of 7 ft (2.134 m). The two lanes next to the side walls may be wider; in such pools, outside lane markers are recommended.

Pool Markings

NCAA. Lines should be placed on pool bottoms to serve as guides for each swimmer, and the color of these lines (preferably black) should be in marked contrast to the general color of the pool. Such lines should be at least 12 in. (30.48 cm) wide and placed in the middle of each swimming lane. As these lines approach the end of the pool, it is recommended that distinctive *T* markings be placed on the bottom. It is recommended that identical target lines 12 in. (30.48 cm) wide be placed on each end wall of the pool or that electronic contact pads be placed in the center of each lane, extending from the top to at least 3 ft 6 in. (1.07 m) below the surface water. The top edge of deck-level pools must be marked with a contrasting color to provide a visual target at the end of the pool. In existing pools where target lines are not present, each end wall must have visible target lines 12 in. (30.48 cm) wide or turning pads so marked. Failure to provide such markings will result in forfeiture of the meet by the host institution. An exception may be allowed where stainless steel gutters overlap the turning target, so long as the overlap does not exceed 18 in. (45.72 cm).

Where practical, lanes should be numbered from right to left as the swimmer stands facing the course. Each lane should be clearly marked so that it may be identified easily by finish judges stationed on the sides of the pool.

USS. Lines should be placed on pool bottoms to serve as guides for each swimmer, and the color of these lines should be marked in contrast to the general color (preferably black) of the pool. Such lines should be at least 10 in. wide and placed in the middle of each swimming lane. As these lines approach the end of the pool, distinctive *T* markings should be placed on the bottom ending 2 m (6 ft 7 in.) from the end wall with a distinctive cross line 1.0 m (3 ft 4 in.) long and the same width as the bottom marker. It is recommended that target lines at least 10 in. wide be placed on each end wall of the pool in the center of each lane, extending from the deck to at least 3 ft 4 in. (1.0 m) below the water surface. The top edge of deck-level pools must be marked with a contrasting color to provide a visual target at the end of the pool. Lanes should be numbered from right to left as the swimmer stands facing the course. Each lane should be clearly marked so that it may be identified easily by finish judges stationed on the sides of the pool.

NFSHSA. Continuous lines at least 12 in. wide (.3048 m) and of a dark color shall indicate the middle of each swimming lane. It is recommended these lines end 60 in. (1.524 m) from the end walls and the last 12 in. (.3048 m) of the line be

36 in. wide (.9144 m), thus forming a broad *T*. The center of each lane shall be indicated on the end walls by a 12 in. (.3048 m) line extending vertically at least 3 ft 6 in. below (1.0668 m) the surface of the water. It is recommended markings on the finishing pad conform with and superimpose on the existing markings of the pool.

Lane Markers

NCAA. Permanent provision should be made to anchor lane lines at the competitive water level in a recessed receptacle. Tightly stretched, easily visible floating lane markers with floats joining to form a continuous cylinder marking the lateral limits of each lane should be provided for dual meets and must be available for championship meets. It is recommended that the last 15 ft (4.57 m) at each end of the lane line be a contrasting color with the remainder of the lane.

USS. Permanent provision must be made to anchor lane lines at the competitive water level in a recessed receptacle. Tightly stretched, easily visible floating lane markers with floats joining to form a continuous cylinder marking the lateral limits of each lane should be provided for all meets and must be available for championship meets. The color of the floats for 15 ft (in 25-yd pools) and 5

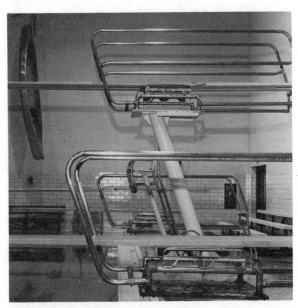

Note extension of dive guardrails over edge of pool. Chesterton High School, Indiana.

m (in 50-m pools) from each end shall be distinct from the rest of the floats.

NFSHSA. Lane markers shall be continuous and clearly visible floats and shall indicate the lateral limits for each lane for all meets. They shall be attached to and stretched between the end walls, anchored at surface water level in a recessed receptacle. It is recommended there be solid-colored floats within 15 ft (4.572 m) of both end walls in contrast with the center portion of the lane markers.

Starting Platforms

NCAA. The front edge of the starting platform should not exceed 30 in. (76.20 cm) in height above the surface of the water and be flush with the end of the pool. The surface of the starting platform should be not less than 20 in. by 20 in. (50.80 cm by 50.80 cm) and maximum slope toward the pool not more than 10° from the horizontal. The top must be covered with a nonskid material. The lane number should be visible from all sides of the platform. Firm starting grips, flush with the end of the pool, for backstroke starts should be placed within 30 in. (76.20 cm) of the surface of the water.

USS. The front edge of the starting platform must not exceed .77 m (30 in.) in height above the surface of the water and shall be flush with the end of the pool for short-course pools. The front edge of the starting platform must be from .50 m to .75 m in height above the water surface and flush with the end of the pool for long-course pools. The surface of the starting platform must not be less than .50 m (20 in.) square and maximum slope toward the pool not more than 10° from the horizontal. The top must be covered with a non-skid material. The lane number should be visible from all sides of the platform. Firm starting grips, flush with the end of the pool, for backstroke starts must be placed .3 to .6 meters above the surface of the water.

NFSHSA. Starting platforms numbered from right to left as viewed from the starting end are required. The top front edge of the platform and backstroke grips shall be no more than 30 in. (.762 m) above the water surface and flush with the pool end wall. The top surface shall be flat with the back-to-front slope not exceeding 10° from the horizontal. It is recommended the top be a mini-

mum of 20 in. square (.508 m) and covered with a nonskid material.

Backstroke Turn Indicators

NCAA. Permanent provision should be made to anchor backstroke flag lines. At least three triangular pennants of two or more alternating colors should be suspended over each lane from a top line approximately 7 ft (2.13 m) above the water surface and 15 ft (4.57 m) from each end of the pool. These pennants should be 6 to 12 in. (15.24 to 30.48 cm) in width and 12 to 18 in. (30.48 to 45.72 cm) in length. In any event where the backstroke is swum, failure to provide these pennants shall result in disqualification of the host competitors.

USS. Permanent provisions should be made to anchor the backstroke flag line. At least three triangular pennants of two or more alternating colors must be suspended over each lane from a line 15 ft or 4.57 m from each end of the 25 yd or m course and 5 m (16 ft 5 in.) from each end of the 50-m course. The flag lines shall be 7 ft above the water surface in the 25-yd course and 1.8 m (5 ft 11 in.) in the 50-m course. Pennants must be 6 to 12 in. in width at the base and 12 to 18 in. in vertical length. For long-course pools, a firmly suspended line (without flags or pennants) extending the full width of the course must be placed 25 m from the finish end of the course at a height of 1.8 m (5 ft 11 in.) above the water surface for all backstroke events, including individual medley and medley relay.

NFSHSA. Backstroke flag lines, suspended 7 ft (2.134 m) above the surface of the water of each lane and 15 ft (4.572 m) from each end wall, shall be required for all events in which the backstroke is swum. At least three pennants of two or more alternating colors shall hang from the line over each lane. The pennants shall be 6 to 12 in. wide (15.24 to 30.48 cm) and 12 to 18 in. long (30.48 to 45.72 cm).

Recall Line

NCAA. Permanent provisions should be made to anchor the recall rope so that it clears the water by at least 4 ft (1.22 m) at its lowest point. A recall rope, which may be dropped across the racing lanes approximately 36 feet (10.97 m) from the take-off in case of a false start, should be available.

USS. Permanent provisions should be made to anchor the recall rope so that it shall be suspended at least 4 feet above the water at its lowest point. A recall rope may be available, which may be dropped across the racing lanes approximately 36 ft from the take-off in the short course and 49 ft in the long course, in case of a false start. A recall rope must be available for national championship meets.

NFSHSA. A recall rope, approximately 42 ft (10.973 m) from the starting point, is required for all swimming events.

Ladders

NCAA. All ladders, steps, or stairs should be recessed in the side pool walls or be easily removable during the competition.

USS. All ladders, steps, or stairs should be recessed in the side pool walls or be easily removable during the competition.

NFSHSA. All ladders, steps, or stairs shall be recessed into side walls or easily removable for competition.

Counter Equipment

NCAA. Visual counters must be provided by the host institution. Each digit must be 12 in. (30.48 cm) high and must be black on a white background. Each set of counters must be equipped with one indicator of solid fluorescent orange color, with or without a numeral, to indicate the

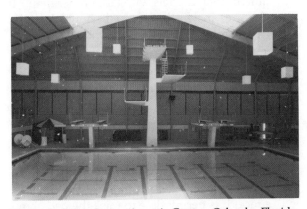

Diving facilities, Justus Aquatic Center, Orlando, Florida

final length of each distance event. Failure to provide visual counters shall result in the disqualification of the host competitors in the events where counters are required.

USS. None required.

NFSHSA. A visual lap-counting system for the 500-yd/400-m freestyle event shall be required for each lane. The system shall consist of a sufficient number of white cards with 12 in. (.3048 m) tall, black, odd, ascending numerals, and one solid fluorescent orange card, with or without a numeral.

Deck Area

NCAA. The deck of the pool should be 6 to 12 in. (15.24 to 30.48 cm) above the surface of the water. Deck space on the diving end should permit sufficient space for installation of all diving equipment and additional area for the free movement of competitors and officials. The recommended minimum is 15 ft (4.57 m) of deck area at both ends of the pool. The width of side-decks must be governed by usage anticipated. If this space is to be utilized for moveable spectator bleachers or other seating, it must be wide enough to accommodate such seating plus sufficient area for free movement of competitors and officials. It is recommended that the maximum amount of space be allocated for spectator seating. If sufficient gallery space is allotted, side-deck width may be limited to 10 ft (3.05 m).

USS. The deck of the pool should be 6 to 12 in. above the surface of the water. Deck space on the diving end should permit sufficient space for installations of all diving equipment and additional area for the free movement of competitors and officials. The recommended minimum is 15 ft of deck area at both ends of the pool. The width of side-decks must be governed by usage anticipated. If this space is to be utilized for moveable spectator bleachers or other seating, it must be wide enough to accommodate such seating plus sufficient area for free movement of competitors and officials. It is recommended that the maximum amount of space be allocated for spectator seating. If sufficient gallery space is allotted, side-deck width may be limited to 10 ft.

NFSHSA. No definition available.

Temperatures

NCAA. The water temperature should be between 79 and 81 °F (26 and 27 °C) for competition. When possible, air temperature at deck level should not be lower than 4 °F below the water temperature. It is recommended that in separate diving pools the water should be between 82 and 86 °F (28 and 30 °C) for competition. Special consideration should also be given to heating and ventilation for the comfort of spectators as well as competitors.

USS. The water temperature should be between 78 and 80 °F for competiton, and there should be adequate heating and/or cooling equipment available to maintain such temperatures. The air temperature at deck level in indoor pools should not be lower than 76 °F, with relative humidity maintained at about 60% and air velocity at about 25 ft/min.

NFSHSA. The water temperature shall be no less than 78 °F (26 °C). It is recommended that the temperature be no more than 82 °F (28 °C).

Lighting

NCAA. It is important that sufficient overhead lighting be installed with concentration directly over both the turning and finish lanes. One hundred (100) footcandles (107.61x) are recommended. Underwater lights may be installed at the sides and at the ends. End lights should be located under lane line anchors and 3 ft 6 in. (1.07 m) deep with a switch for each light. A power source for additional lighting should be available for use with television, movies, and special events. Buildings housing indoor pools should not have deck-level windows in walls facing pool ends. Deck-level windows on the side walls should be the tinted type that reduce glare and reflection on the water surface.

USS. For indoor pools, 100 footcandles illumination is required at the water surface over the entire course. Underwater lights may be installed at the sides and at the ends. End lights should be located under lane line anchors and 3 ft 6 in. deep with a switch for each light. A power source for additional lighting should be available for use with television, movies, and special events. Buildings housing indoor pools should not have deck-level

windows in walls facing pool ends. Deck-level windows on the side walls should be the tinted type that reduce glare and reflection on the water surface.

NFSHSA. None established.

Automatic Judging and Timing Equipment

NCAA. A completely automatic device is one that automatically starts with the starter's pistol and stops when a contestant touches the finish contact pad. A semiautomatic device automatically starts with the starter's pistol or manually stops when one or more official(s) presses a button switch. Both timing and judging systems shall be to 1/100 of a second. All other data shall be disregarded. Any equipment that is installed must not interfere with the swimmers' starts, turns, or the function of the overflow system. This equipment should

- not have any exposed wires on the pool deck;
- be able to display all recorded information for each lane in a vertical or horizontal alignment;
- provide easy reading of a contestant's time (digital readings are recommended); and
- must meet acceptable safety standards.

The finish contact pads for this equipment shall be as follows:

1. *Size.* It is recommended that the finish pad be a minimum of 6-1/2 ft (1.98 m) wide by 2 ft (.61 m) in depth for pools with lanes 7 ft (2.13 m) wide. It is further recommended, but not required, that in pools with lanes other than 7 ft (2.13 m) in width, the pad should be 6 in. (15.24 cm) narrower than the width of the lane.

2. *Tolerance.* The thickness of the pad should not exceed 1/2 in. (1.27 cm), and when installed the pool length must not be less than 75 ft (22.86 m).

3. *Position.* The pad must be located in the center of the lane and be positioned at or below the water level during the progress of the race. The pad must be installed in such a manner as to assure a fixed position for the finish of a race. It is permissible to raise the pad above the water level for the finish.

Diving facility at Meineke Park, Schaumburg, Illinois. Photo courtesy of Kiefer Equipment.

4. *Removable.* The pads may be portable, allowing the pool operator to remove them when there is no competition.

5. *Markings.* The markings on the pad should conform with and superimpose on the existing markings of the pool. The perimeter and edges of the pad will be designated by a 1-in. (2.54 cm) black border.

6. *Sensitivity.* The sensitivity of the pad must be such that it cannot be activated by water turbulence but is activated by a light hand touch. The pad should be sensitive on the top edge.

7. *Safety.* The pad must be safe from the possibility of electrical shock and must have no sharp edges.

Optional accessories that are desirable but not essential for a minimum installation:

- Printout of all information
- Spectator readout board
- Relay take-off judging
- Automatic lap counter
- Readout of splits
- Computer summaries

- Correction of erroneous touch
- Automatic rechargeable battery operation possibility
- TV tie-in system

Note. Appropriate below-deck conduits should be provided for the use of electronic starting, timing, and judging devices, as well as for adequate office space. In some installations, the course measurement may be increased approximately 1 in. (2.54 cm) to meet installation requirements.

USS.

Note: All items marked with an * are required for national championships and international competitions.

Electronic or mechanical officiating equipment includes devices that record the time and/or place of competitive swimming events. Equipment must conform to the requirements of this section.

Types:

1. Automatic*—Activated by the starting device and stopped by the swimmer.

2. Manual-Electronic—May provide any combination of manual and automatic starting and stopping other than completely automatic operation, except that the combined use of manual start and automatic finish is not permitted for competition.

Specifications:

1. Automatic*—Shall provide time and place results to hundredths (100ths) of a second (two decimal places), preferably digital, paper printout for all lanes.

2. Manual-Electronic—Shall provide times and place results as in Automatic (above).

Installation Requirements:*

- Must not interfere with swimmers' starts, turns, or finishes.

- Must not interfere with normal overflow function of pool.

- Shall have no wiring carrying over 12 volts in exposed position on deck.

- In all national championship meets all automatic and semiautomatic equipment supplied by power mains shall be capable of automatic transfer to battery power without affecting continuity of accuracy in the event of line power failure.

Finish Pads*:

1. *Size.* Recommended minimum width for 7-ft lanes is 78 in.; minimum depth is 24 in. In other size lanes, pads should be no more than 6 in. narrower than lanes.

2. *Tolerance.* Thickness should not exceed 3/8 in. When the pad is in position, the course must not be less than 25 yd, or 25 to 50 m in length.

3. *Markings.* Should conform to and superimpose on existing pool markings. Perimeter and edges of pad should be designated by 1 in. wide black border.

4. *Sensitivity.* Should be such that equipment cannot be activated by water turbulence but may be activated by a light touch on both flat surface facing pool and on upper edge.

5. *Safety.* Should be safe from electrical shock and have no sharp edges or corners.

6. *Position.* Pads should be centered in lanes and may be adjustable in height and removable.

Optional Accessories:

- Relay take-off judging capacity
- Automatic lap-counter
- Split readouts
- Correction of erroneous touch
- Constant battery-charge (trickle-charge capacity)
- Television equipment tie-in
- Strobe light in addition to horn start

Back-Up Requirements:

No swimmer must ever be required to reswim a race due to equipment failure that results in unrecorded or inaccurate time or place results.

Automatic and manual-electronic equipment shall be backed up by any available combination of equipment and/or human officials.

NFSHSA. Timing devices, whether manual, semiautomatic or automatic, shall be calibrated to one-hundredth (.01) of a second. The use of automatic electronic timing is recommended for all swimming meets. It is recommended that even when automatic timing is used, a manual timing device be provided each lane as back-up.

It is recommended that touch pads for electronic timing be centered in the lanes, extending to within at least 6 in. of each lane's markers.

Additional Considerations

A number of other factors have a relationship to the overall effectiveness of the competitive swimming course, much of which is covered in other chapters of this book. However, the following points may be further emphasized:

1. The type of outdoor lighting generally provided at most pools is inadequate for competitive swimming. The principal drawback is that lighting is usually achieved by fixtures located on poles that are at the periphery of the surrounding pool area; thus the light intensity on the water's surface is often inadequate. One solution for the championship meets is the temporary installation of lights directly over the pool.

2. Underwater observation windows are desirable from the standpoint of coaching, research, and reporting of swimming meets by television transmission. When at the turning end of the pool, they should be located at 3 ft 6 in. below the surface.

3. Electrical outlets appropriately designed in order to assure safety shall be located around the pool to facilitate the conduct of special events. Only waterproof cable and fixtures should be used. Ground fault interrupters must be included.

4. Microphone jacks that lead to a fixed amplifier in an office should be located at strategic positions around the pool.

Pool with movable bulkhead at University of Nebraska at Omaha.

5. An electrical scoreboard is a desirable addition to the pool facilities. Wall space needs to be provided where spectators will have a clear view of the scoreboard.

6. Swimming officials require considerable space at the end of the pool. Twelve feet of deck space is recommended.

7. Electronic timing systems require a separate elevated area near the finish line. This area should furnish a commanding view of all lanes and afford privacy, yet be readily accessible to officials. Provisions should be made in any new construction for the conduits to carry the necessary wiring for an electronic timing system.

8. Provision should be made to afford deck seating around the periphery of the deck for contestants and officials.

9. Many new installations are featuring glass-enclosed warming rooms for the contestants so that the temperature of the pool area itself can be lowered for the comfort of the specta-tors. Space heaters may also be provided in the diving area where divers will be seated during competition.

10. Drinking fountains should be provided at convenient locations within the pool area and should be recessed.

11. Any items that are of a semipermanent nature should be made so that they are easily and conveniently removable (i.e., lifeguard stands, ladder railings, etc.).

12. Adequate air control should be provided so that temperature, humidity, and air movement may be readily adjusted.

13. Telephones and telephone jacks should be installed where they are convenient for the use of radio, TV, the press, and any other authorized personnel.

14. Provision should be made for the comfort and convenience of radio, television, the press, and any others who would be involved in covering competitive swimming, water polo, synchronized swimming, water shows, and

Illustration of "pike" dive. Note angle of diver's upper torso.

special events. Several electrical outlets should be provided in this area.

15. At least two portable underwater speakers should be provided for synchronized swimming and for recall of competitive swimmers during false starts.

16. There should be at least one double door to the outside or to a hallway so that large items of equipment may be brought into the pool easily.

17. Water outlets (hose bibs) for both hot and cold water should be provided at convenient locations about the deck to facilitate the hosing down of the decks following competition. Some pools are installing hot water lines about the periphery of the pool deck with spray outlets every few feet. This allows the deck to be flushed down quickly and easily by simply opening one valve.

18. Pacing clocks for practice purposes should be fixed on the wall at both ends of the pool and on each side of the pool.

19. At least one large storage room 15 ft by 20 ft should be provided with plenty of shelves and cabinets. Double doors should also be included to accommodate large items such as storage reels for lane lines.

Competitive Diving Requirements

Dimensions

NCAA.
Preferred: 60 ft (18.29 m) in length by 45 ft (13.72 m) in width [long course-75 ft (22.86 m) by 60 ft (18.29 m)]
Acceptable: The diving pool may be separated from or incorporated with the swimming pool. (See figure on page 237 for water depth information.)

USD.
None provided

NFSHSA.
The diving pool may be separate from or part of the swimming pool and the following standards for clearance and water depth are recommended for 1-m diving:

• End of board to anchoring pool wall, 6 ft (1.829 m);

• Side of board to side of another board, 8 ft (2.438 m);

• Side of board to pool side wall, 10 ft (3.048 m);

• End of board to forward pool wall, 29 ft (8.839 m);

• Top of board to ceiling overhead, 16 ft (4.877 m);

• Water depth 2 ft in front of the end of board, 10 ft (3.048 m) with 12 ft or more (3.658 m) preferred;

Note: Pools remodeled or constructed after January, 1987 must have a water depth of 12 ft or more.

• Maximum depth reduction rate of diving pools which do not exceed minimum depth requirements, 6-1/4% for a distance of 20 ft forward (6.096 m) and 6 ft (1.829 m) back and to the sides. Deeper pools may have proportionately steeper depth reduction rates.

Equipment

NCAA.
Preferred: Two 1-m and two 3-m springboards and diving tower, providing take-off platforms at 5, 7.5, and 10 m.
Acceptable: Two 1-m and two 3-m springboards.

USD.
The springboard diving equipment shall consist of not less than two 1-m and two 3-m springboards. The height of the high platform must be 10 m. The intermediate platforms may be from 5 to 7.5 m. For all other classifications of diving competition (e.g., Regional, Association, Invitational, etc.) it is not necessary to have more than one 1-m and one 3-m springboard.

NFSHSA.
The diving board shall be horizontal and 1 m above the water surface, measured from the top of the board.

Water Agitation for Diving

NCAA.
It is recommended that some type of water surface agitation be installed for a zone centered on the longitudinal axis of the board, 2 ft (.61 m) wide, extending for 5 ft (1.52 m) from the tip of the board. Surface agitation may be by underwater air bubblers or above-water spray. Air bubblers should be installed flush with the finished pool bottom with openings of 1/4 in. (.64 cm) or smaller.

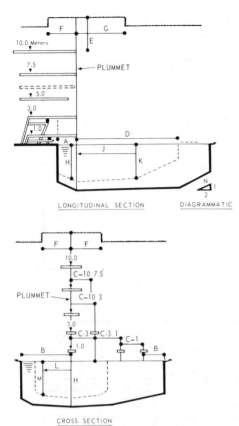

MINIMUM STANDARD DIVING FACILITY DIMENSIONS Adoption by NCAA in 1969		1-METER SPRINGB'D 16'x1'-8'' (4.88m x 50.8cm)		3-METER SPRINGB'D 16'x1'-8'' (4.88m x 50.8cm)		INTER-MED. PLATFORM 16'x5' (4.88m x 1.52m)		7½-METER PLATFORM 18'x 6' (5.49m x 1.83m)		10-METER PLATFORM 20'x6'6'' (6.10m x 1.98m)	
		DIST	DEPTH	DIST	DEPTH	DIST	DEPTH	DIST	DEPTH	DIST	DEPTH
A	FROM PLUMMET BACK TO POOL WALL	6' (1.83m)		6' (1.83m)		5' (1.52m)		5' (1.52m)		6' (1.83m)	
	BACK TO PLATFORM DIRECTLY BELOW							5' (1.52m)		5' (1.52m)	
B	FROM PLUMMET TO POOL WALL AT SIDE	10' (3.05m)		12' (3.66m)		14' (4.27m)		15' (4.57m)		17' (5.18m)	
C	FROM PLUMMET TO ADJACENT PLUMMET	8' (2.44m)		8' (2.44m)		10' (3.05m)				12' (3.66m)	
D	FROM PLUMMET TO POOL WALL AHEAD	29' (8.84m)		34' (10.36m)		34' (10.36m)		36' (10.97m)		45' (13.72m)	
E	ON PLUMMET, FROM BOARD TO CEILING OVERHEAD	16' (4.88m)		16' (4.88m)		10' (3.05m)		10'6'' (3.20m)		11' (3.35m)	
F-E	CLEAR OVERHEAD, BEHIND AND EACH SIDE OF PLUMMET	8' (2.44m)	16' (4.88m)	8' (2.44m)	16' (4.88m)	9' (2.74m)	12' (3.66m)	9' (2.74m)	12' (3.66m)	16' (4.88m)	12' (3.66m)
G	CLEAR OVERHEAD, AHEAD OF PLUMMET	16' (4.88m)	16' (4.88m)	16' (4.88m)	16' (4.88m)	16' (4.88m)	12' (3.66m)	16' (4.88m)	12' (3.66m)	20' (6.10m)	12' (3.66m)
H	DEPTH OF WATER AT PLUMMET		12' (3.66m)		13' (3.96m)		14' (4.27m)		15' (4.57m)		17' (5.18m)
J-K	DISTANCE, AND DEPTH OF WATER, AHEAD OF PLUMMET	20' (6.10m)	10'9'' (3.28m)	20' (6.10m)	11'9'' (3.58m)	20' (6.10m)	11'9'' (3.58m)	26' (7.92m)	13' (3.96m)	40' (12.19m)	14' (4.27m)
L-M	DISTANCE, AND DEPTH OF WATER, EACH SIDE OF PLUMMET	8' (2.44m)	12' (3.66m)	10' (3.05m)	11'9'' (3.58m)	12' (3.66m)	11'9'' (3.58m)	13' (3.96m)	11'9'' (3.58m)	14' (4.27m)	14' (4.27m)
N	MAXIMUM RATIO, VERTICAL TO HORIZONTAL, OF SLOPE TO REDUCE DEPTH 1.2	1:2		1:2		1:2		1:2		1:2	

NCAA minimum standard diving facility dimensions. From *NCAA men's and women's swimming and diving rules* (p. SW-10), 1986, Mission, KS: NCAA. Copyright 1986 by NCAA. Reprinted by permission.

USD.

Mechanical surface agitation is recommended under the diving boards to aid the divers in their visual perception of the pool.

NFSHSA.

A water agitation system that produces water surface agitation extending for 5 ft (1.524 m) beyond the end of the board with a width of 2 ft (.6096 m) is recommended.

Water Polo Requirements

The figures enclosed in parentheses are metric dimensions. All future pools built for water polo should conform to metric dimensions.

NCAA.[4]

The uniform distance between the goal lines must not exceed 100 ft (30 m) and not be less than 75 ft (25 m); the uniform width must not exceed 66 ft (20 m) and not be less than 45 ft (13 m). The minimum depth of the water shall be 6.5 ft (2 m).

While pools built prior to 1976 are exceptions to the foregoing standards, championship events should be conducted in only those facilities that meet the maximum standards.

U.S. Water Polo.

The uniform distance between the respective goal line is 30 m. The uniform width of the field of play is 20 m. The depth of the water must nowhere be less than 1.8 m.

NFSHSA.

Same as NCAA.

---

[4]These field-of-play dimensions for water polo are reprinted by permission of the National Collegiate Athletic Association and are subject to annual revision or change.

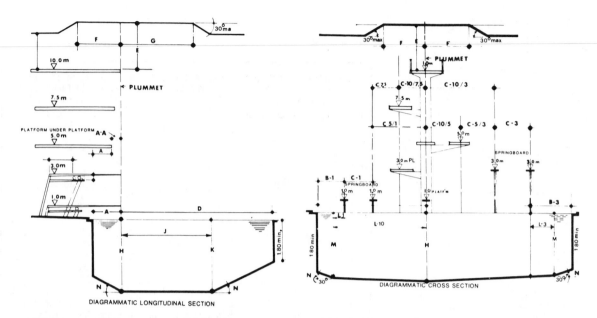

FINA dimensions for diving facilities. From *Constitution and rules governing swimming, diving, water polo, and synchronized swimming*, 1985, Colorado Springs, CO: FINA. Copyright 1985 by FINA. Reprinted by permission.

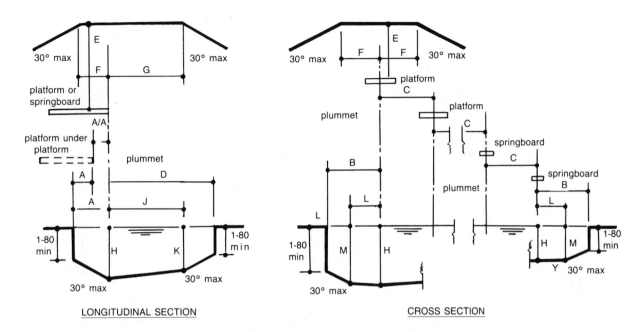

LONGITUDINAL SECTION   CROSS SECTION

			SPRINGBOARD				PLATFORM									
			1 Meter		3 Meters		1 Meter		3 Meters		5 Meters		7.5 Meters		10 Meters	
	Measurements listed in meters	Length	4.80		4.80		4.50		5.00		6.00		6.00		6.00	
		Width	0.50		0.50		0.60		1.50		1.50		1.50		2.00	
		Height	1.00		3.00		0.60-1.00		2.60-3.00		5.00		7.50		10.00	
	Revised to 1 Jan 1981	Dimension	Horiz	Vert	Horiz	Vert	Horiz	Vert	Horiz	Vert	Horiz	Vert	Horiz	Vert	Horiz	Vert
A	From plummet BACK TO POOL WALL	Designation	A-1	—	A-3	—	A-1 pl	—	A-3 pl	—	A-5	—	A-7.5	—	A-10	—
		Minimum	1.50	—	1.50	—	0.75	—	1.25	—	1.25	—	1.50	—	1.50	—
		Preferred	1.80	—	1.80	—	—	—	—	—	—	—	—	—	—	—
AA	From plummet BACK TO PLATFORM plummet directly below	Designation	—	—	—	—	—	—	—	—	AA5/1	—	AA7.5/3/1	—	AA10/5/3/1	—
		Minimum	—	—	—	—	—	—	—	—	0.75	—	0.75	—	0.75	—
		Preferred	—	—	—	—	—	—	—	—	1.50	—	1.50	—	1.50	—
B	From plummet to POOL WALL AT SIDE	Designation	B-1	—	B-3	—	B-1 pl	—	B-3 pl	—	B-5	—	B-7.5	—	B-10	—
		Minimum	2.50	—	3.50	—	2.30	—	2.90	—	4.25	—	4.50	—	5.25	—
		Preferred	—	—	—	—	—	—	—	—	—	—	—	—	—	—
C	From plummet to ADJACENT PLUMMET	Designation	C-1/1	—	C-3/3/1	—	C-1/1 pl	—	C-3/1pl/3pl	—	C-5/3/1	—	C-7.5/5/3/1	—	C-10/7.5/5/3/1	—
		Minimum	2.40	—	2.60	—	1.65 / 1/3 pl 2.10	—	2.10	—	2.50	—	2.50	—	2.75	—
		Preferred	—	—	—	—	2.10	—	—	—	—	—	—	—	—	—
D	From Plummet to POOL WALL AHEAD	Designation	D-1	—	D-3	—	D-1 pl	—	D-3 pl	—	D-5	—	D-7.5	—	D-10	—
		Minimum	9.00	—	10.25	—	8.00	—	9.50	—	10.25	—	11.00	—	13.50	—
		Preferred	—	—	—	—	—	—	—	—	—	—	—	—	—	—
E	On plummet from BOARD TO CEILING	Designation	—	E-1	—	E-3	—	E-1 pl	—	E-3 pl	—	E-5	—	E-7.5	—	E-10
		Minimum	—	5.00	—	5.00	—	3.50	—	3.50	—	3.50	—	3.50	—	3.50
		Preferred	—	—	—	—	—	—	—	—	—	—	—	—	—	5.00
F	CLEAR OVERHEAD behind and each side of plummet	Designation	F-1	E-1	F-3	E-3	F-1 pl	E-1 pl	F-3 pl	E-3 pl	F-5	E-5	F-7.5	E-7.5	F-10	E-10
		Minimum	2.50	5.00	2.50	5.00	2.75	3.50	2.75	3.50	2.75	3.50	2.75	3.50	2.75	3.50
		Preferred	—	—	—	—	—	—	—	—	—	—	—	—	—	5.00
G	CLEAR OVERHEAD ahead of plummet	Designation	G-1	E-1	G-3	E-3	G-1 pl	E-1 pl	G-3 pl	E-3 pl	G-5	E-5	G-7.5	E-7.5	G-10	E-10
		Minimum	5.00	5.00	5.00	5.00	5.00	3.50	5.00	3.50	5.00	3.50	5.00	3.50	6.00	3.50
		Preferred	—	—	—	—	—	—	—	—	—	—	—	—	—	5.00
H	DEPTH OF WATER at plummet	Designation	—	H-1	—	H-3	—	H-1 pl	—	H-3 pl	—	H-5	—	H-7.5	—	H-10
		Minimum	—	3.60	—	3.80	—	3.40	—	3.60	—	3.80	—	4.10	—	4.50
		Preferred	—	3.80	—	4.00	—	3.60	—	3.80	—	4.00	—	4.50	—	5.00
J-K	DISTANCE and DEPTH ahead of plummet	Designation	J-1	K-1	J-3	K-3	J-1 pl	K-1 pl	J-3 pl	K-3 pl	J-5	K-5	J-7.5	K-7.5	J-10	K-10
		Minimum	5.00	3.50	6.00	3.80	5.00	3.30	6.00	3.50	6.00	3.70	8.00	4.00	11.00	4.00
		Preferred	—	3.70	—	3.90	—	3.50	—	3.70	—	3.90	—	4.40	—	4.75
L-M	DISTANCE and DEPTH each side of plummet	Designation	L-1	M-1	L-3	M-3	L-1 pl	M-1 pl	L-3 pl	M-3 pl	L-5	M-5	L-7.5	M-7.5	L-10	M-10
		Minimum	2.50	3.50	3.25	3.70	2.05	3.30	2.65	3.50	4.25	3.70	4.50	4.00	5.25	4.25
		Preferred	—	3.70	—	3.90	—	3.50	—	3.70	—	3.90	—	4.40	—	4.75
N	MAXIMUM SLOPE TO REDUCE DIMENSIONS beyond full requirements	Pool Depth	30 degrees				NOTE: Minimum dimensions "C" (plummet to adjacent plummet) apply for Platforms of minimum widths. For wider Platforms increase "C" by half the additional width(s)									
		Ceiling Ht	30 degrees													

USD recommended dimensions for diving facilities. From *United States Diving rules and regulations*, 1985, Indianapolis, IN: USD. Copyright 1985 by USD. Reprinted by permission.

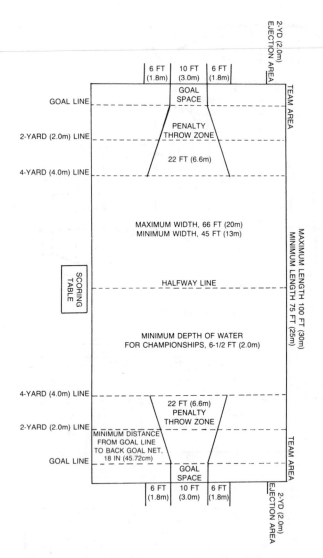

NCAA water polo facility dimensions. From *NCAA water polo rules* (p. 8), 1986, Mission, KS: NCAA. Copyright 1986 by NCAA. Reprinted by permission.

Synchronized Swimming Requirements

Established by U.S. Synchronized Swimming (the only U.S. national agency currently promulgating standards)

Minimum: Pool must have an area of at least 25 ft by 35 ft and not less than 9 ft in depth.

Championship: National championship events shall be held in a pool not less than 25 yd or more

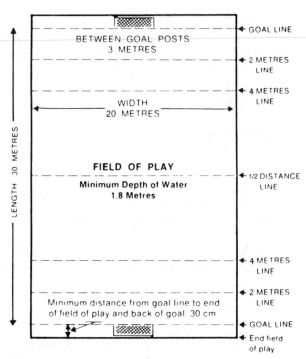

U.S. Water Polo facility dimensions. From *U.S. Water Polo*, 1985, Colorado Springs, CO: U.S. Water Polo. Copyright 1985 by U.S. Water Polo. Reprinted by permission.

than 55 yd in length and not less than 40 ft in width. The pool should have an area of at least 25 ft by 40 ft if not less than 9 ft in depth.

References

Federation Internationale de Natation Amateur. (1985). *Constitution and rules governing swimming, diving, water polo, and synchronized swimming.* Colorado Springs, CO: Author.

The National Collegiate Athletic Association. (1986). *NCAA men's and women's swimming and diving rules* (pp. SW-9–SW-16). Mission, KS: Author.

The National Collegiate Athletic Association. (1986). *NCAA water polo rules* (pp. 7-8). Mission, KS: Author.

The National Federation of State High School Associations. (1986). *Swimming and diving* (pp. 7-10, 28-30). Kansas City, MO: Author.

United States Diving, Inc. (1985). *United States Diving rules and regulations.* Indianapolis, IN: Author.

United States Water Polo. (1985). *U.S. Water Polo rules*. Colorado Springs, CO: Author.

United States Swimming, Inc. (1986). *U.S. Swimming rules and regulations* (pp. 35, 38-43). Colorado Springs, CO: Author.

United States Synchronized Swimming. (1985). *Synchronized Swimming*. Indianapolis, IN: Author.

Photo by Double Sixteen Co., Wheaton, Illinois

Chapter 15

Pool Enclosures

In North America, the largest portion of the population is not favored with a warm climate all year to allow outdoor pools for other than summer use. Pool enclosures, varying from simple tented coverings to formal erected structures, provide the means for allweather or indoor pool activities. Although extending the pool season from partial to full year has many attractions, the cost of conventional structures has become almost prohibitive. Year-round use in the higher latitudes also requires careful consideration of the high energy demands on the natatorium. Various design principles will be discussed in this chapter. For information on pool energy management, refer to chapter 19.

Traditional Designs

Indoor pools built before the 1920s were designed to simulate the elegance of Roman baths or European spas and beaches. Such pools developed pleasant interior environments, but more often they suffered from unanticipated long-term effects of the moist environment. Ceramic tile, marble, and terrazzo hold up well in a moist atmosphere; however, few building facilities could withstand the continually humid environment without experiencing falling plaster, peeling paint, dry rot of wood members, and corrosion of virtually all metallic surfaces. This deterioration is caused by water vapor condensing on or in cool wall or ceiling surfaces. Chemical vapors of chlorine and its nitrogenous compounds add to this problem. This trend of considering the pool function and/or architecture as the principal theory of design persisted until the 1970s. It is possible to upgrade older facilities by design renovation and incorporation of new and more appropriate materials to achieve substantial operating savings and highly effective energy retrofits. The following paragraphs address pool enclosure construction techniques and application of dehumidification/heat recovery equipment.

Relative Humidity and Condensation

In recent years the problems of condensation and humidity control have become increasingly important as high energy costs force more stringent energy conservation measures. Like all buildings, energy conservation requires the walls and ceilings of swimming pool halls to have their insulation values increased. This is particularly true for natatoriums, which have the highest operating temperature (83 to 86°F) of any public building. Unlike other structures, the vapor barrier and the moisture control of the natatorium's relative humidity become critical. Relative humidity is the ratio of water vapor in the air at a specific temperature to the maximum vapor capacity that the air can hold at that temperature (in %). Humidity control in natatoriums of older designs requires large quantities of energy. The building managers involved would be tempted to allow humidity to rise for short-term energy cost savings. This practice may, however, result in gradual damage of the pool-enclosing structure. Owners and operators, as well as designers, should have a working knowledge of condensation and relative humidity and of how they are best controlled for indoor swimming pools.

The air inside all buildings contains water vapor. The measure of comfort experienced by the occupants is a product of the relative humidity and temperature. ASHRAE (1981) has established a range of relative humidity and temperatures for comfortability during different seasons as shown in Figure 15.2. Due to evaporation of water from the large surface area of the pool, the air directly over an indoor pool contains more water vapor than any other location in the building. The amount of water vapor in the air depends on the pool water temperature, air temperature, and the velocity of air passing over the water surface. This vapor, or steam, tends to diffuse uniformly from the water surface into the building volume. The amount of control exercised by the building's heating and ventilation system over the air temperature and relative humidity determines the comfort of the bathers. The temperature of the pool water mass is fairly constant, maintaining a usually comfortable and stable thermal inertia once the tank is raised to the desired water temperature. Water vapor in the air over the pool, however, is not as stable and may condense when it comes in contact with cold surface temperatures below the dew

Figure 15.1 Laminate wood trusses are the highlight of this pool enclosure

point. In areas of a building with very high humidity, water vapor condenses even on a relatively warm surface. Water vapor flows from warm interior areas of high humidity to cooler exterior areas of low humidity. A vapor barrier such as a

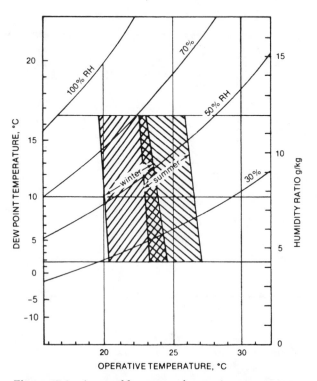

Figure 15.2 Acceptable ranges of operative temperature and humidity for persons clothed in typical summer and winter clothing, at light, mainly sedentary, activity (≤ 1.2 met). (From *ASHRAE Handbook—1985 Fundamentals*, p. 8.19, 1985, Atlanta, GA: ASHRAE Press. Copyrighted 1985 by ASHRAE. Reprinted by permission.)

plastic film or paint must, therefore, be used to prevent this flow of moisture to the colder and drier exterior of the building, and substantial amounts of insulation must also be installed to prevent condensation of moisture on cool interior (hidden) wall and ceiling surfaces. Condensation saturates absorbent materials, causing considerable damage to building materials and equipment, destruction of structural (wood) laminates, oxidation and corrosion of metal building structurals or electrical conduits, dry rot of wood, and freeze damage or spalling to exterior structures, along with general discoloration and deterioration.

Natatorium Humidity Control

A recent design concept for the modern natatorium involves control of the humidity over the pool and also over the deck areas by means of two separate psychrometric zones. An energy-efficient method developed in Germany in the mid-1970s is currently finding its way into American construction. This design addresses the comfort level required by bathers on the pool deck separate from higher, more humid psychrometric conditions that are allowed above the pool water surface and that are less important for user comfort. This concept of separate psychrometric conditions within the same large volume differs markedly from design methods used for over 30 years in the United States and established by ASHRAE national standards. In previously used techniques, well-defined comfort levels of dry-bulb temperature and relative humidity were established throughout the entire volume, uniformly over both the pool and deck areas.

The effectiveness of limiting comfortable temperature and humidity control exclusively to conditioned spaces over the decks is understood by comparing the ratio of natatorium volumes over the pool decks and over the pool(s). The decks may encompass 50% of the building space for a 25-meter pool while decreasing to as little as 30% of the building space in a 50-meter installation. The air volumes to be conditioned above these respective areas are generally proportional to the surface areas. Therefore, conditioning only the volume over the deck obviously results in both a reduction of mechanical equipment and greatly improved effectiveness compared to the same effort required for the entire natatorium. Comfort levels over the decks may be improved and more closely regulated, whereas the annual operating costs for natatorium humidity and comfort control may be reduced.

In this new design technique, two separate conditioned air zones may be identified. One zone is over the decks at a closely controlled comfort level, for example, 86 °F dry bulb and 60% relative humidity. The second air zone is over the pool and is humid space, 3 to 4 °F warmer than the pool water, (approximately 86 °F) with the relative humidity allowed to approach saturation (e.g., ⩾ 90% rh).

The conventional HVAC design approach (ASHRAE, 1981), with six to eight air changes only over the decks, results in a substantial reduction of air ducts, fans, and equipment sizes than otherwise needed when attempting to condition the much larger total building volume with the same criteria. This new design approximates the current European approach: an air flow rate of 3 cubic feet per minute (cfm) per square foot of pool surface area. Figure 15.5 illustrates this energy-efficient natatorium humidity control system, designed with two separate air zones and a heat pump.

This recommended design employs a wide deck-level coping with slotted perforations. The technique also employs an integral surge trench below the coping (rimflow system) or trench cover. (The modern deck-level design for a fast competitive racing pool was first used in Germany at the 1972 Munich Olympics.) The surge trench encircles the pool with its upper section sized as an air duct to provide for adequate return air flow of the HVAC system; the lower portion of the surge trench carries skimmed pool water overflow. The upper volume of the trench serves as the return air duct.

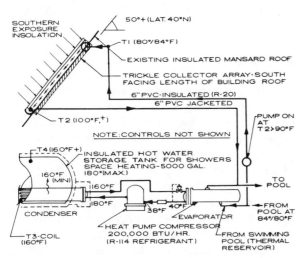

Figure 15.3 Natatorium 2000: energy collection, storage, recovery

Figure 15.4 Brown University Natatorium, Providence, Rhode Island. Architect: Daniel F. Tully Associates.

An overflow pipe at the desired elevation in the trench designates the maximum surge water level and separates the air (duct) volume from the water (surge) volume. In this manner, the flow of humid vapor and chlorine odors off the pool surface is expedited into the return air stream, resulting in minimum attenuation of noxious odors and humidity diffusion into the main natatorium air volumes in either of the two psychrometric zones.

The more humid air just above the pool surface is believed by most coaches to be more comfortable to the throats of active bathers, especially competitive swimmers. In older, conventional designs, hot, dry air is introduced into the building at a low elevation, sweeping across the pool surface in order to pick up the evaporating water vapor. In this design, humid air is discharged through the exhaust fan(s) mounted high on the wall.

With the two-zone natatorium facility, the overhead air supply ducts are located above the surge trench allowing a dry, warm ''air-curtain'' or ''blanket'' to be directed downward around the pool perimeter and into the return air duct—the defined space at the top of the surge trench—thereby effectively sealing off the very humid air over the pool from the relatively drier, controlled atmosphere above the pool deck. As an effective air curtain, it forms an invisible air wall around the

pool, containing the invisible, highly humid air mass over the pool. For large decks an additional supply duct may be located at the outermost building corner, where dry and warm air is directed down to a return air duct below the floor at the wall/floor corner. In this way, a comfortably warm, outside building wall having an elevated mean radiant temperature (MRT) inside the building may be maintained for optimum psychological comfort of wet and bareskin bathers (approximate MRT = 87 °F).

Heat Recovery

Every natatorium design attempts to achieve control of humidity and temperature by well-established, physical principles. A key to control of this natural phenomenon is the evaporative rate of the pool water surface. From the moment the bottom of a swimming pool is covered with water (even if the water is only 1 inch deep), evaporation from the water surface occurs continually and invisibly. The depth of the water is of no consequence because the rate of evaporation is a product of several well-defined parameters: the water temperature, the air temperature, and the velocity of the air over the wet deck and pool water surface. Dalton's law of partial pressures further defines the uniform dis-

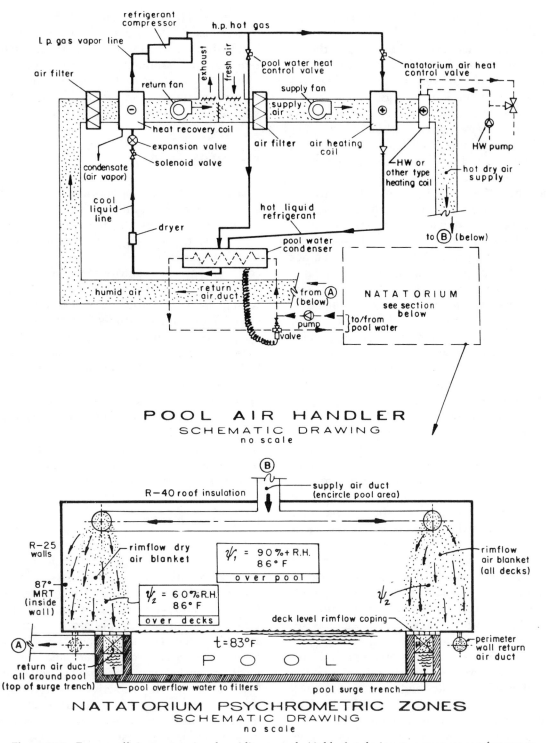

Figure 15.5 Energy-efficient natatorium humidity control. Air blanket design: two separate comfort zones.

bursement of the water vapor or steam (acting like a gas) throughout the containing volume.

In order to remove water vapor from the air and prevent intolerable levels of high humidity in the swim hall, suitable quantities of fresh dry air must be introduced to replace the expelled moist air. In mild seasons or temperate climates this may be ac-

complished in an extremely practical method by the use of large exhaust fans, especially when the outside air is less than 50% relative humidity and not above 95 °F dry-bulb temperature.

In winter, however, it is necessary to heat the cold, dry air before it passes over the wet decks and pool surface so the air picks up the maximum amount of water vapor. When discharging the warm humid air, its measurable warmth, termed sensible heat, is also expelled along with the latent heat in the vaporized moisture. This heat expulsion may be utilized through refrigerant recovery equipment. Furthermore, normal, daily, or seasonal climate changes resulting in very high or low fresh air temperatures, or humidities higher than 70%, lead to uncontrolled swings away from the desired comfort level and result in discomfort to the bathers with this system.

Since the 1970s it has become cost-effective to install heat-recovery equipment to reclaim the sensible heat being wasted in the discharge of warm, humid exhaust air. Several forms of heat-wheels, heat exchangers, glycol ''run-arounds,'' and other passive methods of sensible heat recovery have been effectively used. Mechanical refrigeration is now preferred for dehumidification and heat recovery because it furnishes the lowest long-term, cost/benefit ratio. This is possible because water evaporation is recognized as a cooling process and may be addressed thermodynamically as a heat transfer process. The heat energy needed to evaporate 1 pound of water is 970 BTU. A 50-meter pool complex, when occupied, readily evaporates 500 to 600 pounds of water per hour from the wet decks and pool surface under normal temperature/humidity comfort conditions. When the vapor moisture is condensed by use of refrigeration, all of the latent heat in the water vapor is recaptured and may be transferred back to the air stream for heat supply to the building or heating the water supply.

Heat recovery is accomplished through the use of heat pumps employing a refrigeration cycle. A heat pump is a mechanical apparatus that is rapidly replacing the conventional central AC unit. In this application, heat in the water vapor is removed by the refrigerant flowing through the ''heat recovery coil'' of the evaporator unit. Removal of heat from water vapor extracted from the humid air results in water condensation and allows that reclaimed heat to be returned to the dried air supply by the mechanical equipment (in the refrigerant condenser or ''heating coil'') as it flows back to the natatorium. When refrigeration equipment is operated in this manner, a high coefficient of performance (COP) of 5 to 6 may be realized: For every kilowatt of electrical energy required to operate the mechanical heat pump equipment, 5 to 6 kilowatts of heat energy is returned to the air supply stream after refrigerant dehumidification of the return air.

At times of the day or year when there is no need to add heat to the supply air flow, the heat obtained during mechanical dehumidification of the return air may be added directly to the pool water. This heat is used in turn to overcome the continuous ground heat loss and the heat loss due to pool surface evaporation.

Illumination

The selection of indoor pool illumination, whether natural or artificial, involves issues of safety, task performance, energy effectiveness, lamp efficacy (lumens/watt), cleaning costs of lamps and of fixtures, lamp replacement interval, bulb and labor costs, energy cost, value of money (interest) during period of planned installation, capital cost of wiring, and fixture installation alternatives. In the selection of lighting fixtures and lamps for swimming pool environments another important element is chromaticity and the Color Rendering Index (CRI). The Color Rendering Index is a system that compares how a light source renders the appearance of specified colors when compared to a reference source of the same chromaticity whose CRI value is 100. Lamps having high CRI that accomplish full development of red skin tones are preferable for illumination of the swimming pool area and support facilities.

Natural Lighting

There are two viewpoints concerning the use of large expanses of glass fenestration in indoor/outdoor pools. The first holds that glass walls will increase energy loss, increase dangerous veiling reflections and water surface glare, and promote algae growth and more rapid deterioration of pool sanitizing chemicals. The other view holds that these problems are grossly overstated and are factors that may be easily corrected by proper design. Glass enhances the attractiveness of a pool enclosure. Some design strategies using glass areas require the use of triple-glazing and proper building orientation with respect to sun position and include moveable guard chairs. Overhangs or clerestories to eliminate direct sunlight and glare, blowing warm air curtains at fenestration areas to prevent condensation, and the use of large glass areas rather than small openings have been used. Proponents of expansive glass sections further assert that the pleasant indoor/outdoor atmosphere created by large open expanses of glass increases

Figure 15.6 North Sydney, Australia Olympic swimming pool employs a plastic bubble cover made in Italy.

swimmer satisfaction and pool usage, thus offsetting higher operation costs. As this discussion illustrates, it is necessary to consider the proposed purpose of the pool and other design and cost factors before choosing an enclosure design.

Artificial Lighting

Lighting accounts for 20 to 35% of the energy used by most pools. All of the energy used for lighting—lamps plus ballasts—is developed as heat that must be accounted for in the HVAC system and pool water-heating design. Natatorium lighting may be provided by energy-efficient metal halide high intensity discharge (HID) lamps, color-corrected mercury vapor lamps, or high-efficiency fluorescent lamps. (See chapter 19 for a comparative performance schedule of lamps.) It is suggested that lighting be designed to maintain 50 footcandles (fc) of illumination at deck level for recreation and general pool use. The "maintenance" value is the minimum reading of a photometer (in footcandles) at the specified location when the lamps are at 70% of their rated life and the lamp luminaries are being maintained (cleaned) normally. Increased lighting levels at locations of detailed task performance or instruction stations should be provided with ready access to local on/off switching. Special deck or pool areas for hydrotherapy programs, instruction of disabled individuals, and senior citizen activities must be lighted for higher visual levels. Minimum values for over-deck and above-pool lighting levels recommended by the I.E.S. (1981) at indoor pools are 30 fc for recreation and 50 fc for exhibition. Following is one health department's regulations for minimum area lighting for indoor pools: "Illumination level in indoor pools shall be designed to provide 50 fc intensity over the pool and shall be so designed to eliminate glare and excessive specular reflections. Overhead light sources should be located to provide a minimum of reflected glare or veiling images on the water surface that cause viewing and safety problems" (Suffolk County Department of Health, 1980).

This level of lighting is a minimum requirement, and is in addition to the IES underwater lighting minimum of 100 lumens/sq ft for indoor pools (Kaufman, 1981). Although it is particularly important to provide well-lighted diving facilities, intense direct illumination of this area may cause reflected glare that distracts the diver. Stairs, tower ladders, elevators, and particularly the diving boards and platforms should be safely lighted. Practical provisions should be made for relamping fixtures, particularly when they are located over the pool surface. This may take the form of mechanical devices for lowering fixtures to deck level; catwalks in between roof trusses that access overhead lamps; or scheduled periodic complete replacement of lamps. (See chapter 11 for a discussion of underwater lights.)

Acoustics

The geometry of the building envelope is a major factor in noise control. The larger the space (volume), the greater the reverberation time or length of echo. Proper surface geometry of interior building walls and ceiling and moisture-resistant acoustical ceiling materials may be used effectively to attenuate the sound level. In addition, other means

Figure 15.7 Nylon skin on roof. Columbia, Maryland. Designed by Costello.

of reducing unwanted noise include moisture-resistant curtains and drapes; surface-mounted panels made of sound-absorbing materials such as foamglass placed on the walls and/or ceilings; and water-resistant nonshrink carpet on decks and in spectator areas. Geometric forms of various sound-absorbing materials placed in the over-pool space are an attractive means of sound control. Architectural "space-frames" perform this function and at the same time accentuate the expanse of high ceilings. The use of carpet in and around swimming pools is expected to increase in the future as new types of waterproof and sanitary materials are devised that are easily maintained, do not hold water or support combustion, resist chemical attack, and are fungus-resistant and bacteriostatic.

Enclosure Costs

The preferred types of pool enclosure construction methods follow in ascending order of cost. The order is based on general frame costs but does not account for construction costs due to interrelated mechanical and electrical systems or for insulation requirements in colder climates. Certain precast designs already include insulation.

- Tensile fabric structures
- Air-supported fabric structures
- Arch truss-supported lightweight fabric or plastic skins, either translucent or opaque

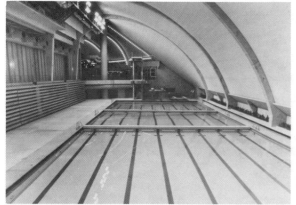

Figure 15.8 Lightweight roof structure, O'Connel Center Pool, University of Florida, Gainesville. Architects: CRS, Moore, May, Harrington, Eng, Geiger-Berger.

- Prefabricated metal frame and metal skin structures
- Pneumatically applied concrete thin shells
- Dome or frame structures with rigid or semirigid plastic panels
- Long-span steel trusses on post and beam construction
- Laminated wood and plastic decking
- Steel frame with masonry sidewalls
- Cast-in-place concrete structurals and masonry sidewalls
- Precast concrete "Tee" beams on load-bearing masonry sidewalls or with precast structural walls

Plastic structures have limited life expectancy due to the deteriorating effects of ultraviolet light. Complex structures that may be moved on and off pools have been developed to allow the use of pools for both indoor and outdoor exposure, but they have had limited success when compared to equivalent, less complex stationary structures in combination with pools. In general, the lower the construction costs are, the greater the maintenance and operating costs.

Building Insulation Selection

The building envelope for an indoor pool requires wall and roof insulation. Typical operating conditions impose a high operating winter temperature difference across the wall and roof of 70 to 85 °F. Coupled with this thermal difference is high inside humidity, posing a potential for dewpoint condensation in the wall unless a complete moisture barrier is installed to prevent migration of water vapor in the air through the wall or roof.

The design parameters required to assess the optimum thickness of insulation needed for the wall and roof of the natatorium thermal envelope can be evaluated by computer program. The cost of the insulation type being used is plotted against the operating savings of a particular insulation thickness.

The planning and construction of an indoor swimming pool are two of the most complex tasks that a recreational or educational agency will undertake. For further guidance in pool planning, refer to other chapters in this book, particularly

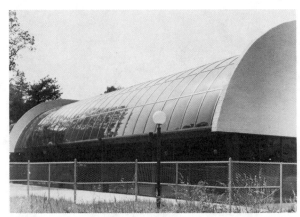

Figure 15.9 Theresa Banks Memorial Pool, Prince Georges County, Maryland. Photo by Steve Abramowitz.

chapters 1, 8, 10, and 16. A design worksheet is provided in Appendix A.

References

American Society of Heating, Refrigeration, and Air-Conditioning Engineers. (1981). *ASHRAE Handbooks—1985 Fundamentals* (p. 8-19). Atlanta, GA: ASHRAE Press.

Kaufman, J.E. (1981). *IES Lighting Handbook* (6th ed.) (p. 291). New York: Waverly Press.

Suffolk County Department of Health. (1980). *State of New York, Standards for the Operation of Swimming Pools, Section 10-E* (p. 15).

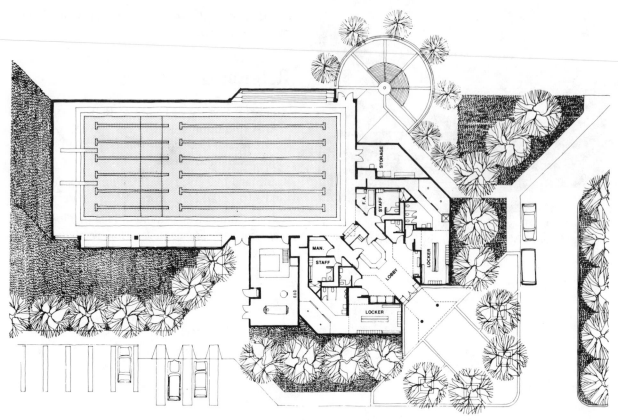

Kent University Pool

Chapter 16

The Pool Bathhouse

The bathhouse functions as a service facility for the activities related to a swimming pool complex. Its purpose is to accommodate the requirements of the people using the pool by providing dressing rooms, lockers, toilets, a first-aid room, a snack bar, and often the pool's administrative facilities. The bathhouse also provides the control center, offices, staff facilities, storage rooms for equipment and supplies, and in many instances the filter room. By properly locating the bathhouse, it also acts as protection from prevailing winds, visual privacy for the pool itself, and can be a focal point to the complex and overall project.

A popular trend, which has considerable merit, is the winterization of the bathhouse so that it may be used as an indoor recreation or community center. Some bathhouses have been designed to serve both a pool and an ice-skating rink located in close proximity to the pool. When this is done, a year-round recreation facility is provided at less cost than if separate facilities were constructed.

The bathhouse structure should be simple, with emphasis on minimum maintenance and maximum durability and energy efficiency. Its design should also permit smooth traffic flow in a controlled and safe setting.

Determining the Overall Size

The size of the bathhouse depends on several factors, beginning with the basic relationship to the size of the pool, the capacity of the pool complex, and ultimately the anticipated peak swimming load. A key factor is the anticipated peak number of people that will be in the bathhouse at one time. For example, the pool complex may have a capacity of 1,000. However, the rate at which people arrive and depart from the pool may indicate that a maximum of 20% (100 males and 100 females) will be in the bathhouse at any one time; hence, the capacity of the bathhouse for planning purposes is 200.

In addition to the peak number of users, such requirements as the type, size, and quantity of lockers; the method of control and checking; the extent of privacy to be afforded the users; and other features determine how large the bathhouse must be.

Between 10 and 15 square feet per person should be allotted for a dressing room. Thus, using the above example, a total of 1,000 to 1,500 square feet for each of the dressing rooms is required. Added to this must be the space needed for lockers, toilets, showers, and other facilities essential to the dressing room.

Although state and local codes vary as to the required number of fixtures, toilets, lavatories, and showers, they generally set their standards according to the number of bathers at capacity. In general, the maximum demand occurs only a few times per year, during which it may be preferable to be overcrowded than to have larger facilities to maintain during the rest of the year.

Components of the Pool Bathhouse

An important consideration in the planning and design of pool facilities is the means of controlling entry to the pool. There are three basic types of admittance procedures designed to provide entrance controls.

1. *Turnstile System*
   - The token or coin-operated turnstile uses a token or minted coin that activates a rotating arm.
   - A plastic-coated magnetic-edged card activates an open latch when inserted in the gate.
   - The key-operated turnstile is similar to a regular door latch.

2. *Attendant System*
   - The infrared technique is primarily used for readmission. When a person leaves, a hand is stamped with ink only visible under infrared light and is checked upon return.
   - Each person is given an admission badge, pin, or tag at the beginning of the season and displays it upon entrance to the area.

- A person pays the admission cost each time the pool is used.
- Prepurchased tickets are presented upon entering the pool facility.

3. *Open Admittance*

   This system permits anyone to enter. This is often the case in large recreation centers.

Clothes Storage Space

Every pool complex that attracts memberships or the general public from a wide area should expect to provide clothes storage facilities. The typical storage systems that have been used are as follows:

1. *Lockers:* This is the most common system for clothes storage. Lockers are usually metal, preferably stainless steel, 12 in. wide, by 18 in. deep by 12 in. high to be stacked 4 or 6 ft high. A bank of 36-in. high and 72-in. high single lockers should be provided to accommodate hanging clothes. Lockers are located within the locker room along the wall or in interior rows. These are operated by key, padlock, coin, or token.

2. *Baskets:* This system usually requires a checkroom, although some modifications have been made to slide the basket into a slot similar to a drawer that locks in place with a key. The basket system is subject to constant sanitary problems unless an easy-to-maintain mesh basket is used, made of stainless steel or vinyl material. Carbon, steel, and other metals rust and stain clothing.

3. *Compartments:* This system is similar to the locker system only smaller compartments are used. These are excellent for small items.

4. *Bags:* Bags may be canvas, mesh, plastic, or vinyl. The patron returns the filled bag to the checkroom where it is hung on a rack according to a number system. Some adaptations have included a rack in the locker room where the bag, when closed, is locked on the rack with key or combination lock.

5. *Envelopes:* The envelope system closely resembles the bag concept except for the difference in shape and their method of storage. One disadvantage is that large pieces of clothing are difficult to store.

6. *Hangers:* A coat hanger is locked onto a rack; or a large pin holds the clothes; or the clothes hook or coatroom concept may be used.

Some pools have provided a combination of locker types. However, the trend seems to be to provide lockers of either system—device-operated or free—because lockers take up less space, keep clothes in better condition, and require fewer personnel to administer than other systems. Where lockers are used, they should be placed on a base, usually concrete, to prevent their getting wet at the bottom and to make floor cleaning easier. Sanitary and health codes in most states require that the floor have a coved base at all walls and edges to facilitate maintenance. All enclosed locker rooms must have some type of ventilation system.

Dressing Area

Individual dressing cubicles are often provided for the women's dressing room but rarely in men's dressing rooms. Cubicles are usually 3 ft by 3 ft with a small seat. Benches the length of the row of lockers are usually included. The number of cubicles should be based on accommodating at least 20% of the capacity of the dressing room.

The locker-room design should provide a maximum of sunlight and air to promote clean and sanitary conditions. Operable skylights provide both natural air and sunlight but offer no protection against the weather. It is, however, an economical design that is often used.

Shower Room

Direct access to the showers from the locker room is essential. The number of showers depends on the number of bathers; usually one showerhead per 40 bathers is the recommended minimum. It should be considered whether individual cubicles for showering or gang or group showers are appropriate. The shower room floor must be pitched to a drain, made of nonslip material, and have a coved base around the perimeter. It is desirable to have the partitions for cubicles wall-hung for easy maintenance. Water temperature for the showers should be controlled to prevent possible scalding: 90 to 100 °F is ideal.

Drying Room

A drying room should be provided next to the shower rooms on both the men's and women's sides. The floor is treated as "wet floor" similar to the shower rooms, but the furnishings consist of benches, hair dryers, mirrors, and hooks. The secret of a "dry" locker room is to keep people in the drying room until they have completely dried themselves. Adequate drains are critical in this area.

Toilets

Toilets should be directly accessible from each locker area and convenient to the pool. They should include or be directly adjacent to the lavatory areas. The number of toilets, urinals, and lavatories required may be calculated as follows: 1 lavatory for each 60 bathers, 1 toilet for each 40 women, 1 toilet for each 60 men, 1 urinal for each 60 men.

Urinals for women are a relatively new development that should be considered because they reduce the requirements for toilets. All fixtures should be wall-hung, and the floors, as in the shower areas and drying rooms, should be pitched and have coved bases around the perimeter.

The floors in the dressing, shower, and toilet areas are potential "wet" areas. Each room must have at least two drains with the floor pitched toward them. Unfinished concrete encourages the growth of fungus and attracts dirt and other undesirable materials that produce objectionable odors and may transfer "athlete's foot" from one bather to another. The ideal floor cover is nonslip ceramic tile. Concrete, if not painted, should be sealed to make it impervious to fungus and to facilitate cleaning. Concrete floors in potentially wet areas should never be troweled smooth (steel finish) because this makes them slippery and hazardous. There are acceptable paint products containing abrasives that produce nonslip surfaces. Epoxy floor coverings have recently been tested and appear to offer a suitable covering and add attractiveness to the locker room. Nonslip carborundum and emery additives applied directly to concrete finishes have been used with success. Open, nonslip plastic floor mats are also being used successfully.

Lobby or Entrance Foyer

The lobby or foyer should be situated at the main entrance to the pool and must be large enough to accommodate all incoming and outgoing patrons. If guests other than swimmers or those using the

locker facilities are anticipated, public toilets are necessary near this area. Seats and other waiting arrangements must be included, as well as public telephones and a bulletin board. If the area is to be used by bathers, it should be designed as a wet surface and be adjacent to the snack bar, concession, or vending machine areas. Checking facilities may also be provided here for those bathers who come dressed in their suits, therefore not requiring use of the locker room.

Control Office Space

The type of activity conducted within the control office dictates that it be located in a position adjacent to the lobby or public access. From here, people are directed to either the men's or women's locker rooms and, depending upon the system used, are either given baskets, a key, and a towel or merely allowed to enter. Visual control over both locker-room entrances must be maintained. If money is collected, tickets or keys distributed, or passes checked, a small, protected booth should be included in this area. The total space required depends on the type of system used. Towels, keys and locks, or baskets should be dispersed from another point, if possible.

The minimum size recommended for the control office is 100 square feet, but the room may easily be 3 times that size, depending on the number of people to be housed and the type of activities to be conducted.

Manager's Office Space

The manager's office should have direct access to the pool area and be situated at a position from which the manager can oversee the entire pool. Raising it to a second level to afford greater visual control is recommended where possible. Com-

munications from this office should be available to all parts of the pool. A phone for outside calls, a microphone for announcements to the swimmers and controls for lighting, heating, and ventilation should be available. This office should be directly adjacent to the lobby and the control office for admissions and basic clerical procedures.

The size of the manager's office may range from a minimum of 80 square feet to 150 square feet or more. The office should contain the necessary equipment to maintain certain records, accommodate visitors, and conduct small conferences. Air conditioning is desirable.

First-Aid Room

A first-aid room is essential in any large pool or beach operation. It must be located where it is accessible from all sections of the pool and also from the street for ambulances. The room should be of sufficient size to accommodate a cot, lavatory, shower with hot and cold water, toilet, and the necessary emergency first-aid equipment. The room should have good air circulation and be designed with materials that are easy to maintain. Communication must be available from this room to all areas of the pool, particularly a nearby hospital. With small pools, it may be necessary for the manager's office to double as the first-aid room.

Lifeguard Room

The lifeguard room should provide a comfortable atmosphere where guards may relax when off duty. In a large pool complex, where a staff of a dozen or more guards of both sexes may be employed, the room should consist of a lounge with a view of the pool for supervision by the chief lifeguard and separate dressing, shower rooms, and toilets for the men and the women. Phone connections to each lifeguard station, the first-aid room, the manager's office, the central office, and the outside are necessary. Microphone control from the guard's room is desirable. The dressing rooms should include some storage space and locker facilities for each guard. Air conditioning and a refrigerator are also desirable.

Instruction Equipment Storage Room

A storage room located at deck level is necessary for the equipment required for pool use and instruction. This includes such items as paddle boards, racing lane markers, water polo goals, ropes, balls, kickboards, extra diving boards, and props for water shows. Shelving and cabinet space should be available for storage of smaller items. A major pool complex requires at least 300 square feet of storage space.

Maintenance Equipment Storage Room

A second storage area is required for maintenance equipment. Space is required for all mechanical equipment including lawn mower(s), portable pool vacuum cleaner, irrigation hose and sprinklers, tools, rakes, and baskets. A multiple-pool complex requires a space of about 300 square feet. An outside rolling door is desirable.

Filter and Mechanical Equipment Room

The filter room houses such mechanical equipment as pumps, filter tanks, water heaters, chemical feeders, surge tank, and control panel and provides storage space for chemicals and sometimes cleaning equipment. It must be separated from areas of public access and yet be convenient to all maintenance facilities such as the chlorine room, maintenance equipment, heating, and utilities. Generally, the utilities for the pool complex, including heating and supply of water and electricity, operate efficiently from the filter room.

The room must be adequately vented and fire-retardant. Ventilation is required for motors and heaters and to ensure fresh air for combustion of fuel-fired units. Its ceiling should be high enough to accommodate any tall equipment, and its floor must be strong enough to support the weight of heavy equipment. Lighting must be adequate for clear visibility of each equipment component and gauge for maintenance purposes. Fifty footcandles of illumination is recommended throughout the mechanical room. Proper drainage is required, and

transformers should be protected against water damage. Groundfault protection of all motors, lighting fixtures, and power receptacles is mandatory at suitable levels to prevent fires and protect personnel.

Sufficient space for the placement, replacement, and servicing of each piece of equipment must be allotted, particularly for bundle pulls of the heat exchanger and the filter tank element. The doors or openings should permit the largest item to be taken in and out.

The Snack Bar

The snack bar is a convenience to the pool patron and may also be a source of income to help in the cost of operating the pool. The following criteria may be used in developing a snack bar.

- The facility and layout are attractive.
- The facility is not excessive in cost.
- The items sold are high profit.
- Good quality items are provided.
- A good but limited menu is available.
- The items will not spoil or go stale.
- The food items can be attractively lighted and displayed.
- The system dispenses items with the minimum amount of personnel.
- Specialized personnel are not necessary.
- The service will require a minimum of the user's time.
- The service will satisfy the user.

Various systems may be employed in dispensing refreshments.

Service system. This type of refreshment stand may be portable or permanent, depending upon which best suits the situation. The stand may be staffed, with the employees on the payroll of the pool as a self-operation; leased, with the employees retained by a concessionaire; or arranged by contract with fixed percentage royalties to municipalities, permit with fee to municipality, or license with fee to municipality.

Vending system. This system includes canteens or servicettes that may be fixed or moveable depending upon the situation. At present these machines are of two types: automated machines that provide hot, cold, and room-temperature snacks and foods such as canned soups, ice cream, and beverages; and semi-automated machines that require occasional servicing.

Although food and beverages are desirable, in most cases they are not permitted in the pool area. However, the eating area should be close to the pool and have its own controlled area, with restricted but direct access to the pool.

In locating the refreshment space, consideration should also be given to servicing the nonswimming spectators and the consequent need for dual access and two separate areas of control. The use of bottles or glass in any form should be avoided because this poses a potential hazard to the pool area.

Saunas, Steam Rooms, and Whirlpools

These three items are popular additions to the pool complex. Generally they are located in the locker room so that people have easy access to them. See chapter 5 for details on construction and operation.

Exercise Room

Exercise rooms and fitness centers equipped with Universal, Nautilus, and other specially adapted exercise equipment are being utilized by physical fitness enthusiasts at an ever increasing rate.

Parking Lot

Parking lots for pool complexes vary depending upon functional and economical considerations. The design of the parking lot itself reflects terrain, climate, grade, groundwater, vegetation, soil, and facilities. The type of vehicle (car, bus, trailer, or truck) and its size and turning radius are also important in the planning of a proper facility. Apart from space for parking, there should be ingress and egress, unloading walks, appropriate signs and markings, curbing, fencing, and barriers. Types of lot controls include automatic gates that may be operated mechanically or electrically; keys used by members to open the gate; and cards, tokens, or coins to insert into a slot to release the gate. Other methods of controlling entrance to parking areas that have proven to be successful include the following:

- Parking meters

- Attendants, used most often when people must be directed to a certain area

- Electronic gates that require that cars be equipped with an electronic device to activate the gates

- Television that employs a closed-circuit screen located in the control office; an operator identifies the car by an appropriate bumper sticker or shield and then opens the gate

Chapter 17

Solar Energy

Solar energy has become more attractive as an energy source for heating pool water, especially as the cost of other commonly used fuels has skyrocketed over the last 10 to 15 years. This chapter explores the use of solar radiation for this purpose, the types of systems available, and the various components of a solar system. Further resources are listed at the end of this chapter.

Why Use Solar Energy?

The apparent high cost of solar equipment and installation has caused some pool owners and designers to decide against the use of solar energy. However, there are several significant reasons for seriously considering the use of solar energy, including the following:

- The temperature desired for swimming pool water (around 80 °F) does not necessitate a great increase in temperature from available summertime water, nor is the demand as great as it is for domestic hot water or for other heating and cooling systems.

- The current life of the average pool solar-heating system is about 15 years. This is expected to increase as further technological advances are achieved.

- Maintenance of solar heaters is minimal. The single greatest concern is the potential corrosion of metal waterways. One way to assure that this is minimized is to make certain that the chemicals added to the pool water for sanitation purposes (chlorine liquid or gas and acids) are introduced to the pool water far from the collector's intake pipes.

Some of the material in this chapter has been adapted from publications of the Florida Solar Energy Center, 300 State Road 401, Cape Canaveral, FL 32920. Used with permission.

Enclosure uses sun effectively. By Sun/Fun Solar Structures, Wheeling, Illinois.

- Once solar equipment is installed there is no further cost. The buy-back time (when the cost of conventional fuels to heat pools matches the cost of the solar system) ranges between 3 and 5 years depending upon the initial cost of the system.

How Solar Radiation Works

Solar radiation is simply the energy derived from the sun. Every year the sun drenches the United States with 500 times more energy than is consumed. If one tenth of this was tapped by only 2% of the nation's surface, the country's energy demands could be met.

The sun is an immense source of energy (radiation, heat, and light) projected in all directions. Its intensity varies as the inverse of the square of the distance from the sun. Weather stations throughout the United States record the amount of solar radiation received at the earth's surface. Solar insulation varies from the solar constant depending on the earth-sun angle and total of direct and diffused sunlight at the bottom of the atmosphere.

Many factors affect the amount of sunlight that finally arrives at the earth's surface, with variations occurring according to the time of day, season, microclimate, latitude, and inclination. Radiation amounts follow the elevation of the sun in the sky—low in the morning and evening, high at noon. Seasonal changes are also twofold; with each season the sun's position in the sky changes and the length of days changes.

There are two sources of heat for swimming pools. First is the absorption of solar energy from the sun by the water. In the summer the water in a swimming pool when exposed to the sun absorbs up to 75% of the solar energy that strikes the surface of the water. The second source is the heat that may be supplied by "collectors," which are the principal elements in the solar energy system. In the latter process, the solar energy absorbed by the collectors or similar device is placed in storage and subsequently used to heat water to a desired temperature for either pools or domestic hot water supply.

Swimming Pool Application

Though governmental programs and funds have been directed toward promoting the use of solar energy for heating and cooling of buildings or heat-

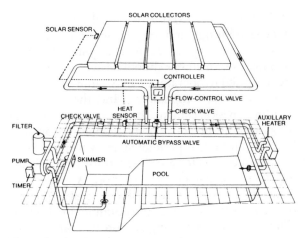

Typical solar system

Solar radiation, when absorbed by a collector or other device, must be placed in storage, either in a monitored storage tank for the pool heating and domestic hot water and/or then in the pool as a storage tank for home heating and domestic hot water in the nonswimming season. This is accomplished with or without the use of a transport medium, and the heated water is distributed to the point of use. The performance of each operation is maintained by automatic or manual controls.

There are many elements and functions that make up a solar system—the collectors; storage; distribution; transport; controls; and auxiliary energy sources, each of which may vary widely in purpose, design, construction, and operation. They may be organized in numerous combinations depending upon component performance compatibility, climate, demands, site, and structure requirements. The systems may be active or passive depending upon whether additional energy for the transfer of thermal energy is used.

Moveable, horizontal panels of weatherable urethane insulation placed on the roof, deck, or yard are used to retain the heat collected on winter days and removed in the summer to permit the absorption of sunshine.

ing domestic hot water, it is estimated that 5 times the square foot of collectors used for such purposes have been used for heating swimming pool water. As a result, a major industry in pool heating has developed with limited published information. As may be expected, the states of Florida and California are the leaders in both research and development in the use of solar energy for heating swimming pools.

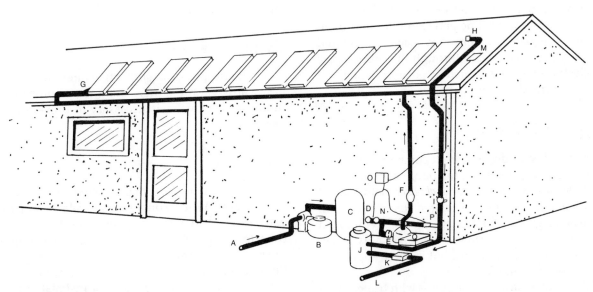

A	Pool Water In	J	Fossil Fuel Heater (if Existing)
B	Pump	K	Chlorinator (if Existing)
C	Filter	L	Warm Water Returns to Pool
D	Check Valve	M	Sensor 1
E	Gate Valve 1	N	Sensor 2
F	Drain Valve	O	Automatic Control Box
G	Solar Collectors	P	Electric or Vacuum Valve (Collector Bypass)
H	Vacuum Breaker & Auto Air Relief	Q	Booster Pump (if Needed)
I	Gate Valve 2		

Typical solar pool heating system with automatic control

Recent developments in equipment and design include the use of aluminum and other materials as collectors; additional compressors; and the use of valves for selecting, draining, and other purposes.

There are four primary solar systems currently in use:

- A *flat plate collector* system, which usually faces south on rooftops. The hot water that is generated may be used for both household needs and pools, through either active or passive systems. The pool filled with water may become a passive collector.

- A *concentrator collector*, which reflects sunlight striking a large area onto a smaller surface. Concentrators trace the sun continually in order to stay in direct sunlight.

- *Pure passive solar architecture* in the forms of windows, glass walls, open water, or other designs.

- *Photovoltaic or solar electric cells*, which are set at the same angle as the latitude of their location.

Typical Pool Solar Heater Plan

A typical pool solar heater is connected by means of tees to the water line between filter and pool. When adequate sunshine is available, the filtered pool water is circulated through the tubes in the collector where it is heated by solar radiation and then returned to the pool.

Types of Collectors

Two collector designs, both commercially available, are in general use for pool heating.

Metal tubes are soldered to metal plates, both painted black and housed in an insulated box covered with plastic or glass. This design is widely employed for "medium-temperature collectors" (MTC) used for domestic water heating but is not the optimum for pool heating applications.

Black "continuous" plastic panels with heaters supplying water through either a large number of small channels that in effect cover the entire panel area, or by larger black plastic pipes connected in series through PVC couplings and U-bends. These designs are often called "low-temperature collectors" (LTC).

Pool heating is characterized by large flow rates and by collector exit-water temperatures only a few degrees above ambient. For such applications, LTCs outperform MTCs from a thermal performance standpoint and are also about half as costly. When seeking an economical system for pool heating, the consumer should be aware that LTCs are designed to operate at a maximum of 15 to 20° above ambient temperature, and therefore, depending on local climate, they may not be suitable for all-year heating of swimming pools. For all-year heating, an MTC is preferable. However, the relatively large collector area needed for winter heating incurs considerable expense. An alternate solution appears to be a combination of LTCs and pool covers that provides the optimum method for extending the swimming season to year-round.

Sizing of pool heaters is related to the pool's surface area. Once the pool has reached the desired temperature, substantially all heat loss is from the surface. Collector sizing is determined to keep the pool at a given temperature above ambient temperature. This practice, also recommended by the National Spa and Pool Institute, is based on the rationale that most larger pools, especially commercial ones, are heated up only once in a season and subsequently maintained at or near the established temperature.

Besides the bank of collectors, the following components are essential to ensure proper functioning of the pool heater.

Check Valve

When the pump is shut off, water may flow backwards via the gutter, skimmer, and/or filter drain. A check valve is necessary to prevent this backflow.

Gate Valve

Gate valves provide manual control over the pool heater. When sunshine is available, a gate valve is closed to divert the pool water through the collectors. At night or during cloudy days when the pump is on, this gate valve should be opened. Simultaneously, gate valves provide control for ground-mounted panels and roof installations as well as serving to insulate the collectors from the piping loop connecting the pool, filter, and pump. Isolation of the collectors may be necessary for their inspection and/or maintenance.

Vacuum Breaker and Drain Cock

When the drain cock is opened, the air-vent vacuum breaker allows air to enter the solar

Collector locations

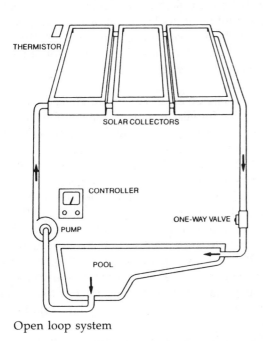

Open loop system

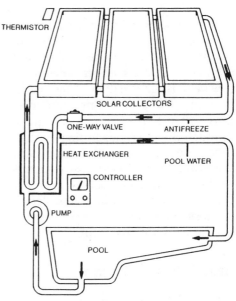

Closed loop system

panels, allowing them to be drained. Draining may be necessary to free the system of air bubbles or to prevent freezing during cold weather. The vacuum breaker is typically installed at the highest point in the return piping from the collector.

Pressure Relief Valve

This valve protects the solar panels against excessive pressure buildup, which may result from water stagnation, blockages from equipment malfunction, or improper maintenance procedures.

Piping

The recommended piping is PVC Schedule 40, 1-1/2 to 2 inches nominal diameter, depending upon existing pool plumbing.

Optional Pump

The decision to install an additional pump depends entirely on the added friction loss created by introduction of the collector panel loop to the existing system. Usually, the average 15,000-

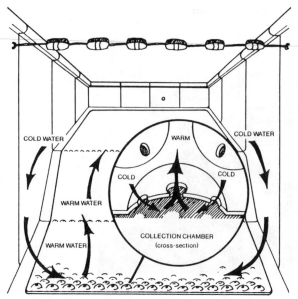

Underwater mat collector

gallon, home pool installation is equipped with a 3/4-hp pump motor. This pump supplies the pressure required to overcome the total pressure loss in the system at the recommended flow rate, which usually is recirculation of the water every 8 to 12 hours. The principal pressure loss in the system is a 10 to 15 psi (pounds per square inch) drop through the filter, depending on the filter's condition. The pressure drop through the collector panel is usually small (4 to 5 psi) compared with the loss through the filter. Pool owners are advised to consult the vendor regarding the collector-panel pressure loss to determine whether it warrants installation of an additional pump.

Optional Automatic Control

An optional automatic control is available with most commercial solar systems. When the temperature sensed at sensor 2 exceeds that sensed at sensor 1 by a predetermined amount (usually 3 to 5 °F), the normally open electric valve is closed, and the pool water flows through the collectors. When sunshine is not available, the control box switches off, and the electric valve opens, allowing the collectors to be bypassed, which is the normal mode of operation.

Indoor Pools

Indoor pools usually require year-round water heating. By contrast, the heating and ventilating loads for pool enclosure space are seasonal.

The low-temperature water required in the pool (80 °F) and the moderate, hot-water temperature required by domestic hot water (105 to 115 °F) correspond to the range of efficient operation for low-cost types of solar collectors. The constant year-round demand for the heating of both pool water and domestic hot water offers a quicker payback than a solar space heating system. Therefore, the recommended priority listing for solar heating for recreational facilities generally is:

- Pool water heating (lowest grade: 80 °F)
- Domestic hot-water heating (105 to 115 °F)
- Building space heating system (180 to 220 °F)

The solar heating system and the pool water hydraulic system interfacing is usually not complex. The pool water itself has large storage capacity for the collection of solar energy year-round. The building or pool conventional heating system should be arranged in conjunction with the solar system and becomes the backup or auxiliary energy system when the solar system cannot carry the load.

Flat plate solar collectors are effective and dependable for year-round application. Glycol water mixtures usually constitute the heat transfer fluid between the collector (in cold climate locations) and the heat exchanger serving the pool and domestic hot-water heat exchangers.

The heat absorbed by the collectors is removed by the heat transfer fluid passing through the collectors. Manifolds at the top or bottom of the collector are balanced to distribute the fluid uniformly to all collectors. For all collectors of equal thermal performance, overall efficiency increases as the ambient temperature rises, the inlet working fluid temperature declines, or the solar radiation increases.

Durability, appearance, ease of installation, mounting, structural supports, controls, and configuration are the prime elements to be evaluated in collector selection. The cost of physically mounting the collectors to the building structure depends on the design of the mounting system selected and the height and slope of the roof or structure on which the collectors are installed. This is an important consideration for existing buildings and requires a detailed analysis by a structural engineer.

Outdoor Pools

Solar heating of outdoor swimming pools involves several unique aspects:

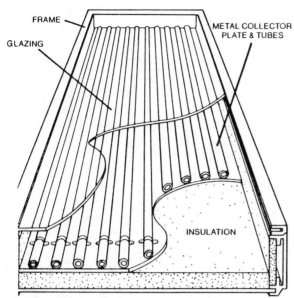

FRAME

GLAZING

METAL COLLECTOR
PLATE & TUBES

INSULATION

Flat plate collector panel

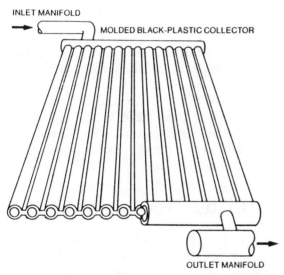

INLET MANIFOLD

MOLDED BLACK-PLASTIC COLLECTOR

OUTLET MANIFOLD

Plastic collector panel

- The desire to swim normally is phased with a warmer trend in the weather.
- The preferred water temperature (80 °F) usually is only a few degrees above ambient (surrounding) temperature.
- The amount of water that must be heated and circulated through the solar energy collector panels is relatively large, the recommended flow rate being a circulation of the entire pool water through the filter about once every 8 hours. This means a flow rate in excess of 30 gallons per minute for an average 15,000-gallon, residential

pool compared with an average flow rate of 1/2 gallon per minute for domestic water heating.

- The volume of water in the pool being relatively large, its temperature is affected only slightly by transient changes in atmospheric weather conditions.
- The need for a storage tank is eliminated because the pool itself serves as the storage.

The goal of any performance analysis of swimming pool solar heating is an estimate of the pool's bulk temperature. Because of its large mass, the pool's water temperature usually changes little during a 24-hour period (a range of about 4 °F). Therefore, the pool temperature can be estimated by calculating an energy balance for a typical day for each month of the year. This is usually done by equating heat gains to heat loss from the pool surface at the equilibrium pool temperature. Obviously, an effective way to maintain high temperatures and thereby provide extensions in the normal swimming season is to maximize heat gains and minimize heat losses. Pools gain heat via the following:

- Absorption of solar energy directly striking the pool surface
- Accumulation of heat supplied by the collector panel

Pools lose heat via the following:

- The long wave, infrared radiation exchange between the pool and the sky. This exchange depends on the emissivity (power of a surface to emit heat radiation) of water as well as ambient weather conditions such as relative humidity, dewpoint, cloud cover, and temperature.
- Radiation loss to surroundings (nearby objects), which depends on the difference between pool temperature and ambient temperature and also on the radiative heat transfer coefficient. When the radiating and absorbing surfaces approach ambient temperature and the radiating surface has a high emissivity (as in pool heating), the value of the radiative heat transfer coefficient is estimated to be 1 BTU/hr sq ft °F.
- Convection loss with the surroundings, which depends on the difference between pool temperature and ambient temperature and also on the convective heat transfer coefficient.
- Conduction loss through the pool side walls and water pipe for circulation, which also must be calculated.

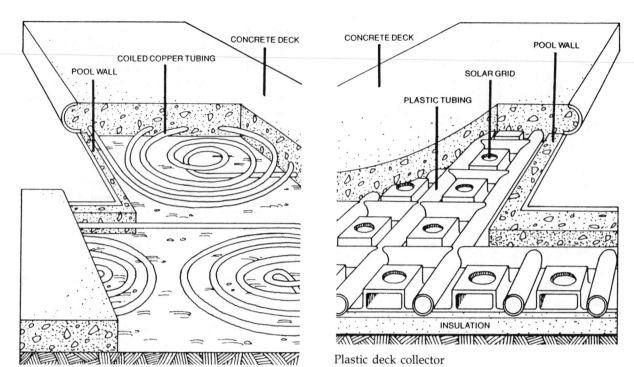

Coil-type deck collector

Plastic deck collector

- Evaporation heat loss from the pool surface, which depends on ambient humidity conditions, the convective heat transfer coefficient, and ambient temperature.

Pool Covers and Blankets

Evaporation accounts for as much as 70% of a pool's total heat loss. Pool covers reduce such loss and are, therefore, an effective means of lengthening the swimming season. Although it is recommended that a single, continuous pool cover be used, it may present a handling problem in larger pools. In such cases, several modular units may be the answer.

Continuous covers and modular units are commercially available at an average cost of $0.50 to $1.00 per square foot and normally have a lifetime of several years. The most commonly used cover material is transparent PVC (polyvinylchloride), which has a high solar radiation transmissivity. For the do-it-yourself pool owner, commercially available PVC film of 4 to 6 millimeters thickness is recommended as cover material. Because it is relatively inexpensive (about $40 per 1,000 square feet), replacement cost is a minor consideration. Water-resistant tape may be used to secure the film

to several modular frames to cover the pool surface. It should prevent tear or collapse if stepped on by any size person.

The inconvenience of covering and uncovering a pool is more than offset by the significantly longer swimming season. Covers also help keep pool water clean, thereby reducing the cost of chemicals and filter maintenance.

Installation and Maintenance

Information on purchase, installation, and maintenance of solar water heating systems is available through published documents. In general, most of this information applies also to pool heating systems. Following are some installation and maintenance tips:

1. The tile angle, that is, the angle that the collector makes with the horizontal, should be close to the optimum value. This value depends on the amount of extension of the normal swimming season that is desired. For continuous plastic panels and for most climates, the optimum value is latitude plus 10 to 15°.

   However, in certain instances, depending on the slope of the roof or personal tastes, it may not be practical to install the collectors at their optimum tilt angle. Fortunately, this does not become a critical factor because as long as the tilt angle is within 15° from the optimum, the overall effect on the heat collected is not significant.

2. The orientation of the collectors normally should be due south. The following list describes how to handle special situations.

   • For locations experiencing afternoon thundershowers, the recommended orientation is 15° *east* of south.

   • For locations experiencing early morning haze, the recommended orientation is 15° *west* of south.

   • For locations experiencing afternoon thundershowers, the recommended orientation is 15° *east* of south.

3. Although most solar pool heating systems do not require much more maintenance than the normal, regular maintenance required by a swimming pool, the following should be observed in sequence when shutting off the system at the end of the swimming season:

   • The automatic control and pump should be switched off.

   • The gate valve should be closed and the drain cock opened so that the solar panels are emptied of water.

   • When restarting the system at the beginning of the swimming season, shut the drain cock, open the gate valve, and switch on the pump and automatic control.

Cost and Life of Solar Systems

The major cost of a solar pool heating system involves the collector panels. Typical low-temperature collector (LTC) costs range from $3 to $4 per square foot of collector area. Medium-temperature collector (MTC) costs are generally 3 to 4 times higher. An automatic control system costs about $350. Gate valves cost $12 to $15, and an extra $75 should be budgeted for the vacuum breaker, pressure relief valve, drain cock, and miscellaneous requirements. A typical figure for installation costs for an average size pool is about $400.

Using the above values, one should be able to determine the cost of a solar pool heating system. For example, in the Miami, Florida area, the total

Light-weight fiberglass roof and walls trap solar energy to heat interior. Photo courtesy of Bill Hedrich, Hedrich-Blessing.

installed cost of a system (assuming $3.50 per square foot of LTC) is:

Cost of collector
405 sq ft of water surface area at $3.50 = $1,417.50	$1,417.50
Valves and plumbing	90.00
Installation	400.00
Total	$1,907.50
Total with optional automatic control	$2,257.50

Solar pool heaters generally are not designed for all-year heating. A large area of collector panels is then required, with consequent higher collector and system costs. The discussion on pool covers suggests that a combination of collectors and pool covers perhaps is the best method for all-year heating. If pool covers are used for an average of 22 hours a day, in conjunction with collectors, the R value is reduced to about 0.5, or 255 square feet of required collector area. Pool covers provide a significant savings in the cost of collector panels required and, therefore, are strongly recommended for use in all-year heating.

These cost figures are only estimates. Ideally, after going through the sizing procedure, anyone planning a solar heating system should contact several manufacturers of solar heating systems to obtain their recommendations and installation prices.

Most of the plastic solar pool heating collectors are made of ABS (acro-butadiene styrene). Plastics have poor resistance to the ultraviolet rays of the sun and, therefore, tend to degrade within a short span of perhaps 2 or 3 years. However, ultraviolet degradation inhibitors normally are combined with the plastic and for such panels, one reasonably may expect a lifetime of about 12 to 15 years.

Other Factors in Using Solar Energy

1. In a screened-in pool the normal heat gain derived from the sun is reduced by as much as 30 to 40%.

2. The performance of unglazed collectors is substantially reduced by cold winds blowing across their surfaces.

3. Swimming pools that are exposed to the sun without shading between 4 hours before until 4 hours after solar noon pick up heat by direct absorption of the sun falling on their surface.

4. The most successful solar heating systems are found in the "Sun Belt" states.

5. The surface required for installation of collectors is about equal to the water surface area of the pool.

6. The heating of pools and spas represents the most cost-effective way of using solar energy.

7. The average pool builder does not have the technical knowledge concerning solar energy. Those interested in exploring the use of the sun should consult with people involved in development and installation of pool solar systems.

Innovations in Solar Energy Use

1. One of the most interesting developments in the solar area is the use of concrete decks surrounding the pool as solar collectors. This idea has been extended to using driveways and even tennis court surfaces as collectors. The way this works is by burying the tubes (usually polyethylene) in the concrete deck. The header of the system is located on the periphery of the deck. This has also been done using asphalt surfaces. The problem with asphalt is that it does not have the lifespan of concrete.

   One of the companies that has successfully accomplished the use of concrete decks and driveways is the Bomanite Corporation of Palo Alto, California. Daniel P. Sieben, vice president of the Bomanite Corporation, suggests two principal benefits of the system. "It is aesthetically pleasing since the solar collectors are out-of-sight, and it keeps the pool deck cool, since the coils remove the heat from the concrete" (Hardesty, 1985). Another method used to cool the water is to divert the return water to a series of sprinkler heads that spray the water over the surface of the pool resulting in a lower water temperature by evaporation.

2. In climates where the ambient air temperature is high (above 90 °F), the water temperature

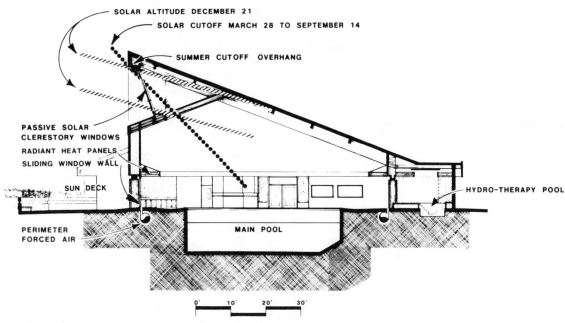

Natatorium designed to use solar energy effectively

Greenhouse structure traps heat of sun

ing the return pipe at ground level where the temperature is about 50 °F, the water returning to the pool can be cooled to provide a more enjoyable water condition.

References

Cromer, C. (1983, July). *Solar heating of swimming pools: A question and answer primer* [FSEC-EN-6-80]. Cape Canaveral, FL: Florida Solar Energy Center.

Cromer, C. (1981, July). *Solar swimming pool heating in Florida, collector sizing and economics* [GP-13-81]. Cape Canaveral, FL: Florida Solar Energy Center.

DeWinter, F. (1980). *How to design and build a solar swimming pool heater.* New York: Cooper Development Association.

Engelhard, R. (1985, July 1). Heat exchangers. *Pool and Spa News*, pp. 84-88.

Hardesty, R. (1985, June 17). Let the sun do it. *Pool and Spa News*, pp. 26-28.

Root, D. (1979). *Solar heating for swimming pools.* Winter Park, FL: Florida Conservation Foundation, Inc.

Root, D. et al. (1982). *Solar water and pool heating manual (Vols. 1 and 2).* Cape Canaveral, FL: Florida Solar Energy Center.

may go as high as 88 to 90 °F. To reduce the water temperature in such cases, experiments have been undertaken that utilize the lower ground temperature to cool the water. By plac-

Solar heating for swimming pools. (1983). Alexandria, VA: National Spa and Pool Institute.

Talwar, R. (1979). Technical considerations—solar sizing and system design. In *Swimming Pool Data and Reference Annual*, pp. 322-323.

Sources of Information

Florida Solar Energy Center
300 State Road 401
Cape Canaveral, FL 32920

National Information Services
5285 Port Royal Road
Springfield, VA 22161

Solar Engineering Magazine
8435 Stemmons Freeway
Suite 880
Dallas, TX 75247

Pool and Spa News
3923 W. 6th St.
Los Angeles, CA 90020

National Spa and Pool Institute
2111 Eisenhower Ave.
Alexandria, VA 22314

Chapter 18

Pool Modernization and Renovation

Pools over 25 years old may need to be renovated and in most instances modernized to eliminate defects that are dangerous or add significantly to the cost of operation. The need for repair or replacement may be related to one or more of the following areas:

- Excessive water loss
- Water turbidity
- Removal of dangerous conditions in the original design
- Increased program usage
- Vandalism
- Chipping, cracking, and other erosion
- Lack of routine maintenance
- Change in state health laws or regulations or city ordinances
- New technological advances

To renovate implies the restoration of a pool to a modern, attractive, functional, and safe facility that meets all existing standards. The basic rule of thumb used to decide between renovation and new construction is if the cost of renovation is more than half the cost of new construction, it is best not to renovate but rather strive for new construction as soon as feasible.

Typical Pool Problems

This chapter will discuss the problems identified above as they relate to the modernization of pools. pools. At the first sign of any of these indicators, professional help should be sought to avoid the

Diving tower at Arizona State University's aquatic center

development of a major problem that may necessitate closing the pool.

Excessive Water Loss

Excessive water loss increases the cost for chemicals and heating of the raw make-up water. The resulting chemical imbalances create unsafe water conditions. The cause of water loss in swimming pools may be classified into three categories.

Pool shell leaks. How water loss occurs depends upon the type of pool shell. Poured concrete pool shells often leak at expansion joints where sealants have disappeared over the years, or where in the original construction water stops between pours had not been used. Concrete, if not placed properly in the original structure, may have voids or air pockets that serve as vehicles for water to escape. Concrete porosity may also be a factor if original paint application, which sealed the surface, has worn off.

Gunite concrete structures offer an advantage over poured concrete because they often eliminate or greatly reduce the expansion joint problem. An improperly placed gunite concrete shell may be porous, but the industry practice of providing a marble-dust plaster finish coat on pool walls and floors helps to seal the pool. Most leaks that occur in gunite pool shells are readily seen by exposed or open cracks that penetrate both plaster finish and gunite concrete shells. These cracks are usually caused by settlement of improperly compacted subgrade at the time of construction, inadequate thickness of transition slabs that slope between shallow and deep water, and exposure to weather by not keeping water in the pool to protect against extreme winter temperatures in northern climates.

Steel shell pools normally have been plagued by a rust-out problem from the outside wall. This occurs by not initially coating the outside shell properly prior to backfilling, thereby allowing water to pocket behind or under the pool shell causing rust areas to develop. Another source of problems with steel pools may be improperly installed welds between sections, allowing pinhole leaks that grow with the age of the pool.

Other pool shell materials include stainless steel, fiberglass, and coated aluminum, all of which are found in modern swimming pool construction. Stainless steel has successfully been used for wall sections and often in conjunction with gutters as a complete wall anchored in a concrete pool floor. Similar arrangements have developed utilizing aluminum coat products. Fiberglass has been used successfully on small pools, but because larger pools require structural shell integrity and the use of field seams, the fiberglass pool is undesirable for large pool applications. Stainless steel wall and/or gutter sections require field welding. Although many pools have been successfully built utilizing this method of construction, a few may suffer from improper field welding by inexperienced welders, and some problems do occur from pinhole leaks in welds from even the most experienced personnel. Most times these areas can be rewelded or spot welded to correct the leak. A discussion of liner type pools is excluded from this section.

Gutter and perimeter piping leaks. Most pools over 20 years old need some amount of repiping. Often it is the pool's recirculation system piping between the filtration plant and the pool structure that has aged. Also, in most cases, the piping has been buried directly in the earth with no pipe case access. This often requires a total repiping job involving renovation of the decks and portions of the pool gutter and shell. Older pools generally used galvanized or cast iron piping. Modern pools use mostly PVC piping and some fiberglass piping, similar to chemical treatment and processing plant piping systems. The older piping used prior to PVC and fiberglass did not tolerate the pool chlorine residuals; and although later use of cement-lined cast iron did prolong pipe life, cement-lined valves and special fittings required were normally not available. Therefore, non-PVC or fiberglass piping subjected externally to the weathering elements of soils and water and internally to chlorine did not last.

The pool piping system may be tested by isolating sections of pipe between the filter room and pool shell to determine if leaks occur and in what pipe. Care must be exercised not to pressure-test old piping under standards for municipal water pipe testing, because pool operations vary between 15 and 30 psi, whereas municipal water piping usually is tested at 150 psi. This higher pressure may cause older pipes to fail when they may have provided additional years of service if not tested at the higher pressure.

Main drain piping may contain leaks and may also be pressure-tested to evaluate its soundness. It is unusual for main drains encased in concrete under the pool shell to develop leaks; if this should happen, there is an option that is far better than jackhammering out the bottom of the pool. If the main drain was oversized in the original construction, it may be possible to provide a liner or new, smaller diameter pipe inside the existing main drain.

Gutter systems in older pools were normally the roll-out type with drains and piping taking the overflow water from the gutter. Some pools only employed recessed skimmers. Both of these overflow systems may need to be converted to a recirculating-type gutter system.

Filtration system leaks.   The most obvious type of leaks are observed in the operation of the filter plant. Here leaks are visible to the operator and generally are accessible to correct. Older filter systems often employed cast iron piping and valves that, over the years of exposure to chlorine and improper pH control, scaled and reduced the effectiveness of the system, thus requiring replacement.

Filter systems below pool-water level, especially vacuum diatomaceous earth (DE) filters, may lose water through a dumping action if the system is shut down and valves between the pool and skimming and main drain lines are not closed. This dumping action may happen with a power failure

if fail-safe, hydraulic, or battery-operated electric valves that close these lines were not installed.

Diatomaceous earth filters most commonly utilized on large pools are a vacuum type that are open concrete, fiberglass, or steel vaults with filter elements stacked on heaters connected to the suction side of the recirculation pump. These filters are the most easily maintained because all working parts are exposed to view. Other filter systems rely on an enclosed tank to house the filter media, such as sand and pressure DE filters. These tanks should be stainless steel, painted, and periodically serviced to ensure long life.

Water Turbidity

Water that lacks clarity, besides being unattractive to users, causes operational problems for lifeguards by reducing visibility of the pool bottom in deeper areas. The most obvious problem of water turbidity may be caused by several different areas of the recirculation system, resulting in cloudy water and often an algae-clad pool bottom. This condition is reflective of an improperly operating filter system, usually including the chemical feed component. Recirculation pumps must be checked to determine if flow in gallons per minute is equal or close to the original design. If pumps are working, then the next step is to determine if old, metallic pipe return lines to the pool have developed scale or rust buildup. This reduces the effective size of the piping and makes an appreciable difference in the amount of water flow they are capable of handling. This condition is evident by a drop in the readings of the flow indicator in the pool equipment room as well as a drop in the volume of water coming into the pool at each of the inlet points. When a flow meter is not available, a simple method of computing the pool water recirculation rate is as follows:

- First, compute the volume of water occupying the upper 6 inches of the pool. For example, the pool measures 75 feet by 45 feet, which equals 3,375 square feet of water surface area. Six inches of water produces 1,687.5 cubic feet of water, or 12,656 gallons.

- Then, drain 6 inches of water out of the pool and refill this 6 inches through the pool recirculation system. Keep track of the exact amount of time required to return the 6 inches that were drained out, and then calculate the flow rate per minute.

If the flow rate should be 300 gallons per minute and is actually 200, it is possible that there is rust in the pipes that prevents the free flow of water.

• Once this has been established, the pipes should be cleaned or replaced in order to bring the circulation up to the level required by the health department.

Filter media may also be the cause of improperly filtering swimming pool water. Vacuum D.E. elements must be checked for overall D.E. application to the precoat cycle, and any damaged or broken elements must be replaced or patched to maintain proper vacuum pressure through filters. Old sand and gravel filters may require replacement of layered sand media disturbed over long years of use and backwash cycles.

Ramp for disabled swimmers at Lido Beach Town Park, Hempstead, New York

Updating Older Pool Designs

Swimming pool designs have evolved over the years due to changing demands of the user, updated competitive swimming rules and diving standards, and research. Some of these conditions have recently been recognized since pool standards have been upgraded, such as diving depths and related deep-water bowl configurations and racing course requirements, including width and depth. Other design problems were proliferated by the ''copy'' syndrome, such as edges inside diving hoppers intended to allow a user to stand and rest next to the pool edge in deep water. Some have developed through careless design practices, for example, protruding seats, float line anchors, and other accessories that protrude into the pool area and cause unnecessary obstructions. Table

18.1 outlines some dangerous pool conditions and suggests possible corrective measures. These corrective measures are only briefly discussed and are presented as a suggestion of the type of remedial work that may be necessary. Owners should seek qualified professional assistance in evaluating and recommending remedial work for their specific pool problems.

Increased Program Usage

Because of increased pool use, program opportunities may need to be expanded including those for diving, competitive swimming, access for disabled swimmers, and night availability. Responses to these needs may necessitate changes in pool configuration in length, width, and depth. For example, the pool basin may need to be modified so that the diving area has greater water depth to accommodate safety in the dive. The pool length may have to be changed so that international competition may be accommodated. Pool lane markings may have to be modernized to introduce new target shapes. The pool shell may have to be modernized with observation windows to allow for the training of competitive divers and to conduct underwater photography. In addition to these program items, pool modernization may be introduced because of changes in the regulations governing competitive swimming activities. For example, the width of the pool may need to be increased to accommodate a regulation number of racing lanes or even an added lap lane.

Dangerously designed diving envelope. Note that the springboard is also misaligned with pool.

Table 18.1 Potentially Dangerous Pool Conditions

Condition	Suggested Corrective Measures
Inadequate water depth and area for springboard diving	Reduce length/height of board Eliminate springboard Redesign/reconstruct bottom
Inadequate lighting for night swimming	Change wattage of lights Add lighting fixtures
Water slide in shallow water (under 5 feet deep)	Place slide in water depth of at least 8 feet
Protruding wall anchors	Recess into wall
Protruding bottom inlets	Recess into pool bottom
Starting blocks in shallow end	Relocate to deep end of pool
Shallow water shelf extends into pool	Prohibit diving in area by placing signs on coping/edge
Constant cloudiness of water	Check filter size and pump capacity
No markings on pool bottom	Paint lines on bottom; use black tile when basin is refinished Paint edge of steps Place line on bottom at breakpoint and on seams of hopper bottom
No depth markers on pool edge	Place markers on coping or edge
Construction ledge extends around pool in deep end	Paint stripes on ledge to make them more visible
Hopper bottom in deep end	Prohibit diving in area by placing warning signs
Spoon-shaped bottom in deep end	Prohibit springboard diving, at least by adults, and add warning signs
No pool rules, inadequate rules, or improper placement	Redo rules and post at every pool entrance
Indoor pools: side windows causing light reflection on water's surface	Tint windows or install curtains

Pool Repairs

Damage caused by persons or natural weathering should be corrected immediately to deter further deterioration. Improved security measures should be implemented to reduce damage due to vandalism.

Outdoor pools, because of their exposure to all kinds of climatic conditions, seem to require repairs or replacement more frequently than indoor pools. Concrete, tile, and other materials such as plaster used in pool basin finishes have a longer life expectancy. When such materials are fabricated, the whole structure has a limited life expectancy. Unless continuous attention is given to such cracks or chipping by removing or repairing the deteriorated areas, resurfacing the pool basin will be necessary.

Routine Maintenance

Lack of routine maintenance may cause staining, unsanitary conditions, broken equipment, loosened parts, pipe and joint failures, moisture collection around electrical installations—all of which may be eliminated by periodic visual, mechanical, and electrical inspection and metering.

The removal of leaves and debris daily eliminates staining. Algae and fungus at their first appearance must be removed to avoid slippery conditions, discoloration, and damage to the pool surface. A strong algicide and scrubbing are required. Cracking, scaling, chipping, and discoloring of the pool basin necessitates sandblasting to remove the old finish before a new plaster surface is applied. New paints that are available may also be used to protect the finishes as well as to provide an attractive appearance.

Advances in Pool Design and Operation

New design concepts may also influence pool renovation such as incorporating surface skimmer conversion to a complete recirculating-type gutter, which could reduce the wave surges so often present in skimmer-type pools. Advances in metal or concrete strength, in filter or valve designs, or in electronic controls often provide ease in maintenance; improve safety and sanitation; and because they require less attention, may result in manpower and cost savings.

Photo courtesy of Keifer Pool Equipment

Other Considerations

In addition to careful consideration of repair or replacement of the pool, equal consideration must be given to the bathhouse, lounge areas, decks, concessions, and other buildings. The modernization of bathhouses and locker facilities often involves new interior finishes, trim, hardware, frames, doors, lockers, and floors and equipment that are more moisture-resistant as well as easy to maintain.

Expansion of new pools may be limited by static population growth and the tax base in many areas, whereas desires for aquatics may be dynamic; therefore decision makers may need to turn to the

modernization of existing pools on the basis of cost versus time benefits.

Existing pool facilities or equipment may require replacement because of these cost factors or because of lack of space, lack of utility services, or for some other reason. Replacement is undoubtedly the easiest direction because all projected current, as well as future, requirements may be incorporated.

Managers and owners of pools that are more than 25 years old should consider having their pools evaluated by a qualified swimming pool engineer. This person can provide a program of rehabilitation or replacement for the pool with cost estimates and a priority of changes needed.

Chapter 19

Pool Energy Management

Conservation of energy through the better design of outdoor pools, natatoriums, and the equipment used in their operation will be an important factor in the planning of swimming pools in the next few decades. Swimming pools and the buildings that house them are large consumers of energy and natural resources. Energy is utilized in the building subsystems for electric lighting, heating, ventilating, air conditioning, plumbing, electrical power and controls, fire protection, waste disposal, communications, horizontal and vertical transportation, and security systems. Energy is also utilized in service operations such as grounds maintenance, snow removal, food service operations, and for transportation vehicles. Energy is utilized to operate the pool itself for pool water heating, filter and circulating systems, backwashing, hot water for showers, wastewater treatment, and chemical water treatment. This chapter examines ways to lower the operating cost of pools through pool energy management.

Component and Climate Analysis

Every pool system must be designed to maintain the consumption of energy and natural resources at the lowest practical level consistent with proper and safe swimming pool operation. A pool energy conservation program should identify specific areas where energy can be conserved, including

- those areas that may be accomplished by the owner's physical plant personnel (operations, maintenance, and preventive maintenance);

- those areas requiring minor alterations, modifications, additions, and retrofits in existing facilities;

Echo Park Pool Complex, Hempstead, New York. Roof design employs acrylic material. Architect: Planning Associates, Bohemia, New York.

- the implementation of an effective space utilization plan;
- the motivation of the recreation staff and users to participate in an energy conservation program.

More details are available in ASHRAE Standards 90-80 and 100 for energy conservation in buildings as well as the bibliography at the end of this book.

The energy consumption of swimming pools and the buildings that house them are largely functions of the local climates to which they are exposed. Local climates generally consist of four cardinal elements that have a major effect on energy utilization: the temperature ranges, humidity ranges, wind speeds, and sunshine. Local climate conditions offer both advantages and disadvantages as shown in Table 19.1. Swimming pools may be designed to be energy utilizing with the local climate as an asset, minimizing disadvantages by energy-conscious design strategies such as proper siting, orientation, wall construction, and window management.

One of the most practical of published weather statistics is the "heating degree-day." Heating degree-days are defined as the number of degrees the average temperature for the day is below 65 °F. For example, a day with a mean temperature of 50 °F has 15 heating degree-days (65 − 50 = 15), whereas a day with a mean temperature of 65 °F or higher has no heating degree-days. Normally, heating is not required in a building when the outdoor mean daily temperature is above 65 °F. The amount of heat required at lower temperatures for any specific temperature is proportional to its degree-day value. A fuel bill is usually twice as high for a month with 1,000 heating degree-days as for a month with 500 heating degree-days. Comparing normal, seasonal degree-days in different locations provides a rough estimate of seasonal fuel consumption. For example, it requires roughly 4-1/2 times as much fuel to heat a natatorium in Chicago, Illinois, where there is a mean annual total of about 6,200 degree-days, as it would to heat a similar natatorium in New Orleans, Louisiana, where the annual heating degree-days total about

Table 19.1 Comparison Climate Components of the United States

Climate Condition	Advantages	Disadvantages
Pronounced daily temperature range	Where daily temperatures shift requiring daytime cooling and nighttime heating (as in very dry areas and at high elevations), the day-to-night temperature swing may be flattened by the use of mass construction materials having thermal inertia to yield reduced fluctuation in temperatures throughout the day.	
Yearly temperature range	Design requirement may be for year-round conditioned building, fully insulated, climate-controlled.	Yearly temperature ranges may be disadvantageous in both hot and cold climates; if it is consistently too hot or cold, building heating or cooling may be required on a long-term basis.
Humidity	Moisture may be an asset when evaporating in hot, dry climates because it will cool and humidify the air—a natural air conditioning.	High humidity at high temperature may be a disadvantage if it causes such discomfort that occupants cannot cool down by sweating in summer, thus requiring air conditioning.
Sunlight		Solar loads in summer are the major factor in cooling loads for most building air-conditioning systems.
Windspeed	Windspeed may be an asset in providing comfort in hot, arid climates; it may be used to provide natural ventilation and to control natatorium humidity.	In cold climates, wind may be a liability because air infiltrates the building, increasing heat losses, and the thermal coefficient of convective heat loss is increased. Wind may be a liability to comfort in hot, dry climates when winds cause bathers to dehydrate and overheat.

1,400. Heating degree-day values are often used for scheduling fuel deliveries and for evaluating power or fuel rates and peak demands of use.

The mean annual heating degree-days total about 100 in the Florida Keys and less than 1,000 in the Florida peninsula and extreme southern Texas. Mean annual heating degree-days increase to 5,000 across most of the middle of the eastern two-thirds of the country, reach over 9,000 in northern New England, and over 10,000 near the Canadian border from the Rockies to the Great Lakes and in the high Rockies. There are usually less than 2,000 heating degree-days a year in southeastern California, southwest Arizona, and along the extreme southern California coast. In Alaska, mean annual heating degree-days range from near 10,000 in the southern and southwestern coastal areas and islands, to over 20,000 in the extreme northern portion. Heating degree-days do not occur in Hawaii, except high in the mountains, or in Puerto Rico and the Virgin Islands.

In contrast to heating degree-days, cooling degree-days as used by the National Oceanic and Atmospheric Administration (NOAA) represent the number of degrees the mean temperature for the day is above 65 °F. For example, a day with a mean temperature of 80 °F has 15 cooling degree-days (80 − 65 = 15), whereas one with an average temperature of 65 °F or lower has no cooling degree-days.

Mean annual cooling degree-days in the coterminous United States total over 3,000 in extreme

U.S. Merchant Marine Academy pool, Kings Point, New York. Equipment by Kiefer.

southeastern California, southwestern Arizona, southern Texas, and central and southern Florida; decrease to 1,500 east of the Rockies as far north as a line from central Kansas through northern Kentucky and to southern Virginia; and to 500 in central North Dakota, lower Michigan, and Connecticut. Cooling degree-days are negligible on the north Pacific coast and in Alaska.

Although the normal definition of "degree-day" cited above is based on 65 °F outside temperature, it is recognized that there is a need for adjusting the degree-days used for heating calculations and determination of optimum insulation thicknesses in buildings such as the natatorium where indoor temperatures required for bather comfort are above 85 °F. The swim hall temperature is generally 15 °F above that of other places of public assembly having clothed occupants. Heating engineers know that the heating plant of a conventional building shuts off at 65 °F or lower during the heating season due to heating additions from lighting power, electrical/electronic equipment, the occupants, and other heat sources incident to the building use. Direct heat addition is only necessary to maintain comfortable temperatures (low

70s) in most buildings when the outside air is below 65 °F.

In the natatorium, however, because bather comfort requires air temperatures above 85 °F, cutoff temperature of the building heat source is not less than 75 °F or even 80 °F. It is therefore critical to the operation of any natatorium that the design for insulation thickness (establishing the U or R factor) be based on heating degree-day information at 75 °F (minimum) and not that value of degree-days normally published for the conventional base of 65 °F. "Degree-hour" heating data is published by NOAA for major geographic locations and may be used to obtain degree-day information for natatorium designs at any base temperature. One apparent difference is noted from this method by the following example. At Virginia Beach, Virginia, available ASHRAE data for nearby Norfolk, Virginia, shows 3,488 degree-days as the normal requirement of the heating season based on 65 °F. Reference to Weather Environment Data (U.S. Government Printing Office) allowed calculation of degree-hours at base temperature 75 °F, from which the natatorium may be designed more realistically (and economically for the owner) at

6,465 degree-days for the higher (operating) base temperature.

Site Topography and Microclimate Analysis

It has been found that recreational facilities tend to develop their own microclimates as they grow through the changing of the natural green areas to swimming pool decks and support areas, buildings, parking lots, sidewalks, and paving. Though these changes usually do not affect the general climate or climatic conditions at the recreational site, these changes may create a local "heat island." The heat-island effect increases in intensity as the facilities grow and is caused by the absorption of solar radiation by swimming pool decks and support areas, buildings, and paved areas having large mass heat-storage capacities as well as the reduction in vegetation—trees or grass—that would utilize a portion of this energy in the process of evaporation. In the evening when the sun is absent, the swimming pool decks and support areas, buildings, and streets cool down slowly, because they have absorbed solar energy during the day and reradiate much of it back and forth between adjacent walls and other man-made surfaces. The recreation facility complex air may not cool significantly, and even by morning it may still be considerably warmer than the air in the surrounding neighborhood. The heat-island effect is generally more clearly defined, therefore, at night than in the daytime. This effect is noticeable in both winter and summer, although it is more pronounced for the summer season.

Although afternoon temperatures are essentially the same at the recreation facility complex as those in the surrounding local two-story residence buildings, the nighttime temperatures average several degrees warmer in the facility complex. Winter conditions, although showing the same heat-island effect, may be the result of somewhat different causes. The heat produced by the buildings contributes greatly to the atmospheric heat in the facility complex. With turbulent mixing in the winter afternoon, this effect is not too great. In the relatively stable winter night, however, the nocturnal inversion, coupled with smoke, water vapor, carbon dioxide, and other impurities in the urban atmosphere, decreases outgoing radiation and results in warmer winter nighttime temperatures in the facility complex than in the nearby neighborhood.

Planning New Pools

For new swimming pool facilities, future additions, and alterations to existing facilities, the designer should include the use of vegetation. Where it is practical, deciduous trees should be specified for summer coolness and coniferous trees for warmth in the winter. Green clearings of any size result in conditions similar to those in the open natural countryside. The following items should be evaluated.

- Provide windbreaks, fences, trees, or shrubs to act as wind barriers and wind pressures on the building envelope and windows.
- Orient the natatorium building with reference to minimizing solar loads in summer and maximizing passive solar heat gains in colder months.
- Planting deciduous trees to provide shade in the summer and to admit sunlight in the winter; plant evergreens to provide shade in the summer and to reduce window heat loss to the night sky in the winter.
- Use light-colored ground surfaces to reflect sunlight into windows, dark-colored surfaces to absorb sunlight and raise outside temperatures.

Water Recirculation and Filtration

The pool water recirculation and filtration system utilizes energy for filtering, heating, and the transporting of pool water. With effective recirculation techniques, the energy consumed may be minimized (see chapter 12 for a discussion of design methods). The water circulation and filtration systems contain fundamental elements that impose pressure drops on the pool water hydraulic system and increase horsepower demand. They include the following:

- main drain outlet grilles
- main drain line

- pool overflows
- flow line to surge tank or to filters
- level or rate control valves
- filters
- hair and lint catcher
- flow meter
- pool water inlets
- pipe, valves, and fittings

An optimizing strategy is to minimize the pressure drop of the above listed items within practical limits and to select pumps to operate at maximum efficiency. Pumps should be run continuously and never shut down as an energy-saving measure.

The water turnover rate determines the water flow rate. A rapid turnover rate results in large pipe and equipment sizes. The turnover rates should be selected to maintain proper sanitary conditions and water quality conditions and at the same time not be oversized. The recommendations for turnover rates are given in chapter 12 of this book, along with hydraulic techniques to optimize the flow and water quality using bottom inlet designs. It may be noted that with the concept of having separate diving pools, turnover rates of one every 6 hours (utilized by most health departments) result in excessive water quantities per bather when considering the actual number of people utilizing the diving pools and the reduced bather load per unit volume.

The following items should be considered and reviewed with local health department authorities in an effort to reduce energy consumption and increase efficiency in the pool's hydraulic systems.

- Turnover rates for diving pools studied and revised; three per day (8-hour turnover) acceptable
- Filters sized large enough initially to have very low, limited pressure drops when approaching the end of the filter run, at not less than 10% below the rated flow
- Hair and lint catcher oversized for minimum pressure drop.
- Flow meters of the Venturi type, or other low head loss type, instead of flow meters with inefficient orifice plates
- Pool water inlets or tubes in the racing lanes of the bottom inlet type sized for the minimum

pressure drop with optimum pool coverage of clean, filtered water

- Uniformly level overflows rim the entire perimeter, discharging directly into an adequate (1 U.S. gallon per square foot pool surface) surge tank (or trench) or large size overflow channel
- Pipe, valves, and fittings sized to optimize the cost of energy. When considering the life-cycle cost for energy, this results in slightly larger pipe, valves, and fittings at a higher initial cost but at a reduced, life-cycle cost of energy charges.

Swimming Pool Water Heating Requirement

The energy for pool water heating is required for the following:

- Initial water heating (usually from 55° ground temperature to 85° in most parts of the U.S.)
- Heat required to offset heat losses from the pool basin to the surrounding ambient (ground, room, sky, etc.)
- Evaporation losses (see chapter 15)
- Water losses (carry-off) from wet bathing suits and vacuum cleaning of the pool
- The heating of make-up water for water lost during backwashing and filter-cleaning processes

The strategies that may be utilized to reduce the pool heating load are as follows:

- The initial heating period should be designed for 1 degree per hour in order to keep the heating plant and heat exchanger sizes to a minimum. The exact heat-up period and equipment sizing should be determined by a balanced judgment taking into consideration the normal pool water heat losses, heating of make-up water, and backwash heat losses, to satisfy the most stringent requirements when considered against the initial fill requirement.
- The pool shell should be insulated outside to minimize the conduction heat losses from the pool water to the ground or surrounding below-deck spaces. (See chapter 12.)
- Evaporation heat losses should be minimized by the utilization of pool covers during periods of nonuse.

- Backwashing losses may be minimized by filter type selection (regenerative cycle) and heat recovery devices in the waste line.

Natatorium Air Heating

Relative humidity and mean radiant temperature (MRT) of surfaces enclosing the pool play a major role in determining comfort levels for indoor aquatic activities. Extensive studies by Fanger (ASHRAE, 1985) on comfort ranges for the naked male body agree on the optimum temperature of comfort at 75 °F. This is in conformity with the generally recommended inside pool enclosure design condition of 86 °F and 60% relative humidity (rh).

The human body loses heat by radiation, convection, evaporation, and the respiratory process. At 80 °F Fanger's study indicates body heat losses are approximately as follows:

radiation	170 BTU per hour
convection	50 BTU per hour
evaporation and respiration	100 BTU per hour
	320 BTU per hour

It has also been shown that skin temperature is approximately 90 °F when the room temperature is 80 °F. As MRT decreases, body heat loss increases. Therefore, if it is desired to maintain the normal balance of 170 BTU per hour loss by radiation at 80 °F, it is important to keep MRT of pool enclosure surfaces as high as practical (near 87 °F). Using an average body surface temperature of 85 to 90 °F and a 170 BTU per hour heat loss or greater, an MRT of 85 to 87 °F is desirable.

Construction elements (walls, roof, and floors) must be selected and designed with overall coefficients of heat transfer (U) that will provide:

- an inside room surface temperature high enough to prevent condensation at worst design condition(s).

- temperature and vapor pressure drops across each constituent wall/ceiling component so that concealed condensation does not occur within the wall. A continuous vapor barrier must be provided inside the pool hall for all the walls and roof.

- an MRT of 85 to 87 °F that will be maintained at all pool hall surfaces. This will keep heat loss

Heat exchanger

by radiation from the unclothed swimmer to his or her surroundings to a minimum, avoiding the discomfort of chills associated with radiation to cold surfaces.

- a thickness of insulation that will be optimized to yield the lowest overall insulation cost plus fuel cost over the anticipated life of the enclosure. (See next chapter heading.)

Swimming pools located in the interior spaces of a building usually are as much a problem for surface temperature and condensate control as pools with wall and roof exposures. The use of glass on pool exposures adds cost in cold climates. Glass walls or exposures make cold draft conditions and vapor condensation difficult and expensive to eliminate. Alternate designs should be studied.

It is desirable to keep air motion within the pool deck area to a minimum to reduce the feeling of drafts on the unclothed occupants and also to reduce the rate of evaporation that increases with air velocity. On the other hand, increased air motion is desirable for the comfort of spectators and is *essential* to water vapor removal.

Because air motion and temperature requirements are different for pool and spectator areas, a complete separation between the two must be made. A third and separate psychrometric zone (ψ_3) should be established to accommodate clothed spectators apart from the bathers' comfort zone (ψ_2) shown in Figure 15.5 (chapter 15). The conditions of the spectator zone should be as recommended by ASHRAE for the local seasonal conditions.

Natatorium Insulation

One of the more practical methods of continuously conserving energy over the life of a natatorium is through the insulation of its outside walls and roof. This is particularly important because a natatorium generally operates at a higher temperature (85 to 87 °F) than any other public building. As a consequence, the heating degree-days to be used in calculations, as previously noted in this chapter, should be based on not less than 75 °F, resulting in substantially higher design values—and a more economical structure to operate—than when using the lower and more common base of 65 °F.

It is generally known that there is a "most economical" thickness for insulation, beyond which any additional energy cost savings does not warrant the additional insulation cost. The method of determining this most economical or optimum thickness is to examine different thicknesses of insulation and for each thickness to calculate both the energy cost of the natatorium when used and the cost of the insulation. These costs, when developed on a current basis, are added together for each thickness to obtain the total cost for that thickness. A plot may be drawn of total cost versus insulation thickness. At the point where the total cost curve is a minimum, the insulation thickness is optimum (see figure below).

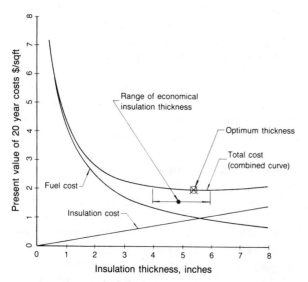

Fuel and insulation cost versus insulation thickness, over 20-year period. EPS board insulation, $0.18/(sf-in); present fuel cost, $0.6332/therm; heating season base temperature, 75 °F; fuel inflation rate, 1%; interest rate, 8.5%.

Whereas the cost of insulation is incurred in the *present*, energy is paid for periodically in the *future*. In order to add together these two costs, the future periodic energy payments are converted to a present value, at a specified interest rate and over a specified time period. Present value may be recognized as the amount required to be deposited in a bank account from which future periodic withdrawals for fuel payments will be made, while interest is earned on the remaining balance.

The present value (Weiss, 1979) of a series of regular escalating payments may be expressed as:

$$\text{present value, } P = p \, c \, (c^n - 1)/(c - 1)$$

where p = the first payment (at the end of the first period)
c = $(1 + r)/(1 + i)$
n = number of periods
r = escalation rate per period
i = interest rate per period

The fuel cost for the first year's energy passing through the insulated walls or roof for a given insulation thickness can be calculated using standard building-load calculation techniques. Seasonal heat conduction through the structure due both to the temperature difference across the walls and roof and the solar gain on these surfaces must be calculated.

The minimum or low point of the curve of total present cost versus insulation thickness can be determined by plotting or by using elementary calculus. This is done by taking the derivative of the right-hand side of the above equation with respect to the insulation thickness, setting the resulting equation equal to 0 and solving for the minimum point where the thickness is optimum. The fact that the variable p, the first period's fuel payment, can be presented as a simple function of the insulation thickness is fortuitous. Weiss and Costello (1980) use this method to present the derivation of the equation shown below from which the optimum insulation thickness can be calculated directly.

$$X_{opt} = \sqrt{Hk/I \times c(c^n - 1)/(c - 1)} - Rk$$

where X_{opt} = optimum insulation thickness, inches
H = $C_h[24D_h - .231Q_{sh}\propto] + C_c[24D_c + .231Q_{sc}\propto]$

k = conductivity of the insulation, (BTU-in.)/(hr-sqft-°F)

I = cost of insulation, $/(sqft-in.)

R = resistance of structure without insulation, (hr-sqft-°F)/BTU

D_h = degree-days for the heating season

D_c = degree-days for the cooling season

Q_{sh} = solar insolation during the heating season, BTU/(sqft-yr)

Q_{ch} = solar insolation during the cooling season, BTU/(sqft-yr) (insolation must account for the orientation of the surface)

$\propto$ = heat absorptivity of the outside surface, wall, or roof

C_h = cost of heating system output energy, $/BTU

C_c = cost of cooling system output energy, $/BTU

Controlling Pool Water Evaporation

The evaporation of pool water from the pool water surface to the pool enclosure ambient air is generally a major contributing element to pool water heating requirements after the pool water is brought up to its operating temperature.

Vapor Transmission

Effective energy conservation requires effective control of vapor transmission during both the occupied and unoccupied periods. Water vapor is low pressure steam and behaves like a perfect gas in many respects, expanding and contracting to fill exactly the space into which it is confined (see chapter 15 for a discussion of natatorium humidity control). The maximum saturation amount of vapor in a given space is a function of temperature: the greater the temperature, the greater the amount of vapor the air can contain.

The more vapor there is in a given space, the greater is its pressure. It tends, therefore, to migrate from regions of greater to regions of lesser vapor concentration. Rate of water vapor flow depends on the vapor pressure differential and the permeability of the structural components.

Water vapor is formed by evaporation from the surface of the pool and wet decks. If pool air is maintained at 86 °F and 60% rh, the vapor pressure in the pool enclosure space above the pool water is .752 in. Hg. If the water temperature is 83 °F, its corresponding vapor pressure is 1.138 in. Hg. The driving force causing migration of moisture, therefore, is .386 in. Hg or 27.29 pounds per square foot in English units, a considerable natural effort to be resisted.

Rate of Evaporation

The rate of evaporation from the pool/wet deck water surface is a function of pool water temperature, room air temperature (at momentary humidity), and air velocity. If air moves across the pool and deck surface in a pattern approaching parallel flow, the relationship of these factors is given by the standard equation published by ASHRAE (1985).

Heat Loss By Evaporation

Theoretical calculations indicate the following heat losses by evaporation from a pool water/wet deck surface of 4,000 square feet, having a water

Photo by Double Sixteen Co., Wheaton, Illinois

temperature range as shown, to a room with ambient air conditions at 86 °F/60% rh:

Water Temperature	Heat Loss
78 °F	93,048 BTUH
80 °F	121,480 BTUH
84 °F	183,355 BTUH
86 °F	216,710 BTUH
88 °F	251,817 BTUH

From the preceding tabulation, it is seen that from 78 to 88 °F water temperature, a rise of only 10 °F, the heat loss almost triples.

Pool covers used on all pools inhibit evaporation and thereby conserve heat, and as a result they reduce heating costs of both indoor and outdoor pools.

Reclaiming Heat Loss

An evaluation should be made to determine if it is economically feasible to reclaim heat in the pool backwash system through a system of heat exchangers to preheat domestic hot water. This is important for filters using granular media that have high backwash water rates for cleaning the filters. In Europe, flat plate heat exchangers are also used to reclaim heat from shower water and wastewater. An evaluation should be made to determine if heat can be reclaimed from the pool air exhaust system to preheat incoming outside air or where potential exists for installation of a heat pump. (See Figure 15.3, chapter 15.) Where a pool is part of a central recreational complex with a refrigeration cycle, as for an ice-skating rink, the following cogeneration technique should be evaluated:

- Can the heat of rejection be utilized to heat pool water?
- Can the heat of rejection be utilized to heat domestic water?

If the pool is part of a complex where selected spaces are air-conditioned, it should also be evaluated to determine if the heat of rejection from the air-conditioning equipment can be utilized by the heat exchangers.

Building Envelope Heating Requirements

The building envelope consists of all outside surfaces enclosing the building such as roof, exterior walls, floors on grade, complete with windows, doors, skylights, louvers, openings for unit ventilators, openings for through-the-wall air conditioners, and other openings. Energy is lost through the building envelope during the winter by the transfer of heat from the inside of the building, through the envelope material, to the outside ambient air. Heat is transferred from the area of high temperature to the area of low temperature or inward to the building on a hot summer day. The heat losses and heat gains through the building envelope are a function of

- heat transmission through the various components of the building envelope;
- infiltration of outside air under the influence of wind and chimney effects; and
- heating and cooling of air changes, required for ventilation.

The thermal resistance of the envelope materials may be calculated from data available on the design drawings for each building. Heat transmission through a building envelope is a function of the thickness, density, and specific heat and surface absorptivity of the envelope materials; the position and thickness of thermal insulation; solar radiation and wind velocity; the U value; and the temperature differential between indoors and outdoors. The standard method of calculating heat loss considers only the last two functions and does not credit the storage effect of masonry or other heavy walls. The standard evaluation process assumes a steady-state heat effect or thermal inertia. The thermal flywheel effects, however, always exist under real weather conditions because of daily fluctuations in dry-bulb temperature and solar radiation intensity.

The combined influence of thermal resistance and thermal storage capacity actually determines the degree by which the building regulates heat gain and loss. Although the impact of resistance insulation on building thermal loads is well understood and reflected in such building standards as ASHRAE 90-80, the thermal storage capacity has not been studied but is recognized as a positive factor, particularly in those buildings having substantial concrete or masonry walls.

The Masonry Industry Committee in their publication "Mass Masonry Energy" offers correction factors to account for the effects of mass. For example, they claim for 5,000 degree-day locations, in a comparison of two walls each having the same thermal resistance, that the heavier or more massive wall loses 13% less heat on an annual basis.

Recommended design factors for minimizing the energy consumption through the building envelope include the following:

- Optimum insulation can reduce summer heat gains and winter heat losses, prevent concealed condensation, and provide a mean radiant wall temperature of 87 °F or greater in pool enclosures. Optimum insulation yields the lowest total insulation plus energy cost over the anticipated life of the building envelope.

- New buildings can be designed with the correct directional orientation to take care of passive solar heating and cooling of glass surfaces.

- A minimum of glass surfaces can reduce heat gains and heat losses.

- Less infiltration can minimize energy consumption.

- Window covers, shades, or blinds should be closed at night in cold climates.

Windows and large, architectural, glass surface areas have a large impact on the amount of energy that is expended in heat losses and heat gains to maintain comfort conditions in recreation buildings. Properly designed and oriented windows may in many cases provide a net daytime energy gain. The major energy functions of windows are to provide solar heat and year-round natural light, to reject summer heat gain by ventilation, and to provide natural ventilation during temperate weather.

Proper window design will reduce energy expenditures and improve occupant comfort levels. The following list includes window design features to be considered with respect to the window's energy functions, the local climate, the time of day and/or seasons, the individual building space utilization, and the internal environmental requirements of the recreational activities being performed.

- Reduce solar heat gains, provide sunscreens, exterior roll blinds, architectural shade projections, exterior shutters or awnings as applicable to new buildings. It may not be practical to apply these items to the existing buildings.

- Provide weatherstripping in all windows and periodically replace those when deterioration occurs.

- Install thermal break in the metal window frame to reduce heat loss and heat gain; however, installation in an existing window is not always practical and, therefore, not recommended except where windows are to be repaired.

- The type of opening operation and window tilt should take advantage of the wind for natural cooling.

- The size and aspect ratio of windows should be proportioned so they approach a square shape to minimize window perimeter, thereby reducing the potential for infiltration. Where windows are to be replaced, the aspect ratio should be considered as well as reduction of glass area. In addition to the reduction of transmission heat loss through reduction in glass area, infiltration heat losses are substantially reduced by approaching the square shape.

- Provide insulating glass and/or storm windows to provide an insulating air space, thereby reducing conducted heat losses on all replacement windows.

- Provide heat-absorbing glass, reflective glass, and applied films of similar performance characteristics for solar control.

- In existing buildings, reduce the glass area by substituting insulated fabric sunshades in a portion of the window.

- Provide venetian blinds, shades, insulated shades, draperies, and the like where practical. Their principal advantage is that they are effective in reducing heat loss in the winter and heat gain in the summer. However, in reducing heat gain, the heat gain absorbed by the device is eventually radiated into the building. It should be noted that for any of these devices to be totally effective as an insulating device, they must trap "hot" or "cold" air between the device and the window, and this is possible only if they are tight fitting and secured in place.

- Opaque roll shades are similar in their principle of operation to shades, draperies, venetian blinds, and the like.

- Wherever practical, massive materials should be located directly in the path of winter sunlight transmitted through the windows in order to store part of the incoming solar heat and provide reradiated heat during nonsunlit hours.

Excessive amounts of glass area are extremely energy-wasteful. However, properly modified window areas can introduce valuable energy to supply solar heating during winter months, a source of illumination during daylight hours to offset the need of artificial illumination, and a means of natural ventilation during temperate weather seasons. The impact of the solar energy that a window receives can be increased by lightly colored adjacent exterior surfaces. The usefulness of sunlight inside the building can be increased by providing mass to store part of the sun's heat. The effectiveness of daylight as a natural source of illumination can be increased by providing light-colored walls and ceilings.

Infiltration heating requirements should be reviewed at all access locations to the building, particularly the main entrance, for opening and closing losses. Inasmuch as traffic rate, building height, and indoor/outdoor temperature difference are uncontrolled, entrance infiltration can be reduced by reducing entrance pressure differentials either by sealing or tightening the building envelope or sealing the entrance with proper doors.

Plumbing Systems and Equipment

The plumbing systems of recreational buildings are large users of water. Water is utilized for:

- toilet flushing
- urinal flushing
- hand washing
- showers
- swimming pool water initial fill make-up (evaporation losses, carry-off water absorbed by bathing suits, and spill losses)
- space cleaning (service sinks, mop sinks, hose bibbs, etc.)
- kitchen and cafeteria (dishwashing, cooking, etc.)
- site irrigation
- evaporative (roof) cooling

The domestic cold water system serves many uses in recreational buildings and their support functions. The cold water, after it is utilized, usually ends up in the sanitary sewage system. A study of sanitary sewage systems has indicated normal building effluent to be 98% water and 2% solids; therefore, any reduction in domestic water results in a reduction in sewage flow rates and total quantities. A reduction in domestic water load results in both a reduction in water and sanitary sewer costs. Every effort should be made to reduce water consumption and at the same time to maintain high standards of safety and health.

Water must be supplied at pressures high enough to satisfy the imposed loads. Excessive pressures result in excessive water consumption. As an example, a faucet with 10 minutes running time delivers the following water capacity at the scheduled water pressure:

Water Pressure	Gallons
50 psi	30
65 psi	36
80 psi	40
100 psi	45

The higher the water pressure, the greater the probability that old materials will leak, water hammer will be created, faucets will drip, and domestic hot water loads will increase resulting in an increase in fuel consumption.

It is recommended that pressure regulators, restrictors, low water flow shower heads, and low water consumption-type sanitary fixtures for new work be provided. All devices must satisfy the pressure requirements of the item served and should be verified before installation.

Water utilized for fixtures can be reduced by the use of flow restrictors (lavatories and showers). Water used for flushing can be reduced by providing water closets and urinals of the low water consumption types. Personnel should be made aware of the importance of their efforts to conserve water and energy. Pool water evaporation losses can be minimized by the application of pool covers as previously noted. The custodial staff should report all dripping faucets, showers, and continuous running water closets for immediate repair.

Hot water is required for sanitary purposes in swimming pool complexes. Domestic hot water is usually generated by heating domestic cold water with a heating medium, generally steam, hot water, and resistance electric heaters. Due to the large quantities of domestic hot water required for showers, the water is usually heated in hot water storage heaters utilizing the available heating. The mass flow rates are regulated by thermostats. If steam is obtained from the central building boiler plant, then one main boiler must be available and on the line at all times for domestic hot water generation in most existing swimming pool buildings. This procedure wastes energy in the summer and in nonwinter periods where the domestic hot water is the only load. Separate water heaters interconnected to the existing storage tanks are recommended for those buildings with heavy summer loads and local electric hot water. The hot water storage heaters should be provided with additional insulation over their existing insulation to keep standby losses to a minimum. Gas-fired water heaters may be selected for minimum firing rates utilizing the concept that the water will be heated at night, and when it is firing during the day it will be fired at peak capacity, keeping its combustion efficiency high at all times.

Hot water temperatures should be generated at the lowest possible temperature consistent with its use. In general, only 105 °F water is required except for kitchens where 180 °F is required at the dishwashers. It is therefore recommended that domestic hot water be generated and stored at 140 °F and circulated to the building at 105 °F to the general use items through three-way mixing valves. A separate line at 140 °F to serve special 140 °F equipment is recommended. The water temperature should be boosted locally from 140 to 180 °F when there is a requirement, as at dishwashers. Where the piping systems do not permit the practical application of this procedure because of the length of piping required, 140 °F water should be distributed and again, local, three-way mixing valves provided. This procedure reduces the heating requirements for domestic hot water.

Where electric boosters and electric hot water heaters are used for kitchen water heating, it is recommended that they be replaced with gas-fired hot water heaters when economically feasible.

Where available, kitchen refrigeration heat-of-rejection can be recovered from the refrigeration cycles by paralleling air-cooled condensers with the water-cooled condensers. The water-cooled condensers become the heat exchange device cooling the refrigerant and heating the domestic hot water. Condensate coolers installed to reclaim steam trap bypass heat and thereby preheat domestic hot water.

Heating Plants

Heating systems are provided in natatoriums and supporting structures to offset building heat losses and maintain the internal thermal environment so that

- the occupants of the building are comfortable;
- the space temperatures are conducive to physical achievement and human performance; and
- the building materials are protected from thermal and vapor damage.

Heating systems are classified in many different ways. The most common method used is to state the heating medium distributing heat to the various spaces and fuel or energy source provided. The most common heating mediums are steam, water, and air. The common fuels normally used are oil, gas, coal, and electrical energy.

All heating systems consist of fundamental elements for the production, distribution, and transmission of heat. They include the following:

- A heat transfer fluid for conveying the heat
- A heat generator in which fuel is burned and from which heat is transferred to the heat transfer fluid
- Pipes or ducts for transporting the heat transfer fluid to the spaces
- Terminal means of transferring the heat in the spaces

Steam, water, and air are heat transfer fluids. Boilers, hot water heat generators, and warm air furnaces are heat generators utilizing either coal, gas, or oil as a fuel or electricity as an energy source. Piping systems and/or ductwork systems distribute the heat transfer fluid to terminal heat transfer elements. Generally the terminal heat transfer elements are radiators, convectors, baseboard and fine pipe radiation, unit ventilators, fan coil units, unit heaters, and central handling units.

Energy is utilized in each of three processes: generation of heat, distribution of heat, and terminal transmission of heat. The objective of an effective energy conservation program is to maximize the efficiency of these processes and at the same time to reduce the consumption of energy. The performance of a heating system is a function of the following parameters:

- Design
- Workmanship and materials
- Extent of wear and use
- User operational methods and habits
- Environmental conditions throughout the climatic year
- Preventive maintenance and maintenance programs

The standard strategy for conserving energy in steam, hot water, and warm air heating systems is to generate and transport the heating medium at maximum efficiency, distributing the heating at the terminal point under the desired temperature conditions corresponding to the maximum efficiency possible. All these items involve effective design, installation, operations, and maintenance procedures. The heating plant design should take the following factors into account:

- Reduce air, steam, and water leaks.
- Reduce steam trap losses.
- Reduce flash steam losses by heat recovery through heating domestic hot water.
- Provide steam and water control valves on heating system surfaces (radiators and convectors).
- Provide condensate coolers to preheat domestic hot water with steam bypassing traps.
- Provide insulation on uninsulated pipe, duct valves, fittings, expansion joints, tanks, etc.
- Upgrade the automatic control systems to provide the maximum fuel savings.
- Retrofit existing condensate, vacuum, and circulating pumps.
- Operate at the lowest practical pressure and temperature conditions.
- Operate boilers and furnaces at the maximum combustion efficiency.

Ventilation Units

Ventilation is the process of supplying air to a space by natural or mechanical means. The purpose of ventilation is as follows:

- To preserve the health, safety, and well-being of the occupants of the buildings
- To dilute odors (locker room, gymnasiums, etc.)
- To protect building materials in swimming pool halls (condensation and frost control)
- To reduce the buildup of heat

The outside ambient conditions should conform to acceptable standards established by the U.S. Public Health Service to be satisfactory for outside air make-up.

Ventilation systems utilize energy in the form of heat for make-up air in the winter and electrical energy for the fans that transport the supply and exhaust air through ductwork to their terminal points. Ventilation systems are usually general or process-type systems. Ventilation air quantities should conform to local, state, and federal codes and should not be less than the recommendations of ASHRAE Standard 62 for natural and mechanical ventilation and ASHRAE Standard 90-80.

If the energy conservation recommendations pertaining to infiltration are implemented, it is mandatory that the ventilation air quantities only be reduced to acceptable "health minimums," not arbitrary "code" minimums.

A summary of energy conservation strategies involving ventilation units includes the following:

- Reduce air flow rates to the minimum consistent with health requirements.
- Change fan speeds on exhaust fans to reflect changes in air quantities. Replace existing motors with smaller motors where practical. Use high efficiency motors.
- Rebalance all air-handling systems for new air quantities.
- Make all efforts to reduce system resistances in order to save motor horsepower.
- Provide economizer cycles on all supply and return systems that have the capability.
- Provide heat recovery devices in 100% outside air systems and large systems with large rates of outside air (see Figure 15.5).
- Provide "night" recirculation ducts to save fuel on locker-room systems designed for space heating with 100% outside air. Load check all fans.
- Run swimming pool exhaust systems on old systems under the control of humidistats and two speed motors to save fuel and power.
- Preheat boiler plant combustion intake air by mixing hot air off ceilings with incoming outside air.
- Retrofit and upgrade when possible, or recondition old fans.
- Clean all ductwork.
- Recalibrate all automatic controls.

Electrical Systems

Electrical systems provide for the following:

- Artificial illumination of sufficient footcandles to create an atmosphere that is safe and pleasant

- The motorized equipment for the operation of heating, ventilating, and air-conditioning systems to maintain space conditions.

- The operation of public address, clock and program, intercom, and related communications systems

- The operation of fire alarm, smoke detection, and related systems to ensure the safety of the building occupants

- The operation of swimming pool recirculation and filtration systems and pool service and maintenance equipment

Lighting systems may typically account for 35 to 40% of the total electrical consumption of build-ings and consequently afford good opportunities for energy conservation. The following are common light sources in use at recreational facilities.

1. *Incandescent*—Incandescent filament lamps produce illumination in the useful range of 16 to 20 lumens per watt. Incandescent lighting is the least efficient but most common source of illumination.

2. *Fluorescent*—Fluorescent lamps are electric discharge lamps. Typically, fluorescent lamps have high efficiency and produce illumination in the useful range of 53 to 78 lumens per watt.

3. *High intensity discharge*—High intensity discharge lamps (HID) include the groups of

Lamp type	Wattage	Lamp size/shape	Life, hrs	Lumens/watt	
				Initial	Mean
Incandescent	100 A-19	A	750	16.9	13.76
	150 A-21		750	19.0	16.34
	300 PS-25		750	21.2	18.2
	500 PS-40		1000	19.8	17.0
	1000 PS-42	PS	1000	23.7	20.4
Tungsten halogen	500 PAR-56	PAR 56	4000	16.0	15.04
	500 T-4	T	2000	20.9	20.3
Metal halide Multi-vapor	175 E-28	E-28	10,000	80.0	59.1
	250 E-28		10,000	82.0	68.0
	100 E-23.5	E-23.5	24,000	42.0	32.0
Mercury	250 E-28	E-37	24,000	48.4	39.6
	400 E37	BT-56	24,000	56.3	32.0
	1000 BT-56		24,000	63.0	40.0
High output multi-vapor	400 E-37	E-37	20,000	100	80.0
Fluorescent	F48T12LW		12,000	72.7	63.3
	F96T12	T12 (1-1/2 in. diameter)	12,000	90.0	78.2
	F96T17		12,000	80.54	59.6
	F96T12CWX	T17 (2-1/8 in. diameter)	12,000	64.1	53.3

Electric lamp comparison

lamps commonly known as mercury and metal halide. Mercury and metal halide lamps are very similar in construction and operation. Each lamp contains two envelopes, the inner envelope (arc tube) and the outer envelope that shields the arc tube from changes in temperature, contains nitrogen that prevents oxidation, provides a surface for phosphor coating, and acts as a filter to eliminate the ultraviolet wavelengths of light emitted. Mercury lamps produce illumination in the useful range of 32 to 40 lumens per watt; metal halide lamps produce illumination in the useful range of 59 to 80 lumens per watt. High pressure sodium lamps yield approximately 108 to 126 lumens per watt. Although this is the most efficient source of illumination, it should not be used extensively at the pool site because the color rendition is unacceptable for interior natatorium use.

Opportunities for energy-efficient illumination systems exist for most areas in natatoriums and other physical education buildings. In natatoriums, the high ceilings afford the opportunity to use high intensity discharge luminaires. The spacing-to-mounting height ratio for certain luminaires is 1.2:1; therefore if a ceiling is 20 feet high, the fixture spacing can be 24 feet on centers. Typical spacing is 18 to 24 feet.

Natatoriums should be illuminated with luminaires affording good color rendition, and the use of metal halide type luminaires is preferred. Generally, natatorium lighting is located around the perimeter of the pool with fixtures equipped with asymmetrical distribution and lenses designed to throw the light across the surface of the water. See chapter 15 for I.E.S. recommendations for the above-deck and above-pool lighting required that is in addition to I.E.S. minimum design provisions for underwater lighting in pools (see also chapter 11).

Locker-room areas may be illuminated to 30 fc by utilizing single-lamp, 35-watt, energy-saver, fluorescent fixtures equipped with "Batwing"-type diffusers. These diffusers provide for wide distribution and the elimination of direct glare normally encountered with standard lenses. Other effective designs are available. Lighting load densities for the bathhouse layout are in the range of 1.0 to 1.4 watts per square foot.

Energy-efficient electrical systems should include the following:

- High efficiency motors
- Photocell control for automatic dimming of luminaires to take advantage of natural light
- Multiple switching for window wall lighting
- Light-colored walls for optimum reflectances
- Equipment sized to actual current loads

It is essential that architects and engineers who design pools and natatoriums become familiar with the techniques and methods of conserving energy through more efficient design. A major task confronting owners and operators of pools is how to reduce energy cost in pools that were built years ago. What rehabilitation is necessary? What equipment needs to be replaced to bring the pool's operating cost down? What instructions should be given to pool managers in order to lower the operating cost? We now have the knowledge and equipment to make effective reduction in energy costs.

References

American Society of Heating, Refrigeration, and Air-Conditioning Engineers. (1985). *ASHRAE guide and data book, 1985 fundamentals*. Atlanta, GA: ASHRAE Press.

Weiss, D. (1979). *Present value of a series of escalating periodic payments*. Massapequa, NY: Dynaflex Scientific Corp.

Weiss, D., & Costello, M. (1980). *Economic considerations in choosing building insulation thickness and material*. Amityville, NY: Milton Costello.

Resources

National Oceanic and Atmospheric Administration (NOAA)
National Climatic Data Center
U.S. Department of Commerce
Asheville, NC 28801

Chapter 20

Innovations in Pool Design

Many of the new developments in pool design and construction have been reviewed in preceding chapters. As talent and science create new manufacturing, fabricating, and building techniques such as laser photo options, microdot transistor batteries, and other devices, they will expedite changes in the materials that will have an impact on the pool industry.

Construction

Following are some of the more recent innovations in pool construction.

Prefabrication of Pool Tanks

Although prefabricated concrete slabs for pool walls were used in the United States for years, the cost of handling and shipping such large slabs made them impractical. By contrast, the system of prefabrication in Germany has proved quite successful. Pool floors are built of prefabricated concrete slabs laid on precast concrete girders. Walls are constructed of large, prebuilt sections, complete with interior finishes and overflow rims that are fitted into place.

A community or organization may choose its pool and components from a catalog. Building details and labor functions are then controlled by information fed into a computer, and the parts are built, assembled, and tested in a factory. The pool is then dismantled, and the parts are delivered to the site for assembly.

Modularization of Pools and Buildings

Now popular in the United States are systems of modular pools and enclosures. Pool contractors

Moveable bulkhead with flow-through system for improved circulation of water by DAF Indal Ltd., Missisauga, Ontario, Canada

and engineers may offer a community or organization a choice of several sizes of pools, including "L" and "T" shapes, with suitable buildings. The complete cost is thus predetermined. Not only is the construction time established in advance, but the time needed for erection is also precisely defined. An organization may decide originally on a small pool, to fit current budgets and needs, and as these grow, both pool and enclosure may be expanded with prebuilt modules at considerably less than the cost of building a new complex.

Moveable Floors

Several German manufacturers have now installed moveable pool floors in the United States. These can be raised or lowered to give an entire pool, or a portion of it, any desired depth or angle. With a system of hydraulic pistons or cog wheels, a portion of the floor as large as 35 feet by 75 feet can be raised within a matter of minutes from a depth of 10 feet to 3 feet and locked in place at any height in between. This system allows a single pool to serve a multitude of purposes and all age groups. An American manufacturer has developed

an aluminum pool floor that works similarly and may even be used to convert a pool into a dance floor or skating rink.

Wave Pools

Based on the accepted theory that it is necessary to provide more than water to keep people happy with swimming pools, a number of devices have been used effectively to add "fun" to swimming. Most spectacular of these machines are those that produce waves, closely resembling ocean surf, in a large pool. Used in the United States as well as Japan, Russia, and Western Europe with apparent success, the wave machines work on several principles, but in all cases they produce waves of 3 or more feet in height, breaking at a predetermined point and continuing to the shallow end of the pool as gradually diminishing surf.

Floating Swimming Pools

A pool that floats in lakes or rivers has been recently introduced. It employs a vinyl liner as the water container and uses the water that it floats

Wave pool by Wave Tek

in as the principal water source. The water is filtered before it is introduced into the pool.

Carpeting

School corridors and locker rooms have been successfully carpeted and now pool planners are beginning to consider carpeting for pool decks. Several companies have perfected carpets that meet most of the criteria for acceptable deck carpets. The essential characteristics that all pool carpets must possess include the following:

- An ability to be sterilized to keep them free of bacteria

- A fungus- and algae-free surface, or at least an ability to be cleaned to eliminate these undesirable organisms when they appear

- A useful life of at least 5 years

- Easy removability to clean the deck underneath

- A nonslip surface when wet

- Availability in a variety of colors

Safety Cushions

As a means of reducing injuries resulting from hitting the bottom of the pool, Nova University at Fort Lauderdale, Florida is experimenting with safety cushions made of closed cellular material. Under diving boards the safety pad is 1 inch thick, whereas in children's pools the pad is 1/4 inch thick.

Automation

Automation of pool operation (water circulation, chemical control, and temperature control) has finally been achieved. Such controllers provide for greater accuracy of water management as well as a reduction in the cost of manpower and are discussed in the following sections.

Filtration and Recirculation

The improvement in filters presents an outstanding example of rapid and successful development. Thirty years ago, swimming pool sand filters were custom designed. Today packaged filters—with face piping installed, simply operated multiport valves, and improved hydraulics—are available for pools of any size, at much lower cost and with greater efficiency than those that were custom designed. Pressure diatomite filters have been greatly improved, providing much longer runs than those available 15 years ago and far simpler operation at lower cost. Vacuum filters have been developed to the point of complete reliability.

Automatic Filtration

Filters have been developed, both in the United States and England, that are sensitive to pressure differentials or changes in flow rates, and which automatically enter the backwash cycle at a predetermined point. These depend on sophisticated instrumentation and are still quite expensive. They will undoubtedly be developed further, however, and should become more readily available and less expensive within the near future.

Widely used on residential pools today are high-rate sand filters (flow rates of 20 gpm and up), which use a single-grade media. Rather than retaining dirt on or very close to the surface, these utilize the entire depth of the media to screen out dirt particles. Other types of filter media, such as calcite, ground blast furnace slag, expanded shale, and ground cinders, may make smaller and more efficient filters feasible.

Experiments with other types of filtration (e.g., ultrasonic and electronic) also indicate that much higher water clarity may be available soon, with smaller vehicles and at lower cost.

Built-In Recirculation Systems

Several manufacturers have developed overflow and recirculation systems that are an integral part of the pool wall, combining overflow rim, skimmer, and supply lines to eliminate perimeter piping. Pools have been designed also with integral surge tanks. With these, controls automatically supply water to the recirculation pump as needed to maintain a constant water level in the pool. This results in a uniform coping rim overflow into the surge tank, eliminating all piping and fitting requirements.

Sanitation

Another example of recent advances in technology is pool chemistry. Chlorine is now available in a variety of forms that are easier to use and are, in many cases, more stable than earlier types. Many of these simplified products are still practical only for smaller pools because of their higher cost. But the desire of the homeowner to spend as little time and effort as possible on the backyard

pool has led to the development of pools that are coming close to complete automation. The higher cost of initial installation of automated equipment is not as significant a factor in residential pools as in larger public pools. The wider recognition of the need for higher standards of purification and clarification of water in public pools will bring about their automation, too, before very long. Some of the labor-reducing products now available for pools are described below.

Automatic Cleaning Systems

These are of two types, those that sweep debris to the main drains by jet pressure, utilizing either hoses or jet inlets; and those that vacuum the pool bottom and collect the debris without sending it through the filter.

Simplified Chemical Feeders

Because of the high acidity and volatility of gaseous chlorine, automatic chlorinators, although considerably simplified and improved, are still not widely used. However, the use of hypochlorinators, which feed solutions of sodium or calcium hypochlorite, is increasing in smaller pools. In addition, a number of dry chlorine feeders have been developed. Some feed granular purifiers in premeasured amounts at predetermined intervals, whereas others function by allowing water to

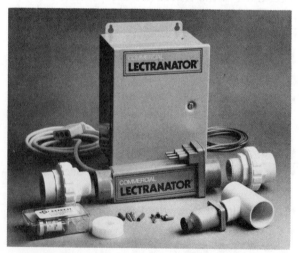

"Lectranator" is an electronic device that uses an electrolytic generation process to produce chlorine from a low concentration of salt in the pool water. Photo by Studio Associates, Inc.

erode chlorine compound tablets or sticks or bromine sticks at precalculated rates. Some types are hooked into the recirculation lines, whereas others are merely placed in skimmers or float on the pool surface. In most cases the cost of using the dry purifiers is prohibitive for public pools, except for supplementary use, but this is expected to change in the future.

Chlorine and pH solution feeders that constantly test the water and feed according to demand are available. Although not too common in the United States as yet, this type of chemical feeder is quite widely used in England and some western European countries.

The Need for Research

There is a great need for research in pool design and operation. Much research will require a coordinated effort among the various organizations, institutions, manufacturers, and individuals involved in the field of aquatics. It is necessary to define the specific areas needing study. However, some areas can only be observed and do not lend themselves to experimentation, such as factors related to drowning prevention and safety of individuals in the water. Following are examples of areas in which research would be valuable.

Water density determines the extent to which a particular individual or object floats. If water density could be reduced, it would have an impact on underwater swimming, scuba diving, and other below-surface activities. Increased water density would be an asset to swimming instruction, diving, and synchronized swimming because natural buoyancy would be increased.

A number of products that increase the surface tension of the pool water, thus reducing loss of heat and of chemicals by evaporation, have been introduced. It is believed that greater water surface control may also help limit wave and splash action, increase skimming action, and perform other valuable functions.

The cost-effectiveness of various pool adaptations should be investigated. For example, what are the most economical methods of adapting a pool for skating, of changing depths to meet the needs of various programs, and of covering the pool during the off-season?

Various methods are claimed to retard wave action in a pool, making it "faster" for competitive swimming. These primarily involve various types of overflow systems or gutter designs, and anti-splash lane floats. Water depths also are known to influence wave action, but the correlation between water depth and pool width and their consequences as to wave action and/or retardation of swimmers is not clearly defined. No comparative information exists in scientific form for any of the "fast" pool claims, yet such data are certainly desirable in relation to many pool activities.

An additional area for research is that of reliable, economical control systems—initiating and response devices—capable of complete and foolproof automation.

In pool chemistry, no absolute criteria have been established for optimum levels of pH, total alkalinity, and free chlorine. It is known that chlorine (HOCl) is more effective at low pH, but how do both factors relate to eye irritation? It is assumed that minimum "free" chlorine levels are desirable (1 ppm plus or minus), but how does the percentage of "free" to "total" chlorine affect "chlorine odors," "reported salty taste," and pH? There is an urgent need for definitive correlations in these areas.

Since the 1920s, state health codes and APHA have promoted the concept of three pool volume turnovers per day and a constant intermixing of incoming (filtered) water with pool water. There is evidence that design criteria based on "bathers per 1,000 gallons of flow per minute" are more reflective of operating conditions. Evidence also suggests that during periods of nonbathing activities, pool volumes may be cleared more effectively in one turnover if filtered water is not mixed with pool water. How soon will new criteria and construction techniques to effect this technical improvement be in common practice?

Sun shields can be collapsed to cover the pool

The Future

Prefabricated metal and plastic pools—using wood, aluminum, or steel walls with vinyl liners, or fiberglass, aluminum, or steel walls without liners, as well as combinations of these—have greatly changed the residential pool market and have affected the nonresidential market as well.

Although these certainly represent a considerable departure from the pools of the 1930s, the majority of home and almost all semipublic and public pools are built almost exactly as they have always been, and except for more sophisticated operational equipment and improvements in aesthetics, they look exactly as they did 40 years ago. Basically, they even operate exactly the same way.

For many pool designers and engineers the present methods of custom building large pools inch-by-inch, using outmoded principles, will soon end. As large companies devote more time and effort to conduct research and development, and as the demand for swimming facilities continues to outstrip the ability to supply them (there is every indication that this will be the case), new products and methods are certain to come.

Plastics, so successfully used for a wide range of pool products today, may eventually supply the answer in regard to complete pools, unless the petrochemical industry is affected by the world oil shortages.

Certainly it is not unreasonable to prophesy that the demand for pools may in the near future be met with rigid plastic tanks with filtration systems and chemical feeders molded into the walls, needing only to be dropped into the ground in one piece, in the case of smaller pools, or in two or three sections for large ones. Easily connected to water and electric sources, these could be made ready for use in a matter of hours.

To one farsighted and very busy recreation complex planner, even this is not enough. He feels that the present system of a tank with holes for water inlets and outlets is archaic. A much improved pool wall, he believes, would be a permeable membrane designed to diffuse the water as it enters the pool. If such a shell were designed for diffusion in inverse ratio to the distance from the source (in other words, more permeable in the center than at the edges), he claims that water circulation would be infinitely better, clarity and purity far superior, and the hydraulics of recirculation greatly simplified.

Evaluation Technique

As these and other new pool designs appear on the market and new products are developed, it becomes increasingly difficult for an organization or community to judge what is good or acceptable. An objective framework must be used. The following questions should be asked by those who must make the final decisions:

1. In products dealing with water handling and sanitation, has the item been approved by the National Sanitation Foundation (NSF)?

World's largest swimming pool cover. 15,460 square feet (92 ft by 170 ft). Made by MEYCO for Maplewood Township Pool in New Jersey.

Rendering of new 63,000 sq ft indoor family-oriented natatorium that contains several innovations. Westminster, Colorado.

2. Has the pool or equipment manufacturer adequately tested the design of the product for safety and durability, and are the test results available?

3. Is the life of the product sufficient to make it economical?

4. Does the product meet local health standards?

5. Does the design conform to standards for competitive swimming if the pool or product is to be used for this purpose?

6. Is the product completely safe for use by a person of any age or ability level?

7. Does the product carry a guarantee or warranty?

8. What do users of the product say about it?

9. Does the product contain the necessary warnings to alert users of potential dangers or hazards?

10. Will it improve the ultimate operation of the pool?

It is generally agreed that the pool of tomorrow must be more economical, safer, and more adaptable. Of these, safety must receive first consider-

ation. The increasing number of injuries and deaths occurring in pool-related accidents demands the attention of all those related to the planning, design, and operation of pools. Some of the unsolved problems, the solutions to which will lead toward attainment of this goal, have been identified in this publication. The challenge lies with the groups mentioned earlier in this chapter, as well as with the pool industry.

Swim-thru-lifeline by Knuckle Pool Co., St. Petersburg, Florida

Appendix A

Establishing a Pool Design Program

This form should be completed by the program staff and submitted to the consultant or architect as the guide to planning and designing the pool. Program design is fundamental to the proper planning and design of a swimming pool. Complete agreement on the nature and scope of the aquatic program must be achieved before the pool can be properly designed.

Consideration must be given to both the immediate and long-range needs. This worksheet is designed to aid communities or schools in arriving at a concise statement of overall goals, objectives, and specific requirements of the program in order that the best possible facility is achieved within the limitations imposed by the budget. Design compromises should be recorded so that everyone involved in planning the facility will be aware of the decision.

People who will be responsible for the conduct and administration of the aquatic program should carefully complete the questions in the worksheet. These requirements will then be translated into design data and characteristics, which then become the guide to the designer and engineer in the preparation of construction plans.

General Description of Pool

The following is an example of a pool description that would normally be prepared by the planning group to indicate the general purpose of the pool.

"This pool is a part of a new physical education building complex consisting of a gymnasium, classrooms, handball courts, and an indoor track. It will be used primarily by three groups: professional physical education students, students enrolled in required physical education courses, and the general student body engaged in recreational swimming."

Functions to be Performed by the Pool Facility

A. Specific Program Areas. Check in appropriate column the activities that are expected to be conducted in the pool.

	No	Yes	Occasionally
1. Instruction of non-swimmers	_____	_____	_____
2. Instruction of swimmers	_____	_____	_____
3. Water safety, lifesaving, and survival swimming	_____	_____	_____
4. Competitive swimming	_____	_____	_____
5. Diving	_____	_____	_____
6. Synchronized swimming	_____	_____	_____
7. Skin and scuba diving	_____	_____	_____
8. Water shows	_____	_____	_____
9. Recreation	_____	_____	_____
10. Instruction for disabled swimmers	_____	_____	_____
11. Teaching young children	_____	_____	_____
12. Canoeing instruction	_____	_____	_____
13. Boating instruction	_____	_____	_____
14. Sailing instruction	_____	_____	_____
15. Bait, spin, and fly casting instruction	_____	_____	_____
16. Water polo	_____	_____	_____
17. Research	_____	_____	_____
18. Other: _____	_____	_____	_____
19. Other: _____	_____	_____	_____

B. Administrative and Supervisory Facilities and Equipment

The proper administration of the swimming pool is essential to assure the health and safety of users as well as to achieve the objectives of the aquatic program. To accomplish these goals, certain controls must be built into the pool, and certain facilities must be provided to house the staff and equipment. In addition, the pool must be furnished with equipment for instruction and safety. This section should contain a list of facilities and equipment related to the above functions that should be carefully studied by the planning group.

Specify the number, and describe the facility or equipment so that the architect and engineer will be able to provide exactly what is needed. If necessary, use a separate sheet of paper to describe the facility.

(1) Offices

Number: _____

Size: _____

Location: _____

Description: _____

Furniture: _____

Special features: _____

(2) Equipment (Indicate number desired and specific manufacturer, if there is a preference.)

    (a) Lifeguard Stands or Chairs

        Number: _____

        Location: _____

        Description: _____

    (b) Safety Equipment

Item	Number	Description
1. Ring buoys	_____	_____
2. Reaching rescue pole	_____	_____
3. Torpedo rescue pole	_____	_____
4. Shepherd's crooks	_____	_____
5. Electronic warning device	_____	_____
6. Ground fault detector	_____	_____
7. Resuscitator	_____	_____
8. Telephone	_____	_____
9. First aid kit	_____	_____
10. Stretcher	_____	_____
11. Back board	_____	_____
12. Safety lines	_____	_____
13. Gas masks	_____	_____
14. Electrical outlets in pool	_____	_____
15. Others (name)	_____	_____

    (c) Instructional Equipment

Item	Number	Description
1. Kickboards	_____	_____
2. Swim "bubbles" or trainer	_____	_____
3. Canoes	_____	_____
4. Boats	_____	_____

　　5.　Swim fins　　　　　　　　　_____　_____

　　6.　Masks　　　　　　　　　_____　_____

　　7.　Goggles　　　　　　　　_____　_____

　　8.　Scuba equipment　　　　_____　_____

　　9.　Snorkels　　　　　　　　_____　_____

　10.　Pace clocks　　　　　　　_____　_____

　11.　Scoreboards　　　　　　_____　_____

　12.　Chalkboards　　　　　　_____　_____

　13.　Bulletin boards　　　　　_____　_____

　14.　Electric clocks　　　　　_____　_____

　15.　Equipment racks, trucks,
　　　　or hangers　　　　　　　_____　_____

　16.　3-meter diving stands　　_____　_____

　17.　1-meter diving stands　　_____　_____

　18.　Platform(s) (give height)　_____　_____

　19.　Diving boards (size and
　　　　type)　　　　　　　　　_____　_____

　20.　Starting blocks　　　　　_____　_____

　21.　Water polo goals　　　　_____　_____

　22.　Water basketball goals　　_____　_____

　23.　Others: (name)　　　　　_____　_____

(3) Maintenance and Operation Facilities and Equipment

　　(a) Storage Rooms (for instruction equipment)

　　　　Number: _____

　　　　Size: _____

　　　　Location: _____

　　　　Special features: _____

　　(b) Public Address System

　　　　Location of microphone input: _____

　　　　Location of central point: _____

　　(c) Benches

　　　　Number: _____

　　　　Location: _____

　　　　Description: _____

(d) Deck Space for Instruction

　　Location: _____

　　Dimensions: _____

(e) Cleaning Equipment

　　Type: _____

(f) Underwater Observation Window(s)

　　Size: _____

　　Location: _____

(g) Deck and Pool Markings (describe): _____

(h) Underwater Sound System: _____

(i) Underwater Lights

　　Indicate number: _____

Requirements and Specifications for Each Program Function

The following data are designed to establish the special requirements of each program area. The activities previously checked need to be fully described and their ''special'' needs identified related to both design and equipment. Place the name of the activity in the space provided under Program Area. Then answer the questions applicable to the activity. Photocopy additional worksheets for each program area.

Program Area: _____

_____

Anticipated peak loads: _____

Age range of users: _____

Size of water area needed: _____

Rules which govern activity: _____

Specific requirements that must be met

Water depth: _____

Pool length: _____

Pool width: _____

Ceiling height: _____

Description of any special features or facilities

Needed: _____

List of special equipment needed: _____

Describe any other special feature of the activity that the architect or engineer should have (such as air or water temperature), in order to design the pool properly for the program to be conducted.

Appendix B

Pool Planning Checklist

This checklist has been developed to serve the person or committee responsible for the planning of the pool facility. It may be used at the very beginning of the project and at various stages throughout the development of the plans and construction. If the answer to the question is "No," immediate action should be taken at that time to correct the deficiency. In addition to this checklist the reader should refer to chapter 8 for specific information on safety features.

Criteria Applicable to All Pools

1. Has a clear-cut statement been prepared on the nature and scope of the design program and the special requirements for space, equipment, and facilities dictated by the activities to be conducted? (See Appendix A.)

2. Has the swimming pool been planned to meet the total requirements of the program to be conducted as well as any special needs of the clientele to be served?

3. Have all plans and specifications been checked and approved by the local board of health and building department?

4. Is the depth of the pool adequate to safely accommodate the activities that the pool serves?

5. Does the design of the pool incorporate the most current knowledge and best experience available regarding swimming pools?

6. Has an experienced pool consultant been brought into the project by the architect or engineer to advise on proper functional layout, safety, and equipment?

7. Is there adequate deep water to safely accommodate springboard and platform diving?

8. Have all requirements for competitive swimming been met?

9. Is there adequate deck space around the pool?

10. Does the swimming instructor's office face the pool? Is there a window through which the instructor may view all areas of the pool?

11. Are the steps or ladders located in the walls of the pool recessed or removable so as not to interfere with competitive swimming?

12. Does a properly constructed overflow system extend around the entire pool perimeter?

13. Where skimmers are used, have they been properly located so that they will not interfere with competitive swimming?

14. Have separate and adequate storage spaces been allocated for maintenance and instructional equipment?

15. Has the spectator area been properly separated from the pool to avoid mixing uses?

16. Have all diving standards and lifeguard chairs been properly anchored?

17. Does the pool layout provide the most efficient control of swimmers from showers and locker rooms to the pool? Are toilet facilities provided for wet swimmers separate from the dry area?

18. Is the recirculation pump located below the "low" water level of the surge trench?

19. Is there easy access to the filter room for both people and materials?

20. Has the proper pitch to drains been allowed in the pool, on the pool deck, in the overflow gutter, and on the floor of shower and dressing rooms?

21. Has adequate space been allowed between diving boards and between the diving boards and sidewalls?

22. Has provision been made for lifesaving equipment?

23. Has pool-cleaning equipment been provided in the plans for the pool?

24. Are inlets and outlets adequate in number and located well below the water line or in the pool bottom so as to ensure effective circulation of water in the pool?

25. Has consideration been given to underwater lights, underwater observation windows, and underwater speakers for the in-ground pool?

26. Have the ends of springboards been covered with a safety pad?

27. Has a pool heater been considered in order to maintain proper water temperature?

28. Have underwater lights been eliminated in the ends of racing courses? If not, are they placed below the 4-foot level?

29. Have provisions been made for access to the pool by disabled persons?

30. Is seating for swimmers provided on the deck?

31. Has the recirculation-filtration system been designed to meet the anticipated future bathing loads?

32. Has the gas chlorinator (if used) been placed in a separate room accessible from and vented to the outside?

33. Has the overflow system been connected to return to the filters in order to conserve water?

34. If the pool shell contains a concrete finish, has the length of the pool been increased by 1-1/2 inches over the "official" size in order to permit eventual tiling of the basin without making the pool "too short"?

35. Has the pool been planned so that it is as safe as possible? This includes not only design of the pool but the equipment placed in the pool.

Concerns Applicable to Indoor Pools Only

1. Has the natatorium been properly ventilated?

2. Have the walls and ceilings been adequately treated acoustically and for energy conservation?

3. Is there adequate overhead clearance for diving?

4. Is there adequate pool deck lighting?

5. Have windows on the side been eliminated in order to prevent light reflection?

6. Are all wall bases coved to facilitate cleaning?

7. Is there provision for proper temperature control in the pool room for both water and air?

8. Can humidity of the pool room be controlled?

9. Is the wall and ceiling insulation adequate to prevent "sweating"?

10. Are all metal fittings of noncorrosive material?

Concerns Applicable to Outdoor Pools Only

1. Is the site for the pool in the best possible location (away from railroad tracks, heavy industry, trees, dusty open fields, and adjacent fixtures)?

2. Has a fence been placed around the pool for proper security?

3. Has subsurface drainage been provided to eliminate runoff to the pool?

4. Is there adequate deck space for sunbathing?

5. Are the outdoor lights placed far enough from the pool to prevent insects from dropping into the pool?

6. Is the deck of the pool of nonslip finish?

7. Is there an area set aside for eating, which is separated from the pool deck?

8. Is the bathhouse properly designed so that the entrance to the pool leads to the shallow end?

9. Are there other recreational facilities nearby for the convenience and enjoyment of swimmers?

10. Do diving boards or platforms face north or east?

11. Are lifeguard stands provided and properly located?

12. Has adequate parking space been provided and properly located?

13. Is the pool oriented correctly in relation to the sun?

14. Have windbreakers been provided in situations where heavy winds prevail?

Appendix C

Organization Addresses

Aquatic Agencies and Organizations

American Alliance for Health, Physical Education, Recreation and Dance
1900 Association Drive
Reston, VA 22091

American National Standards Institute
1430 Broadway
New York, NY 10018

American Public Health Association
1015 15th Street N.W.
Washington, DC 20005

American Red Cross
17th and "D" Streets, N.W.
Washington, DC 20006

American Society of Landscape Architects
1750 Meadow Road
McLean, VA 22101

Athletic Institute
200 Castlewood Drive
North Palm Beach, FL 33408

Council for National Cooperation in Aquatics (CNCA)
901 West New York Street
Indianapolis, IN 46223

International Swimming Hall of Fame
1 Hall of Fame Drive
Fort Lauderdale, FL 33316

National Fire Protection Association
Battery March Park
Quincy, MA 02269

National Recreation and Park Association
3101 Park Center Drive
Alexandria, VA 22302

National Safety Council
444 North Michigan Avenue
Chicago, IL 60611

National Sanitary Foundation
P.O. Box 1468
Ann Arbor, MI 48106

National Spa and Pool Institute
2111 Eisenhower Avenue
Alexandria, VA 22314

National Swimming Pool Foundation
10803 Gulfdale, Suite 300
San Antonio, TX 78216

President's Committee on Employment
  of Handicapped
Washington, DC 20006

Recreation Safety Institute
100 Arrival Avenue
Ronkonkoma, NY 11779

U.S. Consumer Product Safety Commission
  (CPSC)
Washington, DC 20007

Ruling Bodies

Federation Internationale de Natation Amateur
  (FINA)
1750 East Boulder Street
Colorado Springs, CO 80909
Phone: (303) 578-4505

National Collegiate Athletic Association (NCAA)
P.O. Box 1906
Shawnee Mission, KA 66201
Phone: (913) 384-3200

National Federation of State High School
  Associations (NFSHSA)
11724 Plaza Circle, Box 20626
Kansas City, MO 64195
Phone: (816) 464-5400

United States Diving, Inc. (USD)
901 West New York Street
Indianapolis, IN 46223
Phone: (317) 634-3040

United States Swimming, Inc. (USS)
1750 East Boulder Street
Colorado Springs, CO 80909
Phone: (303) 578-4578

United States Water Polo
1750 East Boulder Street
Colorado Springs, CO 80909
Phone: (303) 632-5551, ext. 248

United States Synchronized Swimming
901 West New York Street
Indianapolis, IN 46223
Phone: (317) 633-2000

Appendix D

Bibliography

Swimming Pool Design and Operation

American Alliance for Health, Physical Education, Recreation, and Dance. (1969). *Sports safety—Accident prevention and injury control in physical education, athletics and recreation*. Reston, VA: Author.

American Alliance for Health, Physical Education, Recreation, and Dance. (1980). *Safety in aquatic activities*. (Monograph No. 6). Reston, VA: Author.

American Red Cross. (1977). *Adapted aquatics*. Washington, DC: Author.

American Red Cross. (1981). *Swimming and aquatics safety*. Washington, DC: Author.

American Red Cross. (1983). *Lifeguard training*. Washington, DC: Author.

Armbruster, D.A., Allen, R.H., & Billingsley, H.S. (1973). *Swimming and diving*. St. Louis, MO: C.V. Mosby.

Athletic Institute, & American Alliance for Health, Physical Education, Recreation, and Dance. (1985). *Planning facilities for athletics, physical and health education, and recreation*. Reston, VA: AAHPERD.

Counsilman, J.E. (1968). *Science of swimming*. Englewood Cliffs, NJ: Prentice-Hall.

Data and reference annual. (1972 and 1973 eds.). Fort Lauderdale, FL: Hoffman Publications.

Dawes, J. (1979). *Design and planning of swimming pools*. Boston: CBI Publishing.

Fabian, D. (1958). *Modern swimming pools of the world*. Florence, AL: National Pool Equipment Co.

Gabrielsen, M.A., & Johnson, R.L. (1979, June). Swimming pool safety—professional challenge. *Journal of Physical Education, Recreation, and Dance*, **50**(6), 43-46.

Gabrielsen, M.A., & McElhaney, J.H. (1974, February). *Effects of various water slide configurations on the velocity and depth of penetration of human bodies of different physical characteristics.* (CPSC Report No. 644). Washington, DC: U.S. Consumer Product Safety Commission.

Gabrielsen, M.A., & Miles, C. (1958). *Sports and recreation facilities—For school and community.* Englewood Cliffs, NJ: Prentice-Hall.

Lewin, G. (1979). *Swimming.* Berlin: Sportverlag.

Maglischo, E.W. (1982). *Swimming faster: A comprehensive guide to the science of swimming.* Chico, CA: Mayfield Publishing.

National Aquatics Journal. (1985, Summer), **1**(2). Indianapolis, IN: Council for National Cooperation in Aquatics.

National Swimming Pool Institute. (1972). *Swimming pool operator's handbook.* Washington, DC: NSPI.

Perkins, P.H. (1971). *Swimming pools.* London: Elsevier.

Pool and Spa News. 3923 West 6th Street, Los Angeles, CA 90020.

Ruoff, A.C., III, & Burnstein, S.A. (1973). *Injury potential of swimming pool sliders.* Salt Lake City, UT: Biomedical Test Laboratory, University of Utah.

Ryan, F. (1972). *Swimming skills.* New York: Penguin Books.

Scharff, R.M. (1958). *Swimming pool book.* New York: M. Barrows.

Snyder, R.G. (1965, October). Human tolerance limits in water impact. *Aerospace Medicine,* **36**(10), 940-947.

Swimming Pool Age. Communication Channels, Inc., 6255 Barfield Road, Atlanta, GA 30328.

Swimming pool operator's handbook. Alexandria, VA: National Spa and Pool Institute.

Torney, J., & Clayton, R. (1982). *Aquatic organization and management.* Minneapolis, MN: Burgess.

Troup, J., & Reese, R. (1983). *A scientific approach to the sport of swimming.* Gainesville, FL: Scientific Sports.

U.S. Consumer Product Safety Commission. (1976). Fact sheet no. 8: *Swimming pools.* Washington, DC: Author.

U.S. Consumer Product Safety Commission, & National Spa and Pool Institute. (1985, May 14). *National pool and spa safety conference report.* Washington, DC: U.S. CPSC.

U.S. Lifesaving Association. (1981). *Lifesaving and marine safety.* New York: Association Press.

University of Miami School of Medicine, & Nova University. (1977). *Medical analysis of swimming pool injuries: A report of case studies of 72 swimming pool injuries.* Washington, DC: U.S. CPSC.

Diving

Albrook, O.W., & Walker, J. (1975, November). Underwater deceleration curves in relation to injuries from diving. *Surgical Neurology,* **4**, 36-41.

Batterman, C. (1968). *Techniques of springboard diving.* Cambridge, MA: MIT Press.

Frohlich, C. (1980, March). Physics of somersaulting and twisting. *Scientific American,* **242**(3), 154-164.

Gabrielsen, M.A. (1975). *Photographic analysis of underwater action of international diving champions.* Washington, DC: U.S. CPSC.

Gabrielsen, M.A. (1984). *Diving injuries: A critical insight and recommendations.* Indianapolis, IN: Council for National Cooperation in Aquatics.

Lee, S. (1978). *Diving.* New York: Atheneum Press.

McElhaney, J., Snyder, R., States, J., & Gabrielsen, M.A. (1979). *Biomechanical analysis of swimming pool neck injuries.* Warrendale, PA: Society of Automotive Engineers.

Moriarty, P. (1959). *Springboard diving.* New York: Ronald Press.

New England Spinal Cord Injury Foundation. (1974). *Spinal cord injury registry report* (No. 4). Boston, MA: Author.

Rachman, G. (1975). *Diving complete.* London: Faber & Faber.

Rado, W. (1967). How to handle an injured diver. *Swimming Pool Data and Reference Annual,* **34**.

Shield, C.L., Fox, J.M., & Stauffer, W.S. (1978, September). Cervical cord injuries in sports. *The Physician and Sports Medicine,* **6**(9), 71-76.

Stone, R.E. (1980). *Diving safety in swimming pools: A report to the National Swimming Pool Foundation*. Cambridge, MA: Arthur R. Little, Inc.

Rule Books for Competitive Swimming and Diving

All State Health Departments—Ask for laws or regulations governing swimming pools, write to your state.

See Appendix C for addresses of the various ruling bodies. Because all rule books are revised every year or two, ask for the current edition.

Standards

American National Standards Institute (ANSI). (1972). *Specifications for accident prevention signs*. New York: Author.

American Public Health Association. (1970). *Suggested ordinance and regulations covering private residential swimming pools*. Washington, DC: Author.

American Public Health Association. (1981). Suggested ordinance and regulations covering public swimming pools. Washington, DC: Author.

National Swimming Pool Institute. (1978). *Minimum standards for public spas*. Alexandria, VA: Author.

National Swimming Pool Institute. (1981). *Standards for residential above-ground/portable swimming pools, ladders, and filters*. Alexandria, VA: Author.

National Swimming Pool Institute. (1977). *Suggested minimum standards for public swimming pools*. Alexandria, VA: Author.

National Swimming Pool Institute. (1974). *Suggested minimum standards for residential pools* (rev. ed.). Alexandria, VA: Author.

U.S. Consumer Product Safety Commission. (1976, July 19). *Water slide standard*. Washington, DC: Author.

U.S. Department of Health, Education, and Welfare. (1976). *Swimming pools—safety and disease control through proper design and operation*. Atlanta, GA: Public Health Center for Disease Control.

U.S. Department of Health and Human Services, Center for Disease Control. (1981). *Suggested health and safety guidelines for recreation water slide flumes*. Atlanta, GA: Author.

U.S. Department of Housing and Urban Development. (1966, May). *Minimum property standards for swimming pools*. Washington, DC: Federal Housing Authority.